T0224800

# A Complete Guide to DevOps with AWS

## Deploy, Build, and Scale Services with AWS Tools and Techniques

Osama Mustafa

Apress®

*A Complete Guide to DevOps with AWS: Deploy, Build, and Scale Services with AWS Tools and Techniques*

Osama Mustafa
Amman, Jordan

ISBN-13 (pbk): 978-1-4842-9302-7          ISBN-13 (electronic): 978-1-4842-9303-4
https://doi.org/10.1007/978-1-4842-9303-4

Managing Director, Apress Media LLC: Welmoed Spahr
Acquisitions Editor: Celestin Suresh John
Development Editor: James Markham
Coordinating Editor: Mark Powers

Cover designed by eStudioCalamar

Cover image designed by Shannon Potter on Unsplash (www.unsplash.com)

Distributed to the book trade worldwide by Apress Media, LLC, 1 New York Plaza, New York, NY 10004, U.S.A. Phone 1-800-SPRINGER, fax (201) 348-4505, e-mail orders-ny@springer-sbm.com, or visit www.springeronline.com. Apress Media, LLC is a California LLC and the sole member (owner) is Springer Science + Business Media Finance Inc (SSBM Finance Inc). SSBM Finance Inc is a **Delaware** corporation.

For information on translations, please e-mail booktranslations@springernature.com; for reprint, paperback, or audio rights, please e-mail bookpermissions@springernature.com.

Apress titles may be purchased in bulk for academic, corporate, or promotional use. eBook versions and licenses are also available for most titles. For more information, reference our Print and eBook Bulk Sales web page at www.apress.com/bulk-sales.

Any source code or other supplementary material referenced by the author in this book is available to readers on GitHub (https://github.com/Apress). For more detailed information, please visit www.apress.com/source-code.

Printed on acid-free paper

*I dedicate this book to my mother for her support and constantly encouraging me to work extra hard, and to my family for moral support and encouragement throughout the project.*

# Table of Contents

# About the Author

**Osama Mustafa** The first Oracle ACE in the Middle East. As the first Alibaba MVP, an AWS community builder, the creator/director of the Jordan Amman Oracle User Group (the first group in Jordan related to Oracle technology), and the author of two technology books, Osama is an authority on cloud technology who works with vendors such as AWS, Microsoft, Google, and Oracle. He has experience in automation, has implemented various global projects, and has extensive knowledge of multiple databases.

In addition, Osama is a speaker and author of more than 100 articles published in magazines such as IOUG and UKOUG. He is the author of the book *Oracle Database Application Security*, published by Apress, and has presented at more than 45 conferences around the world.

# About the Technical Reviewer

**Uchit Vyas** is an IT industry veteran, a cloud technologist at heart, and a hands-on enterprise architect and DevSecOps/SRE leader at Accenture Australia. Through his speaking, writing, and analysis, he helps businesses take advantage of emerging technologies. Currently, Uchit works on SRE and DevSecOps practices in the APAC region with presales, delivery, and consulting responsibilities. Uchit loves to play chess and *Age of Empires*, which helps him to clearly see the impact of ideas, research, and automation empowering economies of IT.

Uchit works with large IT organizations to automate traditional datacenter flow, explores new-age tools and technologies, and defines solutions and best practices for small and large enterprises with DevSecOps and enterprise architecture (EA) practices. He has worked at world-class product and service companies such as KPMG, Infosys, and Oracle, during which time he analyzed various cloud platforms, enterprise architecture, infrastructure automation, containers, DevSecOps, and continuous delivery.

He has also written various books about the AWS cloud platform and enterprise service bus including *Mule ESB Cookbook*, *AWS Development Essentials*, *Mastering AWS Development*, *DynamoDB Applied Design Patterns*, and *OpenStack Applied Design Patterns*.

# Acknowledgments

Writing this book was more complicated than I thought and more rewarding than I could ever imagine; it took a long journey to finish. The book focuses on the tools, principles, and more that DevOps teams use.

I would not have been able to get my work done without the continual support and vision of my editor; I want to thank the Apress team and the technical reviewer for working on this book and for the push and support they gave me during this project.

Finally, to the readers who chose this book to be part of their library and support me, thank you, all.

# Introduction

This book is a comprehensive reference for anyone wanting to learn more about Amazon AWS, including AWS services, through real-life examples.

The first two chapters focus on Amazon AWS services; these chapters also cover the Agile methodology and DevOps concepts.

We'll then delve into various aspects of CI/CD, from third-party tools to AWS services, that can create a complete pipeline with real-life examples and projects.

When explaining the test automation process, I offer insight into most of the standard tools used in DevOps.

Infrastructure as code is covered and explained using different tools such as Terraform, CloudFormation, and Pulumi, providing a variety of examples for each and their use cases.

Next, I will help you gain the ability to predict and troubleshoot issues to avoid any downtime. I'll also explain monitoring and observability tools.

In addition, we'll cover security under DevOps, namely, DevSecOps. I'll give an overview and examples that include using third-party tools and AWS tools to create an entire secure pipeline for the company and show how to integrate the solution with the daily pipeline.

Kubernetes plays a significant role in this book and is the standard tool for any DevOps professional. We'll discuss the tool's history, basics, and concepts through a complete solution. Throughout the book, offer incremental examples that allow you to understand how to use and integrate the tools.

Finally, I dedicate a chapter to completing four projects using different DevOps strategies, AWS services, and infrastructure as code; I'll also show how to deploy the solution using CI/CD tools.

# Source Code

All the code used in this book can be downloaded from `https://github.com/apress/complete-guide-devops-aws` or from the author's personal repo, at `https://github.com/OsamaOracle`.

# CHAPTER 1

# Overview of Amazon Web Services

With today's technological boom, the demand for cloud computing services is increasing day by day. Individuals, companies, and multinational businesses are shifting from self-owned web services to cloud services. Among cloud services providers, the most prominent are Amazon Web Services (AWS), Google Cloud Platform (GCP), IBM, and Oracle Cloud.

In this chapter, we'll take a look at cloud services in general and then focus our attention on AWS specifically.

## Cloud Services at a Glance

Why is there a need for online cloud services? The principal function of a cloud service is to provide IT services through the Internet. These services include data storage centers, computing power, and databases. The most prominent feature of cloud services is that the user can place orders and use the services without needing any infrastructure or maintenance.

With the use of cloud providers, IT has seen a rapid shift from costly databases and power units among all major organizations and individuals, regardless of their field of work. The trend toward using cloud services is due to several factors.

- *Cost*: The most significant advantage of opting for cloud services is that it reduces the overall cost for organizations because it allows them to pay only for the resources they use. They no longer have to pay for the hefty infrastructure costs of the powerhouse servers and data centers that were needed earlier, or for the IT experts needed for data management.

© Osama Mustafa 2023
O. Mustafa, *A Complete Guide to DevOps with AWS*, https://doi.org/10.1007/978-1-4842-9303-4_1

- *Speed*: When businesses rely on third-party computing resources, the road from idea to execution takes a matter of minutes. Since planning, management, and maintenance are covered by the on-demand cloud provider, businesses are in a position to deliver faster services to their clients. Similarly, industries can develop innovative ideas that can be transformed quickly with the help of cloud services.

- *Reliability*: As authentic cloud computing companies such as Amazon are fully equipped with the latest configurations to offer the best computing services, they tend to be more reliable. Moreover, the network of cloud services for data backup and retrieval is more reliable than individual databases.

- *Scale*: Another benefit of cloud computing is that both horizontal scaling and vertical scaling are easily possible. For instance, companies can add instances or nodes by adding more space to the existing hard drive in horizontal scaling and can speed up or create wider spaces through adding more machines in vertical scaling easily through cloud computing.

- *Security*: Another highlight of cloud computing is that it provides cyber and data security to its users by protecting the databases from hackers, unauthorized access, and other security breaches. Hence, with reliable cloud computing services such as Amazon Web Services, companies get the most optimal risk management techniques.

## Types of Cloud Computing

*Cloud computing* is an umbrella term used for multiple types of services that cloud providers offer. Organizations use cloud computing not just for databases and servers but for numerous instances, including virtual assistance, software applications, user customizations, and other technological requirements. For this reason, cloud services vary according to the needs of their users, but there is no limitation to the services cloud providers offer. Each cloud computing provider delivers solutions for the specific requirements of the customers.

The first step toward using cloud services is selecting the cloud classification, or type, of deployment. There are three types of cloud computing: public, private, and hybrid cloud.

- *Public cloud*: As the name suggests, public cloud services are provided by third parties such as Amazon Web Services. In the public domain, individuals and firms can use cloud services by logging into their accounts simply through web browsers. The hardware, software, and database systems are not owned by any specific user. These services are accessible to all users as they are controlled and operated by the cloud service provider.

- *Private cloud*: The private cloud environment is accessible only to a specific individual or organization. For example, some organizations require data servers within proximity onsite, while others may opt for third-party hosting. Nevertheless, a private cloud always maintains an exclusive network that caters to the customer's specific business needs. In addition, the privacy of this type of cloud service provides more control and security to its users.

- *Hybrid cloud*: The combination of public and private cloud environments results in hybrid cloud services. Organizations usually choose this type of deployment to conveniently scale up their services during excessive workloads without compromising the privacy and security of their database. Organizations that do not want the cost and maintenance of owning their data centers but require a private network to ensure a controlled environment prefer hybrid cloud services.

## Cloud Service Models

Cloud services can be categorized into three models: *infrastructure as a service* (IaaS), *platform as a service* (PaaS), and *software as a service* (SaaS). In addition, a fourth type of cloud service, *serverless computing*, is sometimes offered by cloud service providers. All models differ from the others in terms of data management, scaling, control, and overall provisioning of cloud services.

- *Infrastructure as a service*: IaaS is the simplest model of cloud services. Through IaaS, individuals, firms, and organizations can become IT tenants of the cloud service providers by hiring the entire IT infrastructure. This includes renting the hardware and software for network services and virtual machines for storage centers and data management. IaaS provides total control over an organization's IT resources, similar to having an onsite data center.

- *Platform as a service*: PaaS is the opposite of the IaaS model. This model requires the clients to focus only on their service provisions and applications rather than worrying about the infrastructure space and costs. Therefore, the computing environment of PaaS is ideal for those individuals and industries that need to concentrate on their product innovations rather than on maintenance, space management, and availability of hardware, software, and network data servers.

- *Software as a service*: The SaaS model delivers the overall structural design and ideas through a software service to its users. As a result, the complete IT process from planning to management to maintenance is covered by the SaaS provider. In addition, SaaS can provide software applications as an end product that can be accessed or downloaded from a website.

- *Serverless computing*: Serverless computing services assist clients by managing and maintaining all their IT requirements, including hardware infrastructure, software applications, and data services. All this is done idly during their subscription tenure and activated only on demand. Usually serverless cloud services are used by clients who want a passive cloud system and then are activated whenever a specific operation occurs. This cloud model environment is cost-effective for small-scale business owners or industries with fluctuating workflow.

Figure 1-1 illustrates the shared responsibility of each cloud category and what you will manage in each model; remember, choosing the suitable model will save a lot of time and money for you and the company.

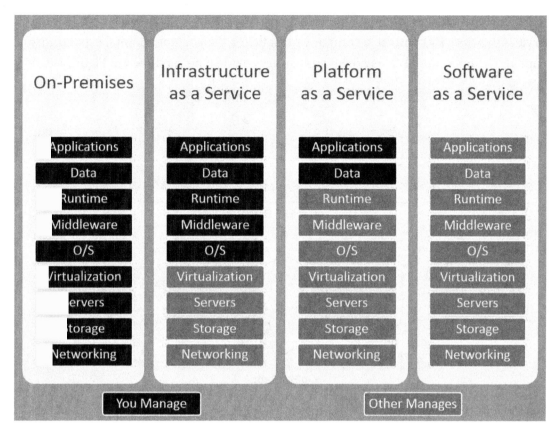

***Figure 1-1.*** *IaaS, PaaS, and SaaS*

My personal experience as a computer engineer has taught me more about cloud computing services than any other resource. Almost every company I have worked at used a cloud service provider to ensure their data was encrypted and secured during my tenure. In addition, the companies preferred to opt for these services as they are cost-efficient compared to owning and maintaining data centers.

Constructing and installing a data center can cost millions of dollars for a company. In addition, the maintenance of virtual machines and servers requires a big expenditure. Therefore, cloud computing services are an ideal choice for all businesses that need IT services but want to save money.

Another downside of having your own data center is that the workflow is not constant. There are times when many computing services are not required. The expense of maintaining data centers 24/7 can lead to monetary losses.

With cloud services, organizations have various options for expenses (opex) for the services they use. By contrast, a company must bear a data center's capital expenditure (capex). The operational costs are high regardless of the type, as shown in Figure 1-2.

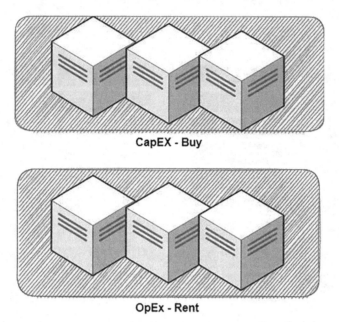

**CapEX - Buy**

**OpEx - Rent**

***Figure 1-2.***  *Capex versus opex*

The benefits of cloud services are clear for organizations that want to run and host their software applications and data operations through the cloud. However, it is equally essential for these organizations to structure their computing needs appropriately. For instance, if organizations do not properly scale, they will be charged for the data space and speed, even if it is not used.

Similarly, switching the apps, notifications, and services on and off is an option in the cloud. When services are not in use, they can be turned off to avoid unnecessary expenses. These power and cost-saving methods are known as *automated techniques*. In short, an automated system allows companies to customize their cloud services so that they pay only for the services they use.

We'll focus on public cloud services in this chapter as they are the most commonly used cloud service type. Public cloud services are simply a group of data centers. Cloud service providers own these data centers and rent them to companies for profit. Even in public cloud services, the same hardware or data servers are shared by all the tenants of the cloud service provider. If someone needs a bare-metal server for individual use and data privacy, for instance, Amazon Web Services would host private cloud services for organizations and individuals.

In this case, a specific computer functions as a separate server for a particular tenant or consumer. Additionally, AWS provides various virtual services with different capacities and designs.

Another significant cloud services company and competitor of Amazon is Microsoft Azure, which provides similar services to its users. Microsoft Azure sells a copy of its cloud operating system so that individuals or organizations can use the services by downloading them to their data centers. In addition to Amazon and Microsoft, many renowned companies and tech giants offer cloud computing services. However, the common aspect among all companies is that they all provide a massive data server setup for database storage and other networking and IT-related operations through the Internet or other private connections.

In another scenario, companies that are operating thousands of virtual machines through hardware such as routers and switches can achieve the same results by using AWS automated services without any hardware devices. The storage, system organization, load distribution, and automated scaling services are provided by AWS with the help of virtual computing (Elastic Cloud Compute [EC2] instances) with massive CPU and RAM resources running in substantial server networks with need-based systems.

This book discusses Amazon AWS inside out and how you can make the switch. The first step is to decide to switch from traditional databases to cloud services. Next, the switch requires awareness and knowledge from the users and IT experts. Finally, shifting from traditional to the latest cloud settings must be done within a specified time. Specifically, the cloud service user organizations should support the AWS virtual resources and help users understand AWS's relevance in the IT world.

The advantages of using cloud services are clear. The next part is choosing a cloud environment and deploying the cloud computing model that best serves users' needs. Generally, the needs of cloud users can be broadly categorized into four cases.

- An organization has all the infrastructural resources, including data centers and IT management, the constantly increasing workflow is leading to more maintenance expenses. In such a case, the organization will look to shift to public cloud services to minimize costs.

- There is no onsite infrastructure when a group of developers is creating a startup. In such a case with no local data centers, cloud services are the best option to start their business immediately.

- Another similar scenario is that of a low-budget startup that cannot afford to set up an onsite data center. Cloud services are the best option for them to start their business.

- Many organizations deal with sensitive databases that require a private network. However, they also need other services such as data analysis, backup, or retrieval. In such a scenario, the hybrid model of cloud services is the best option available for such organizations.

There can be many other situations where the requirements of each user are different from the others. That is why it is vital to understand. A complete service-level agreement (SLA) subscription allows users to customize all the data, applications, and networking services according to their needs. The SLA enables users to design an environment for their IT needs and completely control it.

---

**Note**    If you are new to AWS, you can get a free account for 1500$ credit by signing up at `https://aws.amazon.com/startups/`. This account will also allow you to test the labs and projects in this book.

---

# AWS Cloud Computing's Key Characteristics

Amazon AWS has more services than any other cloud service on the market. Integrating the services with each other will provide a powerful solution.

- *Self-service on-demand*: The self-service on-demand feature in Amazon AWS allows users to order online services at any given time. The users can order through the website, where there is an option for on-demand cloud self-service via a control panel. Figure 1-3 below shows the main page for the AWS portal and some of the services you could use.

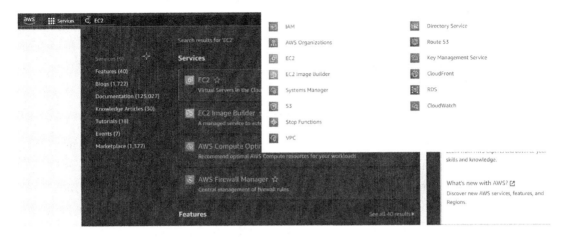

**Figure 1-3.**  *AWS Portal*

- *Broad network access*: The most significant advantage of cloud
  services is that they are available anytime and anywhere through the
  Internet.

- *Resource pooling*: The public cloud infrastructure, including the data
  centers, is distributed across the globe and is installed wherever the
  cloud services are in high demand. For example, a need-based onsite
  cloud service would pool its systems, computing resources, storage,
  and networking applications in the data centers and would provide
  restricted machination from its pool. All public cloud providers have
  many resources to meet diverse demands. For example, AWS features
  data center clusters (known as *availability zones*, or AZs) with
  thousands of bare-metal servers accessible and online, empowering
  clients to operate their computing systems with maximum speed and
  minimum obstruction.

- *Rapid elasticity*: Almost all cloud services require elasticity in the
  public cloud. This means users can increase the capacity and
  optimize performance in accordance with their needs. This process
  is referred as *scaling*. With AWS, automated scaling is provided
  to its customers for both storage and computing resources. AWS
  automatically tracks and regulates the applications and services to
  maintain the better performance of its computing services.

- *Measured service*: You are charged only for what you use in the cloud; this is a metered, or *measured*, service. Cloud service companies make money by selling their services to customers through their data centers. Inbound packet flow, or traffic between subnets housed in different data centers, usually is free; outbound packet flow, or traffic between subnets hosted in various data centers, generally costs an outbound data transfer fee. Charges are calculated per second or minute for computer services such as AWS EC2 compute instances or per gigabyte per month for storage services such as S3 or virtual hard drives, referred to as *Elastic Block Storage* (EBS) at AWS. AWS Billing Dashboard is one of the primary services that allow the cloud engineer to follow up about the services and take action if it crosses.

***Figure 1-4.*** *AWS Billing Dashboard*

Where are you thinking about putting your cloud resources? Before working with AWS, you need to understand the following concepts:

- Regions

- Availability zones

- Edge location

- Location factors

- Compliance factors

- SLA factors

- Costs

# AWS Regions

Amazon Web Services is in more than 240 countries and territories. Millions of active users worldwide are affiliated with AWS, and the number is increasing daily. To exceed the expectations of its clients, the AWS team is constantly working to improve their services and widen their reach among users. In addition, AWS is focused on reducing latency and speeding up its services. Furthermore, AWS is also obligated to store data in the chosen AWS region. See `https://aws.amazon.com/about-aws/global-infrastructure/regions_az/` for more information.

Each of AWS's regions is sizable and located in a different part of the world. Individual Availability Zones within a given AWS Region are designed to be fault-tolerant in an outage in another Availability Zone, check Figure 1-5.

***Figure 1-5.*** *AWS regions*

If you want to explore the region's location more, the AWS website will allow you to do this quickly, as shown in Figure 1-6.

**Figure 1-6.** *AWS website showing regions*

The reach of Amazon Web Services is tremendous, with more than 20 regions worldwide. The regions where AWS is available are known as the AWS *availability zones*. Presently, AWS operates in more than 80 availability zones and aims to double this number in the future. These availability zones are the foundation of the entire AWS structure. Each zone is a geographical location with one or more data centers, making AWS accessible to millions of active users. These data centers are equipped with extra power machines, networks, and connectivity resources. As a result, users can get cloud services with risk-free and latency-free databases, and customers have the option of scaling, which is impossible with any local data center.

The AWS availability zones in each region operate as separate physical entities and are not connected. Even if a region has more than one availability zone, the data centers are located far from each other. This distance ensures that any fault or issue with one data center does not affect the data in any other zone. Moreover, with each AWS as a separate zone, the databases are not shared and remain secure from other zones.

The separate availability zones of AWS provide functional adherence and data security to users. Moreover, stand-alone zones ensure the privacy and protection of user data. Similarly, it conveys to the customers that data protection is taken as a strict rule, which is not compromised at any cost. Hence, AWS guarantees that the user data will not be hijacked or transferred unless the user asks for that.

# Availability Zones

The availability zones of Amazon Web Services are data centers located within a region in one or more location. Each zone is a distinct network and is linked with the other only through a low-latency connection. These isolated networks support data security and speed and are not prone to threats from other networks. Moreover, the separate data centers minimize the workload, resulting in operational stability. In addition, the data centers are carefully located in low-risk areas where data centers can avoid any kind of physical or virtual risks. For instance, the geographical locations for data centers are specifically selected for low risk. However, users are not restricted and can access any regional data center through AWS.

Data centers in each availability zone have power supplies from separate power substations. The intention of having individual power units is to provide an uninterrupted power supply (UPS) to all the data centers. Moreover, different power substations ensure that a power failure in one data center does not affect the power grids in any other availability zones.

Table 1-1 shows some examples of regions and AZs; the list is not definitive. Each AZ is connected to the other within the same region through a customized, excessive, low-remission synthetic network. The inner AWS private cloud network has speeds of up to 40 Gbps. AWS owns and maintains redundant private network lines that connect all AZs within a region.

***Table 1-1.*** *AWS Regions and AZ*

| Region | Region Name | Availability Zones |
|---|---|---|
| us-east-1 | N. Virginia | us-east-1a |
| | | us-east-1b |
| | | us-east-1c |
| | | us-east-1d |
| | | us-east-1e |
| | | us-east-1f |
| us-east-2 | Ohio | us-east-2a |
| | | us-east-2b |
| | | us-east-2c |
| us-west-1 | N. California | us-west-1a |
| | | us-west-1b |
| | | us-west-1c |
| us-west-2 | Oregon | us-west-2a |
| | | us-west-2b |
| | | us-west-2c |
| us-gov-west-1 | US GovCloud West | us-gov-west-1a |
| | | us-gov-west-1b |
| | | us-gov-west-1c |
| ca-central-1 | Canada | ca-central-1a |
| | | ca-central-1b |
| EU-west-1 | Ireland | EU-west-1a |
| | | EU-west-1b |
| | | EU-west-1c |
| EU-west-2 | London | EU-west-2a |
| | | EU-west-2b |
| | | EU-west-2c |
| EU-west-3 | Paris | EU-west-3a |
| | | EU-west-3b |
| | | EU-west-3c |

*(continued)*

***Table 1-1.*** (*continued*)

| Region | Region Name | Availability Zones |
|---|---|---|
| EU-west-4 | Stockholm | EU-west-4a |
| | | EU-west-4b |
| | | EU-west-4c |
| EU-central-1 | Frankfurt | EU-central-1a |
| | | EU-central-1b |
| | | EU-central-1c |
| ap-northeast-1 | Tokyo | ap-northeast-1a |
| | | ap-northeast-1b |
| | | ap-northeast-1c |
| | | ap-northeast-1d |
| ap-northeast-2 | Seoul | ap-northeast-2a |
| | | ap-northeast-2c |
| ap-south-1 | Mumbai | ap-south-1a |
| | | ap-south-1b |
| ap-southeast-2 | Sydney | ap-southeast-2a |
| | | ap-southeast-2b |
| | | ap-southeast-2c |
| sa-east-1 | Sao Paulo | sa-east-1a |
| | | sa-east-1b |
| | | sa-east-1c |

Amazon Web Services customers are given an option to choose from any of the listed regions to subscribe to cloud services for data storage or backup, virtual networking, or any other IT services. However, some online cloud services do not require users to choose a specific region or availability zone, such as Amazon Web Services or Amazon EC2.

In contrast, most of the services in AWS are region specific. This means users will have to choose a particular region or can be operational from only a specific availability zone.

Similarly, AWS makes it possible for users to choose a region that is not in proximity to their geographical location. Some customers select a far-off region as it may cost less than the closer ones. The cost of services in each region at AWS depends upon the pricing of the country.

However, price is not the only factor to consider when choosing different availability zones; security and latency are also driving forces for region selections. After analyzing and evaluating the AWS region selection data, we can say that many multinational companies with global outreach prefer multiple region services. For instance, media and entertainment companies such as Netflix prefer cloud services in several regions simultaneously. Similarly, some users favor selecting a pool of regional databases for data recovery and disaster recovery.

Moreover, businesses with customers of multiple ethnicities also use multiregional cloud services to connect with all their customers globally. Lastly, the rules and regulations of various countries regarding data and information laws are yet another reason to select a specific region. For instance, information is governed differently in some nations and areas, such as the EU, than in other countries. The rules and regulations of a particular region influence how the data moves from one region to another.

We know that AZs are a collection of data centers. When built, they take floodplains and fault lines into account, place each AZ on its own power grid, and link them with private fiber. So, let's take a look at the Oregon region, also known as us-west-2, as shown in Figure 1-7.

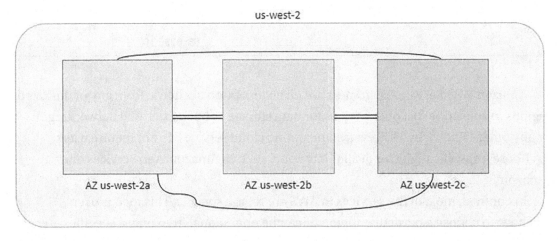

***Figure 1-7.*** *Examples of AZ and region*

Figure 1-7 shows three availability zones in the United States (west 2a, 2b, and 2c) in a particular geographical region. This is a basic system of AWS, and as we analyze Amazon Web Services, we will observe similar patterns of infrastructure. Almost all regions have more than one availability zone; however, as we discussed, these zones are separate entities from each other. For instance, in the United States, there are many states with two availability zones, such as Oregon and Ohio. There are also states that have more than two AZs. Availability zones are integral to high accessibility and risk tolerance, even when regions are the most important infrastructural step.

As there is always a possibility of faults, errors, power shutdowns, malware, hacking, and other threats, customers of cloud services are always looking for reassurance from the service provider when selecting IT services. Therefore, the clients of AWS want to use most of the availability zones within their region so that they can minimize their risk of data loss.

Similarly, clients prefer AWS as it offers not just a powerful computer but also a rigorous data backup system. When shopping around, you want answers to these fundamental issues: "What happens if a data center goes down?" and "What happens if a data center can't be reached?" Well, "We have many data centers," is a decent response to that query. So, suppose we were using the Oregon region. In that case, we'd take advantage of all three availability zones, A, B, and C, and distribute our application across multiple machines, as well as our databases, storage, and content, across all three availability zones, to ensure high availability, fault tolerance, and durability. Again, availability zones are a group of data centers linked by private fiber critical to Amazon Web Services' high availability and fault tolerance.

Is it Amazon's responsibility if your hosted application isn't available? No. It's the customer's problem if the hosted apps don't follow suitable cloud design standards. Failing to design your apps to work effectively in various AZs would void your AWS service-level agreement. Similarly, there is also the option of earning credit on your account for hours of downtime if your app was but you had correctly built it. However, there is a catch: you must show that your program was down by submitting the appropriate network traces.

# Global Edge Services

Customers who want to subscribe to Amazon Web Services must send an online request to Amazon Resource Centers for subscriptions. Users around the world can reach AWS through its edge location service. Edge locations (EVs) are data centers like AZs and are present in various regions worldwide. In 2021, more than 225 edge locations were spread across 47 different countries.

Every edge website is virtually linked with the telecommunication transit network of the specific location. Edge services are spread across the globe like the Internet. Amazon Edge is connected through telecom networks so that they can reach customers worldwide at the lowest cost possible. Accessing Amazon Edge through the Internet is also the slowest way to reach it. However, this has the lowest latency. Moreover, users sometimes use VPN connections or a direct connection from the local data center to connect to the edge site.

Generally, at each edge site, there are three data connection options:

- Internet connections

- Direct Connect connections

- AWS private networks

Various vital services are available at each edge site; some are offered at no cost, while others may be bought and used at each edge location as needed, based on your current and future requirements. The services provided at each edge are covered next.

# Route 53

Route 53 is Amazon's hosted DNS service, named after the standard DNS port number. Route 53 features a public side that receives inbound client queries and then resolves each question to the required AWS resource on the private side.

Let's imagine there's a single DNS server at the edge with complete knowledge of all AWS resources for simplicity. This isn't a highly fault-tolerant design. It would be preferable to have redundant DNS services wired across the globe and have complete awareness of all AWS resources. The Anycast DNS routing techniques were used to create Route 53. All Anycast DNS servers throughout the AWS regions know each target service location in this arrangement. Route 53 will guide you to an edge location based on your site. Once an application request reaches the edge location, it is sent to the selected AWS service location through Amazon's proprietary high-speed network.

The following Figure 1-8 shows the simple architecture of the edge that connected to Route 53.

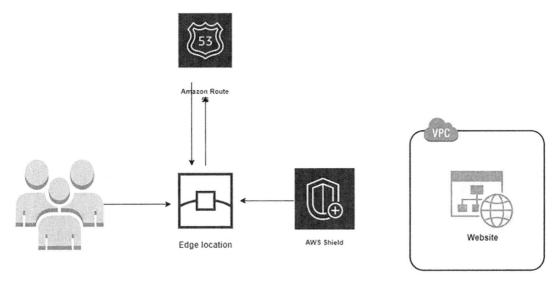

*Figure 1-8.* *Route 53 at an AWS edge location*

# Web Application Firewall

Web Application Firewall (WAF) is a website protection firewall that helps to monitor and guard the user's web applications. WAF functions by filtering the Hypertext Transfer Protocol (HTTP) or website traffic. Hence, it is a protective layer between the potential threats and web applications of the users. These virtual threats include cross-site forgery, cross-site scripting (XSS), file inclusion, and SQL injection. Moreover, there are three types of WAF deployment: network-based, host-based, and cloud-based. However, WAF is not the ultimate solution to all kinds of virtual threats, such as mitigation, etc., as other sophisticated technologies deal with these security hazards.

# CloudFront

CloudFront is another Amazon service that provides high-speed static and dynamic web traffic, including HTML, CSS, JS, and image files. CloudFront is connected to the global edge connections and distributes web data to users. AWS provides the fastest web services through its edge services. For instance, if a customer orders CloudFront web content, the charge is linked up with the low-latency networks through the edge data center and executed without delay to the client. In addition, there is also AWS documentation, which has the following functions:

- As speedy performance is the aim of AWS, the CloudFront services provide immediate content allocation when it is available at the lowest-latency edge location.

- If the web content is unavailable at the edge location, then CloudFront retrieves the data from its source. The user provides the source to get access to the authentic web source.

## Lambda@Edge

Lambda is a SaaS platform that allows user data resource management, such as system maintenance, automated scaling, database provision, etc. More important, Lambda runs on specific code that the user writes; based on that code, Lambda performs multiple automated computing tasks. For instance, the users can launch some code for a Python function to select a particular region for the data center. Later the code will be automatically executed through an edge data center network in the user's proximity. From a few queries per day to thousands per second, Lambda@Edge processes them automatically. Requests are processed in AWS locations closer to the viewer than on origin servers, decreasing latency and enhancing the user experience.

## AWS Shield

AWS Shield provides baseline security to all AWS customers, but AWS does not safeguard each client individually. Instead, it is protecting its edge infrastructure for all clients. What if you want a more tailored DDoS defense? Get your wallet out and contact the AWS Shield Advanced team if you don't know how to handle your security challenges and want AWS professionals to help you with real-time tailored protection.

## AWS Operational Benefits

There are certain advantages to using the public cloud. First, there are unrestricted connections to network and databases. Second, there are various administration options that make operating in the cloud simpler than you probably anticipated. Table 1-1 lists the AWS managed services that might change or supplement your current onsite services and operations.

- *Servers*: It's costly to manage and maintain underutilized servers in your data center. Your on-premise data center will shrink as you move apps to the public cloud. Your overall hosting expenditure will be reduced since you won't be hosting as many physical servers. You won't have to spend as much for software licensing at the processor level since you won't be responsible for operating hypervisor services; Amazon will do that. You might think that switching to the AWS cloud entails merely virtualized resources, but AWS offers a complete range of computing solutions with computing resources of any proportion and capacity, from a single-core CPU with 512MB of RAM to hundreds of times of RAM. You can also purchase a bare-metal server and use it in any way.

- *Storage*: Cloud storage offers many advantages since cloud providers guarantee a limitless quantity of storage. Amazon provides a variety of storage alternatives that are comparable to, but not identical to, your on-premise solutions. Amazon offers shareable file solutions for storage area networks, including the Elastic File System (EFS) for Linux applications and FSx, a shared file service tailored to Windows File Server workloads. EBS allows you to create virtual hard drives. S3 and S3 Glacier provide unlimited storage as well as longer-term archival storage.

- *Managed services*: AWS offers multiple controlled services, as indicated in Table 1-2. These services have the capacity to take the place of the bulky onsite infrastructure after you migrate to the cloud.

***Table 1-2.*** *On-Premise vs. AWS*

| Managing IT | On-Premise | Amazon AWS |
|---|---|---|
| Servers/ compute | Rack, networking, hardware servers, switches, routers. | EC2 with different types, plus complete networking tools. |
| Storage | SAN storage. | EBS, EFS, S3. |
| Monitoring | Different tools, Nagios and SolarWinds. | CloudWatch and X-Ray. |
| Scale | Costly, and usually you can't decrease the resources later. | Provide scale up/down depending on your needs. |
| Identity management | Active Directory, third-party tools if you need to set up SSO. | You can extend your on-premises Active Directory to the AWS cloud with hosted Directory Services. Manage access to popular business apps hosted by third-party cloud providers using AWS single sign-on services (SSO). |
| Backup | It would be best if you used a third-party solution. | AWS manages this part for you for your database or server with snapshots or automatically. |
| VPN | Routers could do this. | AWS provides different services for this such as OpenVPN, Site2Site VPN, and Direct Connect. |

All cloud service providers have a published service level agreement (SLA) that dictates the particulars of what resources are being offered and at which functional level. Moreover, it is the responsibility of the public cloud providers to make a commitment to their clients regarding the data security, standards, and assistance and how other procedures will be reflected in the company's SLA. The service providers are bound to act in accordance with the SLA. Additionally, specifications regarding the allowed duration of technical interruptions and the provider's checks and balances during the interruptions are covered in the SLA. There will also be disclaimers emphasizing the cloud provider's inability to be held liable for situations outside its control.

The cloud provider is answerable for the entire system and arrangement of computing services, resource management, the general administration of the cloud, the protection of data and network services, and the preservation of client privacy, regardless of whatever cloud model is used. The SLA will also include a description of the responsibilities of each client, referred to as the *cloud consumer*, in terms of how they are expected to do business with the cloud provider. Each cloud customer must be completely aware of the features and benefits provided by each cloud service provider; Table 1-3 shows examples of the Amazon AWS SLA, and you can read the SLA agreement at `https://aws.amazon.com/legal/service-level-agreements/`.

***Table 1-3.*** *AWS SLA Examples*

| AWS Service | SLA | Service Credit Percentage |
|---|---|---|
| Amazon Compute (including EC2, EBS, ECS and AWS Fargate) | Less than 99.99% but equal to or greater than 99% | 30% |
| Amazon Database, RDS | Less than 99% but equal to or greater than 95% | 25% |
| Security and compliance | Less than 99% but equal to or greater than 95% | 25% |
| Networking and content delivery | Less than 99% but equal to or greater than 95% | 25% |
| Amazon Storage | Less than 99% but equal to or greater than 95% | 25% |
| Amazon Serverless | Less than 99% but equal to or greater than 95% | 25% |
| Amazon IoT | Less than 99% but equal to or greater than 95% | 25% |

# AWS Data Best Practices

Amazon AWS provides different ways to secure your data; you can't ignore security when moving to the cloud. The AWS cloud is not solely responsible for the overall protection of the computing services; customers share this responsibility. The user controls their own data privacy and must take appropriate measures to protect their data, platform, applications, systems, and networks. Hence, users of cloud services should be just as cautious as they would be when managing their own private onsite data center.

When connected to the AWS public cloud environment, the user can be assured that their data will be in secured hands and will be saved for the longest time possible. Moreover, it is rare to encrypt data from the AWS storage system, except for a few cases like S3 Glacier. Other data cannot be ciphered by default. EBS volumes, on the other hand, use either AWS customer master keys or keys provided by the customer, and both boot and data volumes may be encrypted at rest and in transit, ensuring that the data is protected. Shared storage systems like EFS and DynamoDB tables may also be encrypted while in transit. AWS S3 buckets can be encrypted using keys provided by AWS or keys supplied by the client (if applicable).

Data durability offers special protection; all data saved in the cloud is duplicated across several data centers. EBS volumes are replicated inside the data center in which they are housed. It is possible to achieve high durability by copying S3 items across three sites within the designated Amazon Web Services region. It is amusingly said that for every 1,000 things kept in an S3 bucket, you will lose one of those objects once per 10 million years, according to Amazon's degree of S3 durability. We will be unable to replicate this degree of durability and security on-premises.

The following factors are concerns when moving to the public cloud:

- *Privacy*: The most significant feature of a public cloud service is that the data is stored in a shared data center. This element makes the public cloud different from the private cloud model because there are many tenants of a public cloud service. Nevertheless, genuine cloud service providers like AWS guarantee that the data of each user is protected and segregated from one another.

- *Controlling the data*: Clients have complete control over the storage and retrieval of their data saved on Amazon Web Services. The default setting for all AWS data storage is private unless the clients choose to make it public for some reason; it is the user's responsibility to establish the protection and provision of any data archives kept in AWS.

- *Security*: Data security is one of the most challenging aspects of cloud services. As data encryption threats always exist for public cloud data, reliable cloud service providers like AWS provide the best possible data security policies to their users. AWS provides secured data through shared storage resources. In addition, it offers IAM, which allows users to create permission protocols for their AWS account.

# AWS Network Best Practices

The networking infrastructure of Amazon Web Services is handled at the subgrid level, and all subgrids are formed as personal subnetworks that are inaccessible to the general public. These subgrids are broadband addresses, which are located on the user's personal network, referred to as a *virtual private cloud* (VPC) on Amazon Web Services. Access to subgrids via either the public Internet or any private VPN connection from an onsite system is possible only when a VPC has been configured with a gateway service.

Please keep in mind that it's up to the client to choose a public or private connection, not Amazon AWS. The following Figure 1-9, showing the virtual private network (VPC) creation page.

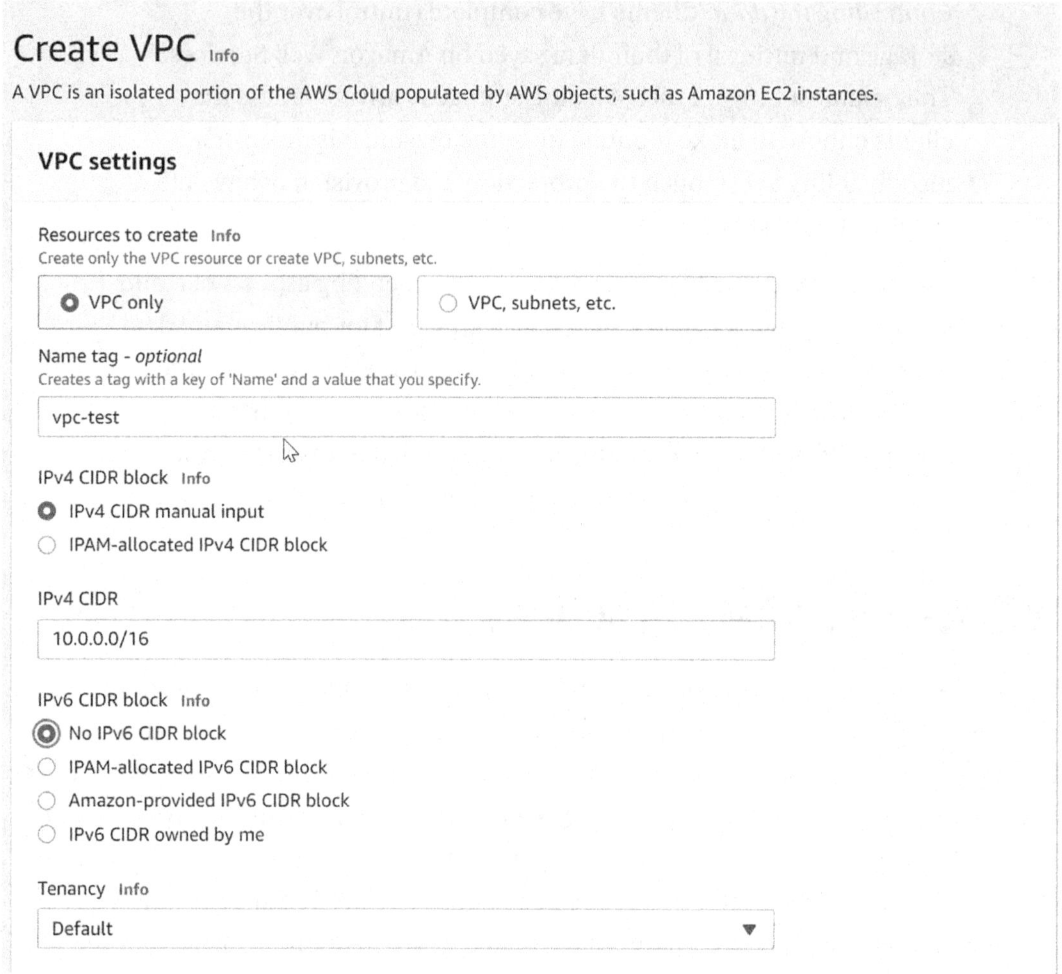

## Create VPC  Info

A VPC is an isolated portion of the AWS Cloud populated by AWS objects, such as Amazon EC2 instances.

### VPC settings

Resources to create  Info
Create only the VPC resource or create VPC, subnets, etc.

| ● VPC only | ○ VPC, subnets, etc. |
|---|---|

Name tag - *optional*
Creates a tag with a key of 'Name' and a value that you specify.

vpc-test

IPv4 CIDR block  Info
● IPv4 CIDR manual input
○ IPAM-allocated IPv4 CIDR block

IPv4 CIDR

10.0.0.0/16

IPv6 CIDR block  Info
◉ No IPv6 CIDR block
○ IPAM-allocated IPv6 CIDR block
○ Amazon-provided IPv6 CIDR block
○ IPv6 CIDR owned by me

Tenancy  Info

Default ▼

***Figure 1-9.***  *Creating a VPC in AWS*

- A type of subnet firewall called a network ACL can control each subnet's ingress and egress traffic, without any previous interaction for the outgoing and incoming packet flow.

- An additional firewall called a *security group* further protects each EC2 instance hosted on a subnet. This firewall specifically dictates which traffic flow will be allowed and where the outgoing traffic will be channelized. Part of creating the VPC is creating the subnet; Figure 1-10 shows the creation of subnets.

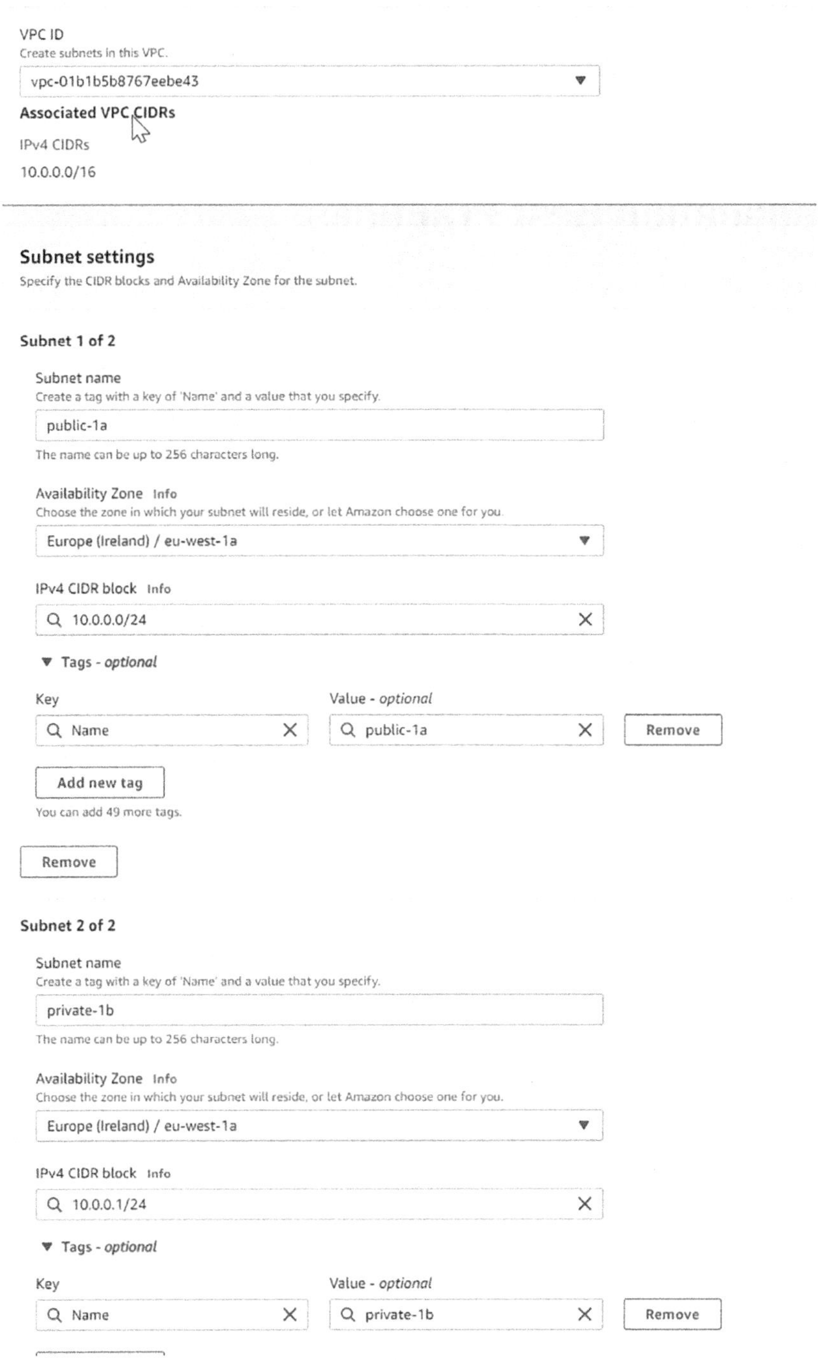

VPC ID
Create subnets in this VPC.

vpc-01b1b5b8767eebe43 ▼

**Associated VPC CIDRs**

IPv4 CIDRs

10.0.0.0/16

**Subnet settings**
Specify the CIDR blocks and Availability Zone for the subnet.

**Subnet 1 of 2**

Subnet name
Create a tag with a key of 'Name' and a value that you specify.

public-1a

The name can be up to 256 characters long.

Availability Zone   Info
Choose the zone in which your subnet will reside, or let Amazon choose one for you.

Europe (Ireland) / eu-west-1a ▼

IPv4 CIDR block   Info

Q   10.0.0.0/24 ✕

▼ Tags - *optional*

| Key | | Value - *optional* | | |
|---|---|---|---|---|
| Q   Name | ✕ | Q   public-1a | ✕ | Remove |

Add new tag

You can add 49 more tags.

Remove

**Subnet 2 of 2**

Subnet name
Create a tag with a key of 'Name' and a value that you specify.

private-1b

The name can be up to 256 characters long.

Availability Zone   Info
Choose the zone in which your subnet will reside, or let Amazon choose one for you.

Europe (Ireland) / eu-west-1a ▼

IPv4 CIDR block   Info

Q   10.0.0.1/24 ✕

▼ Tags - *optional*

| Key | | Value - *optional* | | |
|---|---|---|---|---|
| Q   Name | ✕ | Q   private-1b | ✕ | Remove |

***Figure 1-10.*** *Creating a subnet for a VPC*

Another extra layer of network security from AWS consists of VPC flow logs that can be enabled to capture network traffic for the entire VPC, a single subnet, or a network interface.

# AWS Application Best Practices

It is recommended that web and network servers operated by AWS be situated on personal subgrids. It is not possible to connect to a private subnet from the Internet directly, so you need to set up a VPN such as OpenVPN. A question might arise regarding a public-oriented application that does not have a direct public entry point to the program. It is a best practice at AWS to answer this issue in the following way: for web servers that clients from all over the world access, installing the load distribution system on a public subnetwork next to the web servers gives the optimal configuration option. Users who are looking to get past the system will be routed to the load balancer's DNS name, shown on their computer's screen. When incoming traffic from the public subnet arrives, the load balancer routes it to the targeted web servers located in the personal subgrids. The application load distributor is one of the load balancer types supplied by AWS. It is capable of performing authentication and SSL offload services. Several encryptions and decryption points can be used to construct a three-tier web application's end-to-end flow of communication.

Figure 1-11 shows the most straightforward architecture for an application deployed on AWS.

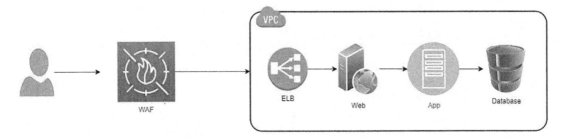

***Figure 1-11.*** *Simple application deployed on AWS*

AWS is accessible in numerous geographical locations and is subject to the laws and rules imposed by states and industry compliance requirements. These regulations rely on the type of company that is being operated. For this reason, there may be various degrees of compliance while using the AWS cloud for your operations. For example, clients of financial, health, and government organizations must adhere to a tight set of rules and regulations. In addition, your organization may have its own set of internal laws and rules to abide by.

In most developed countries, new rules and regulations are implemented regarding the security and protection of databases and virtual information of the corporate sector. Even when there are cybersecurity protection units active, still more restrictions are applied to safeguard user data to protect it from threats of encryption. It is the main responsibility of the service providers to make sure that their client's data is protected effectively.

Cloud service providers have contractual duties to guarantee that such information is kept safe and secure when companies have data records housed in their cloud. They support different compliance standards like the following:

- PCI DSS for payment cards to prevent fraud.

- GDPR is applied in Europe for personal information.

- SOX for Publicly traded companies to protect shareholders.

- GLBA is used by the financial industry to protect personal information.

- HIPPA is usually used for healthcare to protect personal information.

# The Well-Architected Framework

AWS published the Well-Architected Framework a few years ago to assist clients in making informed decisions about transitioning to the AWS cloud. The framework is a set of acknowledged best practices that cloud architects can use to design safe, robust, and decently performing infrastructure for hosting their applications. The best approach should not be mindlessly implemented without comprehending why it has been designated as a best practice; each best practice must still be reviewed to see whether it satisfies your requirements. The latest version of the documentation can be found here: `https://docs.aws.amazon.com/wellarchitected/latest/framework/welcome.html`.

Amazon AWS highly recommends the following for each application that will be deployed on AWS:

- *Operational excellence*: When it comes to AWS application execution, deployment, and monitoring, automatically positioned tracking methods, constant progress, and self-assisted analysis for data retrieval are the best practices. CloudWatch events and alerts, CloudTrail, EC2 Auto Scaling, AWS Config, and the Trusted Advisor are some of the most important AWS services. Successfully supporting the development and operation workloads, exploring their networks, and continually enhancing assistance in operations to generate monetary value are all essential. Always ask yourself questions like the following before implementing anything:

  - What are the best methods to deal with application interruptions? Is it better to do it manually or automatically?

  - How can we keep track of the efficiency of apps and infrastructure components hosted on AWS?

- *Security*: Developing networks that are dependable and safe while preserving client data privacy at the highest possible level is important. Also, it is crucial to use cloud services to secure databases and all computing resources in such a way that it strengthens the protective firewalls, so one could ask themselves questions like these:

  - How do we manage credentials/authentication on AWS?

  - How do we automate things for security?

- *Reliability*: How can the computing services and networks operated by AWS be restored from an outage within the minimum time? Similarly, how can apps fulfill the client's rising demands and perform a task efficiently so that it achieves its target accurately and persistently? The questions to ask include these:

  - How can we keep track of the applications operated by AWS?

  - How can applications hosted on AWS respond to variations in customer requirements?

- *Performance efficiency*: What are the strategies that can fulfill requirements for the cost? Key AWS features include Cost Explorer, Budgets, EC2 Auto Scaling, Trusted Advisor, and the Simple Monthly Calculator. For performance efficiency, you can ask the following:

  - What type of database will this application use?

  - What kind of instance type will we use for this application?

- *Cost optimization*: How do you develop solutions that satisfy your requirements at the lowest cost? Key AWS features include Cost Explorer, Budgets, EC2 Auto Scaling, Trusted Advisor, and the Simple Monthly Calculator. Cost optimization issues to consider are as follows:

  - How can we manage consumption and cost?

  - How are the price goals achieved?

  - Are we up-to-date with current data transfer prices depending on our AWS designs?

- *Sustainability*: You should try to consistently enhance sustainability effects by minimizing the power usage and boosting competency over all elements of a task by adding up the benefits from the given resources and limiting the overall resources needed.

In the case of the AWS Well-Architected Framework, we utilize these terms:

- A *component* is a symbol, grouping, and AWS service that collectively provide a complete unit of technical ownership within a workload in opposition to the demand.

- The *workload* is a segment of elements that collectively creates its monetary worth. A workload is generally the number of features that executives speak about.

- *Milestones* identify significant changes in your architecture as it progresses during the product life cycle (design, execution, trial and error, and application and reproduction).

The Well-Architected Framework provides a group of structurally integrated principles that may help produce a successful cloud architecture.

- If you make a terrible capacity selection while deploying a workload, you risk sitting on costly idle resources or coping with the performance consequences of low capacity. These issues can be resolved using cloud services. You can have the system automatically scale up and down.

- You can establish a production-scale test environment on demand in the cloud, perform your testing, and then decommission the resources. You can imitate your natural environment for a fraction of the expense of testing on-premises since you pay for the test environment only while it's operating.

- Automation helps you quickly build and reproduce your workloads while avoiding physical labor costs. Anyone can keep an eye on the automated processes, assess their effect, and restore to earlier settings as needed.

- AWS can analyze the ways to improve performance and assist in developing organizational experience to deal with events.

The AWS Well-Architected Framework presents infrastructural examples for designing and supporting cloud computing networks that are reliable, protective, competent, economical, and sustainable. The framework raises many relevant and important points for analyzing any present or future infrastructure. This framework is the sum of all AWS best practices. When you use the framework in designing your operational structure, you'll be able to create faster and better systems, while making provisions for the required virtual resources.

## The Well-Architected Tool

The AWS Well-Architected Tool is found in the AWS management dashboard under Management and Governance, as illustrated in Figure 1-12.

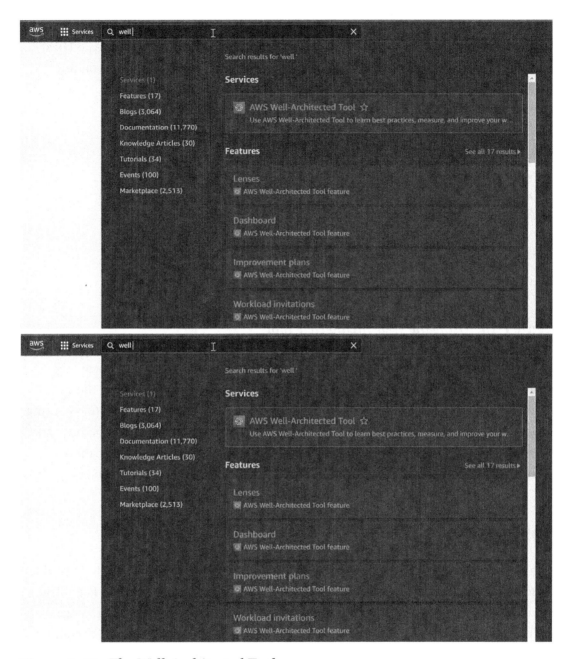

***Figure 1-12.***  *The Well-Architected Tool*

As stated in the Well-Architected Tool documentation, it offers a framework for keeping records and archives of workloads using AWS best practices (see Figure 1-13). Before deploying your application in each of the six pillars, consider several questions. As you examine each question, you can use landmarks to track changes in your design as it progresses through the organization and development life cycle. Using the Well-Architected Tool, you'll get suggestions and assistance following AWS's suggested best practices while doing a comprehensive architectural analysis of a workload you're preparing to deploy on AWS. It is undoubtedly worth your time and effort.

***Figure 1-13.*** *Using the Well-Architected Tool*

When you are choosing where the application will be located, the first stage is identifying the workflow, choosing the industry, and determining whether the application has reached its desired level. Based on the responses to the questions during the workload assessment, the Well-Architected Tool will highlight possible medium and high-risk areas throughout the review process. The plan will also incorporate the six pillars of design success and proposed changes to your original design selections.

# Conclusion

In this chapter, you looked at what a cloud service is and how Amazon fits into the public cloud domain in terms of infrastructural development, particularly IaaS and PaaS. The cloud is indeed a data center. In addition, I covered the cloud models and the usage of each of them, plus the cloud use cases. I highly recommend creating an AWS account and looking for ways to use the free tier before moving to the following chapters (you do need a valid credit card).

Also, review the AWS acknowledgment website to see how your conformity requirements align with what AWS has to offer. Of course, you should thoroughly review the Well-Architectured Framework documentation; I consider this documentation pretty helpful in understanding how AWS works.

We'll move on to the actual implementation of DevOps in the following chapter.

# CHAPTER 2

# Understanding DevOps Concepts

Before we start talking about Amazon AWS and DevOps, you need to have a good understanding of DevOps and why the demand of it is increasing every day.

## DevOps Primer

*DevOps* refers to the departments of development and operations joining together. DevOps can be thought of as the extension of the Agile approach. On the technical side, it will speed up the transition from continuous (Agile) development to integration and deployment and improve the working environment for both the development and operations teams. As you can see from Figure 2-1, there is a gap between the two teams when they are not sharing anything; when implementing DevOps in a company, the gap will disappear, as you can see in Figure 2-2.

O. Mustafa, *A Complete Guide to DevOps with AWS*, https://doi.org/10.1007/978-1-4842-9303-4_2

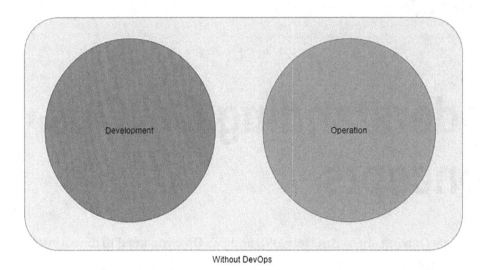

***Figure 2-1.*** *Collaboration without DevOps*

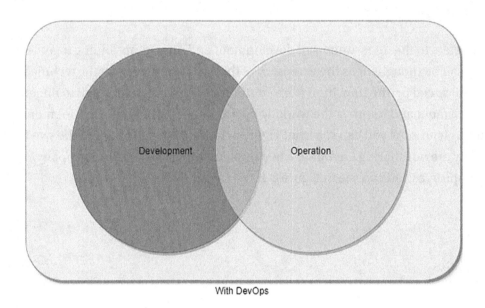

***Figure 2-2.*** *Collaboration with DevOps*

DevOps itself is not a technology. Instead, DevOps tries to apply different methodologies within the company.

Usually, people mix up DevOps and Agile, but they are different from each other, and we will cover this in this chapter's "Agile vs. DevOps" section.

# The DevOps Process

The DevOps methodology is meant to focus on and improve the software development life cycle. You can consider this process an infinite loop.

DevOps often employs specific DevOps-friendly technologies. These solutions aim to improve the software delivery process (or *pipeline*) by streamlining, shortening, and automating the different steps. These technologies also support DevOps principles, including automation, communication, and interaction, between the development and operations teams. Figure 2-3 shows the different phases of the DevOps life cycle.

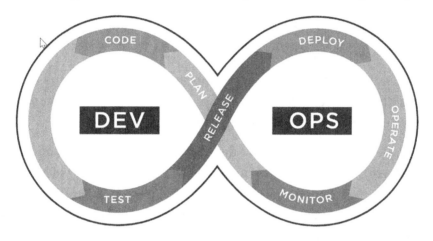

***Figure 2-3.*** *DevOps process*

Let's break the process down and talk about the tools used in each phase:

1. *Plan*: This stage aids in identifying company values and needs. Jira and Git are examples of programs that can monitor known problems and manage projects.

2. *Code*: This stage involves generating software code and software design. GitHub, GitLab, Bitbucket, and Stash are some examples of the tools used.

3. *Build*: In this stage, you manage the software builds and versions and utilize automated tools to compile and package code for eventual production release. You use source code or package repositories to "package" the infrastructure required for product delivery. Docker, Ansible, Puppet, Chef, Gradle, Maven, and JFrog Artifactory are some examples of tools.

4. *Test*: Continuous testing (human or automated) is performed throughout this phase to guarantee the highest possible code quality. JUnit, Codeception, Selenium, Vagrant, and TestNG are examples of test tools.

5. *Deploy*: In this stage, DevOps coordinates, plans, and automates product releases into production. Puppet, Chef, Ansible, Jenkins, Kubernetes, OpenShift, OpenStack, Docker, and Jira are some examples of the tools used.

6. *Operate*: Throughout this phase, the software is managed during the manufacturing process with Ansible, Puppet, PowerShell, Chef, or Salt.

7. *Monitor*: Identifying and gathering information about problems from a particular software release in production is part of this step. New Relic, Datadog, and Grafana are examples of tools used.

To simplify, DevOps means that an IT development team will write code that works perfectly and meets the company standard to do some job. This code will then need a review and will be deployed on one of the environments such as production. This happens without any waiting or downtime. The good thing is that this code will be tested before being deployed to any of the environments.

To achieve this purpose, businesses employ a combination of culture and technology. The Ops team and developers work on the project, and developers work on minor upgrades that go live independently of each other to align the software to the expectations. Plus, to avoid wasting time, Ops configures a CI/CD pipeline that will be run automatically once the developer uploads new code to version control that needs to be reviewed to ensure it's meeting the company's standards.

This permits a business to create a secure piece of work. Small groups can quickly and independently develop, test, and install code and release fast, safely, securely, and reliably to customers. This lets businesses maximize developer productivity, permit organizational learning, create excessive worker satisfaction, and win within the marketplace.

These are the outputs that DevOps produces. However, this is not the world we live in for the majority of us. Our system is frequently dysfunctional, resulting in dreadful outcomes short of our full potential. Testing and infosec operations occur only after a project, which is too late to address any flaws detected. Every necessary action needs too much human labor and too many handoffs, leaving us continually waiting. Not only does this result in incredibly long lead times for getting anything done, but the quality of our work, particularly production deployments, is also troublesome and chaotic, harming our customers.

Consequently, we fall well short of our objectives, and the whole business is unhappy with IT's performance, leading to budget cuts and disgruntled staff who feel helpless to influence the process and its outcomes. What is the solution? We need to transform how we work, and DevOps tells us how.

Let's look at the main elements of a DevOps ecosystem.

# DevOps Goals

The following sections provide a succession of commonly recognized definitions, elaborated on with personal viewpoints.

# Shared Goal

Most businesses can't implement production changes in minutes or hours; it takes weeks or months. Nor can they deploy hundreds or thousands of changes into production daily; instead, they struggle to deploy monthly or quarterly. Production deployments are not routine, instead involving outages, chronic firefighting, and heroics.

These companies are at a substantial competitive disadvantage in an age where competitive advantage means quick time to market, excellent service standards, and constant innovation. This is primarily due to their failure to address a long-standing issue in their technology department.

So, aligning efforts around enhancing system performance and stability, lowering deployment time, and improving overall product quality will result in happy customers and proud engineers; the objective must be reiterated, clarified, and simplified until it is thoroughly understood, defended, and finally adopted by everyone.

DevOps redirects attention away from self-interest and toward that objective. It emphasizes collective accomplishments above individual accomplishments, allowing other teams to see beyond the confines of their cubicle. Have faith in them.

# Collaboration (No Silos Between Teams)

The software approaches that DevOps replaced were missing the benefits that coexisting Dev, Ops, and QA teams can deliver. They did not place a premium on team communication. Thus, it wasn't until DevOps was implemented that solid support for cross-departmental cooperation fundamentally altered how departments operate as a unit.

DevOps extends the Lean and Agile software development approaches since it emphasizes operations. DevOps fosters an atmosphere where diverse teams collaborate to accomplish similar company goals. This implies that your organization's teams will no longer be separated and will no longer strive toward department-specific objectives. However, influential organizations may continue to employ various technologies to do their tasks. DevOps fosters cooperation by dismantling barriers between development, operations, and quality assurance teams and encouraging them to work collaboratively toward a common goal: increasing value for your business. This will eventually help you give more value to your customers.

Collaborative work provides several advantages. Engineers are no longer concerned with the efficiency with which their team completes tasks—because they are all liable for the final result. Also, collaborative work encourages workers from disparate departments to explore ways to enhance a product's operational procedure. This kind of cooperation cross-trains your personnel by allowing them to broaden and update their technical experience in areas not precisely inside their area of competence. As a result, it's a win-win situation for your firm and your workers.

Sometimes there is an organizational silo: One person in the company who is the bottleneck. It is hard for others to fix any bugs because there isn't enough documentation to explain this person's work.

Some people get stuck in a silo because of bad luck. Many engineers had to deal with old systems when they started working; hats off to these engineers because I know how much effort is needed to understand other people's work.

DevOps can solve these issues with concepts such as cross-functional teams. The visibility of what these developers are doing is apparent to all the other groups, and everything is uploaded under one version control repo.

# Speed

One of the main advantages of DevOps is that it speeds up how quickly your business works. For example, let's assume the development team creates new feature branches. They want to deploy manually; this will probably take months, depending on the availability and the risk these features will provide to the system. Assume they deploy this code and after two days find a bug in this new release. What will happen?

Applying the DevOps methodology will solve these issues; the faster you make great software, the sooner you can see how it can help your business. The time it takes to test a product depends on whether there is a place to try it. Updates and upgrades in software usually don't take very long to test if you have a test environment. However, trying a new product takes a lot of time because the operations team must set up a test environment. DevOps makes getting new features and changes into your software easier because it does automated testing and integration, which speeds up the process.

DevOps makes your developer watch your product all the time to ensure it is running smoothly without any issues. This means it takes less time to monitor, find, and fix bugs, which speeds up your time to market. Plus, it will help you find bottlenecks in production and processes that don't add value. Because you can work on fixing them, you'll be able to make money faster.

# Innovation

DevOps is the key to unlocking new ideas in software development. We've seen how DevOps can quickly help you get your software products out. Such quick software delivery frees up some of your developers' time so they can try new features or improve the effectiveness of the ones they already have. Developers can test the feasibility of these ideas by performing a proof of concept and then going on with the project as planned, with little impact on the current project.

A set of rigid rules doesn't bind the developers; a project can permanently be changed if its goals are met. It might not be possible to use an idea one of your employees comes up with for an application with that product, but it might work well with another. When people work together, they develop new ideas and quickly test them. This helps DevOps be more innovative. Thus, DevOps allows for this environment and gives your software delivery the space to work well.

# Satisfaction of Customers

Customer happiness is one of those aspects of the company that may make or ruin it. One of the primary advantages of DevOps is improved customer experience and, ultimately, customer happiness.

Over time, DevOps has shown its capacity to revolutionize and accelerate the software development life cycle (SDLC) process via more flexibility, increased automation, rapid deployment, decreased time to market, and increased productivity.

Figure 2-4 illuminates how businesses attain consumer happiness through six key factors.

***Figure 2-4.*** *DevOps benefits*

- *Customer response time is reduced*: Any delay in responding to client comments or complaints increases consumers' likelihood of moving to another provider or a close rival. This ultimately harms the customer base.

- *It accelerates delivery cycles*: The delayed process was caused by infrastructure problems and resulted in a long time for delivery. In the DevOps environment, releases and innovation occur quicker, with the ultimate business purpose of reaching out to customers early.

Automating repetitive jobs, eliminating routine duties, and streamlining procedures all contribute to the continuous operation of the software delivery chain. This results in a higher pace of innovation and the delivery of more products in shorter time frames. DevOps makes it simpler to achieve faster delivery cycles!

- *It allows for low-priced products*: Because of the shorter periods necessary for minor product launches, the cost aspect should not be a significant source of worry for these businesses. DevOps is precisely what makes this possible. As a result of the shorter manufacturing, operation, delivery, and feedback cycles, less money is spent on product development, reducing the total amount paid. As a result of the decreased development expenses, the customer's price is also lower. This ultimately results in the client being satisfied and interested in future versions.

- *It allows a CI/CD environment*: I will cover more about DevOps continuous integration/continuous development (CI/CD) cycles later in this chapter. CI/CD promises to stabilize the operational environment and respond quickly to production needs. CI/CD cycles reduce lead times and mean recovery time and permit more frequent releases, leading to customer satisfaction.

- *Tests can be automated*: When it comes to DevOps, automation helps to speed up the testing process from integration to staging. Automated testing promotes excellent product testing by preventing bugs from entering production early. Ultimately, this decreases the expenses associated with the launching of new products.

- *Costs are reduced*: Cost and value considerations influence DevOps' return on investment (ROI). One of the most significant advantages of the DevOps approach is the capacity to find and deliver to customers more quickly. This ultimately saves expenses, time, and resources that may be repurposed to identify new consumers and concentrate on providing more excellent value to current customers, among other things.

Before progressing and getting more technical, you should understand the difference between DevOps and Agile, which are connected.

# Agile vs. DevOps

Agile is a way to manage projects and make software based on collaboration, customer feedback, and quick releases. It came from the software development industry in the early 2000s and helped development teams adapt to the market and customer needs.

Agile development is a way to break down a project into smaller parts and assemble them for testing at the end. It can be used in many ways, like Scrum, Kanban, and more.

When it comes to the stakeholders, the two concepts are different. Figure 2-5 explains who the Agile and DevOps stakeholders are.

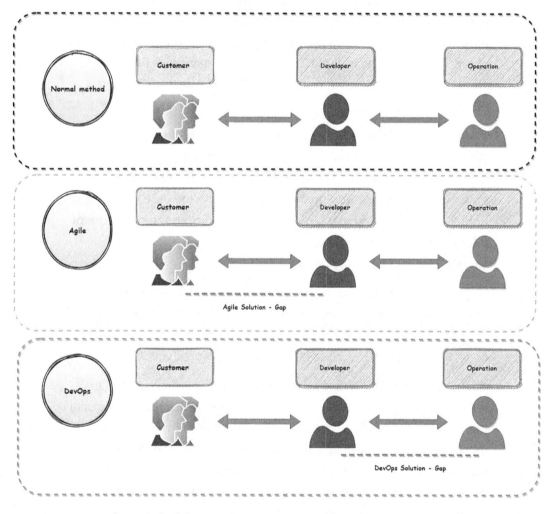

***Figure 2-5.***  *Agile stakeholders vs. DevOps stakeholders*

Table 2-1 highlights Agile and DevOps's different factors to ensure you understand more about these two concepts.

*Table 2-1.* *Key Differences Between Agile and DevOps*

| Factor | Agile | DevOps |
| --- | --- | --- |
| **Definition** | Agile is a way of working that focuses on collaboration, customer feedback, and minor, quick releases. | DevOps is a way to bring development and operations teams together. |
| **Purpose** | Agile is a project management method that helps people work on big projects. | DevOps's main idea is to control all engineering processes from start to finish. |
| **Task** | In the Agile process, changes happen all the time. | DevOps focuses on testing and delivering things all the time. |
| **Implementation** | It can be done using Scrum or Kanboard. | It can be implemented using different software; we will discuss tools later in the chapter. |
| **Feedback** | Feedback is given to clients or customers. | Feedback is presented to the internal team. |
| **Goal** | There is a big gap between what the customer wants and what the development and testing teams can do to meet the goals. | There is a gap between development plus testing and Ops. |
| **Advantage** | There is a shorter development time and better defect detection. | It supports Agile's release cycle. |
| **Tools** | Jira and Kanboard are tools. | Puppet, Chef, TeamCity OpenStack, and AWS are popular DevOps tools. |
| **Automation** | There is no automation built in. | This is the primary goal of DevOps. |
| **Speed vs. Risk** | It supports change and application change. | It should make sure any risk will not affect the application or functionality. |
| **Quality** | It produces better applications that meet the needs of the people who use them. | There is a focus on automation, which reduces human errors. |

There are some new DevOps terms in the previous table, so we will define them in the following sections.

- Continuous integration and continuous delivery

- Infrastructure as code

- Containerization

- Automation testing

- Version control

The person dealing with the software is the DevOps engineer; from coding and deployment through maintenance and upgrades, a DevOps engineer offers methods, tools, and approaches to balance the demands across the software development life cycle.

# Continuous Integration and Continuous Delivery

*Continuous integration* is the process of developers merging changes as often as possible into the code base in the main branch. Developers create a build and then run automated tests against these changes. If these tests fail, the improvements aren't merged, and developers avoid any potential integration issues.

## Continuous Integration's Advantages

These are the advantages:

- Early feedback and build/test automation reduce the time it takes from committing work to properly running it in production.

- Frequent deployment, automated tests, and builds are required for automated deployment.

- Time to restore service and automated pipelines allow for the speedier deployment of patches to production, lowering mean time to resolution.

- Early automated testing significantly decreases the number of problems that reach production.

# Continuous Delivery

*Continuous delivery* is an extension of continuous integration. It automates the deployment of all code changes to a target environment (dev, QA, stage, prod, etc.) after they've been merged. Because the source of truth (your repository) is dependable given your CI process, the artifact may be created as part of CI or this process. This implies an automatic release process on top of the automated testing process. Developers may deploy their changes at any time by simply hitting a button or when CI is complete.

## Continuous Delivery Advantages

These are the advantages:

- Makes the software release process more automated.

- Boosts developer efficiency.

- Enhances the code quality.

- Updates are sent more quickly.

## Continuous Deployment

*Continuous deployment* is the last step of a sophisticated CI/CD workflow. It is an extension of continuous delivery, which automates the release of a production-ready build to a code repository. It also automates the release of an app to production. Continuous deployment depends significantly on well-designed test automation since there is no human gate at the pipeline point before production.

## Roundup of Concepts

Figure 2-6 shows the process for each concept and what the difference is between the stages.

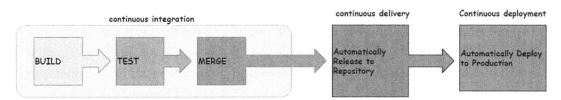

***Figure 2-6.*** *CI/CD stages*

## CI/CD Tools

The following are some standard CI/CD tools:

- Jenkins is an open-source automation server that allows developers to create, test, and deploy their applications with confidence.

- Spinnaker is a cloud-based CD platform for multicloud scenarios.

- CircleCI is a continuous integration and delivery platform that enables development teams to release code quickly and automate build, test, and deployment processes. With caching, Docker layer caching, resource classes, and other features, CircleCI can execute even the most complicated pipelines effectively.

- Concourse is an open-source CI pipeline tool that leverages YAML files for pipeline configuration and configuration-free startup; it has just released version 1.1.

- TeamCity is a general-purpose CI/CD solution that provides maximum flexibility for many workflows and development techniques. You can quickly check the status of your builds, learn what caused them, get the newest build artifacts, and do even more using the Projects Overview feature.

- Screwdriver is a build platform for large-scale continuous delivery. Because it is not bound to any computing platform, it supports an ever-growing variety of source code services, execution engines, and databases. Screwdriver is an open-source project with a well-documented API and a growing community.

## Infrastructure as Code

To explain infrastructure as code, I will give you an example. Before DevOps, if the system administrator wanted to create and deploy two environments, such as development and production, with an average of 12 servers each, the developer needed to repeat the steps for both environments by making the servers, installing the operating system, setting up the network, preparing the tech stack inside the server, configuring everything, and testing it. Usually, these steps would take a month at a minimum, and don't forget the error timeline.

*Infrastructure as code* (IaC) will solve this issue. IaC is about managing and supplying infrastructure using code rather than doing it manually.

Configuration files containing your infrastructure requirements are produced using IaC, making changing and sharing settings easy. This also assures that an identical environment is created every time. IaC supports configuration management and helps prevent undocumented, ad hoc configuration modifications by codifying and documenting your configuration standards.

Version control is a crucial aspect of IaC, and your configuration files, like any other software source code file, should be under source control. Deploying your infrastructure as code also allows you to break it down into modular components that can be combined using automation.

Figure 2-7 illustrates the power of IaC; with a single code base, you can deploy into different environments.

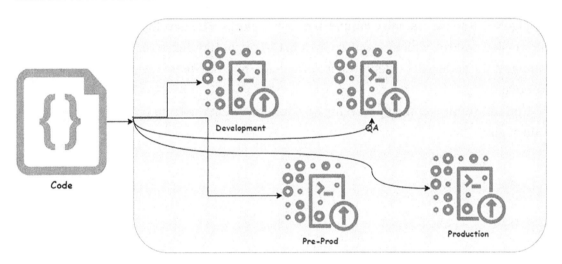

**Figure 2-7.** *IaC power*

System administrators don't have to manually supply and maintain servers, operating systems, storage, and other infrastructure components each time they create or deploy an application since infrastructure provisioning is automated using IaC. Coding your infrastructure establishes a template for provisioning. Although this may still be done manually, automation solutions can handle it.

# How Infrastructure as Code Works

This is how IaC works:

1. The developer/system administrator writes, uploads, and uploads the code to version control.

2. After other developers review the code and ensure it meets the company standard, it will be approved.

3. Their integration with other tools, such as GitHub actions, AWS pipelines, etc., allows the version control to deploy this code automatically.

4. Depending on the tools, the code can be deployed to the cloud or on-premises to create the infrastructure.

Figure 2-8 shows a small example of how IaC works. The developer pushes the code into version control, which could be GitHub, GitLab, or Bitbucket; depending on the company, the code will be deployed automatically after the team reviews and approves the code.

The code author could be working on comments that the team gives to improve the code quality.

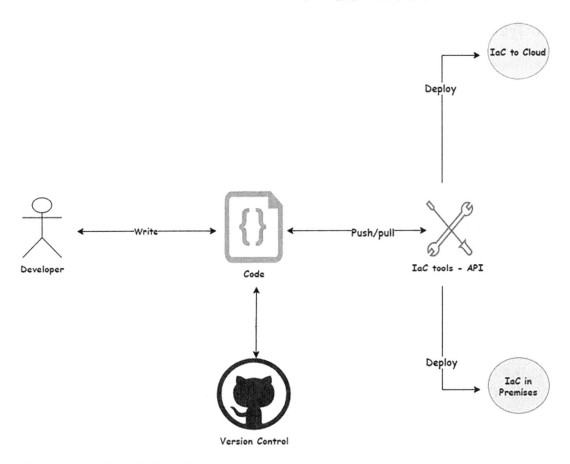

***Figure 2-8.*** *How IaC works*

Regarding how IaC tools function, we may split them into two categories: those that follow an imperative approach and those that follow a declarative approach; you're correct if you believe the previous categories have anything to do with programming language paradigms.

The *imperative approach* specifies a set of commands or instructions the infrastructure must follow to achieve the desired outcome. By contrast, the *declarative method* "declares" the intended conclusion. The declarative approach illustrates the result instead of explicitly detailing the sequence of actions the infrastructure requires to obtain the outcome. I will explain more about these two approaches in Chapter 6.

# IaC Types

There are different types of IaC, each of which can be used for a specific purpose:

- *Scripting*: The most straightforward way to implement IaC is to write scripts. Ad hoc scripts are ideal for performing basic, quick, or one-time actions. However, it's recommended to choose a more specialist option for more complicated configurations.

- *Configuration management tools*: These specialized tools, often known as *configuration as code*, manage software. Typically, they concentrate on setting up and configuring servers. Chef, Puppet, and Ansible are examples of these tools.

- *Provisioning tools*: Infrastructure creation is the focus of provisioning tools. Developers may describe accurate infrastructure components using these tools. Terraform, AWS CloudFormation, and OpenStack Heat are examples.

- *Containers and tools for templating*: I will cover containers in Chapter 9, but what you need to know about this IaC type is that you can build preloaded templates or images with all of the libraries and components required to launch an application. Containerized workloads are simple to distribute and have a fraction of the overhead of a full-size server. Docker, Vagrant, and Packer are some examples.

# Standard IaC Tools

Each of the following tools has advantages and disadvantages. I will not go deep into each tool since there is a complete chapter on IaC with real-life examples and complete projects that allow you to understand more about this powerful DevOps category. Still, I will introduce these tools so you can get a brief look at them now.

## Terraform

I consider Terraform one of my favorite tools; it is the most widely used open-source infrastructure automation technology. It assists with infrastructure-as-code configuration, provisioning, and management.

Terraform makes it simple to design and deploy IaC across numerous infrastructure providers using a single procedure. The needed infrastructure is defined as code using a declarative approach. Before upgrading or provisioning infrastructure, Terraform enables users to do a pre-execution check to see whether the settings fulfill the expected outcome. Customers may have their chosen architecture across numerous cloud providers through a single and uniform CLI procedure. You can swiftly create various environments with the same configuration and manage the whole life span of your desired infrastructure, eliminating human mistakes and enhancing automation in the provisioning and administration process.

## Ansible

Ansible is often the most straightforward method for automating the provisioning, setup, and administration of applications and IT infrastructure. Users can use Ansible to run playbooks to generate and manage the infrastructure resources. It can connect to servers and conduct commands through SSH without using agents. Its code is written in YAML as Ansible *playbooks*, making the configurations simple to comprehend and deploy. You can even extend Ansible's capabilities by developing your modules and plugins.

Red Hat acquired Ansible to promote simplicity. It contributes to IT modernization and aids DevOps teams in deploying applications quicker, more reliably, and with more coordination. You can easily create several identical setups with security baselines without worrying about meeting compliance standards. Ansible provides a competitive edge in business by freeing up time for the company to implement innovation and strategy and align IT with business requirements.

## Chef

Chef is one of the most well-known IaC tools in the business. Chef employs a procedural-style language, in which the user must write code and define how to attain the desired state step-by-step. It is up to the user to select the best deployment method. Chef enables you to build recipes and cookbooks using its Ruby-based DSL. These recipes and cookbooks detail the processes necessary to configure your apps and utilities on existing servers to your liking.

This infrastructure management solution is designed to help you implement and model a scalable and secure infrastructure automation process in any environment. Chef allows DevOps teams to supply and deploy on-demand infrastructure quickly. Chef is a configuration management technology many businesses utilize in their continuous integration and delivery operations.

## Puppet

Puppet is another open-source configuration management solution widely used to manage several application servers simultaneously. It also employs a Ruby-based DSL, like Chef, to define the intended end state of your infrastructure. Puppet differs from Chef in that it utilizes a declarative approach, in which you must first determine how you want your settings to appear, and then Puppet will figure out how to get there.

Puppet is a collection of IaC tools for delivering infrastructures rapidly and securely. It has a large community of developers who have created modules to enhance the software's capabilities. Puppet connects with almost every major cloud infrastructure as a code platform, including AWS, Azure, Google Cloud, and VMware, allowing for multicloud automation.

## SaltStack

SaltStack is a Python-based open-source configuration management application that provides a simple solution for quickly provisioning, deploying, and configuring infrastructure on any platform.

SaltStack focuses on automating an organization's infrastructure, security, and network. It's a simple IaC tool that comes in handy to mitigate and resolve typical infrastructure problems. It's a safe and cost-effective IaC system that automates and orchestrates processes while reducing human work. It can automatically identify issues with event triggers and restore the appropriate state if necessary. Salt also provides SSH support, which allows for agentless mode. It contains a scheduler that allows you to define how frequently your code should be performed on the managed servers.

## Vagrant

Vagrant is another excellent IaC tool built by HashiCorp. Vagrant focuses on creating computing environments with a few virtual machines rather than enormous cloud infrastructure settings with hundreds or thousands of servers spread across several cloud providers.

Vagrant is a simple yet effective tool for creating development environments. It encourages the use of unified workflows by using declarative configuration files that include all of the necessary setup information. It ensures state consistency across environments and integrates with popular configuration management technologies such as Puppet, Chef, SaltStack, Ansible, etc.

Now, let's talk about the built-in tools of each cloud provider; you need to understand that each cloud provider has its own IaC tools that allow the system administrators, SRE, or DevOps to work on it; some cloud providers provide more than one in the same cloud, for example, Amazon AWS.

## AWS CloudFormation

AWS CloudFormation is an integrated IaC solution inside the AWS cloud platform that allows you to rapidly and easily deploy and manage a group of connected AWS and third-party resources using infrastructure as code. It enables you to apply all needed DevOps and GitOps best practices. By connecting CloudFormation with other essential AWS resources, you can manage the scalability of your resources and even automate additional resource management. AWS CloudFormation also lets you develop resource providers using its open-source CLI to provision and manage third-party application resources alongside native AWS resources.

CloudFormation is written in YAML or JSON format. All you have to do is create your desired infrastructure from scratch using the appropriate template language and then utilize AWS CloudFormation to provide and manage the stack and resources indicated in the template. CloudFormation also uses rollback triggers to restore infrastructure stacks to a previously deployed state if errors are observed to ensure that deployment and upgrading of infrastructure are controlled.

## Azure Resource Manager

The Azure Resource Manager service allows you to install and manage Azure resources. Instead of deploying, maintaining, and tracking resources separately, an Azure-specific IaC solution enables them to be deployed, maintained, and followed in a single collective operation. Role-based access control (RBAC) is built into the resource management system, allowing users to apply access control to all resources within a resource category.

Resource Manager lets you utilize declarative templates instead of scripts to manage your infrastructure. You may reinstall your infrastructure solution several times during the application development life cycle using Azure resource management while maintaining state consistency.

## Google Cloud Deployment Manager

Google Cloud Deployment Manager is a solution that automates resource creation, setup, provisioning, and administration for Google Cloud. You can create a group of Google cloud services and manage them as a single entity. You may develop models using YAML or Python, preview changes before deploying, and examine your deployments through a console user interface.

Choosing the right tool depends on your expertise and why you need to use this tool.

## Tool Roundup

Table 2-2 lists several tools and briefly explains how they work; you either need to configure an agent to make them work or install the tools on the server.

***Table 2-2.*** *Tools*

| Tools | How It Works | Focus |
|---|---|---|
| **Terraform** | Agentless | Admin focused, IaC |
| **Ansible** | Agentless | Admin-focused configuration management |
| **Jenkins** | Agentless | Dev focused and can work for admin also, CI/CD |
| **Puppet** | Agent-based | Dev focused |
| **Chef** | Agent-based | Dev/admin focused |
| **Saltstack** | Agent, agentless | Admin focused |

# Benefits of Infrastructure as Code

IaC creates a standardized, repeatable infrastructure definition. Why is it necessary to be repeatable? Because with infrastructure as code, you can be confident that you'll always have the same infrastructure. Developing and maintaining an infrastructure specified as code is more efficient than manually maintaining it.

Changes can be tracked, versions compared, security ensured, and rules enforced using IaC. The following are the advantages of IaC:

- *Speed*: Organizations that adopt IaC spend less time on manual procedures, allowing them to accomplish more in less time. Iteration is quicker since there is no need for an IT administrator to finish manual activities.

- *Consistency*: Every stage of the process is handled and finished automatically, removing the possibility of human mistakes and sick days and weekends. Changes are made widely and quickly, allowing development teams to focus on adding value.

- *Efficiency*: Following a more consistent approach to provisioning infrastructure can save time and concentrate on nonrepetitive, higher-order jobs.

- *Less headache*: Anyone can deploy the IaC; there is no need for a system administrator to deploy it, which means there will be less overhead on each department in the company.

- *Accountability*: This one is simple and fast. You can track each configuration's changes because IaC configuration files may be versioned like any other source code file. There will be no more guesswork as to who did what and when.

- *Low cost*: Undoubtedly, one of the most significant advantages of IaC is the reduction of infrastructure administration expenses. You may drastically lower your expenditures by combining cloud computing with IaC. You'll save money because you won't have to spend money on hardware, pay people to run it, or rent physical space to hold it. However, IaC decreases your expenses differently and more subtly.

## Infrastructure as Code Examples

Let's look at a quick example of a basic AWS EC2 instance setup scenario; I will cover three different tools for the same example.

## Terraform

Figure 2-9 shows how the file structure will look. I will not explain the files since Chapter 6 will cover this part.

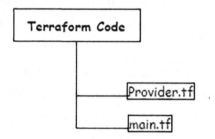

***Figure 2-9.*** *File structure example*

This is the code in `provider.tf`:

```
1. terraform {
2.    required_providers {
3.      aws= {
4.        source  = "hashicorp/aws"
5.        version = "~> 3.27"
6.      }
7.    }
8. }
9.
10. provider "aws" {
11.    region = "us-west-1"
12. }
```

This is the code in `main.tf`:

```
1. resource "aws_instance" "web_server" {
2.    ami                     = "ami-0123456"
3.    instance_type           = "t3.micro"
4.    subnet_id               = "subnet-14322"
5.    vpc_security_group_ids = "sg-143224"
6.    key_name                = "server-key"
7.    tags = {
```

```
 8.     Name = "Web_Server"
 9.   }
10. }
```

## Ansible

For Ansible, we will use a fundamental YAML file; please note the indentation is significant in YAML.

```
 1. - hosts: localhost
 2.   gather_facts: False
 3.   vars_files:
 4.   - credentials.yml
 5.   tasks:
 6.   - name: Provision EC2 Instance
 7.     ec2:
 8.       aws_access_key: "{{aws_access_key}}"
 9.       aws_secret_key: "{{aws_secret_key}}"
10.       key_name: server_key
11.       group: test
12.       instance_type: t3.micro
13.       image: "ami-0123456"
14.       wait: true
15.       count: 1
16.       region: us-west-1
17.       instance_tags:
18.         Name: Web_Server
19.     register: ec2
```

## AWS CloudFormation

AWS CloudFormation is a service from Amazon AWS that makes it simple for developers and companies to construct a group of linked AWS and third-party resources and provide and manage them logically and predictably; you can use YAML or JSON.

```
1. AWSTemplateFormatVersion: "2010-09-09"
2. Resources:
3.   WebInstance:
```

```
4.     Type: AWS::EC2::Instance
5.     Properties:
6.        InstanceType: t3.micro
7.        ImageId: ami-0123456
8.        KeyName: server_key
9.        SecurityGroupIds:
10.       - sg-143224
11.       SubnetId: subnet-14322
12.       Tags:
13.         -
14.           Key: Name
15.           Value: Web_Server
```

As you can see from the previous examples, the tools lead to the same results; it's great to know different ones, but not mandatory. If you are thinking about deploying resources to cloud computing, the next step is to understand IaC because it will save time and money. Now it's time to jump into the next topic in this chapter, automation testing.

# Automation Testing

Once upon a time, the only testing step in the development cycle was QA testing, which was one of the most extended steps in this cycle; the developer finished their work and uploaded it to version control, and the QA team needed to make sure the code met the company's standard depending on the testing scenario.

That took time and probably caused issues between the teams because no one likes to repeat work; DevOps solved this problem between the groups with a straightforward approach called *automation testing*.

What is automation testing? It is a software testing approach for comparing the actual result to the predicted outcome; it can be accomplished via test scripts or another automation testing tool. Automating repeated processes and other testing duties that are not easy to complete manually is what test automation is for.

Manual testing entails a single person evaluating the software's functioning in the same manner as a user would. Automated testing uses an automation tool, allowing more time on higher-value jobs such as exploratory tests, while time-consuming tests such as regression tests are automated. While updating test scripts will take time, you will improve your test coverage and scalability.

Manual testing allows the human mind to derive conclusions from a test that might otherwise be overlooked by test automation. Large projects, projects that repeatedly need testing in the same regions, and projects that have previously undergone a human testing procedure benefit from automated testing.

## Advantages

Why do you need to use automation testing in the first place?

Some of the advantages of automated testing are as follows:

- Automation testing minimizes the time it takes to complete a test because automated testing is more efficient than manual testing.

- It lowers the project's cost and resource needs since a script produced once may be made to execute an unlimited number of times as long as the application remains unchanged.

- It allows you to deal with many inputs, which is impossible with manual testing.

- It helps create a continuous integration environment in which the new build is automatically tested after each code push. You can develop jobs using CI/CD technologies like Jenkins that tests when a build is deployed and emails the test results to stakeholders.

- You can save time by automating your tests. Automated tests are quick to perform and can be repeated. Put another way, you won't have to wait weeks to do the tests again—only a few hours will be enough, which will lead to different results.

  - The software development cycle is shorter.

  - Releases occur more often.

  - Changes and upgrades to the app are made more quickly.

  - Deliveries have a shorter time to market.

- Because automated testing doesn't need human participation while running, you may test your app late at night and get the findings the following morning. Software developers and QA may spend less time testing since automated tests can frequently run independently.

Basically, with automation, your engineers can focus on critical tasks. Fixing current app functionality isn't as thrilling as adding new features, as we all know.

- An immediate response provides immediate feedback. Developers get testing information instantaneously with rapid execution to respond swiftly if a problem happens. Forget about deciphering the code that was written three weeks ago.

- Test automation makes you more likely to have error-free releases with more precise tests. Automated testing is more accurate than manual testing because it requires less human interaction. The problem is that a human tester may make errors at any stage of the review process. The machine, on the other hand, will not cooperate. Because generated test cases are more exact than human testers, you may lower the likelihood of failure by removing human mistakes.

- Your app's excellent quality and performance will be ensured through automatic testing. It lets you run hundreds of automated test cases simultaneously, allowing you to test your app across different platforms and devices quickly. Choose cloud-based device farms to get the most out of test parallelism and concurrency. They can assist you with covering all of the needed OS and hardware setups.

## Misconceptions

Since I mentioned the benefits of automation testing, I will discuss some misconceptions about it.

- *You will have more free time as a result of automation*: You need to understand that there is always something to automate; you can always enhance your infrastructure, and automation will allow the team to focus on other things and the quality of your code and infrastructure. Most manual testing time is spent on exploratory and functional testing, which involves manually searching for faults. Once that procedure is finished, the manual tester must perform the same actions repeatedly. That time is significantly reduced with automated testing. Instead of writing tests, automated testers code them and improve them. However, after the test is completed, automated testing enables the reuse of tests, eliminating the need to repeat the whole procedure. Instead of spending time on the highly repetitive activities that a human tester would do, you may concentrate on broader, more fundamental problems with your building product.

- *The price of automated testing is excessive*: I don't understand why people think the automation options are expensive. You can use open-source software, and automated testing allows you to concentrate on more important topics such as client demands, functionality, and enhancements. Automated testing also lowers the cost and requirements for repeated code modifications, so the investment pays off over time. Furthermore, the software tests may be run once the source code is amended. Performing these tests is time-consuming and expensive, whereas automated tests may be done repeatedly at no extra expense. Parallel testing is another method to check how much money your automated testing makes. Similar testing allows you to perform numerous automated tests simultaneously rather than executing them one after another; this significantly reduces the time it takes to run your automated tests.

- *Manual testing isn't as good as automated testing*: This misconception makes me laugh whenever I hear it. We are not in competition here. Sometimes you need manual testing inside your company; it just depends on your business needs. Each method has its own set of benefits and drawbacks. A person sitting in front of a computer does manual testing by methodically walking through the program using SQL and log analysis, experimenting with different use and input combinations, comparing the results to the intended behavior, and documenting the findings. After the original program has been produced, automated testing is often employed. Unattended testing may execute lengthy tests that are generally avoided during manual testing. They may even be installed on several computers with various settings.

- *There is no need for humans*: Because automated testing is more precise and quicker than what people can achieve without incurring significant human error, this misunderstanding is understandable. On the other hand, complex applications are built to support a collaborative approach by incorporating tools that enable co-workers to walk through a piece of test code and provide feedback on the script. This automation does not replace the need for in-person contact or communications in software development. Instead, it increases that characteristic by giving an additional communication route. Consider it this way: email did not replace the telephone; it is only a different means of communication.

## Stakeholders

Automation testing is different from any other automation; it requires expertise with QA and experience with scripting. The question in this section is, who should be part of the test automation process?

- *Developers*: They understand what kind of application the company has and the screens inside the application; therefore, integrating testing into the development process necessitates integrating development environments. It's part of the developer's job.

- *QA (manual or automated)*: For manual testers, those new to automation, recording, and replaying, utilizing the same recorded script with various input data may be helpful when finding and correcting issues in different contexts.

- *Automation experts*: These engineers will use a scripting language and interface with continuous integration platforms. The ability to scale testing might be critical for automation engineers.

## Disadvantages

Automation is not always the solution for your business. The following are some scenarios where automated testing is not recommended and some of automation's drawbacks:

- *Inexperience with the automation tool*: One of the most common reasons for not using a tool and programming language to construct powerful scripts is a lack of experience with the tool and a particular programming language. These and other factors contribute to the failure of automated testing.

- *Applications that often change*: Choosing test automation for an application that undergoes frequent modifications necessitates ongoing maintenance of the test scripts, which may or may not result in the required return on investment. DevOps comes with the Agile methodology, which is not recommended.

- *Wrong test case*: The effectiveness of automated testing depends on the test cases selected for automation. Incorrectly specified tests result in a waste of resources and time spent automating.

- *Test scripts created inefficiently*: For this point, you need to understand the difference between DevOps and automation testing; both have different job responsibilities. Test scripts with insufficient or no validations might result in false-positive test results. These false-positive findings hide the underlying flaws, which might have been readily detected if manual verification or better scripting had been used.

## Test Automation Process

Figure 2-10 shows the test automation cycle that can be added to the DevOps process, as I will show later in this chapter.

All operations are included in the automated testing process. We'll go over each step, from understanding requirements to automated scripting and CI/CD integration.

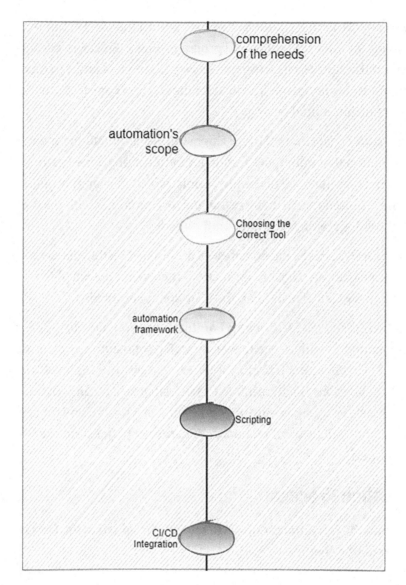

**Figure 2-10.** *Test automation process*

Let's break the process down:

- *Comprehension of the needs*: The first and most crucial step in test automation is fully comprehending the market. Understanding the demand will aid in defining the extent of automation and selecting the appropriate technology.

- *Automation scope*: Finding the correct test cases for automation is the first step in defining the area. All test cases under the test case classes specified in the "What to Automate?" portion of this chapter would fall under this category.

- *Choosing the correct tools*: The choice of tool is influenced by several variables, including the project's requirements, programming skills, project budget (whether to use a free or commercial tool), etc.

- *Automation framework*: We need to build an automation framework to produce comprehensive test automation suites. These frameworks aid in test scripts' reuse, maintenance, and robustness. Depending on the project requirements, we may pick from various automation frameworks; I will briefly describe these frameworks later in this chapter.

- *Scripting*: After the previous setup of the automation framework, we begin scripting the test cases that will be automated. The automation tester usually does scripting depending on the QA engineer, which will give the work to the automation tester.

- *CI/CD integration*: Although we can run the test cases on demand, CI/CD is widely used in almost every product or service-based company. This involves setting up the test suites on a CI/CD tool like Jenkins from a testing point of view. A significant advantage of combining the automation suite with the CI/CD pipeline is the ability to automatically trigger test cases for execution after deployment. The automated test suites in this configuration assess the build's stability with just one click right after deployment.

## Automation Framework

After discussing the steps of automation testing, we need to learn more about the framework that this kind of DevOps category usually uses; we need to establish a set of guidelines for manual testing on any application. Examples include the structure of test cases, the prioritizing of test execution, and many strategies for improving the whole software testing process, to name a few. In the same way, we employ automation frameworks in automation testing to assist in reducing the expense of maintaining automated scripts. Improving the whole automated testing process is also a priority.

Ask yourself a few things before implementing the solution:

- What should be done to make this automation testing work?

- What is the report output?

- What should I do in case of failure?

- How can we test the data/output?

- How can we use these scenario functionalities over and over again?

To respond to the concerns mentioned, the type of framework is relevant.

- *Modular framework*: Modular frameworks are a kind of automation framework in which widely used capabilities such as database connection, login flow, reading data from an external file, and so on, are recognized and developed as methods. Instead of repeatedly writing the same line of code, we call the reusable functions whenever needed.

- *Keyword-driven framework*: You can write test cases; for example, create test cases in an Excel spreadsheet. The framework will already have methods designed for each phrase, such as automation code for the OpenBrowser and other keywords. Once the framework is set up, a nontechnical user may develop plain-text automation test scripts.

- *Data-driven framework*: The test data in a data-driven framework is stored in external files. The test case is performed numerous times with various datasets in each iteration, depending on the number of rows in the external files (fetched from the file). The term *data-driven framework* comes from the fact that data drives automation.

- *Hybrid framework*: As you can tell from the name, this is the combination of multiple frameworks. So, a variety of any two of the previous frameworks would be termed a *data-driven framework*. Mainly when we say a *hybrid* framework, it relates to a data-driven framework merged with a keyword-driven framework.

We have talked about almost everything related to automation testing; the one thing that is missing is the tools. Next I will cover some common tools I have used during my career.

# Test Automation Tools

Let's start with one of the most common tools used for automation testing.

## Selenium

Selenium is in demand and frequently utilized. It is one of the best QA automation tools available. It can automate across many operating systems, including Windows, Mac, and Linux, as well as browsers such as Firefox, Chrome, Internet Explorer, and headless browsers.

Selenium test scripts can be developed in Java, C#, Python, Ruby, PHP, Perl, and JavaScript, among other computer languages. Selenium's browser add-on Selenium IDE has record and playback capabilities. Selenium WebDriver is a sophisticated tool for constructing more complicated and advanced automation scripts.

## Cucumber

Cucumber is a free behavior-driven development (BDD) tool. Cucumber is an open-source testing automation tool supporting languages such as Ruby, Java, Scala, Groovy, and others.

Testers, developers, and customers collaborate to write test scripts. Cucumber works only in a web environment. Gherkin is a simple English language used to write test code. Cucumber code may be run on various frameworks, including Selenium, Ruby, etc.

## Watir

Pronounced "water," Watir is an open-source web automation testing tool. Watir is one of the top automation scripting tools for Windows and supports Internet Explorer. Watir + WebDriver is compatible with Firefox, Opera, and the HTML Unit headless browser.

Although Ruby is the scripting language, you may automate web applications written in any language; Watir allows you to connect to a database, read flat files, and use Excel, which is helpful for data-driven testing. You can create reusable test code that you can use in several test scripts. Watir is considered one of the best QA automation tools.

## Mabl

If you don't like to code, Mabl is the right tool; it is an intelligent, low-code test automation solution for quality engineering. Agile teams can improve application quality using Mabl by including automated end-to-end testing in the development process.

# Version Control

Another important DevOps category is probably used in every company nowadays, so what is it? Version control systems are software tools that aid in recording file changes by keeping track of code changes. Without version control, it's tough to automate things and create CI/CD pipelines.

## Significance of a Version Control System

As we all know, a software product is produced collaboratively by a group of developers who may be based in various places. Each contributes a particular set of functionality/features. As a result, they modify the source code to contribute to the product (either by adding or removing it). A version control system is a kind of software that aids the development team in quickly communicating and managing (tracking) any changes made to the source code, such as who made a change and what it was. Every contributor who made the modifications has their own branch, and the changes aren't merged into the source code until all of them have been evaluated. Once all the changes have been given the green light, they are merged into the main source code. Version control organizes source code and boosts productivity by streamlining the development process.

Here are more impacts of version control on how a company works:

- It increases the pace of project creation by facilitating practical cooperation.

- It offers improved communication and support, increased staff productivity, expedited product delivery, and enhanced employee capabilities.

- Tracking every tiny change will reduce the risk of mistakes and disputes while the project is being developed because more than one person will review the code and ensure no errors (a third eye).

- It assists in the recovery in the event of a calamity or unforeseen circumstance.

- The most crucial point is that it tells us who, what, when, and why modifications were done.

As DevOps team members, you must know two different use cases for version control; each depends on the company. I have seen companies using both use cases simultaneously, ensuring nothing will be lost.

- A repository can be compared to a change database. It includes all of the project's modifications and historical versions.

- The personal copy of all the files in a project is a copy of the work (or checkout). You can modify this copy without harming other people's work, and when you're done, you can submit your changes to a repository.

Are these the same tool? Let's look at examples of each one of them and the pros and cons of each one of these tools.

## Git

Git is one of the most popular version control systems today.

### Features

- It is a model for a distributed repository.

- HTTP, FTP, and SSH are compatible with current systems and protocols.

- The history may be verified via cryptography.

- Direct object packing regularly takes place.

### Pros

- Performance is both quick and efficient.

- It offers `git bash`, a fantastic command-line tool.

- Changes to the code can be monitored.

**Cons**

- Keyword expansion and timestamp preservation are not supported.

- If the project is big, it is tough to follow up and trace.

## SVN

**Features**

- Metadata is versioned in a free-form manner.

- Branching is not affected by file size and is a low-cost procedure.

- Versioning is applied to directories.

**Pros**

- It's simple to set up and manage.

- When compared to Git, it has superior Windows support.

- It has the advantage of excellent GUI tools such as TortoiseSVN.

**Cons**

- The modification time of files is not saved.

- Signed revisions are not supported.

## Bitbucket

**Features**

- Code review and comments are included in pull requests.

- Bitbucket Pipelines is a service that provides continuous delivery.

- Two-step verification and two-step verification are necessary.

**Pros**

- It allows you to work on the repository as a team.

- It's tightly integrated with Atlassian products like Jira and Confluence.

**Cons**

- It no longer supports HTTPS-based authentication and now only supports SSH.

- When there are several code conflicts, merging code might be complicated.

## GitLab

**Features**

- Git is used for version control and repository management.

- Issue management, issue tracking, and bulletin boards are all available.

- The Review Apps tool and the Code Review feature are helpful.

- GitLab CI/CD is a CI/CD tool.

**Pros**

- It supports Kubernetes.

- It has an integrated CI platform with support for both default and custom runners.

- It includes helpful features such as built-in CI/CD assistance, which allows us to install and test our apps quickly.

- There are fewer code conflicts since it enables local checkout and several developers to work simultaneously on the same software file.

**Cons**

- The documentation could be improved.

- It is expensive.

- GitLab needs a dependable support center that is simple to find and use.

Sure, there are more tools than this, but I will not mention all of them here. I tried to cover the common ones, and I will now discuss different types of version control, because as a DevOps engineer, you need to know about each one of them.

# Version Control System Types

When you are part of a development team, the team members can work on the same pieces of code during a project. As a consequence, changes made to one section of the source code may be incompatible with alterations made to the same section by a different developer working on the project simultaneously.

Let's discuss the version control types to understand more about version control.

## Local Version Control Systems

This is one of the most basic types, and it uses a database to track file changes. One of the most widely used VCS tools is RCS. Patch sets (differences between files) are stored in a particular format on a disk. It can then re-create what any file looked like by adding all the fixes.

This kind of version control offers backup and testing benefits.

## Centralized Version Control Systems

Centralized version control systems (CVCSs) have a single repository, with each user having a working copy (see Figure 2-11). You must commit to updating the repository with your modifications. Others may be able to view your changes if you update. To make your improvements visible to others, you'll need two things.

- You will commit.

- Others will update or request a change.

The CVCS benefits vary from one company to another, but the general one is that it is easy to set up. In addition, it provides work transparency and allows the team to follow up. On the other hand, if one server goes down, the developer can't save the work, and the remote commit is usually slow.

## Distributed Version Control Systems

Distributed version control systems (DVCSs) have many repositories (see Figure 2-11). Each user has a working copy and repository. Simply committing your modifications does not provide anyone access to them. This is because the commit will only reflect those changes in your local repository, and you'll need to push them to the central repository to see them. Similarly, until you have previously pulled other people's modifications into your repository, you do not receive other people's changes when you update.

Four elements are necessary to make your modifications apparent to others.

- You commit.

- You push.

- They pull.

- They update or request a change.

This type of version control is the most common one; it's like a two-in-one tool because of local version control. The whole history is always accessible thanks to local contributions; there is no need to access a remote server. This saves time, mainly when dealing with SSH keys, and is an excellent approach for people who work remotely or offshore.

The centralized repo stores everything in one place depending on the working directory and the file structure that the company has, and it's considered one of the simplest forms of version control; on the other hand, the distributed version controls where the code will be mirrored on every developer's computer.

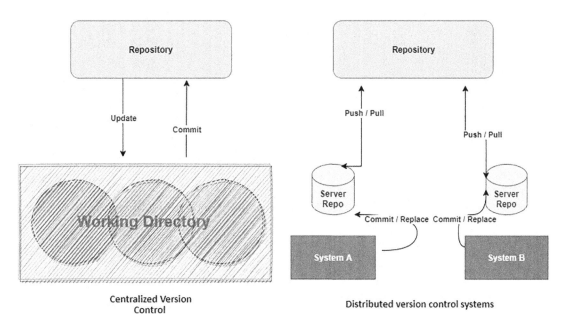

*Figure 2-11.* *How a centralized repo works*

# Summary

In this chapter, we covered the most topics for the DevOps category and the tools that can be used; depending on each category, there are tons of tools that can be used. To summarize, whether you are a novice or an expert looking to learn more, DevOps is a mindset and a profession that allows you to be creative with no boundaries; there is always something you can improve and expand. Knowing all of the tools isn't required, but understanding how they function and how to utilize them will be a strength when implementing DevOps.

The following chapters will explain more about DevOps. For example, I didn't discuss containerization in this chapter, which is part of DevOps as well. Let's not waste any time getting to the technical part.

# CHAPTER 3

# AWS Services for Continuous Integration

In the previous chapter, we reviewed DevOps and AWS concepts. In this chapter, I will cover DevOps continuous integration, particularly the following core topics:

- What is continuous integration?
- Continuous integration concepts
- Amazon AWS services for CI
- Examples of these CI services

By embracing DevOps methods, AWS delivers configurable services that allow enterprises to create and deliver products quicker and more reliably.

Provisioning and managing infrastructure, deploying application code, automating software release procedures, and monitoring the performance of your application and infrastructure are all made easier with these services.

You can deploy AWS resources using different methodologies; one of these methods is infrastructure as code (IaC), which we discussed earlier. Others are Terraform, CloudFormation, and AWS Cloud Development Kit, which help a company track the resources.

AWS CodeBuild, AWS CodeDeploy, AWS CodePipeline, and AWS CodeCommit are some services that aid continuous deployment, and we'll cover each in this chapter.

## Continuous Integration and Continuous Deployment

Continuous integration (CI) and continuous delivery (CD), commonly joined as CI/CD, are a culture, set of operating principles, and practices used by application development teams to deliver code changes more frequently and reliably.

© Osama Mustafa 2023

O. Mustafa, *A Complete Guide to DevOps with AWS*, https://doi.org/10.1007/978-1-4842-9303-4_3

For DevOps teams, CI/CD is a best practice. In Agile methods, it's also a best practice. CI/CD allows software development teams to focus on satisfying business needs while maintaining code quality and security by automating integration and delivery.

Continuous integration developers integrate their modifications back to the main branch as often as feasible. The developer's modifications are verified by building a build and running automated tests against it. You avoid integration issues if you wait until release day to integrate changes into the release branch.

When new commits are incorporated into the main branch, continuous integration focuses on testing automation to ensure the application is not damaged.

This is considered a programming methodology and technique set that regularly encourages development teams to commit tiny code changes to a Git repository. Because most current applications include writing code on various platforms and tools, groups want a standardized method for integrating and validating changes. Continuous integration allows developers to efficiently create, package, and test their applications.

Developers are more likely to commit code changes more often when they have a consistent integration procedure, which leads to improved cooperation and code quality.

Continuous delivery is an extension of continuous integration. It distributes all code changes to a testing/production environment immediately after the build step, which means you have an automatic release process and automated testing. You can deploy your application at any moment by just pressing a button.

In principle, continuous delivery allows you to distribute daily, weekly, biweekly, or monthly, depending on your company's needs. Suppose you genuinely want to reap the advantages of continuous delivery.

In such instances, you should deploy to production as quickly as possible to guarantee that little batches of code are published that are simpler to debug in the case of a problem.

The environment-specific parameters that must be bundled with each delivery are stored using CI/CD technologies. After that, CI/CD automation performs any required service calls to web servers, databases, and other services that must be restarted. Following deployment, it may also run additional tasks.

CI/CD necessitates *continuous testing*, as the goal is to produce high-quality code and apps. Automated regression, performance, and other tests are run in the CI/CD pipeline during continuous testing.

# CI/CD and DevOps

Every DevOps approach is built on the foundation of continuity. Continuous integration, continuous delivery, and continuous deployment are all part of the DevOps process. Let's take a closer look at each in Figure 3-1, which offers a snapshot of which stage each one of them is applied in and the advantages of incorporating them into the software development process.

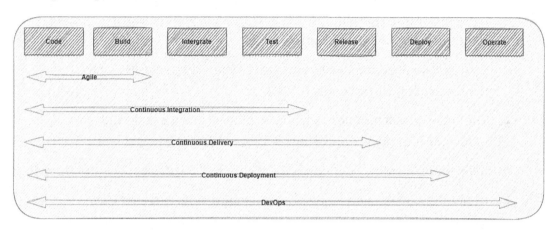

***Figure 3-1.***  *CI/CD big picture*

One benefit of CI/CD is being able to automate things. For example, if CI/CD is applied, there is no need to interrupt production for releases; therefore, you can build quickly. Deployment pipelines are triggered automatically for every change. Because you deploy small batches of changes, releases are less risky and simpler to correct in the event of a problem; plus, customers see a steady stream of changes, and quality improves daily than monthly, quarterly, or annually.

Each process comes with specific requirements. To implement continuous integration in your company, you need the following:

- Your team must build automated tests for each new addition, enhancement, or bug correction.

- You'll need a continuous integration server to monitor the main repository and execute tests on every new commit.

- Developers should integrate modifications as often as feasible, at least once a day.

Satisfying these requirements will provide the following benefits to a company:

- As automated testing catches regressions early, fewer problems are submitted to production.

- The release is simple since all integration difficulties were addressed early on.

- Developers are warned when they break the build and can concentrate on repairing it before moving on to another activity, resulting in less context switching.

- Testing costs are dramatically lowered, as your CI server can execute hundreds of tests in seconds.

- The QA team will be able to spend less time testing the code and more time improving the quality culture and the code itself.

Next, before implementing continuous delivery, you'll need to address the following:

- Continuous integration requires a solid foundation, and your test suite must cover enough with your code.

- Automated deployments are required. Although the trigger is still manual, human involvement should not be needed after the deployment.

- Your team will undoubtedly require feature flags to ensure that unfinished features do not affect consumers in production.

Satisfying these requirements and implementing continuous delivery offers these benefits:

- The difficulty of software deployment has been removed. Your team no longer needs to spend days preparing for a release.

- You can release your code more often.

- There will be less pressure on the development team, especially for small changes.

Lastly, here are the elements you will need to consider before implementing continuous deployment:

- The environment should be implemented as the best practice to avoid many issues; if this is not done later, it can affect the automation quality, which is supposed to simplify the infrastructure.

- Documentation, documentation, documentation: it must stay current with the deployment schedule.

- Define the process of each release and what changes should be made such as feature flags, bug flags, etc.

By addressing all of these needs, there's no need to interrupt production for releases, and for every modification, deployment pipelines are launched automatically.

This means you can build quickly. Installing and maintaining a continuous integration server are typical continuous integration costs. But you can significantly reduce the cost of adopting these practices by using a cloud service, which we will discuss in this chapter.

Jenkins users, for example, establish their pipelines in Jenkinsfiles, which explain several steps such as build, test, and deploy. The file declares environment variables, choices, secret keys, certificates, and other factors, subsequently referenced in stages. Error circumstances and alerts are handled in the post section.

Build, test, and deploy are the three steps of a typical continuous delivery pipeline. At various phases, the following activities might be included:

- You can execute a build after cloning the code from version control.

- You can use stage gates to automate the needed and supporting approvals when required.

- All essential infrastructure tasks are automated as code to set up or pull down cloud infrastructure.

- You can get code to run in the desired environment (staging, QA, Prod).

- Managing and customizing environment variables depend on the environment.

- The components of an application are pushed to their relevant services.

- Updating the configuration depends on the infrastructure side.

In the next section, we'll explore cloud services covering CI/CD; specifically, we'll focus on Amazon Web Services, specifically, what services you need to use and how to configure them to meet your company's needs.

---

**Note**    You'll find the projects I cover in this book much easier to follow if you already have an AWS account. For more information on signing up for an AWS account, navigate to `https://docs.aws.amazon.com/AWSCloudFormation/latest/UserGuide/cfn-sign-up-for-aws.html`.

---

# Continuous Integration

I mentioned CI, a software development method in which developers regularly merge code changes into a shared repository before running automated builds and testing. CI shortens the time to detect and fix defects, enhances software quality, and approves and deploys new software upgrades.

AWS provides the following three services that relate to CI.

## AWS CodeCommit

AWS CodeCommit (Figure 3-2) is a managed source control service that hosts private Git repositories and is safe and highly scalable. CodeCommit removes the need for you to run your source control system, and there is no hardware to provide or scale and no software to install, set up, or run. CodeCommit can be used to save everything from code to binaries, and it supports all of Git's essential features, enabling it to operate in tandem with your current Git-based tools. Your team may also use CodeCommit's online coding tools to read, modify, and work together on projects.

***Figure 3-2.*** *AWS CodeCommit*

AWS CodeCommit provides several advantages.

- You can use HTTPS or SSH to send your files to/from AWS CodeCommit. Your repositories are automatically secured at rest using customer-specific keys through AWS Key Management Service (AWS KMS).

- CodeCommit uses AWS Access Control AWS Identity and Access Management (IAM) to govern and monitor who has access to your data and how, when, and where they have access. CodeCommit now uses AWS CloudTrail and Amazon CloudWatch to help you keep track of your repositories.

- AWS CodeCommit saves your repository in Amazon Simple Storage Service (Amazon S3) and Amazon DynamoDB for high availability and durability. Your protected data is kept in numerous locations for redundancy. Thanks to this design, the data in your repository will be more available and more durable.

- You may now be notified when anything happens in your repositories. Amazon Simple Notification Service (Amazon SNS) notifications will be used for notifications. Each notice will provide a status message and a link to the resources that caused the notification to be produced. You can also use AWS CodeCommit repository triggers to send alerts, generate HTTP webhooks, and call AWS Lambda functions in response to your selected repository events.

- AWS CodeCommit is a collaborative software development platform. You can commit, branch, and merge your code, allowing you to keep track of the projects in your team. Pull requests, which offer a method for requesting code reviews and discussing code with collaborators, are now supported by CodeCommit.

# Creating a CodeCommit Repository on AWS

You can create a new CodeCommit repository using the AWS CodeCommit GUI or AWS Command Line (AWS CLI). After you've created a repository, you can add tags to it.

Let's start with the GUI option.

## Create a Repository (Console)

To create a CodeCommit repository using the GUI, you need to follow these steps:

1. From the AWS Portal, search for AWS *CodeCommit*; it's essential to choose the correct region for you (Figure 3-3).

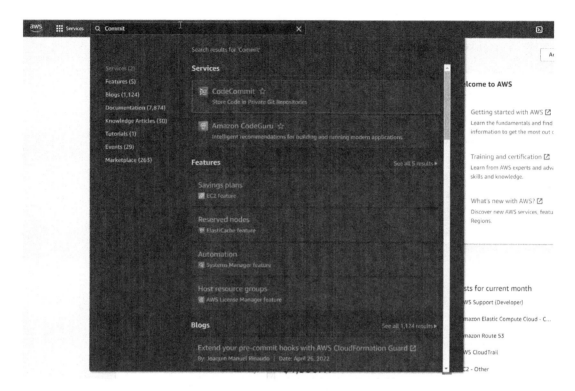

***Figure 3-3.***  *Choosing CodeCommit from the AWS Portal*

2.  Choose to create a repository from the page, as shown in
    Figure 3-4.

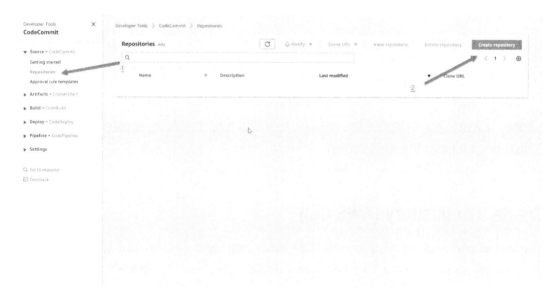

***Figure 3-4.***  *Creating a CodeCommit repository*

3.  In the Create repository dialog (Figure 3-5), specify a name for the repository in the "Repository name" field.

    The description is optional, but I usually prefer to write something explaining what this repo is for and which project, especially if you have more than one; tags are essential to make AWS management more efficient. When you are done, click Create.

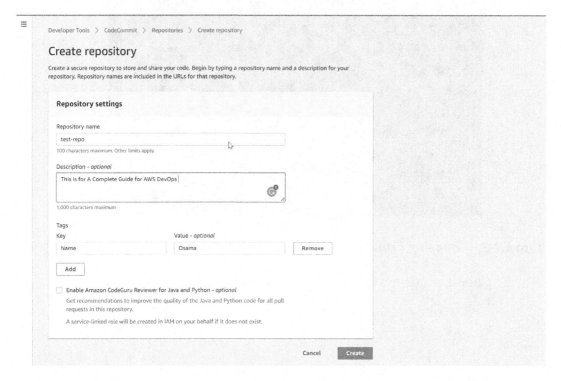

***Figure 3-5.***  *Choosing the repository name*

---

**Note**    Case is important when naming repositories. Your AWS account's name must be unique in the AWS region.

---

## Create a Repository (AWS CLI)

The first step to working with the AWS CLI is configuring the command-line tools to allow you to connect to the AWS Portal and deploy things, so let's quickly go through that process.

1.  Open the IAM console (Figure 3-6) in the AWS Management
    Console after logging in.

***Figure 3-6.***  *IAM page*

2.  After creating a user and assigning them the appropriate
    permissions, select the user. The new screen will be shown in
    Figure 3-7; choose the security credentials and click "Create
    access key."

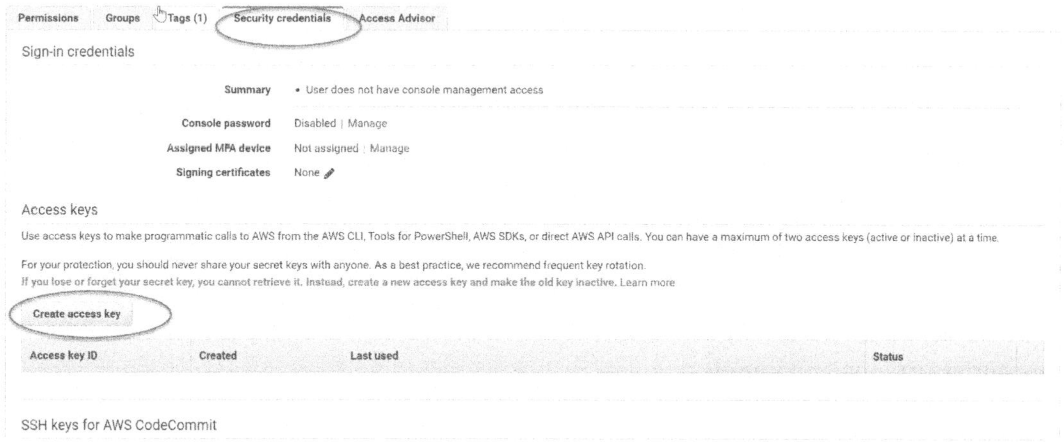

***Figure 3-7.***  *Creating access key and secret key*

3.  Choose Show to see the new access key pair. After this dialog box closes, you can no longer access the secret key. This is how your credentials will appear.

    -   *Access key ID*: AKIOMKOUSMP7COURSE

    -   *Secret access key*: kdasdasm9nmasdc/lkCOURSEKEY

4.  *Optional*: Choose the `Download.csv` file to get the key pair. Place the keys in a safe place. After this dialog box closes, you can no longer access the secret key.

Now you have the access key and secret key, but before moving on, let's also go through the installation process for the AWS CLI. I prefer using v2 instead of v1.

When using the latest Amazon command-line interface (CLI) version, all timestamp response values are returned in ISO 8601 format. In the first release of the Amazon CLI, commands returned timestamp values in whatever format the HTTP API response supplied. This format might be different for each service.

To Install the AWS CLI, you can check the AWS documentation at `https://docs.aws.amazon.com/cli/latest/userguide/getting-started-install.html`.

Once you install the tool on your machine, you can set it up; it's simple using the following snippet:

```
1. $ aws configure
2. AWS Access Key ID [None]: AKIOMKOUSMP7COURSE
3. AWS Secret Access Key [None]: kdasdasm9nmasdc/lkCOURSEKEY
4. Default region name [None]: eu-west-1
5. Default output format [None]: json
```

As a DevOps team member, you need to understand the AWS CLI, and it's highly recommended to use it instead of the GUI since the GUI has some limitations; it's mandatory to mention this is the direct way to configure the CLI.

With experience, CLI setup may be much quicker than GUI configuration. The user may set up the network's inbound and outbound connections and any necessary routing protocols and access controls with only a few simple instructions. With a graphical user interface, accessing these features would need many clicks and a search for the appropriate menus and panels.

Imagine, for example, having multiple accounts under the AWS organization, a service from Amazon AWS that allows companies to have various accounts such as Prod, Dev, and QA; in that case, you may be the easiest way to use AWS SSO.

After configuring the AWS CLI, you can run the commands to create the repository, but there are some elements you should consider first.

- Choose a name that distinguishes the CodeCommit repository from others using the --repository-name option; this name must be unique across all AWS services.

- The --repository-description attribute is optional and will allow you to add comments or explain how this repository is being used.

- Another optional attribute is --tags, which, naturally, allows you to add tags and key values.

The command that will be used to create the code commit repository is shown here:

```
1. aws codecommit create-repository --repository-name test-repo
--repository-description "first repo for AWS DevOps" --tags Team=DevOps
```

If the command ran successfully without any issues, the output would have the following information:

```
1. {
2.     "repositoryMetadata": {
3.         "repositoryName": "test-repo",
4.         "cloneUrlSsh": "ssh://git-codecommit.eu-west-1.amazonaws.com/
           v1/repos/test-repo",
5.         "lastModifiedDate": 1336081622.594,
6.         "repositoryDescription": "first repo for AWS DevOps",
7.         "cloneUrlHttp": "https://it-codecommit.eu-west-1.amazonaws.com/
           v1/repos/test-repo",
8.         "creationDate": 1336081622.59,
9.         "repositoryId": "d897513-c95w-1002-aaef-799cBook",
10.        "Arn": "arn:aws:codecommit:eu-west-1:111111111111:test-repo",
11.        "accountId": "111111111111"
12.    }
13. }
```

One of the most common cases using the AWS CLI is that the DevOps team member forgot the name or the ID. To retrieve them using the CLI, follow these steps:

1. To see a list all of CodeCommit repositories, run the following; you can use `--sort-by` or `--order`:

```
1. aws codecommit list-repositories
```

The output will be formatted as JSON, like the one below.

```
1.  {
2.      "repositories": [
3.          {
4.              "repositoryName": "test-repo"
5.              "repositoryId": "d897513-c95w-1002-aaef-799cBook",
6.          },
7.          {
8.              "repositoryName": "Book-repo"
9.              "repositoryId": "fgf0024c-dc0v-44dc-1191-799cBook"
10.         }
11.     ]
12. }
```

2. If you need more information about a single CodeCommit repository, use this:

```
1. aws codecommit get-repository --repository-name test-repo
```

The output will be JSON, as the previous is related to the repository.

3. To get information about numerous CodeCommit repositories, use this:

```
1. aws codecommit batch-get-repositories --repository-names test-repo book-repo
```

If it is successful, this command produces a JSON with the following information: any CodeCommit repositories that could not be located and the CodeCommit repositories that can be found with information such as repository name, repository description, repository's unique ID, and account ID.

When you initially link to a CodeCommit repository, you usually clone the repository's contents to your local workstation. Straight from the CodeCommit console, you may add and modify files in a repository. You may also add a CodeCommit repository as a remote repository if you already have a local repository. This section explains how to connect to a CodeCommit repository.

Before connecting to CodeCommit, these are the prerequisites:

- You must install the necessary software such as Git and settings on your local computer to be able to link to CodeCommit. You can do this at `https://git-scm.com/book/en/v2/Getting-Started-Installing-Git`.

- You'll need the clone URL for the CodeCommit repository you'd want to connect to. To access information about available repositories, use the AWS CodeCommit GUI, AWS CLI, or Git from a local repo linked to the CodeCommit repository.

Once you set up Git, the user needs to be configured to use CodeCommit; from IAM, choose the username, and under the username, choose the security credentials; check Figures 3-8 and 3-9; both show how to configure the needed to grant access to the user.

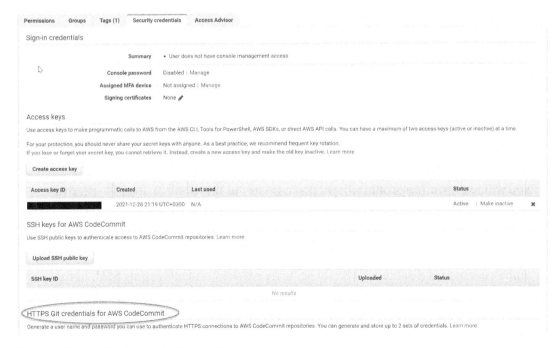

***Figure 3-8.***  *IAM user information*

SSH keys for AWS CodeCommit

Use SSH public keys to authenticate access to AWS CodeCommit repositories. Learn more

Upload SSH public key

| SSH key ID | Uploaded | Status |
|---|---|---|

*No results*

HTTPS Git credentials for AWS CodeCommit

Generate a user name and password you can use to authenticate HTTPS connections to AWS CodeCommit repositories. You can generate and store up to 2 sets of credentials. Learn more

Generate credentials

*No credentials have been generated.*

***Figure 3-9.*** *IAM code commit configuration*

Copy the username and password IAM produced for you by displaying, copying, and pasting this information into a secure file on your local computer or selecting "Download credentials" to download this information as a `download.csv` file. To connect to CodeCommit, you'll need this information.

Now to connect, you have two options.

1.  Connect to the CodeCommit repository by cloning the repository.

2.  Connect a local/existing repo to the CodeCommit repository.

Let's start with the first part, connecting using the clone option:

3.  Once you complete the prerequisites, you can choose any directory or location on your PC, Linux, Mac, or Windows and run the clone commands; remember `First-Repo,` the folder name.

    1. git clone https://git-codecommit.eu-west-1.amazonaws.com/v1/
    repos/test-repo First-repo

You can also configure the AWS CLI to set a default profile and region; I don't prefer that, especially if you have multiple accounts and need to switch between them.

You will use a source profile we will discuss later in this book, using `git-remote-codecommit` via HTTPS, with the AWS CLI default profile and AWS region set as follows:

1. git clone codecommit://test-repo First-repo

Some companies disable HTTPS for security reasons and allow only SSH; in that case, each DevOps within the team needs to provide a public key, such as this:

1. git clone ssh://git-codecommit.eu-west-1.amazonaws.com/v1/repos/test-
repo First-repo

Figure 3-10 shows that the test-repo has been created and the options that we have to clone the repository.

***Figure 3-10.*** *Repository information*

## Connect a Local/Existing Repo to the CodeCommit Repository

There are two other options that pertain to creating a CodeCommit repo: if you currently have a local repository and want to make a CodeCommit repository the remote repository, ad if you already have a remote repository and want to push your changes to both CodeCommit and that remote repository.

One of the most common use cases is to keep utilizing your current Git repository solution while experimenting with AWS CodeCommit.

1.  Run the Git `remote -v` command from your local repo directory. It would be best if you got something like this as a result:

    **HTTPS**

    ```
    1. origin  https://git-codecommit.eu-west-1.amazonaws.com/v1/
    repos/test-repo (fetch)
    2. origin  https://git-codecommit.eu-west-1.amazonaws.com/v1/
    repos/test-repo (push)
    ```

**SSH**

```
1. origin  ssh://git-codecommit.eu-west-1.amazonaws.com/v1/
repos/test-repo  (fetch)
2. origin  ssh://git-codecommit.eu-west-1.amazonaws.com/v1/
repos/test-repo  (push)
```

2. Once you run the previous command, run the following command, which specifies where you want to host your code:

```
1. git remote set-url --add --push origin some-URL/repo-name
```

To modify a Git remote origin using an HTTPS URL, one must first open the Git terminal and verify the current remote URL, for example.

```
1. git remote set-url --add --push origin  https://git-
codecommit.eu-west-1.amazonaws.com/v1/repos/test-repo
```

3. Rerun the `git remote -v`.

**HTTPS**

```
1. origin  https://git-codecommit.eu-west-1.amazonaws.com/
v1/repos/test-repo (fetch)
2. origin  URL/RepoName (push)
```

**SSH**

```
1. origin  ssh://git-codecommit.eu-west-1.amazonaws.com/v1/
repos/test-repo   (fetch)
2. origin  URL/RepoName  (push)
```

4. The CodeCommit repository should now be added; run `git remote set-url --add --push origin` again but with the repository URL.

**HTTPS**

```
1. git remote set-url --add --push origin https://git-
codecommit.eu-west-1.amazonaws.com/v1/repos/test-repo
```

**SSH**

```
1. git remote set-url --add --push origin ssh://git-
codecommit.eu-west-1.amazonaws.com/v1/repos/test-repo
```

5. Run the `git remote -v` command again.

6. Make sure you're pushing to both remote repositories now by adding a dummy text file.

7. After creating the text, run the following:

```
1. Git add .
2. git add dummy.text
```

8. Run the following command and choose a proper comment:

```
1. git commit -m "Added dummy text file for texting."
```

9. You need to push this file from the local to the CodeCommit repository. To do this, run the following command:

```
1. git push -u remote-name branch-name
```

Once you run the previous command, the file will be uploaded, and you will see output like the following (remember this for HTTPS; it is almost the same for SSH):

```
1. Counting objects: 5, done.
2. Delta compression using up to 4 threads.
3. Compressing objects: 100% (3/3), done.
4. Writing objects: 100% (3/3), 5.61 KiB | 0 bytes/s, done.
5. Total 3 (delta 1), reused 0 (delta 0)
6. To URL/RepoDestation
7.    a5ba4ed..250f6c3  main -> main
8. Counting objects: 5, done.
9. Delta compression using up to 4 threads.
10. Compressing objects: 100% (3/3), done.
11. Writing objects: 100% (3/3), 5.61 KiB | 0 bytes/s, done.
12. Total 3 (delta 1), reused 0 (delta 0)
```

```
13. remote:
14. To https://git-codecommit.eu-west-1.amazonaws.com/v1/repos/
test-repo
15.     a5ba4ed..250f6c3  main -> main
```

## View Repository Details (Console)

Follow these steps to see some details about the repository:

1. Open the CodeCommit console as mentioned before in this chapter.

2. Select the repository's name from the Repositories menu.

3. Choose the Clone URL and the protocol to clone the repository.

4. Choose Settings in the navigation pane to see the settings for the repository and data, such as ARN and ID.

## View CodeCommit Repository Details (AWS CLI)

It's crucial as DevOps team members to know all the available options; sometimes, you need to use CLI for things not supported using the GUI and Git commands previously mentioned in this chapter.

I prefer to use CLI since it's everything you need; once you start using CLI, you will find everything else easy.

Now dealing with CodeCommit, it's like you are dealing with Git, but for AWS, which is the same concept. However, in this case I need to change the settings for the repository.

After going through a couple of code commit configurations, you can share a CodeCommit repository with other users once you've established it. First, choose the protocol, either HTTP or SSH, to propose to users when cloning and connecting to your repository using a Git client or an IDE.

The URL and connection details should then be sent to the people you want to share the repository. You may also need to create an IAM group, apply managed policies to that group, and update IAM rules to refine access, depending on your security requirements.

Here is a summary of what is needed by both protocols:

**HTTPS**

1. Install the Git tool on your local PC.

2. Generate HTTPS credentials for the users, which were covered earlier.

**SSH**

1. It would help if you generated a public-private key using one of the tools, such as Putty keygen.

2. Save these keys for later.

3. The public key will be connected with your cloud IAM user.

4. Configure the local PC, as mentioned earlier.

# View CodeCommit Repository Details (Git)

You should be familiar with Git commands to connect and start using the code commit using Git commands.

Run the `git remote show remote-name` command from a local repo to get information about CodeCommit repositories.

The output for this command will look like the following, formatted for HTTPS:

```
1. remote origin
2.    Fetch URL: https://git-codecommit.eu-west-1.amazonaws.com/v1/repos/
      test-repo
3.    Push  URL: https://git-codecommit.eu-west-1.amazonaws.com/v1/repos/
      test-repo
4.    HEAD branch: (unknown)
5.    Remote branches:
6.      MyNewBranch tracked
7.      main tracked
8.    Local ref configured for 'git pull':
9.      MyNewBranch merges with remote MyNewBranch (up to date)
10.   Local refs configured for 'git push':
11.     MyNewBranch pushes to MyNewBranch (up to date)
12.     main pushes to main (up to date)
```

# Configuring Notifications for AWS CodeCommit

It's imperative to understand code commit basics and the configuration; you may establish notification rules for a repository to email users about repository event types you define. When occurrences fit the notification rule parameters, notifications are delivered. To utilize notifications, you can either establish an Amazon SNS subject or use one already in your Amazon Web Services account. Utilize the CodeCommit console or the AWS CLI to set up notification rules.

From the AWS Portal, go to CodeCommit and choose the repository you want to set up notifications for, as shown in Figure 3-11.

***Figure 3-11.*** *AWS CodeCommit notification*

Next, click "Create notification rule." A new screen will open, as shown in Figure 3-12. Enter a name for the rule in the "Notification name" field.

For "Detail type," you have two options.

5. Basic if you want only the information provided to Amazon EventBridge included in the notification

6. Full if you want to include information provided to Amazon EventBridge and the CodeCommit or notification manager might supply it

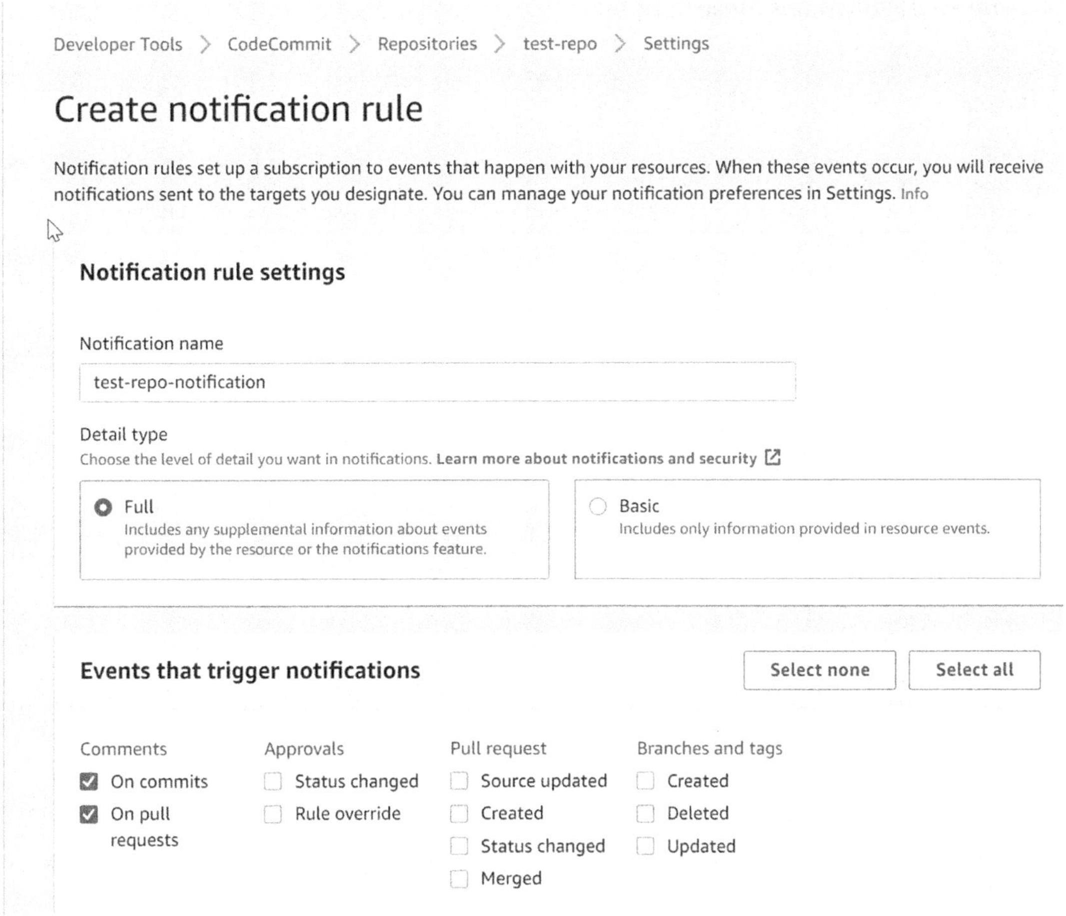

Developer Tools  >  CodeCommit  >  Repositories  >  test-repo  >  Settings

# Create notification rule

Notification rules set up a subscription to events that happen with your resources. When these events occur, you will receive notifications sent to the targets you designate. You can manage your notification preferences in Settings. Info

## Notification rule settings

Notification name

| test-repo-notification |

Detail type
Choose the level of detail you want in notifications. **Learn more about notifications and security** ⤤

○ Full
Includes any supplemental information about events provided by the resource or the notifications feature.

○ Basic
Includes only information provided in resource events.

## Events that trigger notifications

[ Select none ]    [ Select all ]

| Comments | Approvals | Pull request | Branches and tags |
|---|---|---|---|
| ☑ On commits | ☐ Status changed | ☐ Source updated | ☐ Created |
| ☑ On pull requests | ☐ Rule override | ☐ Created | ☐ Deleted |
| | | ☐ Status changed | ☐ Updated |
| | | ☐ Merged | |

***Figure 3-12.*** *CodeCommit notification settings*

The next step is to select the events you want to send alerts under events that trigger notifications; for the target type, you have two options if you have already configured the target.

7. *Slack*: If you want to get a notification for this repository on the Slack Channel, use the webhook.

8. *SNS topic*: This is provided by AWS, which allows you to send emails or SMS.

Figure 3-13 illustrates these options.

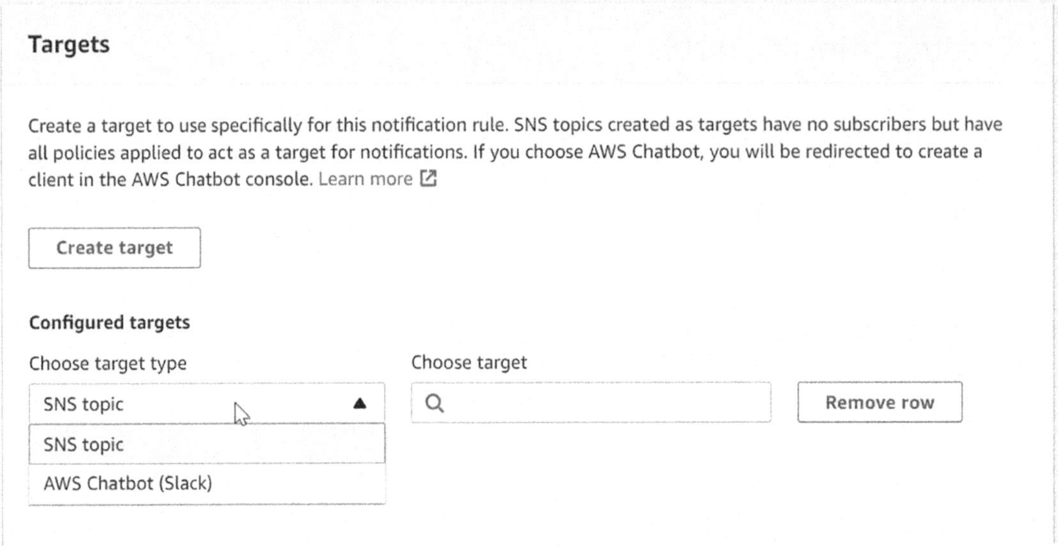

**Targets**

Create a target to use specifically for this notification rule. SNS topics created as targets have no subscribers but have all policies applied to act as a target for notifications. If you choose AWS Chatbot, you will be redirected to create a client in the AWS Chatbot console. Learn more ☑

Create target

**Configured targets**

| Choose target type | Choose target | |
| --- | --- | --- |
| SNS topic ▲ | Q | Remove row |
| SNS topic | | |
| AWS Chatbot (Slack) | | |

*Figure 3-13.*  *Notification target*

I've now covered the elements essential to using CodeCommit, but know that it's a vast topic I encourage you to explore further. For the needs of this book, however, you should now be set in terms of using CodeCommit.

Now that you've established your CodeCommit repository, it's time to start coding. We'll be utilizing AWS CodeBuild.

# AWS CodeBuild

AWS CodeBuild is a managed service continuous integration solution that generates code, performs tests, and creates ready-to-deploy software packages. You don't have to maintain, scale, or provision your development servers. CodeBuild may utilize Git or any version control as a source provider.

CodeBuild grows indefinitely and can handle several builds at once. CodeBuild provides several preconfigured environments for Windows and Linux. Customers may also use Docker containers to transport their customized build environments. Open-source technologies like Jenkins and Spinnaker are also integrated with CodeBuild.

Unit, functional, and integration tests may all be reported using CodeBuild. These reports show how many test cases were run and whether they succeeded or failed. The build process may also occur if your integrated services or databases are placed within a VPC.

Your build artifacts are secured with customer-specific keys maintained by the KMS using AWS CodeBuild. You may provide user-specific rights to your projects with IAM.

Like any other service, Code build provides different benefits for any company, such as the following:

9.  CodeBuild sets up, patches, updates, and manages your build servers.

10. CodeBuild grows to match your build requirements on demand. You pay for the amount of construction time you use.

11. For the most common programming languages, CodeBuild offers predefined build environments. To begin your first build, all you have to do is point to your build script.

# How CodeBuild works

Like any other services on Amazon AWS, you can manage/run code build using different ways:

12. Console/GUI

13. AWS CLI

14. AWS SDK

15. CodePipeline

All of them will lead to the same results, but it's good to know them; see Figure 3-14.

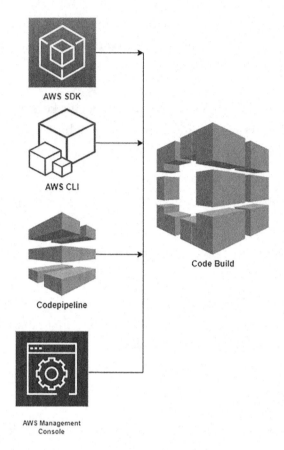

***Figure 3-14.***  *Which AWS services you can use to run CodeBuild*

Before you start using CodeBuild, you need to answer questions that will help you understand more about what you will do with the configuration and setup.

**Where will your code be stored?**

CodeBuild supports a different version/source code repository, but the build specification (*build spec*) file must be included in the source code so the code build will understand the stages.

A *build spec* is a YAML-formatted collection of build commands and associated parameters used by CodeBuild to conduct a build.

The following are the supported version control/source code repositories:

16.  CodeCommit

17.  Amazon S3

18.   GitHub

19.   Bitbucket

**Which build commands should you use, and in what sequence should you execute them?**

When we talk about the commands, buildspec files are necessary; they indicate how these commands will be executed, and in which order.

**What do you need to complete the build, either tools or runtimes?**

You code in Python, Java, or even Ruby.

**Do I need an extra package such as Maven, or am I good with what I have now?**

The following is an example of what buildspec look like; this a sample for a small Node.js application. Remember, it's YAML.

```
1. version: 0.2
2. phases:
3.   install:
4.     runtime-versions:
5.       nodejs: 10
6.     commands:
7.       - echo Installing Mocha...
8.       - npm install -g mocha
9.   pre_build:
10.     commands:
11.       - echo Installing source NPM dependencies...
12.       - npm install
13.       - npm install unit.js
14.   build:
15.     commands:
16.       - echo build started on 'date'
17.       - echo Compiling the Node.js code
18.       - mocha test.js
19.   post_build:
20.     commands:
21.       - echo build completed on 'date'
22. artifacts:
```

```
23.   files:
24.     - app.js
25.     - index.html
26.     - package.json
27.     - node_modules/async/*
28.     - node_modules/lodash/*
```

Now that you have a high-level understanding of CodeBuild, let's explore it in more detail. First up is how to use CodeBuild with a code pipeline. As was the case with setting up the repository, you have multiple options, and again we'll focus on using either the GUI or AWS CLI.

## Using CodeBuild via the Console

CodeBuild services allow DevOps to build an entirely different version depending on the configuration so that the release will be known to the company.

For example, the company added a new feature called a *menu*, known as a code change. This was added so that CodeBuild will generate from the source code a release called menu-v1.0.zip; this release will be deployed later, and so on.

Configuring CodeBuild is straightforward, but sometimes the setup differs from one company to another.

As you can see later in this chapter, some integrate cloud build with various tools or services such as CodePipeline or Jenkins to automate the whole process. There are common steps you need to follow, shown here:

1.  You need to have source code.

2.  Create a buildspec file.

3.  Create an S3 bucket (the best practice is two buckets).

4.  Upload your source code to version control such as GitHub or CodeCommit.

5.  Create and configure the build project.

6.  Test the build project by running it.

7.  Check the summary information.

8.  Check the output for the generated artifact.

# Step 1: You Need to Have the Source Code

Let's go with the first step, which is the source code; either you will create a free account on GitHub and upload the code you want to use there or you will go to my GitHub account at `https://github.com/OsamaOracle`.

Clone the repo called `CodeBuild-repo-example` (`https://github.com/OsamaOracle/CodeBuild-repo-example`).

Inside the repository, you can check and see Java code plus the buildspec file.

See Figure 3-15, which shows the repository structure.

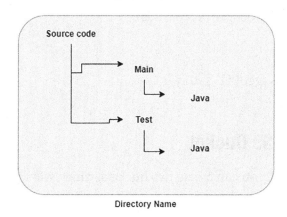

***Figure 3-15.***  *Repo folder structure*

# Step 2: Create a Build Specs File

At this process stage, you will construct a build specification file, also known as a *build spec*. CodeBuild utilizes this document to execute a build. A build spec is a collection of instructions and parameters formatted in YAML.

CodeBuild cannot correctly transform your build input into build output or identify the build output artifact in the built environment so that it may be uploaded to your output bucket if you do not provide it with a build spec.

```
1. version: 0.2
2.
3. phases:
4.   install:
5.     runtime-versions:
6.       java: corretto11
```

```
 7.   pre_build:
 8.      commands:
 9.        - echo nothing to do in the pre_build phase...
10.   build:
11.      commands:
12.        - echo Build started on 'date'
13.        - mvn install
14.   post_build:
15.      commands:
16.        - echo build completed on 'date'
17. artifacts:
18.    files:
19.      - target/messageUtil-1.0.jar
20.
```

## Step 3: Create an S3 Bucket

In a straightforward step, you can create two buckets, which will allow you to understand and organize the output.

## Step 4: Upload Your Code

You must upload the code to the version control tool, such as GitHub, Bitbucket, or CodeCommit.

## Step 5: Create the Code Build Project

AWS CodeBuild performs the build when you create a project, so let's do this:

1.   Go to the CodeBuild service from the console, as shown in Figure 3-16.

Services
CodeBuild
Search results for 'CodeB'
Services (14)
Features (11)
Blogs (965)
Documentation (6)
Tutorials (8)
Events (9)
Services
See all 14 results
CodeBuild
Build and Test Code
CodeCommit
Store Code in Private Git Repositories
CodePipeline
Release Software using Continuous Delivery
AWS Signer
Ensuring trust and integrity of your code
Features
See all 11 results
Actions
lcome to AWS
Getting started with AWS
Learn the fundamentals and find valuable information to get the most out of AWS.
Training and certification
Learn from AWS experts and advance your skills and knowledge.
What's new with AWS?
Discover new AWS services, features, and Regions.

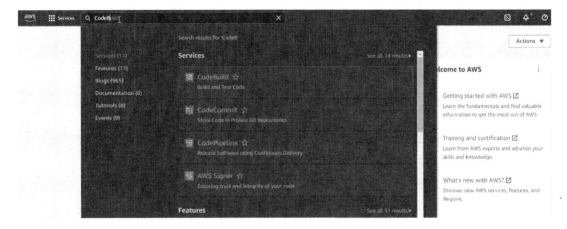

***Figure 3-16.*** *AWS Portal*

2. Create the project, as shown in Figure 3-17.

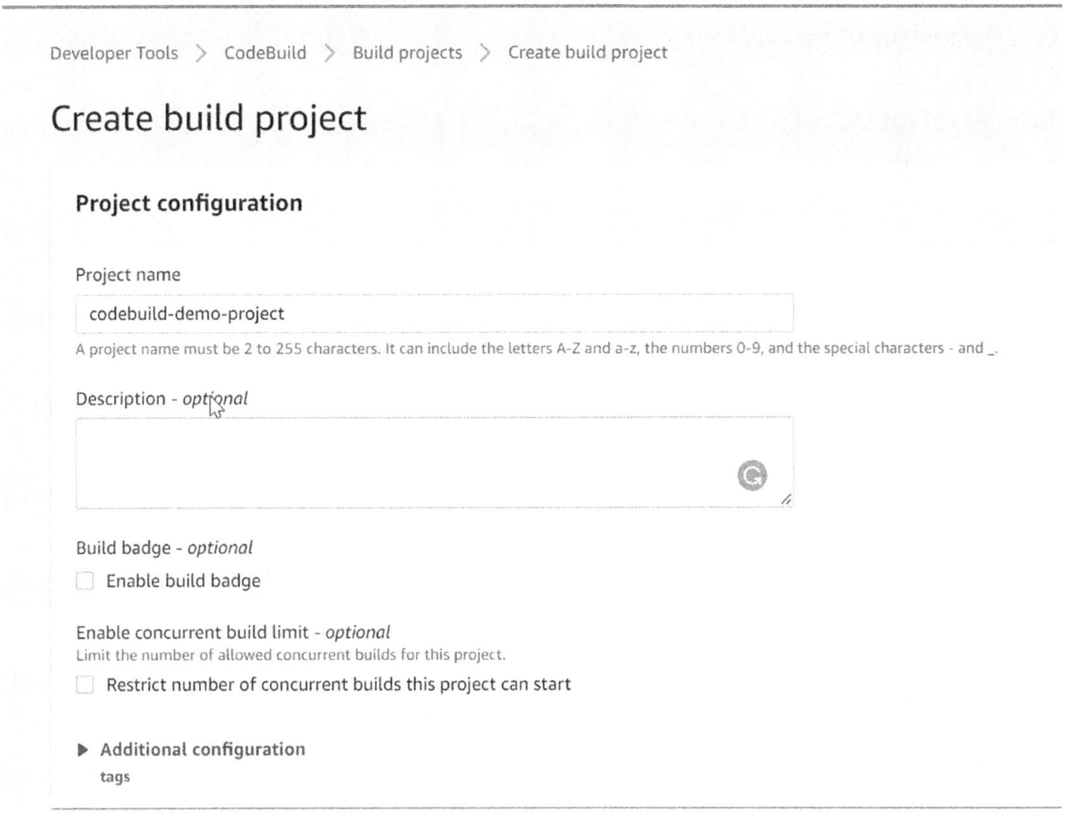

Developer Tools > CodeBuild > Build projects > Create build project
Create build project
Project configuration
Project name
codebuild-demo-project
A project name must be 2 to 255 characters. It can include the letters A-Z and a-z, the numbers 0-9, and the special characters - and _.
Description - optional
Build badge - optional
Enable build badge
Enable concurrent build limit - optional
Limit the number of allowed concurrent builds for this project.
Restrict number of concurrent builds this project can start
Additional configuration
tags

***Figure 3-17.*** *Creating a project*

# Using CodeBuild via the AWS CLI

With the help of the create-project command and the –generate-cli-skeleton option, you may construct a skeleton JSON file:

```
1. aws codebuild create-project --generate-cli-skeleton
```

The output of the first command will generate a JSON file and copy the JSON file.

Switch to the directory where you stored the file and then execute the create-project command again.

```
 1. {
 2.    "name": "codebuild-demo-project",
 3.    "source": {
 4.       "type": "S3",
 5.       "location": "codebuild-region-ID-account-ID-input-bucket/
          MessageUtil.zip"
 6.    },
 7.    "artifacts": {
 8.       "type": "S3",
 9.       "location": "codebuild-region-ID-account-ID-output-bucket"
10.    },
11.    "environment": {
12.       "type": "LINUX_CONTAINER",
13.       "image": "aws/codebuild/standard:4.0",
14.       "computeType": "BUILD_GENERAL1_SMALL"
15.    },
16.    "serviceRole": "serviceIAMRole"
17. }
```

Please copy the previous code, and modify it depending on the project name, location of the bucket, and environment configuration as the project needs.

Save this file inside the exact repository location (GitHub, Bitbucket, etc.) and run the following command:

```
1. aws codebuild create-project --cli-input-json file://create-project.json
```

Execute the create-project command once again while specifying your JSON file, and the project will be created.

Next is the project's source; as mentioned, we created an S3 bucket before so that will be our source, check Figure 3-18.

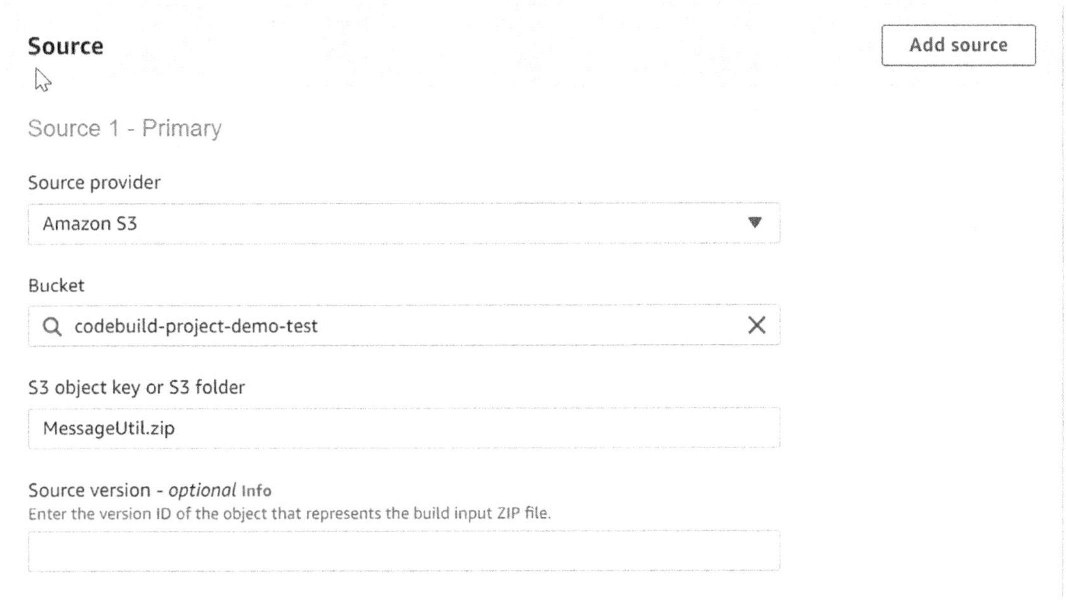

*Figure 3-18.*  *CodeBuild source configuration*

## Step 6: Test and Run the Code

Now, where will you run the code build is called the *environment*. For this one, you have two options.

20.  A managed image, selections from the operating system, runtime(s), image, and image version.

21.  A custom image, such as Windows, Linux, Linux GPU, or ARM. If you choose another registry, enter the data and tags of the Docker image in Docker Hub as the external registry URL.

If you check the privileged box, because you want to use this building project to create Docker images, the building environment image you selected does not include Docker support from CodeBuild. Otherwise, all builds trying to communicate with the Docker daemon will fail. To interact with your builds, you must also run the Docker daemon. The following build commands can be used to establish the Docker daemon during your build spec install step. Do not perform these instructions using a CodeBuild build environment image with Docker support.

The last section is the service role, an AWS service that takes on a service role when it performs activities on your behalf. As a service that conducts backup operations on your behalf, AWS Backup requires that you pass it a role to assume when performing backup operations. If you have already created one, there is no need to do it again; choose it.

You could do extra configurations such as VPC, timeout, compute options, and variables. See Figure 3-19.

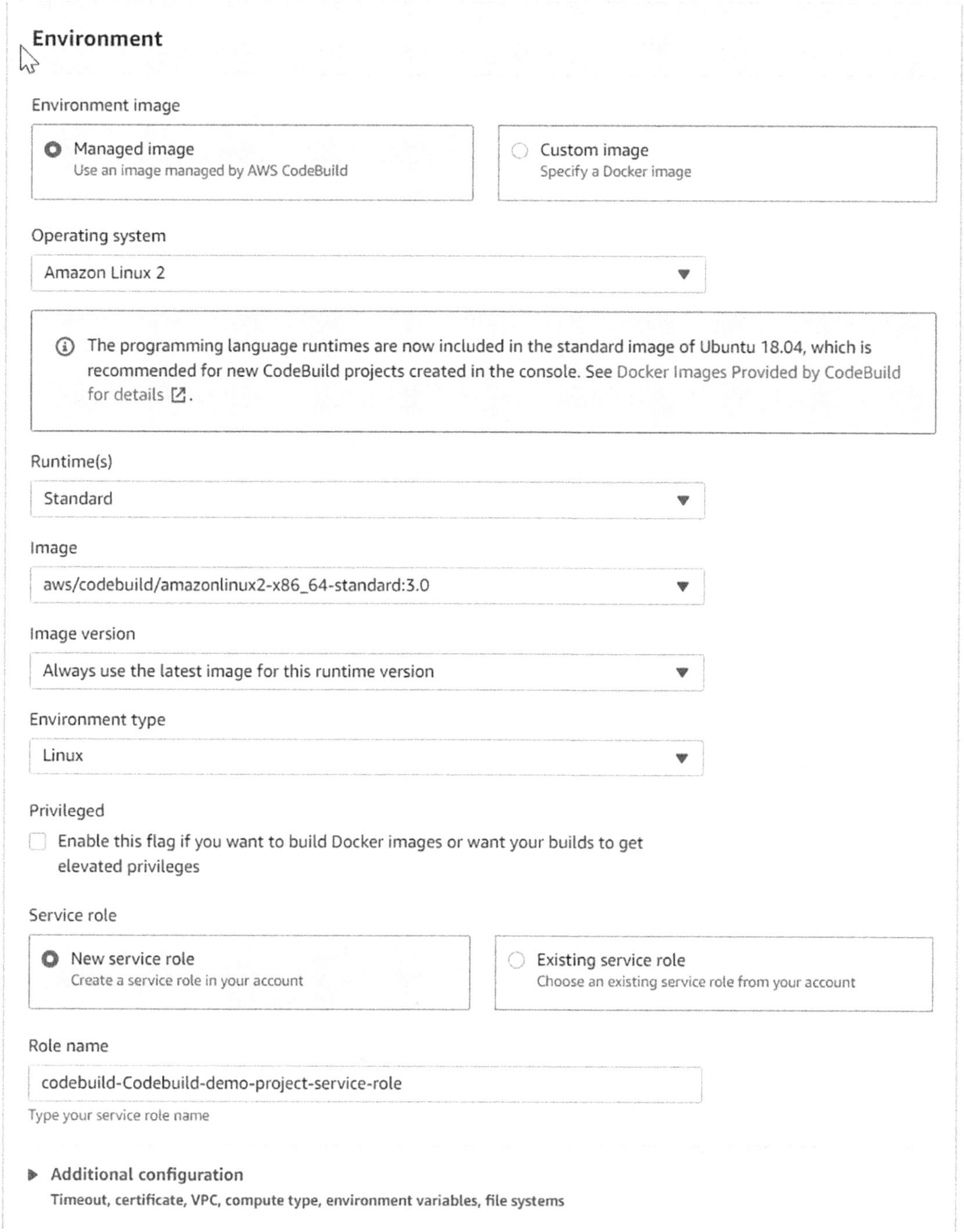

**Environment**

Environment image

○ **Managed image**
Use an image managed by AWS CodeBuild

○ **Custom image**
Specify a Docker image

Operating system

Amazon Linux 2 ▼

ⓘ The programming language runtimes are now included in the standard image of Ubuntu 18.04, which is recommended for new CodeBuild projects created in the console. See Docker Images Provided by CodeBuild for details 🗗 .

Runtime(s)

Standard ▼

Image

aws/codebuild/amazonlinux2-x86_64-standard:3.0 ▼

Image version

Always use the latest image for this runtime version ▼

Environment type

Linux ▼

Privileged

☐ Enable this flag if you want to build Docker images or want your builds to get elevated privileges

Service role

○ **New service role**
Create a service role in your account

○ **Existing service role**
Choose an existing service role from your account

Role name

codebuild-Codebuild-demo-project-service-role

Type your service role name

▶ **Additional configuration**
Timeout, certificate, VPC, compute type, environment variables, file systems

***Figure 3-19.*** *CodeBuild environment configuration screen*

The next step is to specify the build spec file; if you check the repository, you will find a file with that name responsible for telling CodeBuild what to do; there is no need to mention the filename unless you change the default name.

You can insert the command manually, or you can enter the filename if your source code/repository already includes the file with the default name (`buildspec.yml`).

If your build spec file has an alternative name, for example, `buildspec-project-one`, YAML, or location, enter the path to it in the build spec name starting from the root. See Figure 3-20.

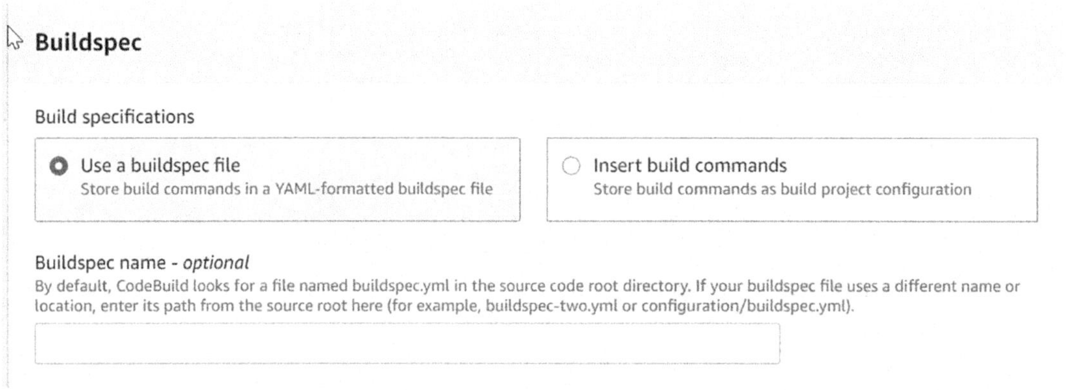

**Buildspec**

Build specifications

○ Use a buildspec file
Store build commands in a YAML-formatted buildspec file

○ Insert build commands
Store build commands as build project configuration

Buildspec name - *optional*
By default, CodeBuild looks for a file named buildspec.yml in the source code root directory. If your buildspec file uses a different name or location, enter its path from the source root here (for example, buildspec-two.yml or configuration/buildspec.yml).

*Figure 3-20.* *Defining the buildspec file*

A batch configuration is a collection of builds that may be executed as a single operation. When starting the build, the advanced option also allows for batch configuration, and once you choose it, the following options will appear:

- You create a service role or choose the existing one.

- Set the allowed compute type(s) for batch, with optional compute types

- Set the maximum builds allowed in batch.

- Set the batch timeout.

The next option is the artifact, a product created during development. A data structure, a prototype, a flow chart, a design specification, or a configuration script are all examples.

Some artifacts are necessary throughout the development cycle and must be conveniently located.

As you can see from Figure 3-21 and Figure 3-22 we chose S3 as our artifact destination, in the same bucket; you can set a name for the output in case you want it to be compressed.

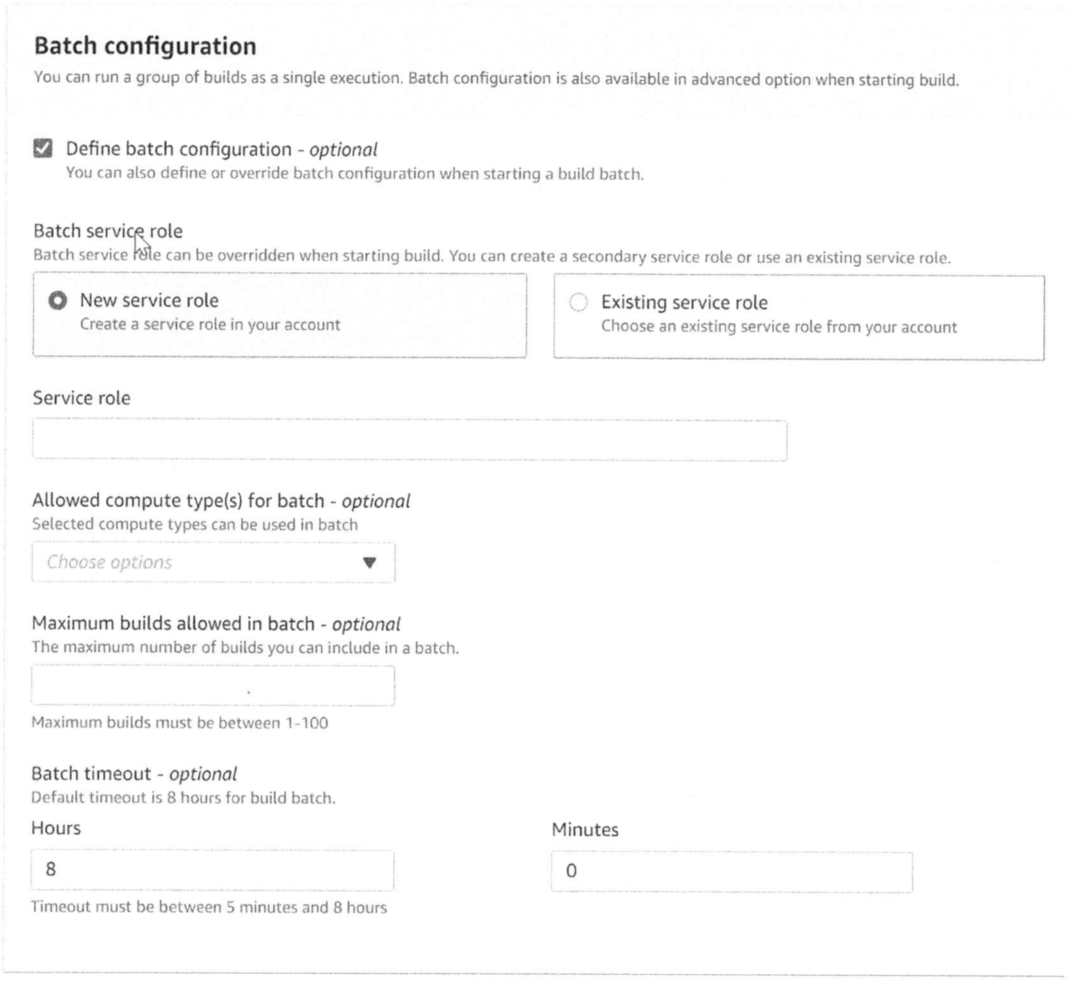

**Figure 3-21.** *Batch configuration*

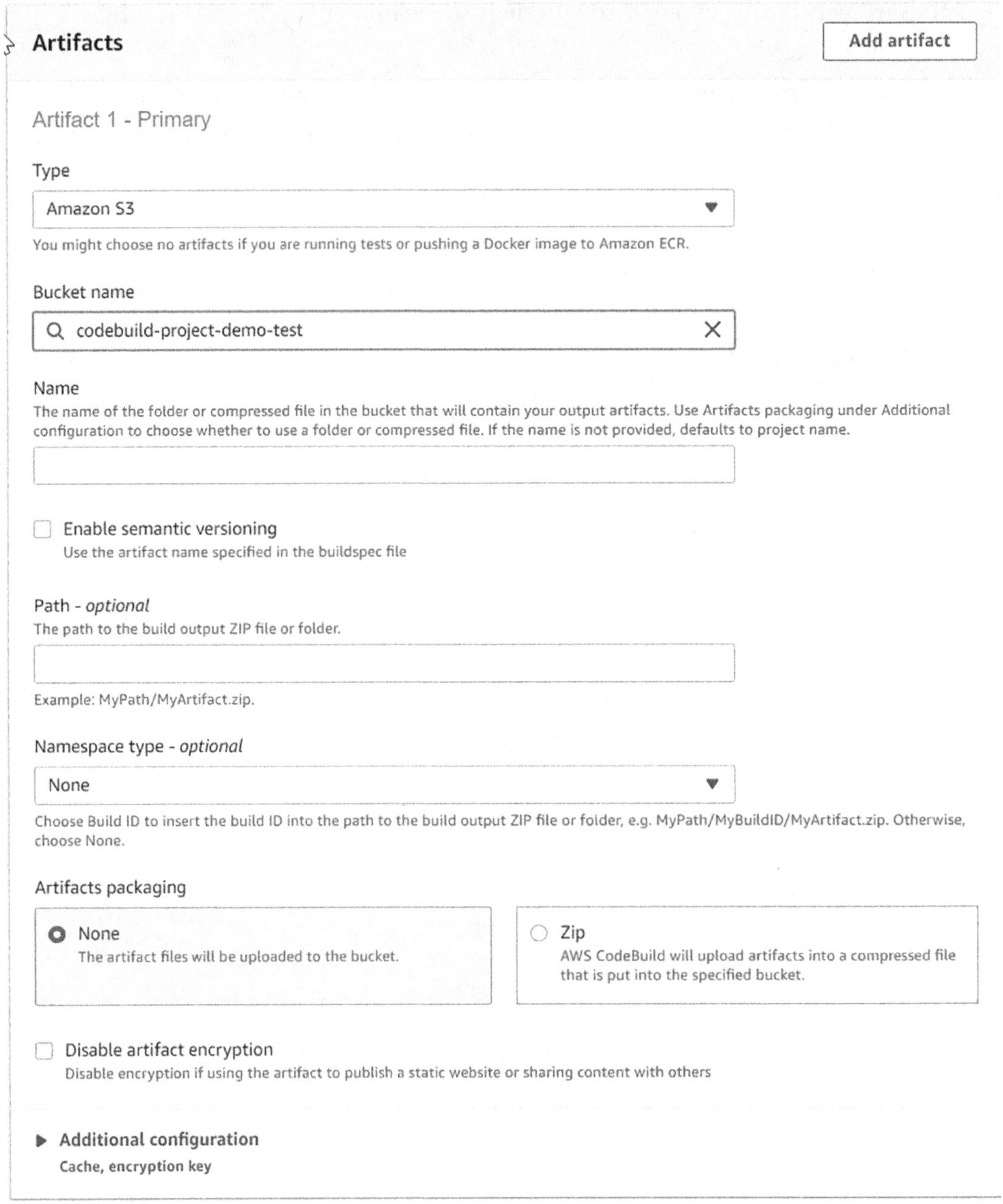

**Artifacts**                                                    [ Add artifact ]

Artifact 1 - Primary

Type

| Amazon S3                                                 ▼ |

You might choose no artifacts if you are running tests or pushing a Docker image to Amazon ECR.

Bucket name

| 🔍  codebuild-project-demo-test                          ✕ |

Name

The name of the folder or compressed file in the bucket that will contain your output artifacts. Use Artifacts packaging under Additional configuration to choose whether to use a folder or compressed file. If the name is not provided, defaults to project name.

| |

☐ Enable semantic versioning
   Use the artifact name specified in the buildspec file

Path - *optional*
The path to the build output ZIP file or folder.

| |

Example: MyPath/MyArtifact.zip.

Namespace type - *optional*

| None                                                      ▼ |

Choose Build ID to insert the build ID into the path to the build output ZIP file or folder, e.g. MyPath/MyBuildID/MyArtifact.zip. Otherwise, choose None.

Artifacts packaging

| ⦿ None | ◯ Zip |
| The artifact files will be uploaded to the bucket. | AWS CodeBuild will upload artifacts into a compressed file that is put into the specified bucket. |

☐ Disable artifact encryption
   Disable encryption if using the artifact to publish a static website or sharing content with others

▶ **Additional configuration**
   Cache, encryption key

*Figure 3-22.* *CodeBuild artifact screen configuration*

Finally, I disable the CloudWatch monitor because of the cost, but in case this is production, so you may need to enable it for troubleshooting in the future, Check Figure 3-23.

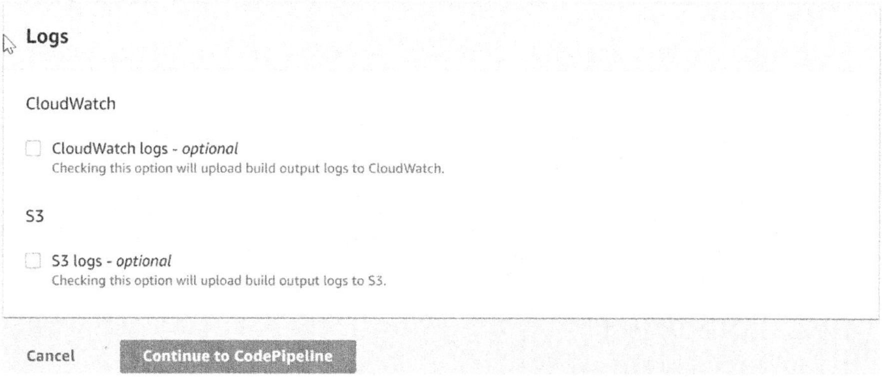

### Logs

#### CloudWatch

☐ CloudWatch logs - *optional*
  Checking this option will upload build output logs to CloudWatch.

#### S3

☐ S3 logs - *optional*
  Checking this option will upload build output logs to S3.

Cancel    **Continue to CodePipeline**

***Figure 3-23.*** *Logs*

Once you are done with creating the project, click Start, check Figure 3-24.

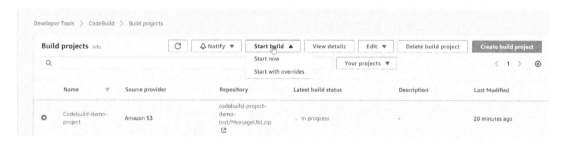

***Figure 3-24.*** *Starting the build*

You can run the following command line to start the build using the command line:

```
1. aws codebuild start-build --project-name project-name
```

# How to Create a CodeBuild-Based Pipeline

The following steps will show you how to create a pipeline using CodeBuild for the company code:

1. Access the AWS Portal with the proper user permission to work with CodeBuild:

   a. Working as an Administrator/root account is usually not recommended by AWS.

   b. You might be an Administrator user with specific permission; we will discuss this later in this book.

    c. You might be an IAM User with permission assigned to it and the permission; you need the following (based on AWS best practices):

1. `codepipeline:*`
2. `iam:ListRoles`
3. `iam:PassRole`
4. `s3:CreateBucket`
5. `s3:GetBucketPolicy`
6. `s3:GetObject`
7. `s3:ListAllMyBuckets`
8. `s3:ListBucket`
9. `s3:PutBucketPolicy`
10. `codecommit:ListBranches`
11. `codecommit:ListRepositories`
12. `codedeploy:GetApplication`
13. `codedeploy:GetDeploymentGroup`
14. `codedeploy:ListApplications`
15. `codedeploy:ListDeploymentGroups`
16. `elasticbeanstalk:DescribeApplications`
17. `elasticbeanstalk:DescribeEnvironments`
18. `lambda:GetFunctionConfiguration`
19. `lambda:ListFunctions`
20. `opsworks:DescribeStacks`
21. `opsworks:DescribeApps`
22. `opsworks:DescribeLayers`

2. Search for CodePipeline (we will cover it deeply later in this book).

3. Create a pipeline and follow the screens and instructions depending on your setup and configuration; if you are unsure what you are doing, leave things as default, at least for the first time; Check Figure 3-25.

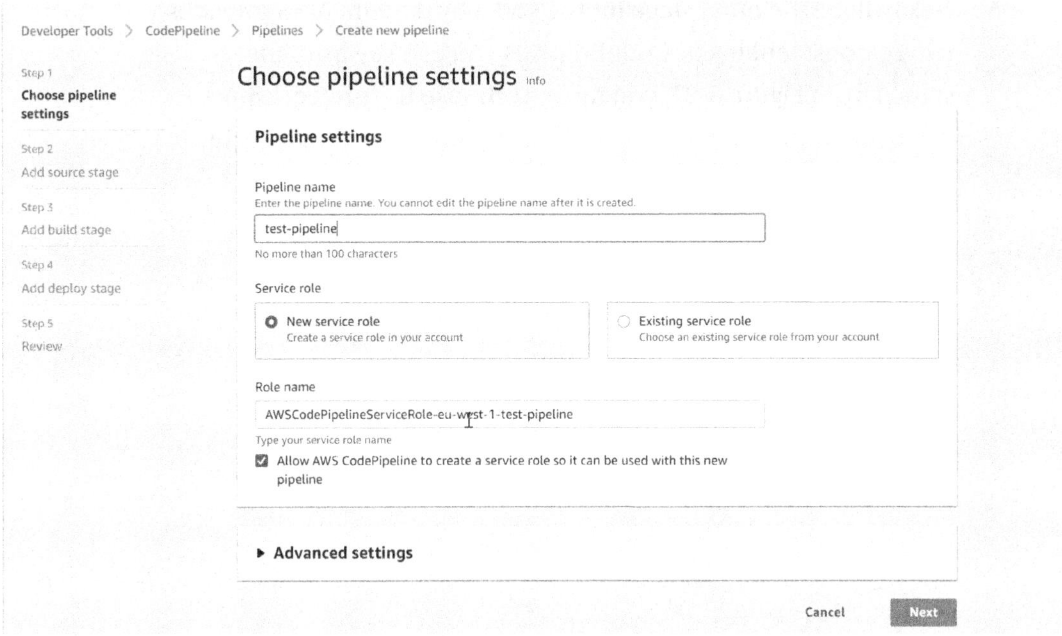

**Figure 3-25.** *Creating a pipeline*

4. Next, choose the code source; if you save your code on ECR, S3, or CodeCommit, then select it, and once you do this, a new screen will pop out, including the configuration part for the repository; Check Figure 3-26.

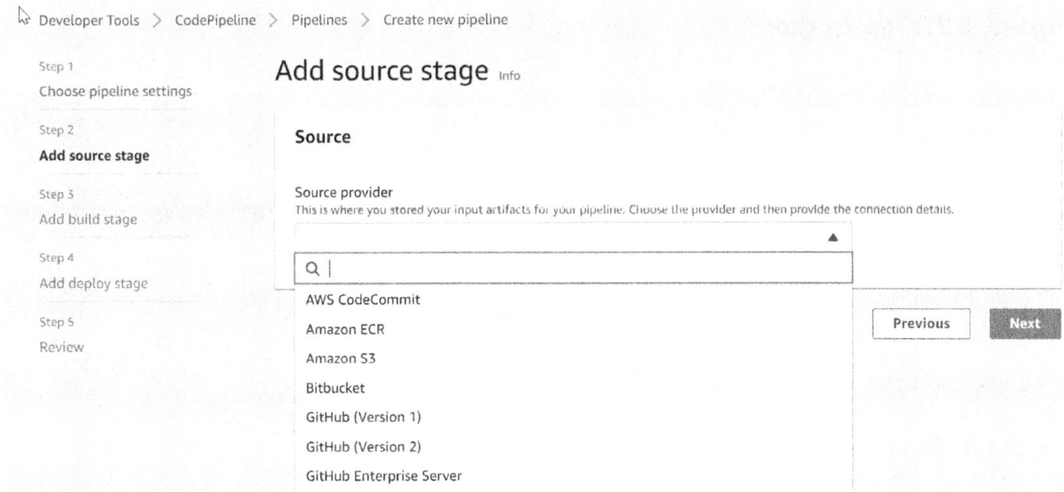

**Figure 3-26.** *Source stage*

5.  Next will be the build stage for the code; by default, AWS provides two options: Jenkins or CodeBuild; as you can see from the screen from Figure 3-27, you need to choose the project name if you already have created one. Otherwise, you need to create one; check Figure 3-28.

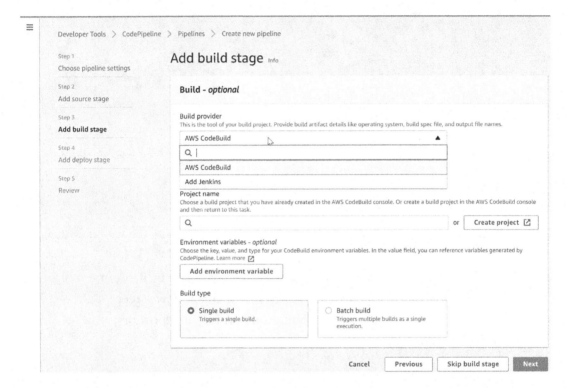

***Figure 3-27.*** *Build stage*

**Project name**
Choose a build project that you have already created in the AWS CodeBuild console. Or create a build project in the AWS CodeBuild console and then return to this task.

| 🔍 | | or | Create project ☑ |
| --- | --- | --- | --- |
| aws-perspective-575086934169-eu-west-1-TaskStack-5J2O9L9YWQ0H | | | |
| PipelineAssetsFileAsset185A-nW7YztydSp8S | | | ✕ |
| PipelineBuildSynthCdkBuildP-fN333lWNgwhX | | | |
| MySesEmailPipeline-selfupdate | | | |

***Figure 3-28.*** *Project name already exists*

**Note**    The "Create project" button will allow you to create a new CodeBuild project that meets your configuration; click it and follow the previous screenshots mentioned earlier in this chapter.

6. Now, you create the project; the last step is to deploy the provider, choose to skip it, and accept this decision when offered if you do not want to deploy the build artifact.

   The second option is to choose a deployment provider for the deploy provider and then enter the parameters when requested if you want to deploy the build artifact.

7. Review your options on the Review screen before clicking "Create pipeline."

8. Once the pipeline runs successfully, open the S3 services; for each pipeline, you are creating by default, create a bucket. The format of this bucket name is as follows:

   ```
   codepipeline-region-ID-random-number
   ```

   Or you can find out the bucket name by retrieving the information for this pipeline using the AWS CLI command; this is the power of the command line.

   ```
   aws codepipeline get-pipeline --name my-pipeline-name
   ```

Navigate to the folder corresponding to your pipeline's name. Then access the folder corresponding to the value you noted before for the Output artifact. You can download and extract the file's content (`filename.zip`).

As mentioned earlier, you can add and test actions to CodeBuild, allowing DevOps to automate and eliminate the manual process.

It's simple to do this. To add a build action or test action, all you have to do is follow these steps:

1. Open CodePipeline Services.

2. Choose the pipeline you want to edit.

3. Choose the tooltip from the details pages and the source action and click Edit.

4. Now, between the source and Build stage, add another stage.

5. Choose the stage name and add an action; enter the action name.

6. For the Action provider, choose CodeBuild.

7. Choose the output artifact you identified previously in this method under "Input artifacts."

8. Enter a name for the output artifact in the "Output artifacts" field.

9. Choose to add an action.

10. Save and release the change.

## Use AWS CodeBuild with Jenkins

Not all companies will use CodePipleine; AWS allows you to integrate the services with other solutions such as Jenkins, one of the most common CI/CD tools.

Jenkins is an open-source DevOps automation software designed in Java for CI/CD. It's used to set up CI/CD processes and provides many plugins that allow DevOps to use them for different solutions.

1. To use Jenkins, you should install and configure it; you can set up an EC2 cluster. To do that, follow the official documentation at `https://www.jenkins.io/doc/book/installing/linux/`.

2. Next, install the CodeBuild plugin for Jenkins, which is done by following the official instruction: `https://github.com/awslabs/aws-codebuild-jenkins-plugin`.

3. Next, use the installed plugin, following the instructions mentioned earlier.

## Use AWS CodeBuild with Codecov

I have seen another typical case used for CodeBuild, Codecov, a free application for open-source software that helps contributors enhance test coverage and maintain code quality.

And you can sign up for free at `https://about.codecov.io/sign-up/`; check Figure 3-29.

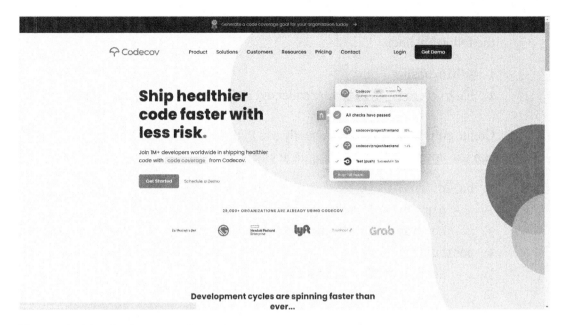

***Figure 3-29.*** *Codecov main page*

Follow these steps:

1. Add the repository to Codecov for which you require coverage.

2. Choose Copy when the token information appears; check the below Figure 3-30.

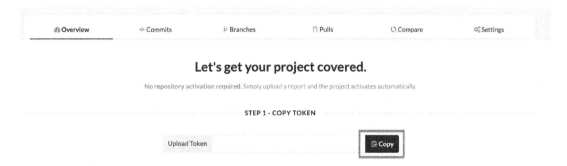

***Figure 3-30.*** *Generate token and copy it*

3. Once you have copied the token, add this token as an environment variable called CODECOV_TOKEN to your project.

4. Create a bash script, for example, `codecov_script.sh`, and insert the following lines:

```
1. #/bin/bash
2. bash <(curl -s https://codecov.io/bash) -t $CODECOV_TOKEN
```

5. Create your buildspec file; I usually use Python for DevOps. You can use any programming language you want.

```
1. build:
2.    - pip install coverage
3.    - coverage run -m unittest discover
4. postbuild:
5.    - echo 'CodeCov Connection.'
6.    - bash  codecov_script.sh
```

6. Run the build; it should be working now.

We discussed AWS CodeCommit and CodeBuild as part of continuous integration; now, we will go for the last part, CodeArtifact.

# CodeArtifact

CodeArtifact securely saves, distributes, and shares software packages used in the software development process. So that developers have access to the most recent versions, CodeArtifact can be set to download software packages and dependencies from public artifact repositories automatically.

Software development teams increasingly depend on open-source packages to conduct routine operations in their application package. It is increasingly vital for software development teams to retain control over a specific version of open-source software free of vulnerabilities. You can use CodeArtifact to create rules that enforce those mentioned earlier.

In addition, CodeArtifact works with package managers and building tools such as Maven, Gradle, npm, yarn, and pip.

Before working with CodeArtifact, you need to understand the concept of this service so it will be much easier for you to deal with it.

### Domain

The first concept you need to understand is the domain. Repositories are grouped into a domain, which is a higher-level object. The domain stores all package assets and information, making managing numerous repositories within a business more straightforward. You may apply permissions to several repositories held by distinct AWS accounts using a domain. Even though an object is accessible from several sources, it is kept only once in a domain.

This is useful for copying, unique names, and storage, and you can apply policy across multiple repositories.

### Repository

CodeArtifact repositories are not the same ones we are using in version controls; a CodeArtifact repository has a collection of package versions, each corresponding to a group of assets. Using tools such as the NuGet CLI, the npm CLI, the Maven CLI (mvn), and pip, each repository offers APIs for acquiring and publishing packages. Each domain has a limit of 1,000 repositories.

### Package

A package is a collection of software and information for resolving dependencies and installing the program, consisting of a package name and description.

### Package Version

A package version allows the DevOps to identify the package version, for example, @types/node 1.2.3.

### Package Version Revision

A new package version revision is produced each time a package version is modified.

For example, a recent version revision is created if you release a new source code for Python and want to add another package to the source code by default.

### Upstream Repository

When the package versions in one repository can be accessed via the downstream repository's repository endpoint, the contents of the two repositories are essentially merged from the client's perspective. Create an upstream connection between two repositories using CodeArtifact.

### Asset

An asset refers to an individual file stored in CodeArtifact and associated with a package version.

### Package Namespace

To understand this concept, let me give you a much more straightforward example; CodeArtifact usually organizes packages into logical groups to disallow name conflicts.

For example, if you have an npm package, CodeArtifact will create the name like @types/node, and @type will indicate the package scope and name of the node; this depends on the following documentation: https://docs.npmjs.com/cli/v7/using-npm/scope.

For Maven, the approach is different; for example, org.apache.logging.log4j:log4j is divided into two things:

- Group ID: org.apache.logging.log4j

- CodeArtifact ID: log4j

Each package manager has a unique namespace to allow DevOps to understand the type of these packages and their meaning.

## Configure CodeArtifact

The first thing you need to do is open the AWS account if it isn't already. Then access CodeArtifact; check Figure 3-31.

***Figure 3-31.*** *CodeArtifact AWS Portal*

To create your first domain and repository, open the CodeArtifact interface, choose to create a domain and repository, and follow the instructions in the launch wizard.

Also, don't forget to install AWS CLI.

If you want to provide IAM users with access to CodeArtifact, you need to create an IAM policy; you can use the default one provided by AWS, AWSCodeArtifactAdminAccess.

The following policy is a custom IAM policy that will allow users to get information about repositories and domains of the CodeArtifact:

```
1.  {
2.      "Version": "2012-10-17",
3.      "Statement": [
4.          {
5.              "Effect": "Allow",
6.              "Action": [
7.                  "codeartifact:List*",
8.                  "codeartifact:Describe*",
9.                  "codeartifact:Get*",
10.                 "codeartifact:Read*"
11.             ],
12.             "Resource": "*"
13.         },
14.         {
15.             "Effect": "Allow",
16.             "Action": "sts:GetServiceBearerToken",
17.             "Resource": "*",
18.             "Condition": {
19.                 "StringEquals": {
20.                     "sts:AWSServiceName": "codeartifact.amazonaws.com"
21.                 }
22.             }
23.         }
24.     ]
25. }
```

Another policy example will allow the user to retrieve specific information about the domain you defined in the policy.

```
1.  {
2.      "Version": "2012-10-17",
3.      "Statement": [
4.          {
5.              "Effect": "Allow",
```

```
 6.            "Action": "codeartifact:ListDomains",
 7.            "Resource": "arn:aws:codeartifact:eu-west-1:account-
               number:domain-name*"
 8.        }
 9.    ]
10. }
11.
```

The last step for configuring the CodeArtifact is related to what package you will use.

- *Python*: You can use pip to install the package.

- *Maven*: You should Gradle or mvn.

- *Npm*: You can use the npm CLI.

- *NuGet*: You can use dotnet or AWS toolkit in Visual Studio Code, as
  you can see in Figure 3-32.

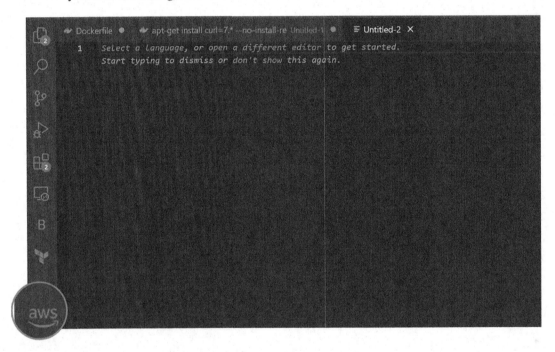

*Figure 3-32.* *Visual Studio Code, AWS toolkit*

## Create a CodeArtifact Domain

Configure a domain by clicking "Create domain," as shown in Figure 3-33.

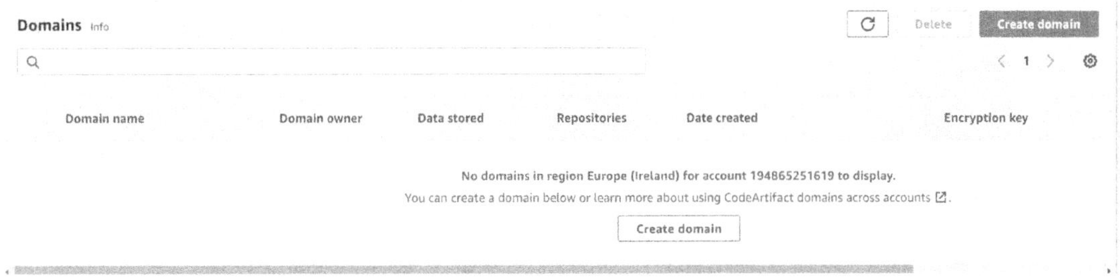

***Figure 3-33.*** *Creating a CodeArtifact domain*

Once you do this, a new screen will show up; check Figure 3-34, and all you have to do is choose a name and KMS; or you can use the command line, as shown here:

1. `aws codeartifact create-domain --domain my_domain`

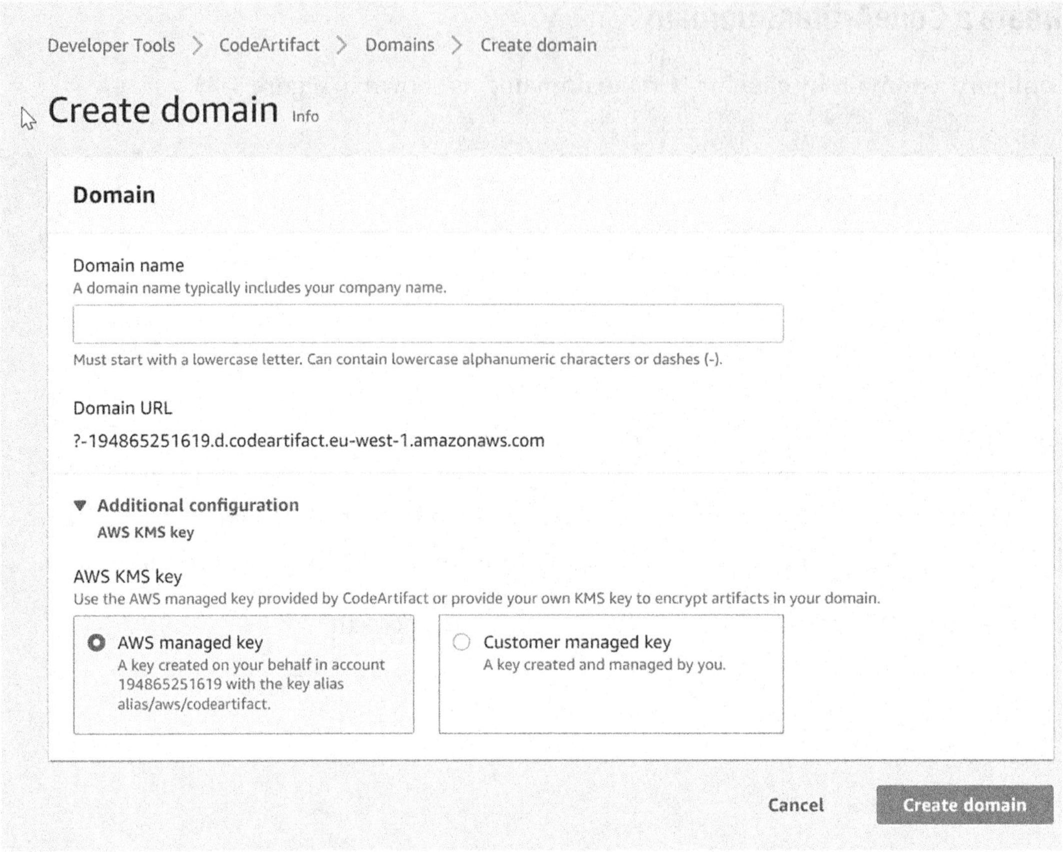

Developer Tools  >  CodeArtifact  >  Domains  >  Create domain

## Create domain  Info

### Domain

Domain name
A domain name typically includes your company name.

Must start with a lowercase letter. Can contain lowercase alphanumeric characters or dashes (-).

Domain URL

?-194865251619.d.codeartifact.eu-west-1.amazonaws.com

▼ Additional configuration
   AWS KMS key

AWS KMS key
Use the AWS managed key provided by CodeArtifact or provide your own KMS key to encrypt artifacts in your domain.

⦿ AWS managed key
   A key created on your behalf in account
   194865251619 with the key alias
   alias/aws/codeartifact.

○ Customer managed key
   A key created and managed by you.

Cancel    Create domain

*Figure 3-34.*  *Creating a domain screen*

## Create a CodeArtifact Repository

The CodeArtifact console or AWS CLI can be used to establish a repository. There are no packages in a repository when you create it.

In the left panel, choose Repository; check Figure 3-35.

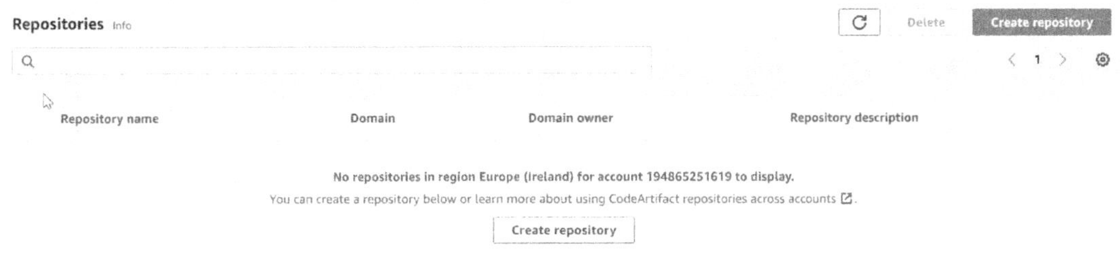

*Figure 3-35.* *Creating a CodeArtifact repository*

Click "Create repository." Enter your repository's name in the "Repository name" field Enter an optional description for your repository in the "Repository description" field. Publish upstream repositories and add intermediate repositories to link your repositories to package authorities like Maven Central and npmjs.com; check Figure 3-36.

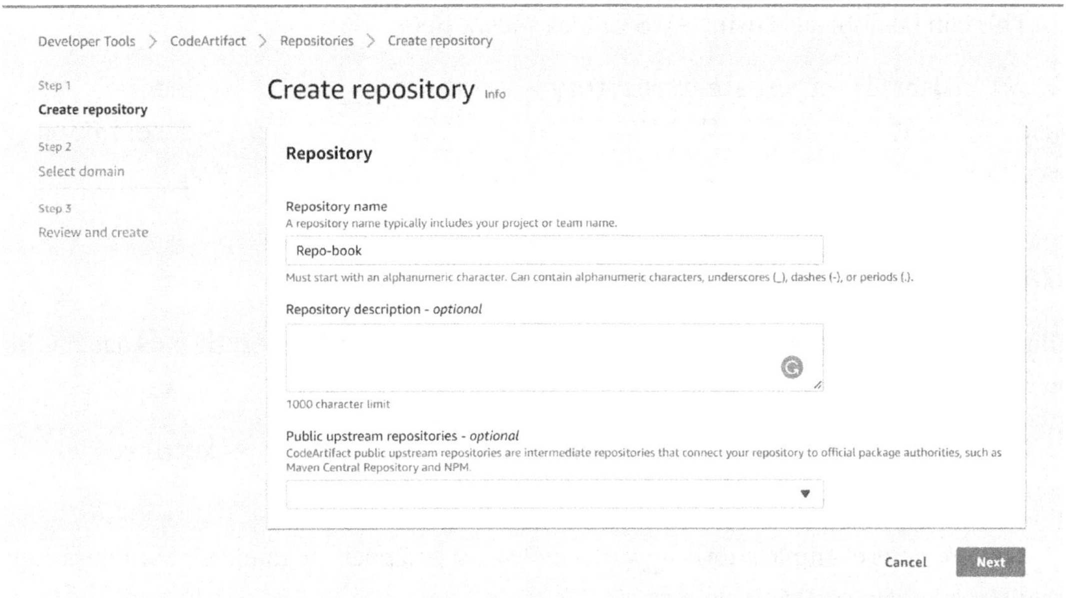

*Figure 3-36.* *CodeArtifact repository screen*

The domain screen will allow you to choose a domain within the account or a different account, as shown in Figure 3-37. Once you are done, review what CodeArtifact is making for you in the "Review and create" step.

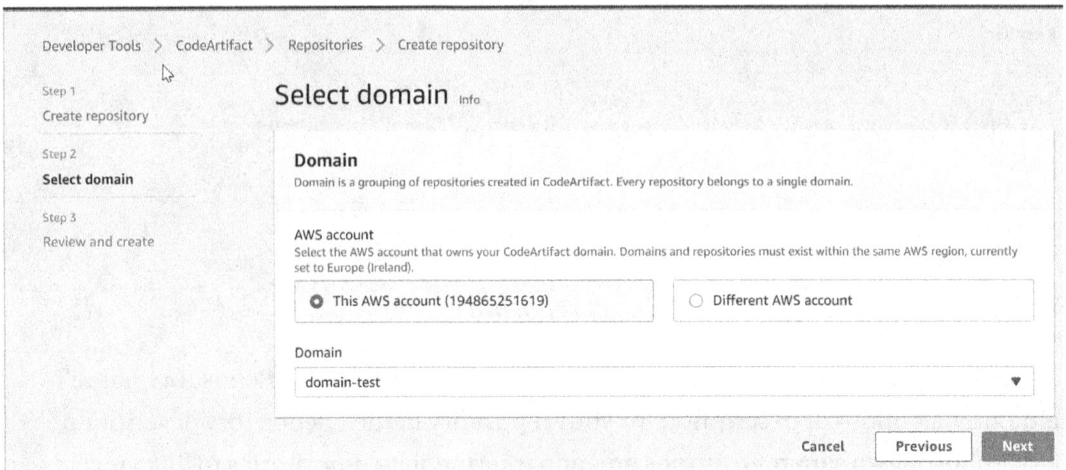

*Figure 3-37.* *Domain screen*

This can be done also using AWS CLI, as shown here:

```
1. aws codeartifact create-repository --domain book_domain --domain-
owner account-number-for-the-domain --repository book-repo  --description
"Book Repo"
```

## Example CodeArtifact for Python

There is no console for this, so you need to use AWS CLI; each supporting package has its own configuration.

```
1. aws codeartifact login --tool pip --domain book_domain --domain-owner
account-number-for-the-domain --repository book-repo
```

The previous example shows how to use Python as a package manager configuration; it's different if you use Maven or npm.

Before we end this chapter, you should know each artifactory has something called *dependency caching*, limiting the number of dependencies that must be retrieved from CodeArtifact for each build activating local caching in CodeBuild.

Each package manager has a Cache folder; if you use this folder, then you will enable the dependency caching.

| Package Manager Tool | Folder |
|---|---|
| pip | /root/.cache/pip/**/* |
| mvn | /root/.m2/**/* |
| Gradle | /root/.gradle/caches/**/* |
| npm | /root/.npm/**/* |
| NuGet | /root/.nuget/**/* |

For example, you can use dependency caching by mentioning it in the buildspec file, as shown here:

```
1.  cache:
2.   paths:
3.    - '/root/.cache/pip/**/*'
```

# Summary

In summary, technology businesses should adopt DevOps ideas and techniques to make the transition to the cloud as easy, efficient, and successful as possible; with this, you will make your life easier. Most IT organizations, if not all, now practice continuous integration.

Applying this solution benefits any company. AWS provides different solutions and services. As mentioned earlier in this chapter, any company can offer a complete automation cycle without a third-party solution.

But at the same, CI/CD offers a simple and efficient method to deploy new app code in minutes. AWS CodePipeline, AWS CodeCommit, AWS CodeBuild, AWS CodeDeploy, and several additional tools may assist developers in integrating, testing, and deploying new code. You can even use these solutions to combine them with infrastructure as code, which will automate the process in the company.

We rarely have the time or talent to plan ahead of time in business, especially for new product development. We can estimate more accurately and confirm more often by completing fewer steps. A shorter feedback loop allows for more iterations. Learning is driven by the number of iterations, not the hours spent.

In the next chapter, I'll cover AWS for continuous deployment concepts and what Amazon AWS can offer as services for continuous deployment. I will also share an example and configuration for these services.

# CHAPTER 4

# AWS Services for Continuous Deployment

In the previous chapter, I covered CI/CD, focusing on continuous integration, its benefits, and AWS as a cloud provider for constant integration, and I showed some examples.

In this chapter, I will discuss continuous deployment. You already have an idea of what the difference is between CI and CD and when you should use each one.

The isolated modifications integrated and confirmed during CI can be coupled with the remaining product code in a continuous delivery cycle. The pair is then put through a series of more thorough tests. Continuous delivery aims to demonstrate that the ultimate product is deployable, not necessarily to deploy it. The continuous delivery pipeline (CDP) is the method for continuous delivery.

First, however, I'll explain what continuous deployment is, what continuous delivery is, and the difference between the two.

In this chapter, I will cover the continuous deployment and delivery of Amazon Web Services. I'll also walk you through projects that will give you a complete understanding of the different relevant services and how to use them.

## Introduction to Continuous Deployment

Continuous deployment is the last step in an automated software development process. Each check-in on a successful build to your source control is delivered to a production-like environment using continuous deployment; you'll deploy the program to production sooner or later. The sooner you do this, the more likely you are to be able to resolve errors quickly. It is simpler to recall what you did yesterday that may have created the issue than to recognize what you did two months ago. Imagine checking some code into source control and receiving error signals from your production environment five minutes later.

© Osama Mustafa 2023
O. Mustafa, *A Complete Guide to DevOps with AWS*, https://doi.org/10.1007/978-1-4842-9303-4_4

You'll be able to discover and correct the issue right away, and the production program can be up and running without bugs in five minutes. Unfortunately, the concept of automatic deployment, let alone automated deployment on every check-in, makes most managers and software owners uneasy.

When should you change to continuous deployment?

- *Manual inspections*: There are restrictions to what can be done here if a deployment is not automated. Even if it is automated, an organization may decide not to deploy every version, in which case a human check can be implemented. A user acceptance test (UAT) is typically used to perform such a check early in the pipeline.

- *Deployment in stages*: Even if you want to deploy the newest version from the pipeline automatically, you can do it in stages. You can, for example, publish it to a site that is available only to a subset of users who want to check out the new version, or you can transparently redirect select users to the latest release. If any issues arise during the evaluation period, only a subset of users will be impacted and can be referred to the prior version. The remaining users can be forwarded to the new version if everything seems OK. This is called *canary deployment*.

- *Deployment strategy*: We will have a chance to discuss the deployment strategies in the next chapter; each strategy will need a different configuration and setup.

# Continuous Delivery

Continuous delivery and continuous deployment are sometimes confused. Modifications through the pipeline are automatically sent to production, resulting in many daily production deployments. With continuous delivery you can often conduct frequent deployments or choose not to if you want a slower deployment pace. Continuous delivery is required for continuous deployment.

The isolated modifications integrated and confirmed during CI can be coupled with the remaining product code in the continuous delivery cycle. The pair is then put through a series of more thorough tests. Continuous delivery aims to demonstrate that the ultimate product is deployable, not necessarily to deploy it. The continuous delivery pipeline (CDP) is the method for continuous delivery.

With continuous delivery, such as DevOps, you have the capability to change the type of deployment you use, and you can deploy new features, bugs, fixes, and more to production or any other environment.

When continuous delivery is implemented, the following occurs:

- Software is deployed through a cycle.

- Your team emphasizes software deployment above new feature development.

- Anyone can obtain instant, automatic feedback on their system's production readiness whenever they make a change.

- On-demand deployments of any version of the program to any environment are possible.

The following are the main advantages of continuous delivery:

- *Reduced deployment risk*: Because you're making more minor changes, less can go wrong, and correcting errors is quicker.

- *Noticeable progress*: Many people keep track of their success by logging their hours worked. It is considerably less credible if "done" implies "developers announce it to be done" than if it is deployed into a production environment and works.

- *Feedback*: The greatest danger of every software project is that you will create something useless. The sooner and more often you put functional software in front of actual users, the faster you will learn how beneficial it is.

Developers can use continuous delivery to automate testing beyond unit tests, allowing them to evaluate application improvements across several dimensions before releasing them to users. UI testing, load testing, integration testing, API reliability testing, and other tests allow developers to test upgrades and identify concerns ahead of time extensively. Automating the creation and replication of many environments for testing, which was hard to achieve on-premises, is now simple and cost-effective in the cloud.

Amazon AWS provides two services for continuous delivery: AWS CodeDeploy and AWS CodePipeline.

# AWS CodeDeploy

AWS CodeDeploy is a fully managed service tool that automates program deployments to Amazon Elastic Compute Cloud (Amazon EC2), AWS Fargate/ECS, AWS Lambda, and your on-premises servers.

CodeDeploy may deploy application content stored in Amazon S3 buckets, GitHub repositories, or Bitbucket repositories that run on a server. A serverless Lambda function can also be deployed using CodeDeploy. CodeDeploy can be used without making any modifications to your current code.

You can use CodeDeploy to make it simpler to do the following:

- Release new features on time.

- Update versions of AWS Lambda functions.

- Avoid any downtime during application deployment.

- Take on the complexity of upgrading your apps while avoiding many of the hazards of manual deployments.

The service grows with your infrastructure, allowing you to quickly deploy one or hundreds of instances. You can use almost any application material, including code, serverless AWS Lambda functions, web and configuration files, executables, packages, scripts, and multimedia files.

CodeDeploy offers various advantages that support the DevOps idea of continuous deployment, starting with deployments being automated using CodeDeploy, enabling you to deploy software reliably and quickly. CodeDeploy gives you centralized management over your application deployments.

CodeDeploy allows you to effortlessly create and check the progress of your deployments using the AWS Management Console or the AWS CLI; you can see when and where each application revision was deployed using CodeDeploy's full report. You can also set up push alerts to obtain real-time deployment changes.

On the other hand, to reduce downtime, CodeDeploy assists you in maximizing the availability of your application throughout the software deployment. It gradually introduces updates and monitors application health using customizable rules. Software deployments can be halted and turned back if there are any issues.

You can halt and roll back deployments automatically or manually if there are issues.

In addition, CodeDeploy works with multiple deployment strategies, discussed in the next chapter.

There is a different use case for CodeDeploy. However, I will show how to use a couple of examples so you can understand when you need to use it.

## AWS CodeDeploy Project

Imagine development teams frequently asking you to deploy a web page on an EC2 instance repeatedly. This is a repetitive, tedious manual task. To automate this process, we will use CodeDeploy; the infrastructure is pretty simple and will be as follows:

- The application is based on WordPress, which requires PHP and MySQL.

- The operating system is Amazon Linux or Red Hat Enterprise Linux.

- There is a single EC2 instance.

The high-level steps for this project are as follows:

1. Configure an EC2 instance and install the CodeDeploy Agent.

2. Configure what needs to be deployed to the EC2 instance.

3. Upload the WordPress code to S3.

4. Update the WordPress applications depending on the needs.

## Step 1: Configure an EC2 Instance

Sign in to the AWS Console, choose EC2, and click "Launch instances" (Figure 4-1).

***Figure 4-1.***   *Creating an EC2 instance*

Next, you need to fill in some information, such as the name, network, and key pair (SSH); what you need depends on your configuration, as shown in Figure 4-2.

- Choose an Amazon Machine Image (AMI), and choose an OS that is supported by CodeDeploy; you can check here for supported versions: https://docs.aws.amazon.com/codedeploy/latest/ userguide/codedeploy-agent.html#codedeploy-agent-supported- operating-systems.

- Choose an instance type.

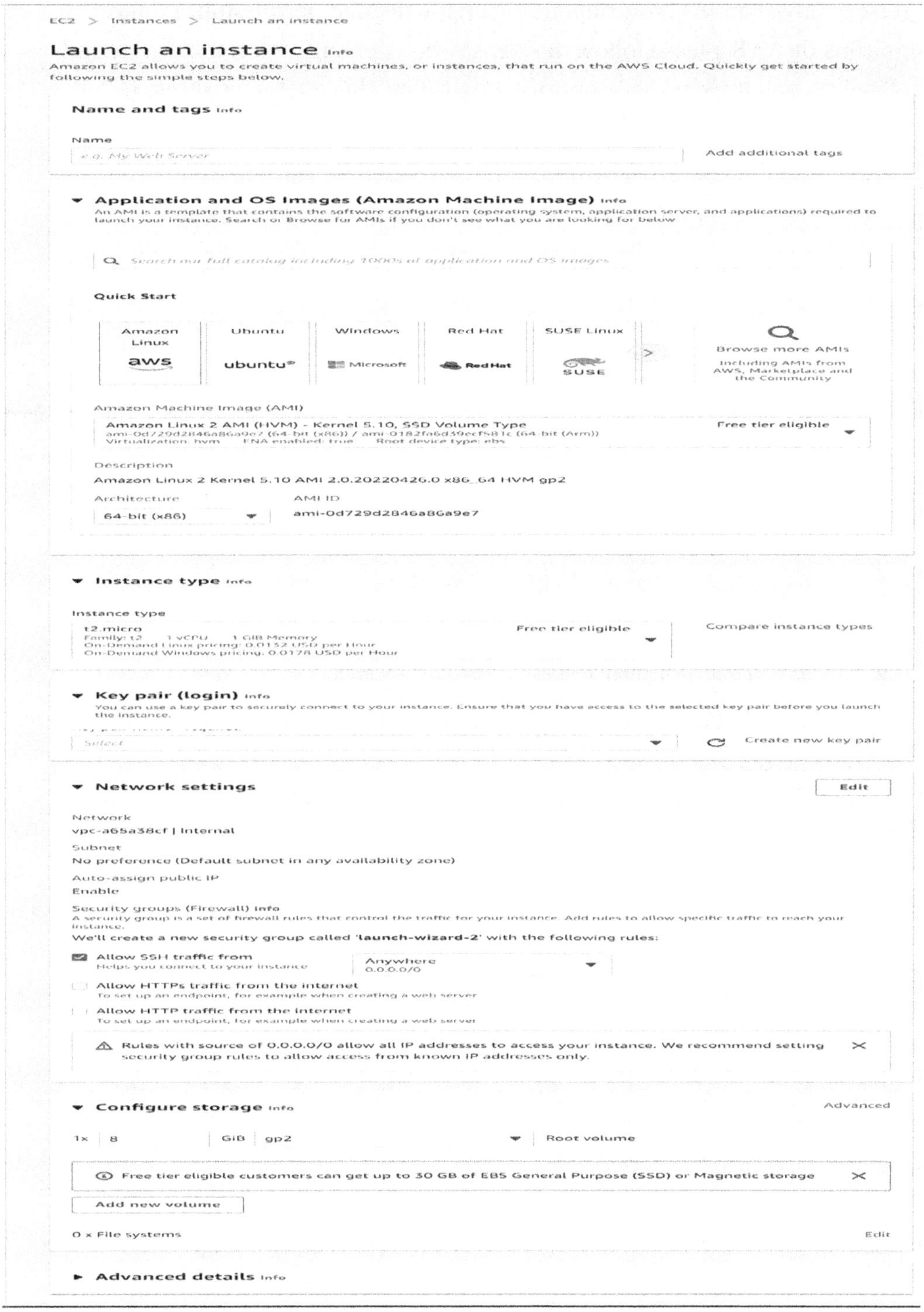

**Figure 4-2.** *EC2 configuration*

You can create an IAM role depending on the needed permission. To make an IAM role inside AWS, please follow the steps; when dealing with CodeDeploy and CodePipeline, you must provide permission to allow these services access to the required resources.

---

**Caution**   You may notice that some steps are repeatable for CodePipeline and CodeDeploy. Nevertheless, the idea is to show how easy the configuration is for both.

---

**CREATE AWS ROLES**

If you are familiar with these steps, skip this section.

1. From the console, choose IAM, or you can access it at `https://console.aws.amazon.com/iam`.

2. The IAM screen will open; choose a role. See Figure 4-3.

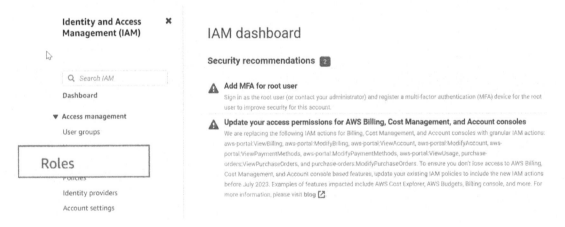

*Figure 4-3.*   *Creating an IAM role*

3. Choose Roles from the left menu, and then select "Create role." On the "Create role" page, choose the services you will be using for the role, which is CodeDeploy here, as shown in Figure 4-4.

IAM > Roles > Create role
Step 1
Select trusted entity
Step 2
Step 3
Select trusted entity Info
AWS service
Allow AWS services like EC2, Lambda, or others to perform actions in this account.
Web identity
Allows users federated by the specified external web identity provider to assume this role to perform actions in this account.
Use case
Allow an AWS service like EC2, Lambda, or others to perform actions in this account.
Common use cases
EC2
Use cases for other AWS services:
CodeDeploy
CodeDeploy
Allows CodeDeploy to call AWS services such as Auto Scaling
CodeDeploy - ECS
Cancel
Next

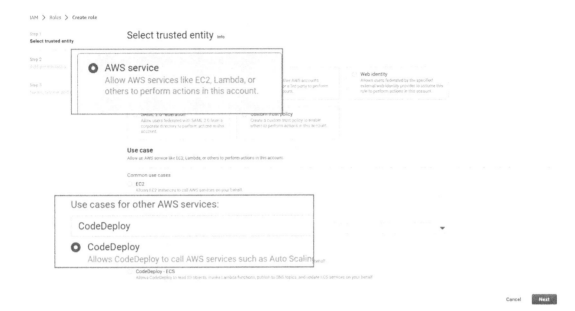

*Figure 4-4. Choosing CodeDeploy*

4. The next screen will be for adding permission; leave everything as is, as shown in Figure 4-5.

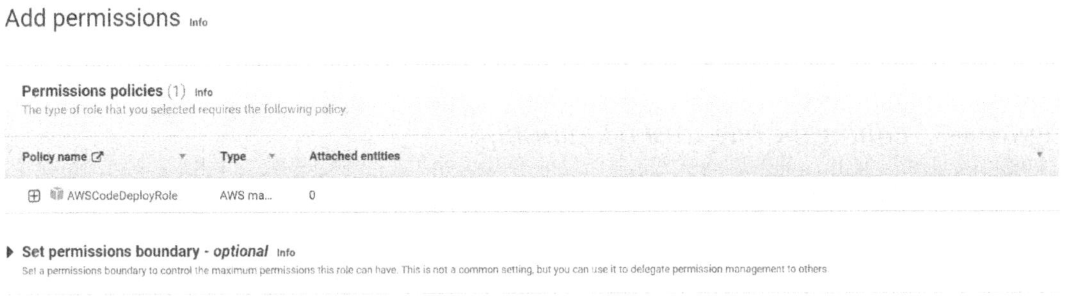

Add permissions Info
Permissions policies (1) Info
The type of role that you selected requires the following policy.
Policy name
Type
Attached entities
AWSCodeDeployRole
AWS ma...
0
Set permissions boundary - optional Info
Set a permissions boundary to control the maximum permissions this role can have. This is not a common setting, but you can use it to delegate permission management to others.

*Figure 4-5. Adding permission to a role*

5. Type the service role's name (**CodeDeployServiceRole**, for instance) into the "Role name field" on the Review screen, and then click "Create role," as shown in Figure 4-6.

**Figure 4-6.**  *After creating the role*

6. Now, click the role, which will open a new screen that allows you to edit the role and insists on a trust relationship; see Figure 4-7.

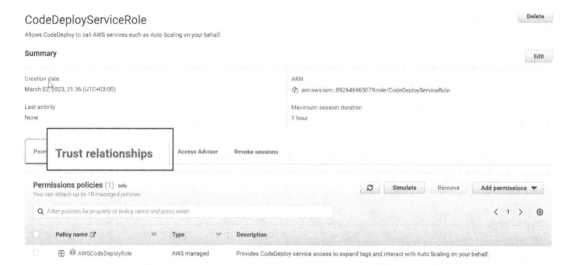

**Figure 4-7.**  *Editing the role-trust relationships*

You will see the current policy attached to the role; you can add a different one as shown here, which allows the code deployment to access an additional AWS resource.

For example, if I need to give permission for CodeDeploy for EC2, I use this:

```
1. {
2.     "Version": "2012-10-17",
3.     "Statement": [
```

```
4.        {
5.            "Sid":" ",
6.            "Effect": "Allow",
7.            "Principal": {
8.                "Service": "ec2.amazonaws.com"
9.            },
10.           "Action": "sts:AssumeRole"
11.       }
12.   ]
13. }
14.
```

After that, you need to grant access to S3 so CodeDeploy can access the bucket and deploy the code to EC2.

```
1. {
2.      "Version": "2012-10-17",
3.      "Statement": [
4.          {
5.              "Action": [
6.                  "s3:Get*",
7.                  "s3:List*"
8.              ],
9.              "Effect": "Allow",
10.             "Resource": "*"
11.         }
12.     ]
13. }
14.
```

Note that for the next configuration for EC2 Storage, I recommend leaving it as is to ensure no extra cost.

- Using tags will make your life easier later.

- Configure the security group as shown in Figure 4-8.

  - For now, open ports SSH, HTTP, and HTTPS.

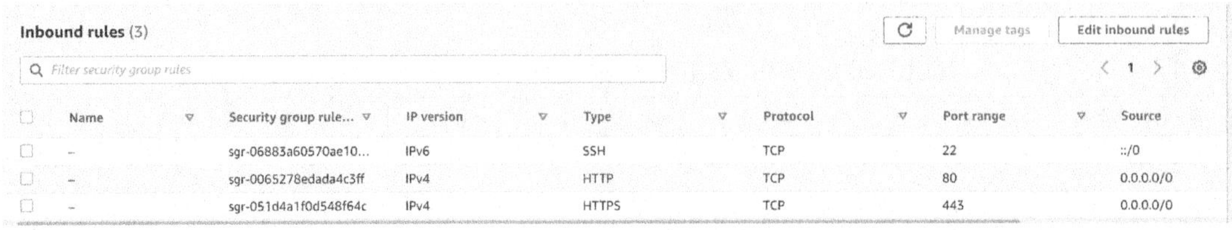

| | Name | Security group rule... ▽ | IP version | Type | Protocol | Port range | Source |
|---|---|---|---|---|---|---|---|
| ☐ | - | sgr-06883a60570ae10... | IPv6 | SSH | TCP | 22 | ::/0 |
| ☐ | - | sgr-0065278edada4c3ff | IPv4 | HTTP | TCP | 80 | 0.0.0.0/0 |
| ☐ | - | sgr-051d4a1f0d548f64c | IPv4 | HTTPS | TCP | 443 | 0.0.0.0/0 |

*Inbound rules (3)*   Manage tags   Edit inbound rules

***Figure 4-8.***  *Security group*

Continue to the "Instance launch" page and click Launch.

Do not forget to keep the private key in a secret place.

After launching the instance using the private key or SSM, we need to install the CodeDeploy Agent; if you choose to install it and follow the steps here, the installation for the agent will be different from one operating system to another.

The link in command 5 in the following snippet is a generic link, so make sure to change it depending on where the resource will be deployed and the bucket's name.

```
1.  sudo yum update
2.  sudo yum install ruby
3.  sudo yum install wget
4.  cd/home/ec2-user
5.  wget https://bucket-name.s3.region-identifier.amazonaws.com/
    latest/install
6.  chmod +x./install
7.  sudo./install auto
8.  sudo service codedeploy-agent status
9.  sudo service codedeploy-agent start
10. sudo service codedeploy-agent status
```

The name of the Amazon S3 bucket containing your area's CodeDeploy Resource Kit files is `bucket-name`. `region-identifier` is the identifier for your region, such as West Europe Region.

For example, `aws-codedeploy-eu-west-2` is the bucket name, and the region is
`eu-west-2`. To find the bucket name and the available region to download the agent, please
refer to the AWS documentation shown here:

```
https://docs.aws.amazon.com/codedeploy/latest/userguide/resource-kit.
html#resource-kit-bucket-names
```

## Step #2: Configure the Source Content to Be Deployed on EC2

To clone your WordPress code, you need to use the `git` command.

To install the `git` command, follow these steps. Each Linux command has its
package manager, but the concept is the same (I am using Ubuntu).

Git packages are available using the `apt` command, commonly used in Ubuntu.

1. `sudo apt-get update`
2. `sudo apt-get install git-all`

Now, with the `git` command, you can clone the repo; you can choose to clone to
any folder.

```
git clone https://github.com/WordPress/WordPress.git /home/ec2-user
```

After cloning the code and moving to the next step, you need to stop and start
scripting for the application, which will be used later in the appspec YAML, the same as
the buildspec discussed previously in other chapters.

1. The first script you will need is for the dependencies. This script
   will be responsible for installing Apache, MySQL, and PHP;
   you can call the script `WordPress-dependencies.sh` to install
   dependencies. Save all the scripts in one folder.

   1. `#!/bin/bash`
   2. `sudo amazon-linux-extras install php7.4`
   3. `sudo yum install -y httpd mariadb-server php`

2. The following script, which is straightforward, starts the
   application: `start-script.sh`.

   1. `#!/bin/bash`
   2. `systemctl start mariadb.service`

```
3. systemctl start httpd.service
4. systemctl start php-fpm.service
```

3. Shut down the application with `stop-script.sh`.

```
1. #!/bin/bash
2. systemctl stop httpd.service
3. systemctl stop mariadb.service
4. systemctl stop php-fpm.service
```

4. Create a WordPress database script called `create-database.sh`.
   This script will be used to create a database called `Wordpress_DB`
   to be used by the application; we notice that you also need to
   create a folder called `scripts` and create this file under it.

   MariaDB on Amazon Linux 2 does not have a root password
   by default. If you create a root password for MariaDB and lock
   yourself out of your database, you must reset the root password.

   And you can do that by running the following command; if you do
   not want to set the MariaDB password, you can do that and leave
   it blank.

```
ALTER USER 'root'@'localhost' IDENTIFIED BY 'new_password';
1. #!/bin/bash
2. mysql -u root -p your-password
3. CREATE DATABASE IF NOT EXISTS test;
4. CREATE_WordPress_DB
```

5. The last step is that you need to change the script's permission to
   make them executable.

```
1. chmod +x//home/ec2-user/scripts/*
```

6. If you use CodeDeploy, CodePipeline, etc., you need to write
   either the buildspec or AppSpec, depending on which services
   you will use; this time, I will use CodeDeploy.

Using the appsec file will be our choice because we are deploying to EC2; before continuing with the example, let's look at what the difference is between then.

**buildspec.yml**

The pipeline generates an artifact at the source, and this file is used to build it. Remember, only applications that need a build (such as Angular, React, etc.) will need this. It is unnecessary to download this file using a Node.js application.

**appspec.yml**

If you want to deploy your software to an EC2 instance, you will need this file. When the files are replaced in the EC2 instance, the deployment group will seek this file in your root, which contains instructions. In the case of a Node.js application, for instance, you would need to issue the command run application again.

```
1. version: 0.0
2. os: Linux
3. files:
4.    - source:/₩
5.      destination:/var/www/html/WordPress
6. hooks:
7.    Before Install:
8.      - location: scripts/WordPress-dependencies.sh
9.        timeout: 300
10.        runas: root
11.    ApplicationStart:
12.      - location: scripts/start_script.sh
13.      - location: scripts/create_database.sh
14.        timeout: 300
15.        runas: root
16.    ApplicationStop:
17.      - location: scripts/stop_script.sh
18.        timeout: 300
19.        runas: root
20.
```

## Step 3: Upload WordPress Code to S3

Now you'll prepare your source code and submit it to a place where CodeDeploy can deploy it; the following steps demonstrate how to create an Amazon S3 bucket, prepare the application revision files for the bucket, bundle the revision files, and finally push the modification to the bucket.

1. Creating the s3 bucket is a straightforward step either by using the command line (AWS CLI) or by using console.

   ```
   1. aws s3 mb s3://test-wordpress-code
   ```

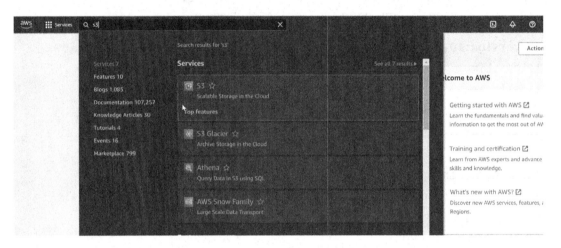

***Figure 4-9.***  *Creating the S3 bucket from the console*

2. Choose S3, as shown in Figure 4-9, and the new screen will display. Click "Create bucket," as shown in Figure 4-10.

***Figure 4-10.***  *S3 Dashboard*

3. The configuration screen will open; choose the same bucket name and the region as your CodeDeploy region, and leave the other settings as the defaults. See Figure 4-11.

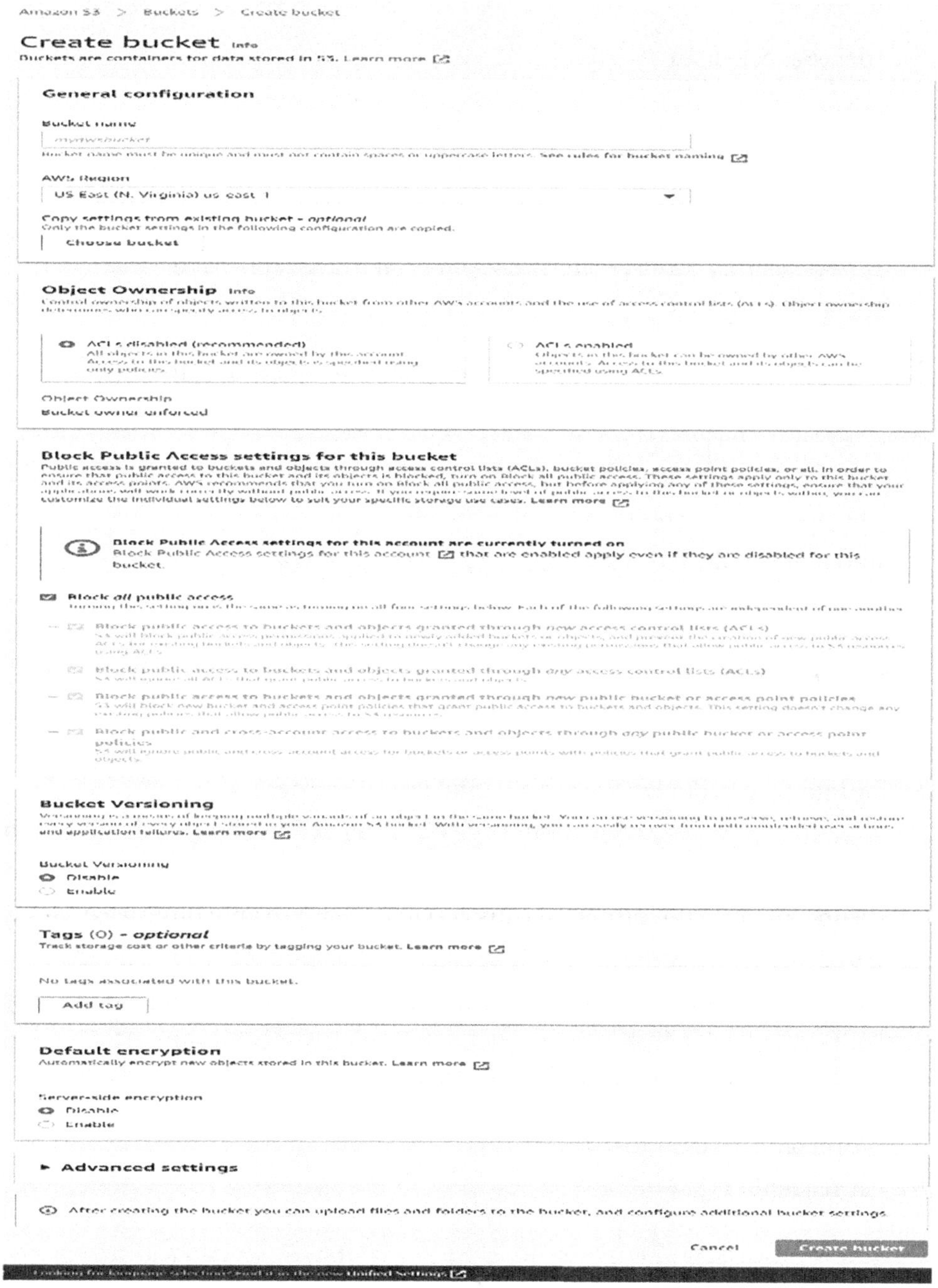

*Figure 4-11.* *S3 configuration screen*

4.  Create an archive file with the WordPress application files and the AppSpec file, and we will register the app called WordPress. The last command will call the push command to create a bundle for all the files.

```
cd/home/ec2-user
```

If you had not created the role mentioned in step 1 of this example, you would face a "permission denied" error when running this command.

```
1. aws deploy create-application --application-name
WordPress_App
```

```
1. aws deploy push --application-name WordPress_App
--s3-location s3://test-wordpress-code/WordPressApp.zip
--ignore-hidden-files
```

The previous command compiles the files in the current directory into a single file. WordPressApp.zip is a single archive file that contains everything you need.

## Step 4: Deploy the Code

The next step is now deploying an application. You can use the AWS CLI or the CodeDeploy interface to deploy the version and track its progress.

If you want to deploy the application using AWS CLI, follow the instructions in this section.

First, ensure you have the proper permission to deploy the app; otherwise, you will not be able to do that; you should create a service role needed for the next step.

The following is one of the examples for the Services role (saved under a file called accessrole.json), which will give access to CodeDeploy under all supported regions:

```
1. {
2.     "Version": "2012-10-17",
3.     "Statement": [
4.         {
5.             "Sid": "",
6.             "Effect": "Allow",
```

```
 7.             "Principal": {
 8.                 "Service": [
 9.                     "codedeploy.amazonaws.com"
10.                 ]
11.             },
12.             "Action": "sts:AssumeRole"
13.         }
14.     ]
15. }
16.
```

Then, run the following command, which will create a service role:

```
1. aws iam create-role --role-name CodeDeployServiceRole --assume-role-policy-document file://accessrole.json
```

We need to create a deployment group connected to the previous service role. It is possible to delegate authority to a service by assigning it a special identity and access management (IAM) role. CodeDeploy can connect to your Amazon EC2 instances thanks to the service role.

```
1. aws deploy create-deployment -group
2.   --application-name WordPress_App
3.  --deployment group name WordPress_DepGroup
4. --deployment-config-name CodeDeployDefault. OneAtATime
5.  --ec2-tag-filters Key=Name,Value=CodeDeployDemo,Type=KEY_AND_VALUE
6.  --service-role-arn serviceRoleARN
```

After applying the earlier steps, refer to Figure 4-12, which explains the application deployment step.

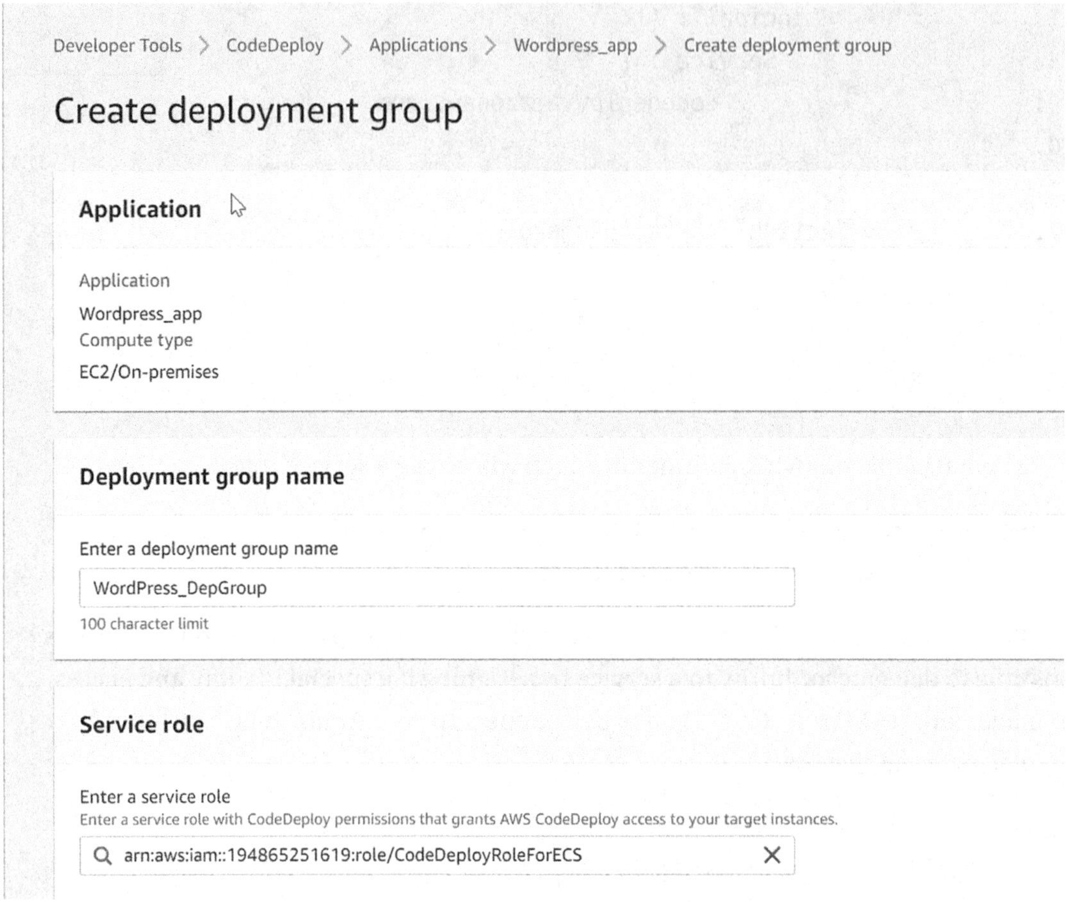

*Figure 4-12.* *Creating a deployment group from the console*

Before creating a deployment, ensure the CodeDeploy Agent is installed and running; otherwise, an issue will appear.

```
1. aws ssm create-association
2.    --name AWS-ConfigureAWSPackage
3.    --targets Key=tag:Name,Values=CodeDeployDemo
4.    --parameters action=Install, name=AWSCodeDeployAgent
5.    --schedule-expression "cron(0 2? * SUN *)"
```

On the same screen of CodeDeploy, you will see the system manager section, which is responsible for deploying the CodeDeploy Agent via System Manager; see Figure 4-13.

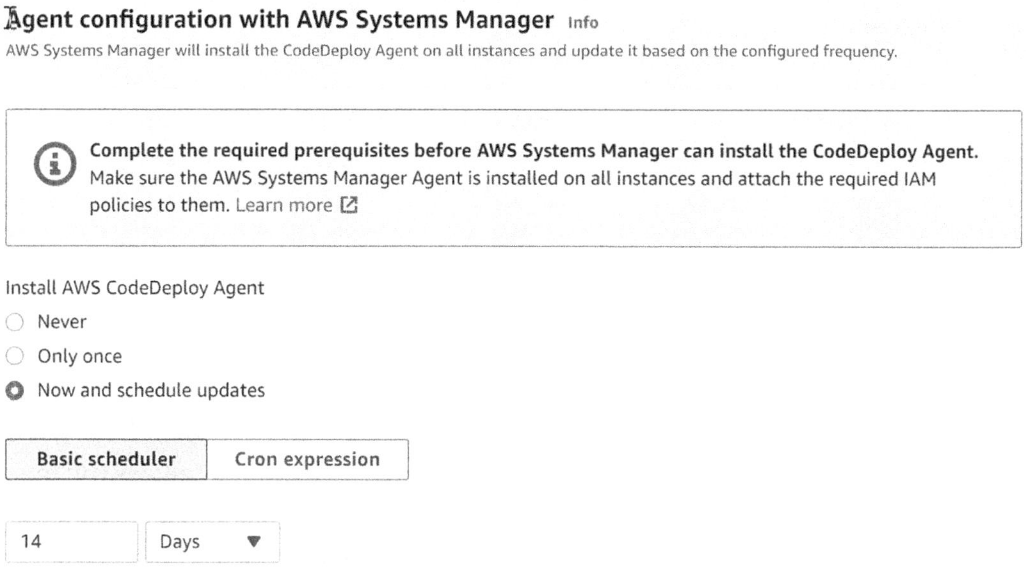

**Agent configuration with AWS Systems Manager** Info

AWS Systems Manager will install the CodeDeploy Agent on all instances and update it based on the configured frequency.

> ⓘ **Complete the required prerequisites before AWS Systems Manager can install the CodeDeploy Agent.**
> Make sure the AWS Systems Manager Agent is installed on all instances and attach the required IAM policies to them. Learn more ☑

Install AWS CodeDeploy Agent

○ Never

○ Only once

◉ Now and schedule updates

| Basic scheduler | Cron expression |

| 14 | Days ▼ |

***Figure 4-13.*** *Installing the agent through the console*

Let's deploy now by running the following command:

```
1. aws deploy create-deployment
2.   --application-name WordPress_App
3.   --deployment-config-name CodeDeployDefault. OneAtATime
4. --deployment-group-name WordPress_DepGroup
5.   --s3-location bucket=codedeploydemobucket, bundleType=zip,
     key=WordPressApp.zip
6.
```

The following section concerns deployment settings and how fast the application will be deployed; see Figure 4-14.

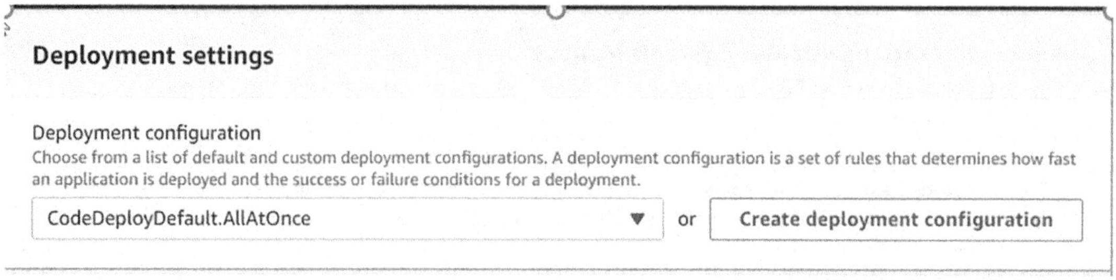

**Figure 4-14.** *Deployment settings*

## Step 5 (Optional): Redeploy the Code

The question is, what will happen if you change something inside the code? How can you redeploy again; the answer is simple, as Amazon AWS CodeDeploy allows you to redeploy again using AWS CLI or the console.

Using the same command as earlier, you can redeploy your code without issues.

```
1. aws deploy create-deployment
2.  --application-name WordPress_App \
3.  --deployment-config-name CodeDeployDefault. OneAtATime
4. --deployment-group-name WordPress_DepGroup
5.  --s3-location bucket=codedeploydemobucket, bundleType=zip,
    key=WordPressApp.zip
6.
```

Or, in the console, select your application and click "Deploy application," as shown in Figure 4-15.

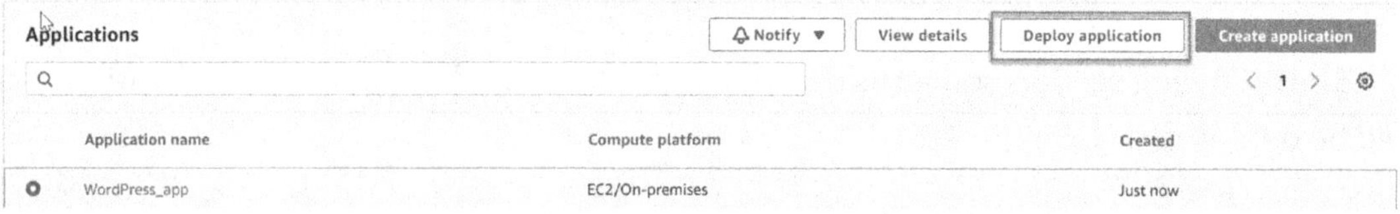

**Figure 4-15.** *Deploying the WordPress application*

Overall, once the application is deployed and you try to access using the public DNS of the EC2 instance, the first page will be like that; this page will allow you to configure the connection to the database and enter a username and password.

Since the next page is HTTP, you need to open the port under the security group to make it work; otherwise, it will not be open.

In Figure 4-16, you can see the application home page (configuration page).

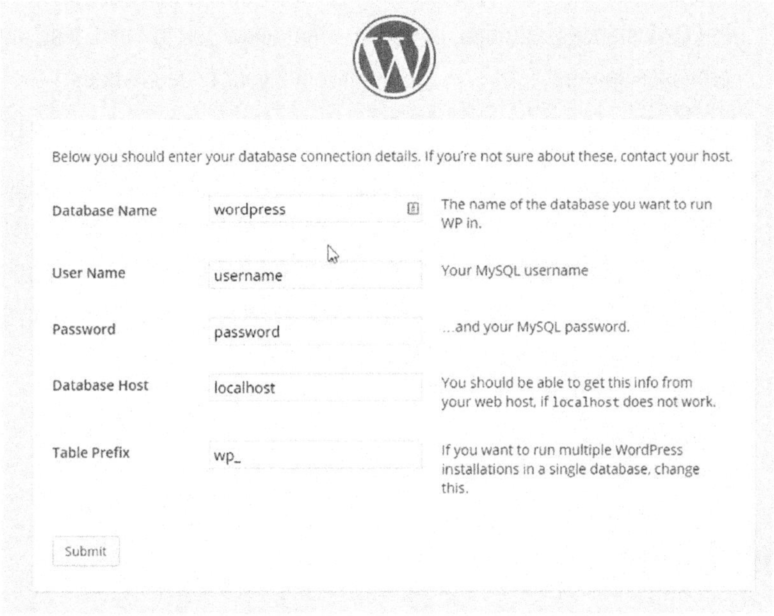

**Figure 4-16.**   *The WordPress configuration page*

You can also use CodeDeploy for on-premises servers; for sure, you will need a VPN in that case, and it can be used to automate Lambda functions; at the end of this chapter, I will include one of the projects for CodeDeploy.

Before starting with the following topic, I will explain the difference between CodeDeploy and CodePipeline, as you can see from Table 4-1, which shows a difference between CodeDeploy and CodePipeline and will allow you to understand each one of them.

***Table 4-1.*** *CodeDeploy vs. CodePipeline Key Differences*

| Factors | CodeDeploy | CodePipeline |
|---------|------------|--------------|
| Usage | Use to automatically deploy code to EC2 instances, Lambda, or on-premises servers. | This is one of the continuous deployments that allow you to build, test, and deploy once your code changes. |
| Known name | Deployment as services. | Continuous deployment. |
| Features | Helps to minimize downtime during deployment. Can work with any complexity of code update. Track application health status. Accessible to roll back updates across EC2 instances. | Provide different prebuilt plugins that allow you to integrate with other tools. Integration with third-party solutions. Can follow up with the deployment via workflow model. |

# AWS CodePipline

The previous table gave you an idea about what CodePipeline provides. This service allows you to automate the manual step to release your software so you can quickly configure stages for the automation software release process. But what else can you do with CodePipeline, or what is the use case for this service?

First, you can automate your software releases. As a company, you want to minimize the potential for human error; automating your software releases does that.

Uploading your code source to version control allows you to test, build, or deploy that code. The workflow differs from company to company. Some companies will make the approval manual to ensure the code meets the standard; others integrate the workflow with other QA automation tools, and so on.

One of the most critical use cases is speeding up the delivery time and making the development team focus on the code quality more than the deployment time.

After the development cycle, CodePipeline allows you to check the deployment status using the console and check which stage has been implemented thus far (see Figure 4-17).

***Figure 4-17.*** *Checking the deployment*

Integration with third-party software is another consideration. For example, the company can use GitHub, Gitlab, or Bitbucket to upload the code to CodeCommit and trigger action on Jenkins. Again, the configuration could differ from one company to another; it all depends on the use case.

One more critical feature of CodePipeline is that it allows you to check the deployment history, see whether it has failed or succeeded, and review what has been deployed to the server and what changes the development team made. As shown in Figure 4-18, the history has three statuses.

- Succeeded means the pipeline has been deployed to the target without any issues.

- Failed means one or more stages has failed for some reason.

- Superseded means the user should stop this pipeline or eliminate one of the stages.

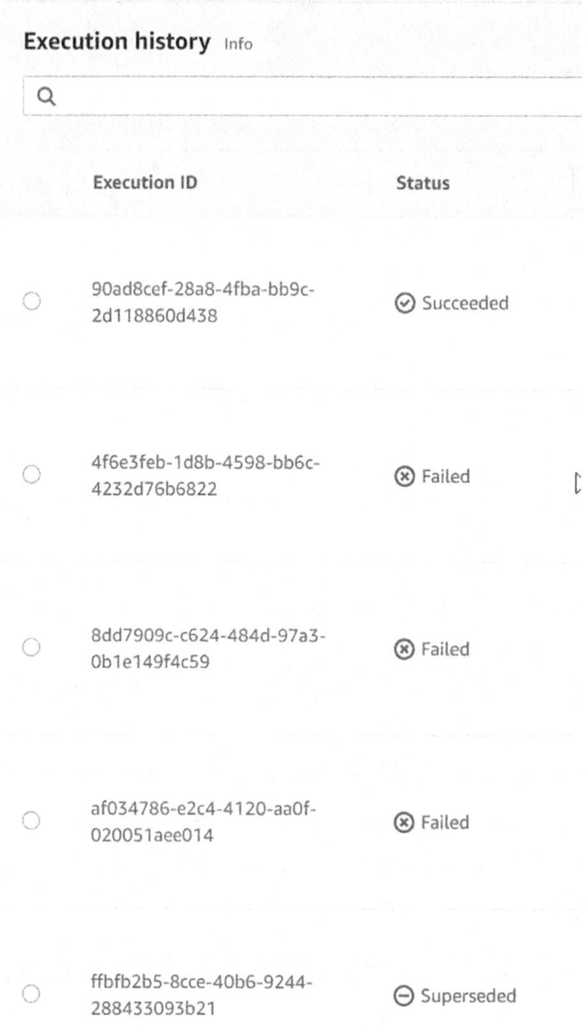

**Execution history** Info

| Execution ID | Status |
|---|---|
| 90ad8cef-28a8-4fba-bb9c-2d118860d438 | ⊘ Succeeded |
| 4f6e3feb-1d8b-4598-bb6c-4232d76b6822 | ⊗ Failed |
| 8dd7909c-c624-484d-97a3-0b1e149f4c59 | ⊗ Failed |
| af034786-e2c4-4120-aa0f-020051aee014 | ⊗ Failed |
| ffbfb2b5-8cce-40b6-9244-288433093b21 | ⊖ Superseded |

*Figure 4-18.*  *CodePipeline history*

## CodeDeploy Component

When talking about CodeDeploy, a different component, starting with the application, is considered the first part of the CodeDeploy component, a collection of deployment groups such as EC2 instances or on-premises servers; moreover, a deployment configuration is how your deployment will work.

Another component mentioned earlier, the buildspec, is the most important part; it is responsible for how the application will be deployed to the instance or target. Last but not least, the deployment group acts like an environment such as Prod, QA, UAT, or Dev.

When working with deployment, you must understand the deployment types or strategies and which DevOps will be used to meet the company's needs. The deployment strategies define the network traffic to the environment, such as production, which can control the downtime and minimize it as much as possible. When you replace the old deployment with the new one, how will this be done?

To understand more about the deployment strategies, refer to Chapter 5.

# Project: Create an Essential Pipeline Using AWS CodePipeline

One of the easiest ways to create a pipeline in CodePipeline is to use AWS's Setup Wizard setup. In this section, I'll show you how to deploy a web application in the S3 bucket to an EC2 instance using CodePipeline.

The steps are as follows:

1. Create an S3 bucket.

2. Install the CodeDeploy Agent on the EC2 instance.

3. Create the application inside CodeDeploy.

4. Create a pipeline to deploy the application to EC2.

# Step 1: Create the S3 Bucket

This step is straightforward; from the console, choose S3, as shown in Figure 4-19.

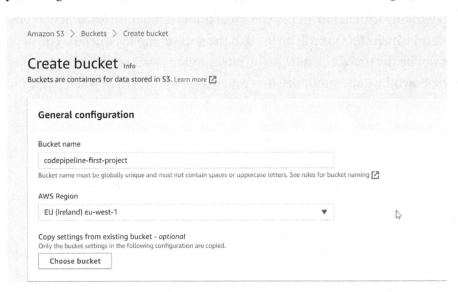

***Figure 4-19.*** *Creating the S3 bucket code pipeline*

Download the application, which is already uploaded to GitHub (`https://github.com/OsamaOracle`). I am using an application that will be deployed on the Linux operating system. Then, upload the file to the S3 bucket we created before, as illustrated in Figure 4-20.

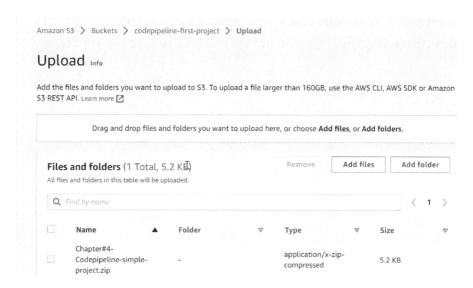

*Figure 4-20.* *Uploading the application to S3*

# Grant Access to EC2

The next step will be creating an IAM role to grant access to the EC2, as demonstrated in Figure 4-21. (You can skip this if you're already familiar with this process.)

---

**Caution**    You may notice that some of the steps in this section are the same for CodePipeline and CodeDeploy. The idea is to show and allow you to understand how easy the configuration is for both.

---

*Figure 4-21.* *Creating an IAM role*

Once you click "Create role," a new screen will appear, as shown in Figure 4-22. Click Next; making this role allows EC2 instances to call AWS services on your behalf.

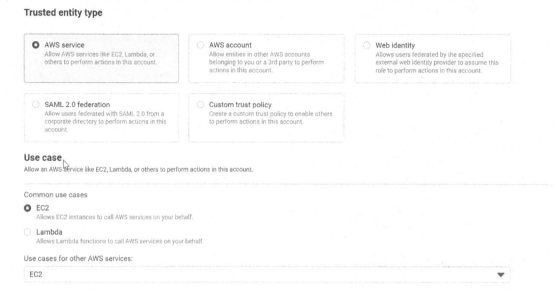

*Figure 4-22.* *Creating a a role for EC2*

On the next screen, you need to add permission to this role and search for a policy called *AmazonEC2RoleforAWSCodeDeploy* plus another policy called *AmazonSSMManagedInstanceCore*; see Figure 4-23 and Figure 4-24.

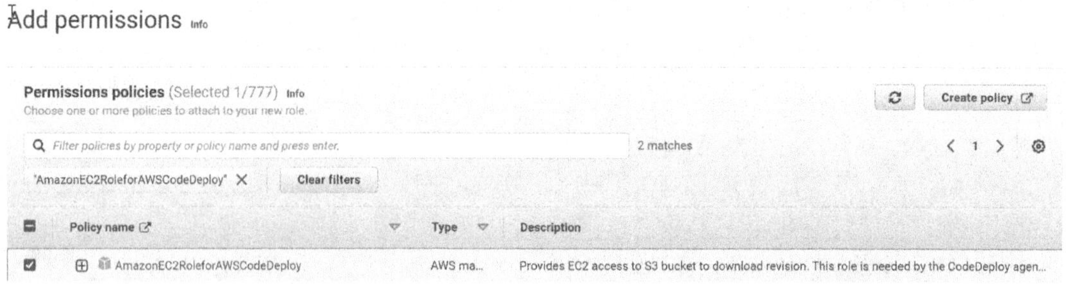

Add permissions Info

| Permissions policies (Selected 1/777) Info | | | |
|---|---|---|---|
| Choose one or more policies to attach to your new role. | | | |

| | Policy name ⬈ | Type ▽ | Description |
|---|---|---|---|
| ☑ | ⊕ 📄 AmazonEC2RoleforAWSCodeDeploy | AWS ma... | Provides EC2 access to S3 bucket to download revision. This role is needed by the CodeDeploy agen... |

*Figure 4-23.* *Adding the AmazonEC2RoleforAWSCodeDeploy policy*

*Figure 4-24.* *Adding the AmazonSSMManagedInstanceCore policy*

Once you add these policies, name the role something you will remember later; for me, I called it **Ec2Codepipeline**, as shown in Figure 4-25.

Name, review, and create

**Role details**

Role name
Enter a meaningful name to identify this role.

```
Ec2Codepipeline
```

Maximum 64 characters. Use alphanumeric and +=,.@-_ characters.

Description
Add a short explanation for this role.

```
Allows EC2 instances to call AWS services on your behalf.
```

Maximum 1000 characters. Use alphanumeric and '+=,.@-_ characters.

Step 1: Select trusted entities                                                                           Edit

```
 1 ▾ {
 2       "Version": "2012-10-17",
 3 ▾     "Statement": [
 4 ▾         {
 5               "Effect": "Allow",
 6 ▾             "Action": [
 7                   "sts:AssumeRole"
 8               ],
 9 ▾             "Principal": {
10 ▾                 "Service": [
11                       "ec2.amazonaws.com"
12                   ]
13               }
14           }
15       ]
16   }
```

*Figure 4-25.* *Naming the role*

## Step 2: Launch the EC2 Instance

Next, we need to launch the EC2 instance; I will not repeat the steps since they were discussed earlier in this chapter with two differences: assign the role to the EC2 instance, and the instance number needs to be 2. See Figure 4-26.

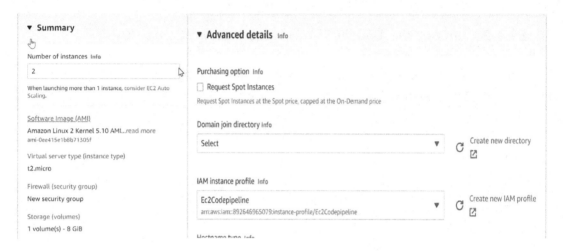

***Figure 4-26.***  *Creating an EC2 instance for the CodeDeploy project*

## Step 3: Install the CodeDeploy Agent on EC2

In this step, we need to create the application in CodeDeploy.

We will allow CodeDeploy to install the agent inside EC2 and choose the deployment strategy that CodeDeploy supports.

To do this, choose to create an application; the name is up to you. In our case, it will be the first project, but the compute platform should be EC2/on-premises, as shown in Figure 4-27.

***Figure 4-27.*** *Choosing an application, CodeDeploy*

- After creating the application, we need to create a deployment group for the application to choose the appropriate name.

- The services role should be created before.

- Under the deployment type, choose In-place.

- Set the deployment setting to CodeDeployDefault.OneAtOnce.

- Disable the Load Balancer settings.

    Figure 4-28 illustrates all of this.

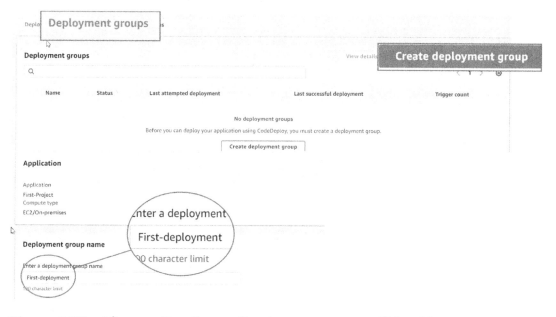

***Figure 4-28.*** *After creating the application screen, you will be able to create a deployment group*

You need to configure the deployment type as shown in Figure 4-29.

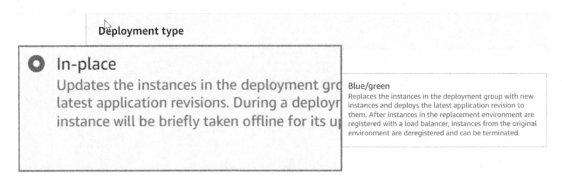

***Figure 4-29.*** *Deployment type*

The next section is "Environment configuration," as shown in Figure 4-30.

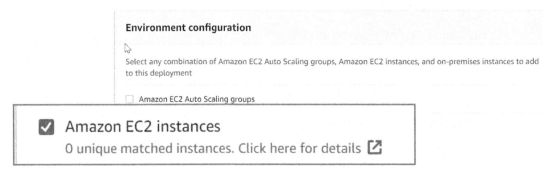

***Figure 4-30.*** *Environment configuration settings*

Deployment configuration will be responsible for installing the CodeDeploy agent with AWS System Manager; you can choose how to install it. See Figure 4-31.

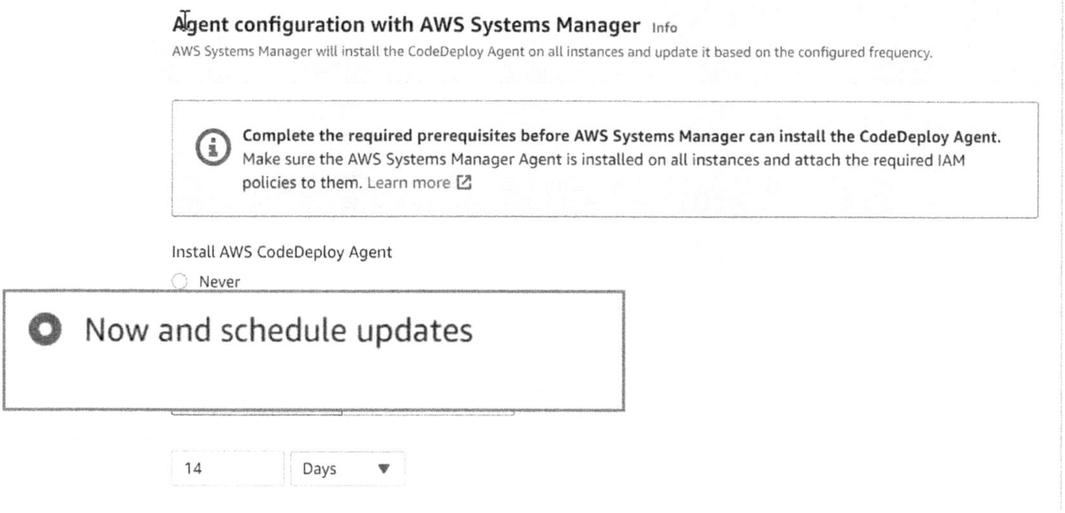

**Agent configuration with AWS Systems Manager**  Info

AWS Systems Manager will install the CodeDeploy Agent on all instances and update it based on the configured frequency.

> (i)  **Complete the required prerequisites before AWS Systems Manager can install the CodeDeploy Agent.**
> Make sure the AWS Systems Manager Agent is installed on all instances and attach the required IAM policies to them. Learn more ☑

Install AWS CodeDeploy Agent

○ Never

◉ **Now and schedule updates**

| 14 | Days ▼ |

**Figure 4-31.**  *Installing the CodeDeploy Agent*

The last step in the deployment group is to set the deployment settings, such as how fast an application is deployed and the success or failure conditions for deployment; see Figure 4-32.

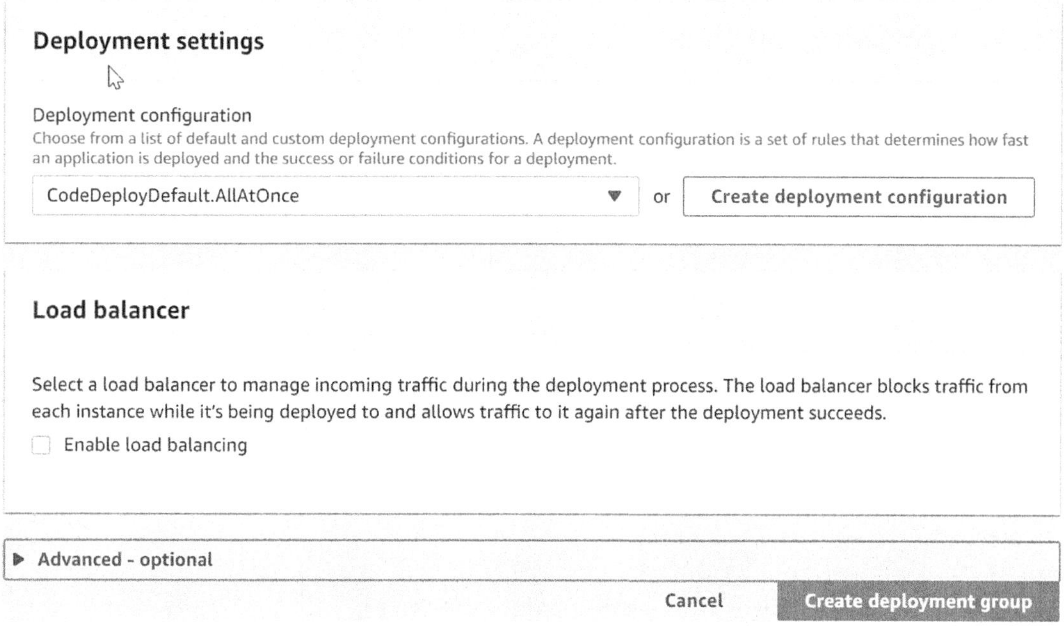

**Deployment settings**

Deployment configuration

Choose from a list of default and custom deployment configurations. A deployment configuration is a set of rules that determines how fast an application is deployed and the success or failure conditions for a deployment.

| CodeDeployDefault.AllAtOnce ▼ | or | **Create deployment configuration** |

**Load balancer**

Select a load balancer to manage incoming traffic during the deployment process. The load balancer blocks traffic from each instance while it's being deployed to and allows traffic to it again after the deployment succeeds.

☐ Enable load balancing

▶ Advanced - optional

Cancel    **Create deployment group**

**Figure 4-32.**  *Deployment group, deployment setting*

# Step 4: Create the Pipeline

Now, we will create the pipeline from the console and choose CodePipeline, as demonstrated in Figure 4-33.

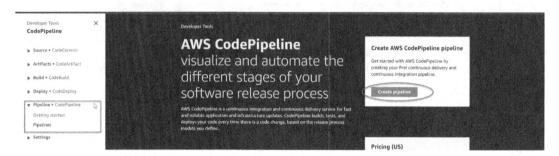

***Figure 4-33.*** *CodePipeline main page*

Once you click to create a pipeline, a new screen will appear, asking you to choose a name for your pipeline.

For the role of the service, you have two options: create a new one or choose a previously created one; see Figure 4-34.

For the advanced settings, leave everything with the default values.

## Choose pipeline settings Info

### Pipeline settings

Pipeline name
Enter the pipeline name. You cannot edit the pipeline name after it is created.

```
demo
```
No more than 100 characters

Service role

○ New service role
Create a service role in your account

○ Existing service role
Choose an existing service role from your account

Role name

```
AWSCodePipelineServiceRole-eu-west-1-demo
```
Type your service role name

☑ Allow AWS CodePipeline to create a service role so it can be used with this new pipeline

***Figure 4-34.*** *CodePipeline settings*

Next, we must choose the application we need to create the pipeline for, which we already uploaded to the S3 bucket; see Figure 4-35.

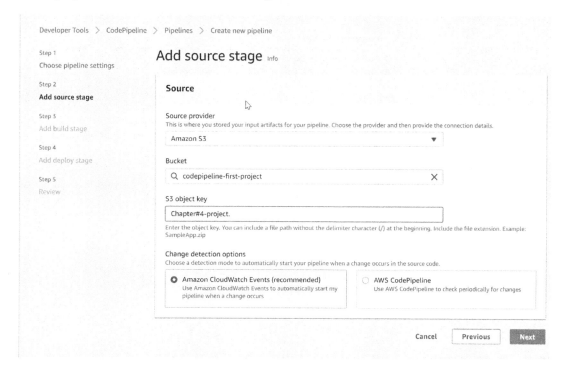

***Figure 4-35.***  *CodePipeline's Add Source stage*

For the build stage, skip the build stage since we will not build anything; then click Next and confirm.

In the last step, the "Add deploy stage" page, choose CodeDeploy, the application name we created before, and the associated deployment group, as shown in Figure 4-36.

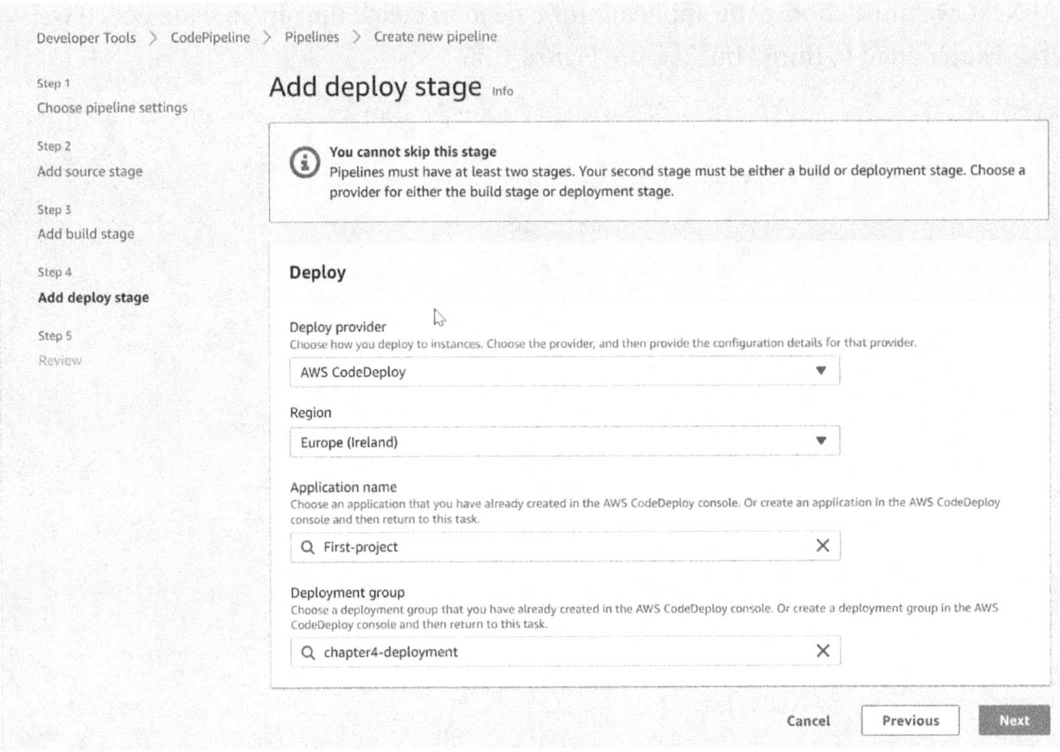

*Figure 4-36.  Deployment stage for CodePipeline*

Congratulations, you have just created your first project with CodePipeline. You can add stages to your pipeline, allowing you to understand CodePipeline more.

The previous examples are straightforward and allow you to understand how CodePipeline works. I will demonstrate another example, but let's use CI/CD and integrate CodePipeline with GitHub this time.

# Integrate CodePipeline CI/CD with GitHub

The idea of this project is to deploy a simple static website written in HTML from GitHub to Amazon S3; when the developer makes a code change, they will create a GitHub pull request to merge the code with the master/main branch. The merge will trigger an event (GitHub integration within CodePipeline) and push these changes depending on the configuration we wrote to S3.

The first step is to create the bucket that will host the website; in my case, I called it **website-static** with no particular configuration; the S3 bucket properties will be as follows and are shown in Figure 4-37.

- No public access.

- No version.

- No policy or security features are enabled.

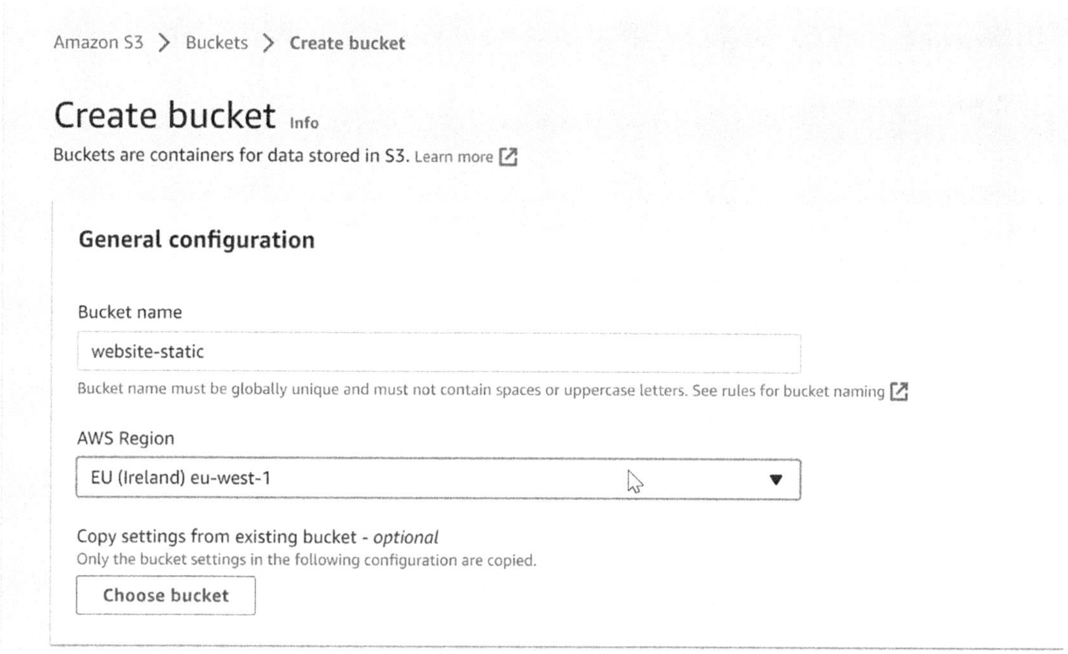

*Figure 4-37.* *Creating a website-static bucket*

The next step will be to create the code pipeline from the console. Select CodePipline and click "Create pipeline," as shown in Figure 4-38.

*Figure 4-38.* *Creating a pipeline for the project*

173

After clicking the button, the console will redirect you to another page, the configuration page; see Figure 4-39.

Choose a clear name for your pipeline so you will understand its purpose.

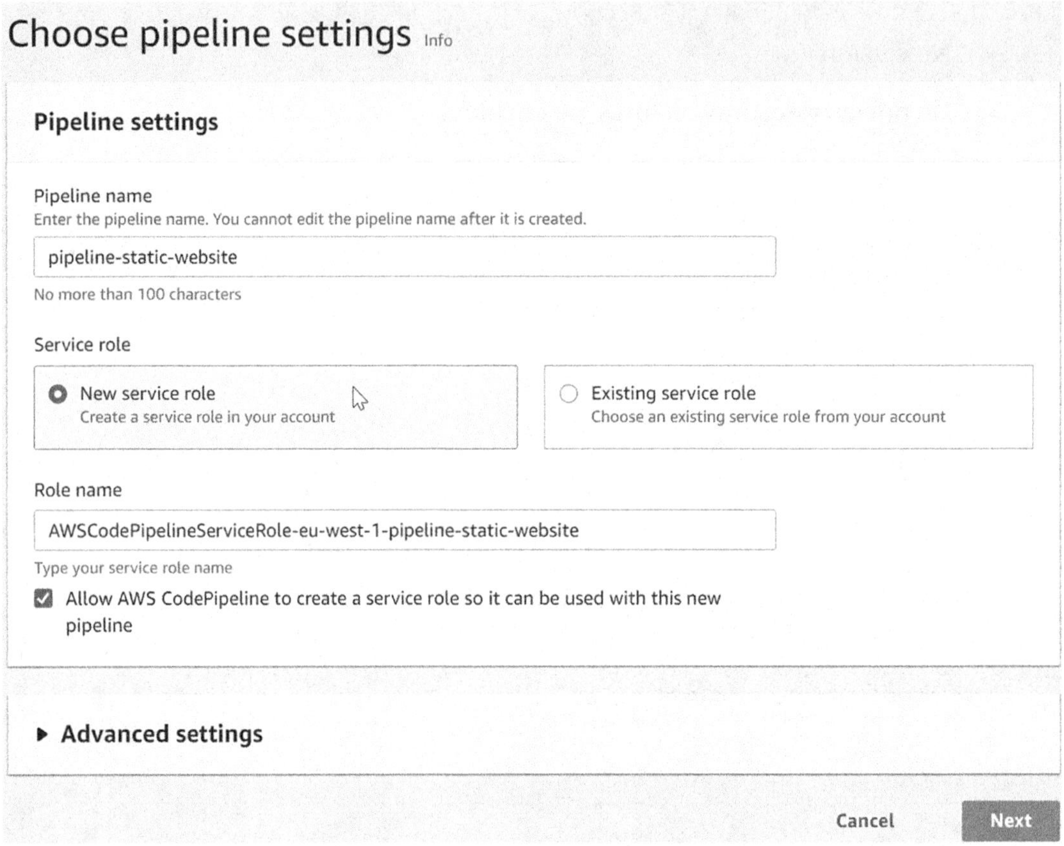

## Choose pipeline settings  Info

### Pipeline settings

**Pipeline name**
Enter the pipeline name. You cannot edit the pipeline name after it is created.

pipeline-static-website

No more than 100 characters

**Service role**

( • ) New service role
Create a service role in your account

( ◯ ) Existing service role
Choose an existing service role from your account

**Role name**

AWSCodePipelineServiceRole-eu-west-1-pipeline-static-website

Type your service role name

☑ Allow AWS CodePipeline to create a service role so it can be used with this new pipeline

▶ **Advanced settings**

Cancel          Next

***Figure 4-39.*** *Pipeline configuration, choosing a pipeline name*

On the same page, AWS will require you to create a service's role, which is a set of permissions to allow CodePipeline to interact with other AWS services; either you can keep the services role name set to the default or you can choose the name by yourself.

In the advanced settings, you will choose the bucket, as shown in Figure 4-40, or you can allow a pipeline to create one for you, but CodePipeline will set the name.

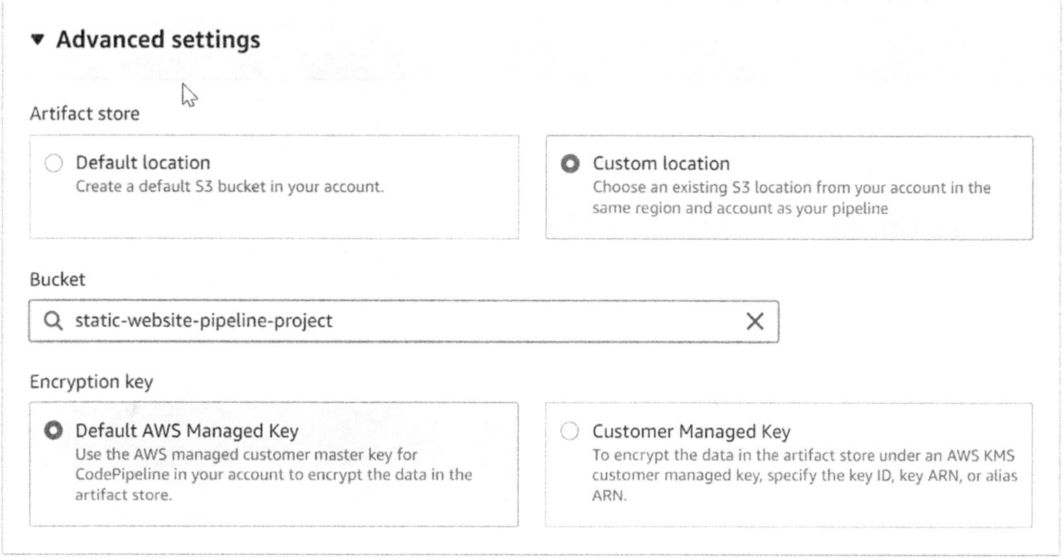

▼ **Advanced settings**

Artifact store

| ○ Default location<br>Create a default S3 bucket in your account. | ● Custom location<br>Choose an existing S3 location from your account in the same region and account as your pipeline |
|---|---|

Bucket

🔍 static-website-pipeline-project                               ✕

Encryption key

| ● Default AWS Managed Key<br>Use the AWS managed customer master key for CodePipeline in your account to encrypt the data in the artifact store. | ○ Customer Managed Key<br>To encrypt the data in the artifact store under an AWS KMS customer managed key, specify the key ID, key ARN, or alias ARN. |
|---|---|

***Figure 4-40.*** *Choosing an S3 bucket name*

Click Next, and the following screen will allow you to choose the source provider where the code was uploaded; in our case, it will be GitHub version 2.

The screen will be expanded to allow you to connect GitHub with the pipeline and create the connection, as shown in Figure 4-41.

Select the Connect to GitHub button on the right if this is your first time connecting to GitHub using CodePipeline. Doing this will enable a new AWS Developer Tools window, allowing you to establish a new connection. You will be requested to log into GitHub if you are not already.

---

**Note**    The difference between GitHub version 1 and GitHub version 2 is that in GitHub version 1, you can download only the source; GitHub version 2 will allow you to clone it so you can access the metadata.

---

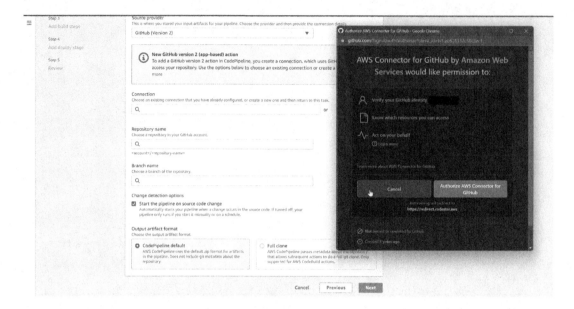

***Figure 4-41.*** *Pipeline configuration, GitHub integration*

Allow AWS to install the connector when you create the connection, as shown in Figure 4-42.

***Figure 4-42.*** *Installing the AWS connector*

Once you are done with the connection, you will be redirected back to the screen; you need to choose the information of the code repository and which branch, as shown in Figure 4-43. Click Next once you are done.

Remember to choose the right repository name; once you create the connection, your repository names will be shown in the field, as well as which branch you will use for this code.

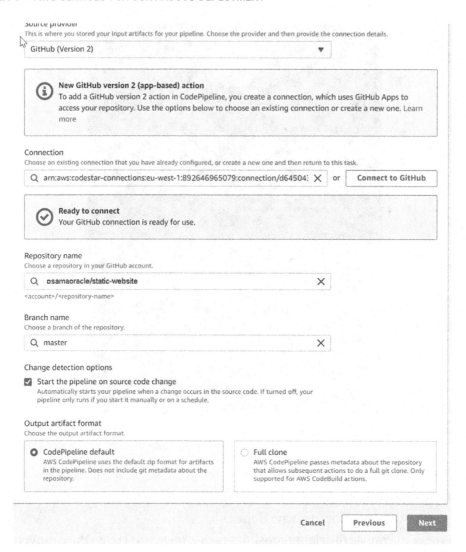

***Figure 4-43.*** *Pipeline configuration, GitHub connection*

Once you click Next, the following configuration will be the build stage, and since this is a static website and we will not build anything or have any artifactory, we will skip, confirm, and click Next. See Figure 4-44.

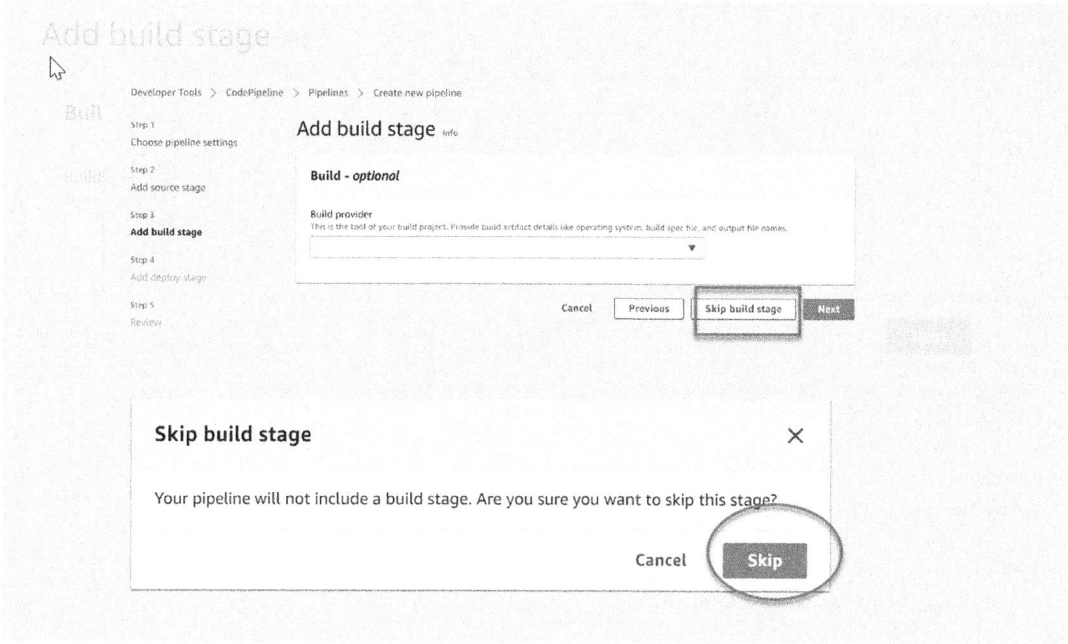

***Figure 4-44.*** *Pipeline configuration, skipping the build stage*

On the next screen, AWS provides a different deploy provider; in our case, it will be Amazon S3. Choose the correct region for the created bucket, the bucket name, and the development path in case you deploy to a specific folder inside S3.

Select "Extract file before apply." This option will hide the S3 object key; see Figure 4-45.

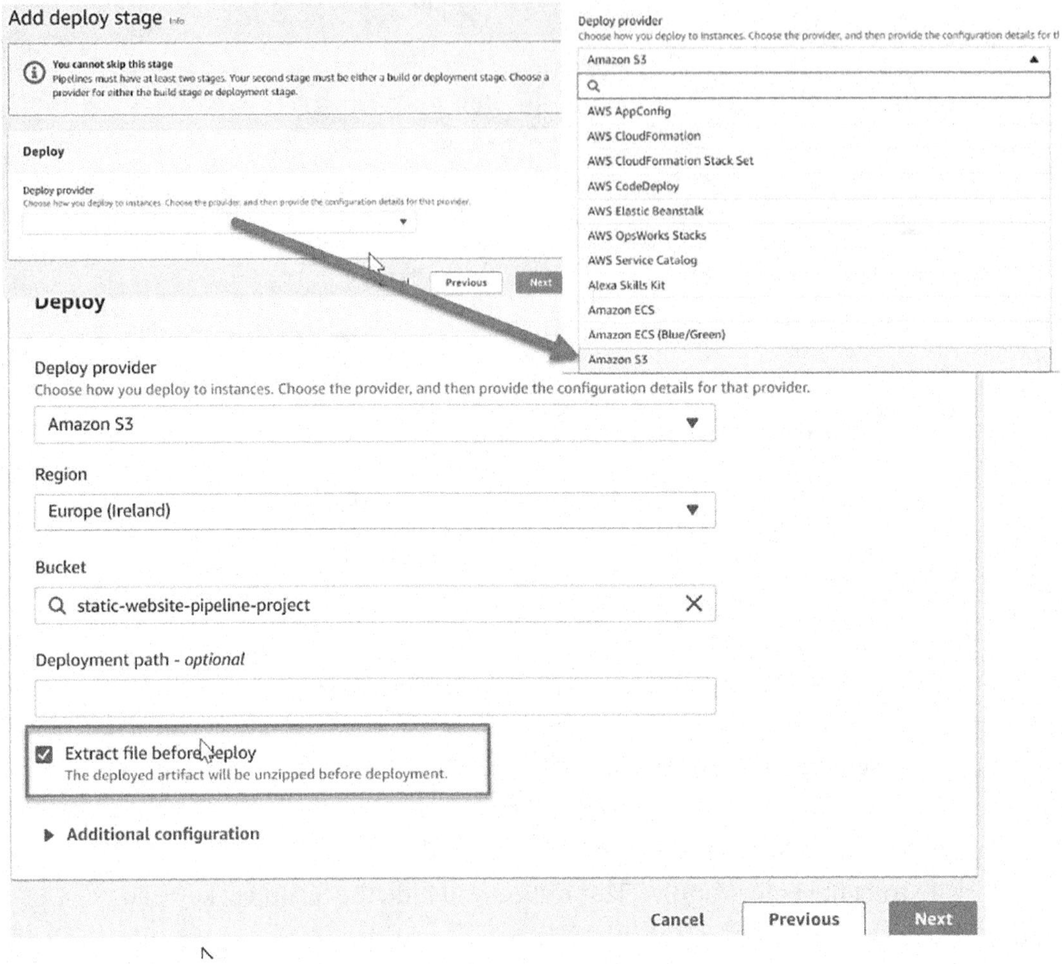

***Figure 4-45.***  *Pipeline configuration, deployment stage*

Review all the information. If you are happy with the configuration and setup, click "Create a pipeline." The first trigger will be automatic once you click the button; see Figure 4-46.

***Figure 4-46.*** *Pipeline configuration, CodePipeline results*

If you check the S3 bucket after the pipeline run is finished, you will see the code has been uploaded there.

# Summary

In this chapter, you learned more about using continued deployment inside Amazon AWS and learned what kind of services match this concept.

Additionally, we reviewed the deployment strategy in general and the one AWS provides; in this chapter, I tried to cover the concepts with real-life examples to allow you to understand the use case and the different configurations each time.

In the next chapter, we will cover one of the essential parts of the deployment, which are the different deployment strategies. In general, we will discuss each one of them in detail, compare them, and discuss the use case for them. After discussing the strategies in general, I will cover them from Amazon AWS's point of view.

# CHAPTER 5

# AWS Deployment Strategies

In the previous chapter, I covered deployment and how to create a pipeline. Still, one of the central concepts when building the pipeline is understanding the deployment strategy and which type you will use, because there are multiple deployment types, each serving a different purpose depending on the use case and the company approach.

In this chapter, I will discuss general and specific deployment strategies. I'll also cover the types offered by AWS.

## What Is a Deployment Strategy?

A deployment strategy is the method by which a company, development team, or DevOps department releases a new version of its software. This method will depend on how network traffic will be distributed to the latest release and how to deal with it.

These are the deployment types:

- Blue/green deployment

- Canary deployment

- A/B testing deployment

- Re-create deployment

- Ramped deployment (rolling upgrade)

- Shadow deployment

Let's look at each in detail.

© Osama Mustafa 2023
O. Mustafa, *A Complete Guide to DevOps with AWS*, https://doi.org/10.1007/978-1-4842-9303-4_5

# Blue/Green Deployments

One of the most common deployment strategies is when the software's new version runs next to the old version.

Once the QA team tests the latest version and ensures it's running without any errors, the load balancer will switch the traffic from the old version to the new version. This is also called *red/black deployment*.

- The blue environment is running current application version.

- The green environment is running the new application version.

The first, more outdated version is the blue environment, while the latest, most up-to-date version is the green environment.

As shown in Figure 5-1, the subsequent action is to transition to a green environment by routing all user traffic to the new setting. Because this move can take place extremely rapidly, there won't be any downtime for the users. In addition, if you need to undo the changes, you can do so immediately by redirecting the traffic to the previous version.

This approach offers several advantages.

- You will have two versions of your application, so you can roll back anytime and test without affecting the live version.

- You avoid having multiple versions of the application.

However, there are some potential disadvantages.

- Replicating the environment makes the process complex and requires extra work.

- It is useful for a stateful application.

- It requires careful testing.

- There is an extra cost.

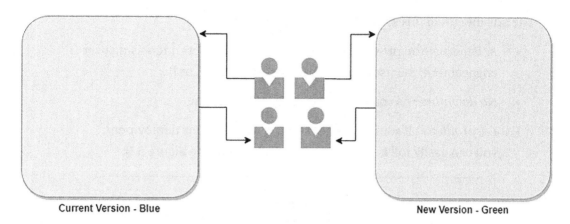

Current Version - Blue                                                    New Version - Green

**Figure 5-1.** *Blue/green (red/black) deployment*

# Canary Deployments

One of my favorite deployment strategies is *canary deployment*. In this type of deployment, the development team will prepare the new version, but they will gradually shift it into production based on a percentage.

For example, the DevOps will start deploying the new version gradually, say, 10 percent of it; then the QA will test that much and inform the team if there are any bugs or errors.

The percentage will be increased to 15 percent, 20 percent, up to 100 percent; this will help the team test the new version's stability bit by bit. Canary deployments offer a significant level of control. However, it may be challenging to put this into practice. See Figure 5-2.

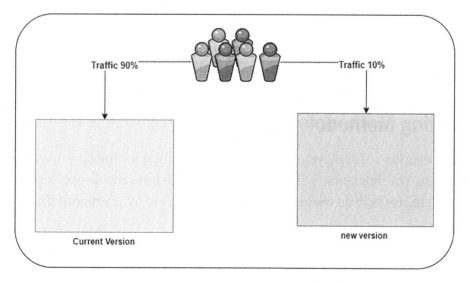

Traffic 90%                                                    Traffic 10%

Current Version                                              new version

**Figure 5-2.** *How canary deployment works*

The advantages of this kind of deployment are many.

- *A/B testing*: You provide two alternatives to the users, increasing user engagement; the users will be assigned to group A or B.

- *No downtime*: As you can see, there is no downtime.

- *Easy rollback*: If something goes wrong with the new deployment, you can easily roll back to the previous version. See Figure 5-3.

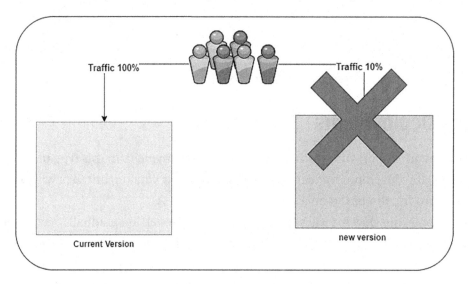

**Figure 5-3.** *Fast rollbacks in case of errors*

- *Fast feedback*: The QA will provide quick feedback about each stage, which makes updating the application much more effortless.

The disadvantage is that it can be slow to roll out.

## A/B Testing Methodologies

In an *A/B testing* kind of deployment, the developers will deploy the new release next to the old release. The difference is that the new release will be available only for certain people, most likely QA to do testing and some developers to fix any reported issues; see Figure 5-4.

The good thing about this kind of deployment is that it's a different environment, like the blue/green deployment. This does consume more resources while the team is testing, but once the testing is done, the old version can be deleted.

Another downside is that it does create more work, because the developer will have to maintain and work on two different environments to ensure both of them are performing correctly.

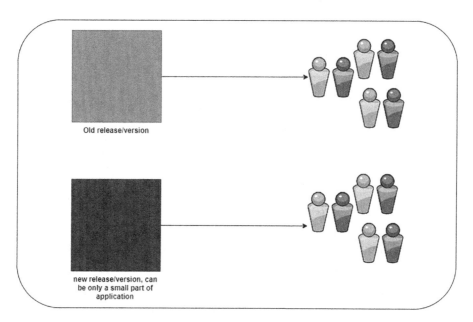

*Figure 5-4.* *A/B testing deployment example*

The advantage is that you can control the traffic.

These are the disadvantages:

- The load balancer setup can be complicated.

- Troubleshooting is not easy for this deployment.

# Re-create Deployments

This type is straightforward; the system administrators will shut down the old system, deploy the new release, and immediately reboot the servers, as shown in Figure 5-5.

There will be downtime between the shutdown and the machine's startup.

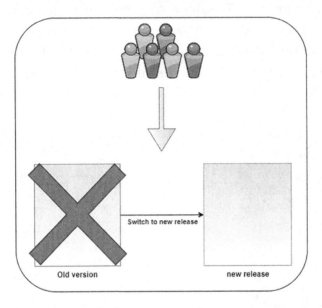

***Figure 5-5.*** *How the re-create deployment works*

The good thing about this deployment is that it's cheaper, with no need for a load balancer to shift the traffic from one to another environment; the bad thing about it, as you can see, is the downtime, which is not reasonable for some companies.

The advantage is that it's an easy deployment to set up.

The disadvantage is that downtime may be extended and affect the users.

## Ramped Deployments (Rolling Upgrades)

Please don't mix this deployment type up with canary deployment. By using canary deployment, early adopters can get their hands on a new software version before the general public. Rolling deployments focus on specific servers, while a canary technique selects a subset of users to test the new software before rolling it out to everyone.

Compared to canary deployment, rolling/ramped deployment gives certain users the updated program version.

This approach will gradually replace the old version/release with the new version/release; see Figure 5-6.

After replacing the environment entirely with the new version, the old one can be shut down; using this deployment will allow the team to monitor the performance of the new release and roll out quickly in case something happens.

IT departments need to worry about only one production environment for a web program when using the rolling deployment method. In other words, IT administrators first stagger change releases to install a new application version on select servers or instances. Some servers run the new program; others run the old one. Some users utilize the updated code, while others use the production version.

This type comprises a network of computers or instances in the cloud, each running its own copy of the program. In addition, a load balancer is often used to distribute user requests over many servers.

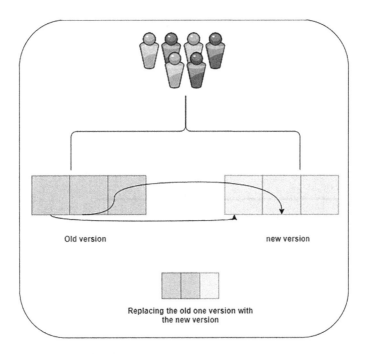

**Figure 5-6.**  *How ramped deployment works*

Here are the advantages:

- It's an easy deployment to set up.

- The new version will be replaced slowly and needs time to be tested.

- It's one of the best deployments for stateful applications.

These are the disadvantages:

- Supporting the application can be exhausting for this kind of deployment.

- You cannot control the traffic.

# Shadow Deployments

One of the most complex deployments that DevOps can do is a shadow deployment.

The team will deploy the new and old versions together, but the users cannot connect to the latest version immediately, meaning it will stay "in the shadows" (where the name comes from); see Figure 5-7.

After that, the developer will send a copy of the requests to the shadow version, which will help test the new version and the performance of the latest release.

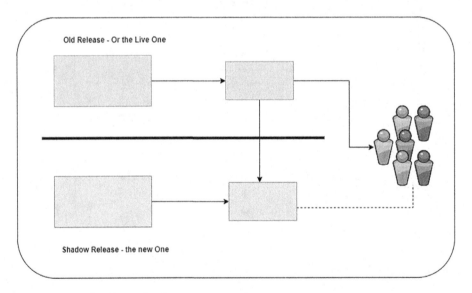

*Figure 5-7.* *How shadow deployment works*

These are the advantages:

- There is zero impact on the users.

- You can monitor the performance with real production traffic.

These are the disadvantages:

- Supporting this kind of development isn't straightforward.

- It is complex to set up.

The previous deployment strategies are for DevOps in general. We need to discuss the Amazon AWS deployment strategies, which are similar to the previous ones.

In the next section, I will discuss the deployment strategies from Amazon AWS's perspective; you will notice that the names are the same. In addition, Amazon AWS added a new deployment strategy to its cloud, which will be discussed in the next section.

Amazon AWS uses the strategies mentioned earlier in this chapter with an addition or a new name; this will be explained as it comes up.

# Amazon AWS Deployment Strategies

To create a deployment solution that is complete and fully functional, you have first to establish the required deployment methods. Your ideal equilibrium of management, efficiency, price, tolerance for risk, and other variables may influence the deployment strategies you choose to utilize to update your application. Each deployment service offered by AWS is compatible with several different deployment techniques.

The following are the deployment options offered by AWS:

- In-place deployments

- Prebaking versus bootstrapping AMIs

- Blue/green deployments

- Canary deployments

- Linear deployments

- All-at-once deployments

# In-Place Deployments

From the name, you can understand that this deployment will update the application without providing any new infrastructure; the old one will be stopped and then updated with the latest version. This kind of deployment is similar to the re-creating deployment method.

Deployment settings for one at a time, half at a time, and all at once are available with AWS CodeDeploy and AWS Elastic Beanstalk.

The following are the advantages:

- The cost remains the same; there is no need to provision new infrastructure.

- The infrastructure and administration/management will be the same.

The following are the disadvantages:

- Rollback will be slow since you need to reinstall the old version.

- The application needs to be tested well.

- Downtime may occur depending on the infrastructure setup on the cloud.

# Prebaking vs. Bootstrapping AMIs

When application components are prebaked into an Amazon Machine Image (AMI), it may reduce the time needed to start and run an Amazon EC2 machine. During deployment, it is possible to rapidly pair the prebaking and bootstrapping methodologies to construct new instances adapted to the current environment.

Deploying your application with any necessary dependencies or updates when an Amazon EC2 instance is started is known as *bootstrapping* an EC2. It is possible for deployments and scaling events to be delayed if a complicated application or substantial downloads are necessary.

The following are the advantages:

- Bootstrapping lets you quickly reproduce the Dev, QA, and Production environments.

- You can construct a setting where one may heal and learn about oneself.

- It improves Amazon AWS resource management.

- It is considered a low-cost option in the cloud.

The following are the disadvantages:

- It is not a consistently smooth option and comes with a risk of failure.

- The administration's efforts probably will increase due to the complexity.

# Linear Deployments

Linear is considered part of blue/green deployment with some canary deployment features; when traffic is moved via a linear deployment, each increment takes the same amount of time. The proportion of traffic transferred in each increment and the interval in minutes between each increment are specified in predefined linear options.

The following are the advantages:

- There is no downtime.

- Few users will be affected if the new environment doesn't work correctly.

The following are the disadvantages:

- The deployment will take time.

- There is an extra cost.

# All-at-Once Deployments

In another type of blue/green deployment, the traffic will be moved from the old version to the new one.

The following are the advantages:

- There is no downtime.

- A few users will be affected if the new environment doesn't work correctly.

The following are the disadvantages:

- The deployment will take time.

- There is an extra cost.

**Note**   During the writing of this book, Amazon AWS announced fully managed blue/green deployments in Amazon Aurora and Amazon RDS, something new and not yet implemented. This type of deployment will eventually make our lives much easier.

To understand what this means, you can build a distinct staging environment that is fully controlled, synchronized, and a reflection of the production environment by using blue/green deployments. The staging environment will make a copy of the primary database used in your production environment and any in-region read replicas. Blue/green deployments use logical replication to ensure these two environments remain in sync.

You won't have to worry about losing any data if you make the staging environment the production environment instead. Blue/green deployments will prevent writes from being made on both the blue and green environments to prevent any data from being lost during the switchover.

Once you do the configuration, the green environment will catch up to the blue one. The production environment's traffic is then redirected to the newly promoted staging environment using blue/green deployments, which occurs without any modifications to the application's code.

## Blue/Green Deployments for MySQL RDS

Search for *RDS* in the AWS Management Console, choose the databases that must be modified in the console, and then select Create Blue/Green Deployment from the Actions drop-down option, as shown in Figure 5-8.

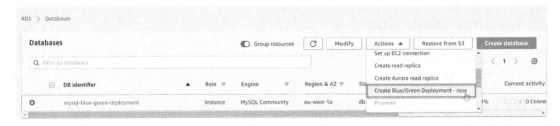

***Figure 5-8.*** *Amazon AWS new feature RDS blue/green deployment*

You can modify the properties of your database, like the engine version, DB cluster parameter group, and DB parameter group for green databases. You can also establish a blue/green deployment identification associated with your database.

To utilize a blue/green deployment in your Aurora or RDS instance, in our case MySQL, you will need to switch on binary logging by changing the value for the `binlog_format` parameter in the DB cluster parameter group from `OFF` to `MIXED`.

Once you choose this option, the configuration is straightforward (Figure 5-9).

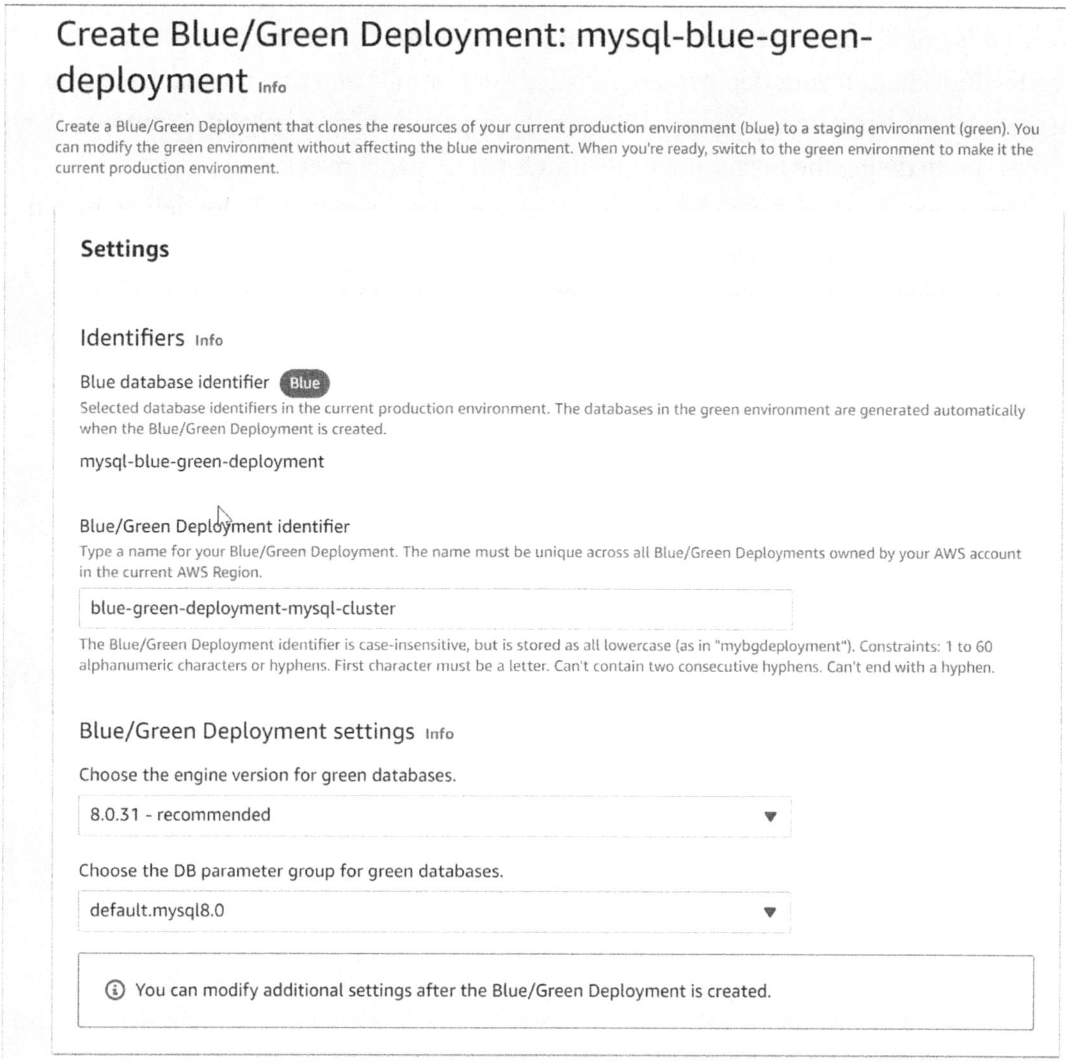

**Figure 5-9.**  *Amazon AWS blue/green deployment configuration*

The database will be ready for production when you choose Create Blue/Green Deployment from the drop-down menu since it will create a new staging environment and execute automatic operations. Note that you will have to pay for this feature of the database, which includes reading replicas and DB instances in multi-AZ deployments and any additional options you may have activated on the green one, such as Amazon RDS Performance Insights.

When the creation process is finished, you will have access to a staging environment prepared for testing and validation before it's promoted to the new environment.

At this point, you are close to being ready to move your green databases into production; check if your deployment finished successfully and that the databases are prepared for the transition. There is also another option which is helpful, "timeout," that allows you to define the maximum time limit for your switchover.

Plus, once you do the switchover, the blue/green deployment will not delete the old production environment, just in case you still need access.

The RDS blue/green deployment option is beneficial when you need to create, for example, a DR solution or a staging environment that will allow the developer to work on it and sync with production instead of performing manual work.

If you want to do this using AWS CLI, it's simple, as shown here:

```
1. aws rds create-blue-green-deployment
2. --blue-green-deployment-name blue-green-deployment-mysql-cluster
3. --source arn:aws:rds:eu-west-1:223344555:db:mysql-blue-green-deployment
4. --target-engine-version 5.7
5. --region eu-west-1
```

# Summary

In this chapter, we discussed the ways I could deploy an application into the cloud or even on-premises; in addition, we talked about types of deployment strategies.

We covered the types of deployments offered by Amazon AWS and compared each, mentioning the cons and pros.

Before deciding what to implement in your system, you need to investigate a variety of facets and contrast the possible deployment strategies. Using one of them depends on the use case and business needs.

In the next chapter, we will go through different DevOps categories. One of the most common uses is infrastructure as code; the next chapter will also cover a variety of tools, such as Terraform, CloudFormation, and Pulumi, as show how to use them.

# CHAPTER 6

# Infrastructure as Code

Infrastructure as code (IaC) is one of my favorite subjects; in this chapter, I'll break it down and focus on the most important details regarding how it works with AWS.

In this chapter, I will cover IaC in general, the benefits of using IaC, and why you need to use it. I'll also cover IaC tools, such as Terraform, CloudFormation, Pulumi, and Ansible, and the difference between them, as well as when you should use each one of these tools.

## What Is Infrastructure as Code?

As a DevOps engineer, you will hear about IaC a lot, especially if you or your team is deploying multiple resources such as databases, virtual machines, load balancers, and more.

Say you have different environments such as QA, UAT, development, preproduction, production, and maybe more. Imagine redeploying the same resources to these environments over and over again. Figure 6-1 shows the effort you need to make without IaC.

© Osama Mustafa 2023
O. Mustafa, *A Complete Guide to DevOps with AWS*, https://doi.org/10.1007/978-1-4842-9303-4_6

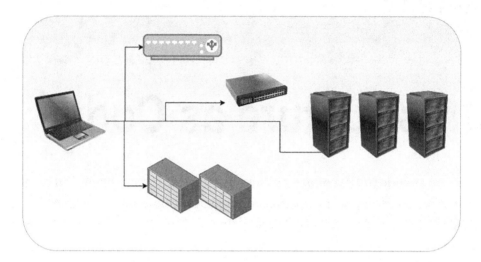

**Figure 6-1.** *The old way of deploying resources one by one*

You should be able to produce more value in less time using cloud and infrastructure automation. This allows you to do it more reliably, saving money and time for your company. In reality, however, using the cloud results an ever-increasing volume, level of complexity, and variety of items that need to be managed.

One of these advantages is automation. Other advantages are that the cloud can solve the resource and life-cycle management complexity, versioning, and configuration. Basically, the method of infrastructure automation known as *infrastructure as code* is modeled around and borrows techniques from the field of software development. It emphasizes the importance of consistent processes that can be repeated for modifying the configuration of resources such as compute, storage, network, load balancing, and provisioning. When changes are made to the definitions, those modifications are subsequently "pushed out" to the systems by making use of processes that are unattended and include rigorous validation. Figure 6-2 shows you how you can use IaC to deploy to different environments.

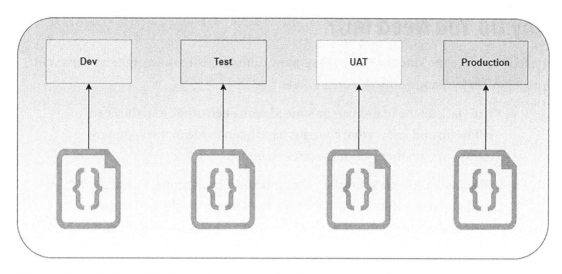

**Figure 6-2.** *IaC multiple-environment deployments*

DevOps engineers write the IaC files; upload them to the company version control, for example, GitHub or GitLab; and share the changes done on the code with the other team members so that the deployment and code enhancements will start.

After that, the DevOps engineer needs to keep updating the code based on the team review and pushes the changes to the pull request/merge requests; once the team comments are finished, the pull request will be approved and merged with the main branch.

To simplify, Table 6-1 shows the cloud approach versus the classical one.

**Table 6-1.** *Apporach Followed in the Cloud*

| Factor | Classical Approach | Cloud Approach |
|---|---|---|
| **Hardware** | Physical hardware; the company needs to wait to set up this hardware. | Virtualized resources and quick setup. No need to wait. |
| **Provisioning** | It will take time at least two weeks, depending on the environment. | Fast; probably will take minutes. |
| **Provisioning type** | Manual configuration. | It can be a manual or automated configuration. |
| **Changes** | It will be risky, and you need to have a rollback plan in case the changes fail. | Can be done to improve the infrastructure; very fast rollback; most of the changes automated. |
| **Architecture** | Monolithic. | Microservices and monolithic. |
| **Change cost** | High. | Low. |

# Why Do You Need IaC?

The following are the kinds of results that many different teams and organizations want to accomplish by using infrastructure as code:

- With IaC, all the teams can be synced with each other, and they can follow up and know what changes have been made to the company infrastructure; there are no secrets anymore.

- Developers will have visibility over infrastructure resources and their configurations; they will also be able to define, provide, and organize their needs, eliminating the need to rely on IT employees to carry out these tasks on their behalf.

- Rollback and failure accidents are easy to fix; if you deploy something and cause an issue with IaC, roll back.

- Enhancement and improvement never stops with IaC; the time spent by IT staff members is not wasted on mundane, routine work but on activities that put their skills to good use.

- Instead of discussing potential solutions in meetings and documents, it is more effective to put them into action, testing them and measuring their effectiveness.

There are a couple of things you need to understand before you start working with infrastructure as code. Let's look at some myths about the process.

**Myth 1: I will use IaC to deploy first, followed by automation.**

I have seen clients writing the code for infrastructure and using it to deploy the application. It's good practice and an automated one, but don't expect to make changes from the console later or make changes manually.

Ask your DevOps engineers to update the code; everything must be done using IaC once you decide to use it.

There are three main problems in implementing automation later:

- Automation should allow quicker delivery times for everything; automation's advantages are lost if executed after the bulk of the job has already been completed.

- When you use automation, creating automated testing for your software is much less of a hassle. And when issues are discovered, they can be fixed and rebuilt more rapidly. If you include this in the construction process, you will have a superior infrastructure.

- It is challenging to add automation to an established system. Automation occurs during the planning and execution of a system. Adding automation to a system not designed initially with automation in mind requires significant changes to the system's architecture and implementation.

In the cloud, infrastructure that isn't automated quickly becomes a loss. The price of manual upkeep and repairs may add up rapidly. That is, if the function it performs goes off without a hitch.

IaC solves the problem of release pipeline environment drift. Teams must manage deployment environment parameters without IaC. Each habitat becomes a "snowflake" that can't be replicated automatically.

Environment inconsistency might hinder deployment. Manual infrastructure maintenance is error-prone and hard to monitor.

IaC infrastructure deployments are repeatable, avoiding runtime difficulties from configuration drift or missing dependencies. Release pipelines configure target environments. The team modifies the source, not the target.

Why are people trying to avoid IaC while making the changes? As shown in Figure 6-3, it's simple: fear.

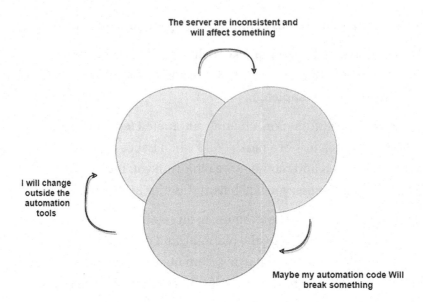

**Figure 6-3.** *The automation fears*

Code complicates things and requires support engineers to know a lot. This is new ground for some, but it is the most critical component for backup, feature requests, and resources. Support and code don't always match.

No one can remember every configuration of every resource in an infrastructure; thus, if you want to change a resource, you can do this without IaC and by hand in the portal without much thought about restoring this at some time.

**Myth 2: It's one way, either speed or quality.**

Writing the IaC will take time, only at first, and it's normal to think that delivering quick code will make it low-quality code, as you can see in Figure 6-4, which is incorrect.

**Figure 6-4.** *Speed versus quality*

202

Teams prioritizing speed over quality produce flawed systems due to the inefficiency of their plans. It's common for established firms to feel that they've lost their "mojo" after adopting this strategy. Because of the system's complexity, even relatively straightforward modifications that used to be implemented in a matter of hours now require days or weeks.

**Myth 3: A task is not repetitive so there's no need to automate it.**

Ideally, after you've built a system, it will be complete. According to this theory, you don't make that many adjustments and thus automating them is not worth the effort.

In real life, when a company creates a system, it tries to enhance it as much as possible to reach a point of stability; these changes need to be documented somehow to avoid any misconfiguration in the future.

The best way to document the infrastructure is IaC; sometimes, these changes will be verified from one company to another.

- You can make changes on the network layers, either by open security port, ingress, or egress.

- You must update the servers or virtual machine with a new application upgrade or operating system.

- You've tweaked the database's configuration, which dramatically boosts its speed.

- Updating the application server is necessary to access the latest features.

One of the golden rules in the cloud is that modifying conditions creates stability.

If you can't patch your application and database regularly, then your system/application is not stable at all; if small changes cause downtime, then your system is not stable.

# IaC Types

When you work with IaC, you will notice that not all tools are the same. This is the power of IaC. Each one of them has a different purpose.

# Scripts

One of the most famous approaches of IaC is considered simple because the script is usually written to do only one task.

# Configuration Management

Some of the most familiar IaC tools were designed to do complex tasks such as upgrade the database, install servers, apply patches, and much more. Examples of these kinds of tools are Ansible, Chef, and Puppet.

# Provisioning

If you want to create a complete infrastructure, this is the category you are looking for; you can deploy any infrastructure components such as a load balancer, EC2, and much more. You could even retrieve a value deployed manually and use it inside your code; examples of these tools are Terraform and CloudFormation.

# Containers and Templating

All these types of tools don't provide image templates. Assume you have an EC2 image and want to use it as an image for another infrastructure; what will you do? With the help of tools, you can generate templates and images that already have all the libraries and components an application needs to be installed; one of the best types of tools is a packer.

# Tool Examples

Table 6-2 explains the differences between the tools from a high level. These are the most common tools worldwide.

***Table 6-2.*** *DevOps tools examples and how these tools are working*

| Tools | How It Works | Focus |
|---|---|---|
| **Terraform** | Agentless | Admin focused |
| **Ansible** | Agentless | Admin-focused configuration management |
| **Jenkins** | Agentless | Dev and can work for admin also, CI/CD |
| **Puppet** | Agent-based, agentless (not all the features will work) | Admin and dev focused |
| **Chef** | Agent-based can be agentless (not all the features will work) | Dev and admin focused |
| **Salt** | Agent, agentless | Admin focused |

After explaining the IaC concepts, how it works, and its benefits, it's time for the technical stuff. I will divide the tools into two main categories.

- *Cloud tools*: Cloud tools will support only cloud-native solutions. These tools will allow you to deploy to different cloud providers, and some of the tools even work on specific clouds only.

- *On-premises tools*: These tools on only on-premises, allowing DevOps to configure the infrastructure components.

While infrastructure as code has many benefits, selecting an IaC solution can be complicated, because the functions of several IaC tools are similar. Many of them are free and available to the public. Some of them provide business assistance. Without firsthand experience, it's difficult to determine how to choose between them.

While it's technically accurate that you might be just as productive with any of these tools, most comparisons you see list their general features, giving the impression that you could be just as effective with any of them.

I actually use several IaC tools, but it will also work if you want to stick only to one simultaneously. I'll now cover how to how the best one (or several) for your job.

# How to Choose an IaC Tool

I will compare different IaC tools, such as Terraform, Ansible, Pulumi, and CloudFormation, in this section. When you choose a tool, you'll want to consider the following factors:

- Provision versus configuration management

- Agent versus agentless

- Integration with other tools

- Mutable infrastructure versus immutable infrastructure

- General IaC language versus specifically designed language

- Paid version versus free version

## Provision vs. Configuration Management

When talking about this provisioning versus configuration management, there are lots of examples. Terraform, CloudFormation, Azure Resource Manager, and Pulumi are provision tools, but also Ansible, Puppet, and Chef are configuration management tools.

IT infrastructure provisioning is a way of introducing the necessary hardware and software. Likewise, it might mean the processes involved in facilitating the access to and use of information by people and machines. Configuration follows provisioning.

Virtual machines (VMs), load balancing, databases, and so on, can all be provisioned with the help of these technologies. You can let configuration management and its tool handle the setup.

On the other hand, configuration management guarantees that hardware, software, and network infrastructure always perform as intended, where the services they deliver use the code in a manner that is both repeatable and consistent.

Simply, configuration management is not the same as provisioning.

The configuration management can still deploy the infrastructure, but it's more about controlling things such as where the application configuration should be located and where to install it.

Provision tools, Terraform, for example, provision a virtual machine called a *database instance* with specific networking requirements and instance size.

```
1. resource "aws_instance" "database-instance" {
2.    ami           = "ami-12345f4433dd1f123"
3.    instance_type = "t2.micro"
4.
5.    network_interface {
6.       network_interface_id = aws_network_interface. database-
         instance-nw.id
7.       device_index         = 0
8.    }
9.
10.   credit_specification {
11.      cpu_credits = "unlimited"
12.   }
13. }
14.
```

If you convert the previous code to configuration management, the easiest way to do this is to use a tool such as Ansible.

```
1.  ---
2.  - name: EC2_instance_creation
3.    hosts: localhost
4.    gather_facts: false
5.    tasks:
7.    - name: EC2_Specs
8.      block:
9.        - name: EC2_infomation
10.
11.         ec2_instance_info:
12.         register: ec2_info
13.       - name: Print info
14.        debug: var="ec2_info.instances"
15.
```

You need to complete the YAML code and create the EC2_Block, which will be responsible for the operating system. This is only a tiny section of the complete YAML file to provision only EC2, so usually the provision tools are much easier to use than the configuration when it's related to the infrastructure section.

```
1.   - name: EC2_Specs
2.     block:
3.       - name: Launch ec2
4.         tags: chapter_IaC
5.         ec2:
6.           region: us-east-1
7.           key_name: Osama-PrivateKey
8.           group: ec2_secuirty_group
9.           instance_type: t2.micro
10.          image: ami-12345f4433dd1f123
11.
```

# Agent vs. Agentless

Some of the IaC tools require you to install agents to work correctly. Chef and Puppet, for example, require an agent. For sure, they are powerful tools that can do many things, but there is a disadvantage to these agents' tools.

Although Chef and Puppet provide varying degrees of functionality for agentless modes, these modes appear to be an afterthought. They do not cover the whole set of features of the configuration management solution. Because of this, the default setup for Chef and Puppet usually contains an agent.

- *Administration*: Having an agent is an extra job for the system administrator or site reliability engineer (SRE). This agent requires updates occasionally, and agents should be in sync with the primary node, especially if the number of servers is significant.

- *Security aspect*: It would be best if you opened an additional port to make this agent work, which sometimes is a concern to the security team.

- *Setup*: The architecture of the agent tools work can seem complicated; see Figure 6-5, which illustrates how the Chef architecture works.

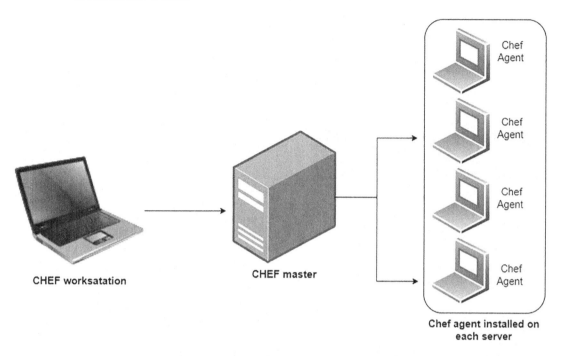

***Figure 6-5.***  *An example of agent tools: Chef*

# Integration with Other Tools

IaC is a powerful tool, but it can't do everything for you. Let's look at Terraform as an example; it can do many things and provides a complete infrastructure.

However, Terraform has limitations related to configuring the virtual machine or application, such as if you need to configure the template.

Figure 6-6 shows a different IaC use case depending on what is needed; from the bottom, Terraform can be used to provision the cloud infrastructure.

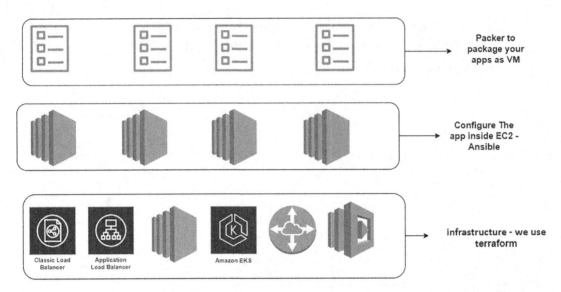

**Figure 6-6.** *A complete solution can be provided using different IaC tools*

Ansible can provision cloud resources, provision on-premises infrastructure, or even inject commands to the servers; moreover, a packer, which is open-source software, can replicate a machine's exact setup across various platforms.

## Mutable Infrastructure vs. Immutable Infrastructure

Chef and Ansible are considered mutable tools, but what does this mean? Let's assume you want to install a Linux package using Chef. Chef will update the software on all of your servers that are in use. The changes will take effect without you having to do anything. Each server eventually develops its unique history of modifications as more and more upgrades are applied to it with time; it is *idempotent*.

Because of this, each server becomes slightly different from all the others, which can result in subtle configuration bugs that are challenging to detect and replicate. (This is the same configuration drift problem that occurs when you manage servers manually; if you have different environments, these environments will not be in sync with each other and will be hard to troubleshoot.)

On the other hand, *immutable infrastructure* refers to a method of managing service and software deployments on IT resources in which components are swapped out rather than modified in any way. Microsoft developed this method.

A perfect example of immutable infrastructure is a container because any changes to a container can be made only by creating a new version of that container.

For instance, if you want to update an image using Terraform, it will not update the image. It will just create a new one with the latest update and delete the old one. Although it is theoretically conceivable to coerce configuration management software into doing immutable deployments, this is not the approach that is often taken by such tools.

## General IaC Language vs. Specifically Designed Language

Chef and Pulumi allow you to write IaC with the programming language you already know. Chef supports Ruby, but Pulumi offers support for a broad range of general-purpose programming languages (GPLs), including JavaScript, TypeScript, Python, Go, C#, Java, and more.

Moreover, there is another type called a *domain-specific language* (DSL); for example, YAML is used by Ansible and CloudFormation (which also supports JSON), and Terraform uses HCL. Puppet makes use of the Puppet language.

**GPL Pros**

- If you know the language, you don't need to learn anything extra.

- It has professional mature tooling because of the community and overall level of quality.

- It can be applied to the completion of virtually any programming endeavor.

**DSL Pros**

- It has organized and structured code.

- The code is easier to understand since it's more straightforward and less wordy.

## Paid Version vs. Free Version

There are different IaC options, and which you use depends on the goal the company wants to meet. Most IaC vendors provide two options, either paid or free. For instance, the open-source version of Terraform is free to use on its own, or you can pay for HashiCorp's Terraform Cloud.

I think the free versions of Terraform, Chef, Puppet, and Ansible can be used well for production; commercial services can make these tools much better, but you can get by without them. Alternatively, without the premium service known as Pulumi Service, it is more challenging to utilize Pulumi in production.

## Comparison of Tools

Table 6-3 summarizes the main differences between the IaC tools we've discussed so far.

***Table 6-3.*** *IaC comparison based on different aspect*

| Factors | Terraform | Ansible | CloudFormation | Pulumi | Chef | Puppet |
| --- | --- | --- | --- | --- | --- | --- |
| Free/Paid | Both | Both | Paid | Both | Both | Both |
| Cloud | All | All | AWS | All | All | All |
| Category | Provision | Configuration Mgmt | Provision | Provision | Configuration Mgmt | Configuration Mgmt |
| Infra type | Immutable | Mutable | Immutable | Immutable | Mutable | Mutable |
| Agent | No | No | No | No | Yes | Yes |
| Community | Huge | Huge | Large | Small | Large | Large |
| Maturity | Average | Average | minimal | minimal | High | High |
| DSL/GPL | DSL | DSL | DSL | GPL | GPL | DSL |
| Procedural/ Declarative | Declarative | Procedural | Declarative | Declarative | Procedural | Declarative |

## Terraform

When we are talking about IaC, the first tool that comes to your mind is probably Terraform, which is an open-source IaC tool created by a company called HashiCorp. It is generally used by DevOps engineers to automate infrastructure-related activities. You can use Terraform to create cloud infrastructure, and it works with any cloud providers, including AWS, Google Cloud, Azure, and more.

With Terraform, you can provide a programmatic description of your whole network's setup. Terraform allows you to construct and manage resources in parallel across providers, even if your servers originate from various providers such as AWS or Azure. Terraform is the glue that holds together your IT infrastructure and the universal language with which you can communicate with all your teams.

Terraform was developed using the Go programming language. The Go source code is compiled into a Terraform binary (or multiple binaries for each supported OS).

You don't need to run any additional hardware to use this program to deploy infrastructure from your laptop, a build server, or any other computer. The Terraform binary automatically performs API calls on your behalf to various cloud providers such as Amazon Web Services, Microsoft Azure, Google Cloud Platform, DigitalOcean, OpenStack, and more. Terraform can use the infrastructure these providers already have for their API servers and the authentication procedures you currently use (e.g., the API keys you already have for AWS).

You next question probably is, where does Terraform get its API call? Terraform configurations are the solution; they detail the architecture you want to build. The "code" in "infrastructure as code" refers to these settings. Let's look at how to set up Terraform; the API used here is for the AWS cloud provider.

While initializing a working directory, the Terraform CLI searches for and installs the necessary providers. It can automatically download providers from a Terraform registry or load them from a local cache or mirror.

The operation of Terraform is accomplished by constructing a graph database that gives operators insight into the relationships between resources. In addition, it produces an execution plan, showing operators the order in which Terraform's activities will be carried out in response to a setting being applied or modified.

```
1. resource "aws_s3_bucket" "example_bucket" {
2.   bucket = "terraform-code-chapter"
3. }
```

Transparent portability across cloud providers is a typical concern for Terraform users because of the wide range of cloud services it supports. In other words, if you use Terraform to specify a set of AWS resources such as servers, databases, and load balancers, can you then use the exact instructions to deploy the same resources in another cloud provider like Azure or Google Cloud?

I find this is a question that leads nowhere. However, since various cloud providers provide different kinds of infrastructure, it is impossible to implement the same infrastructure in multiple cloud providers.

The functionality, configuration, administration, security, scalability, availability, observability, and so on, of AWS's servers, load balancers, and databases differ vastly from those of Azure and Google Cloud. Terraform's approach is to standardize the language, toolset, and IaC techniques behind the scenes while letting you write provider-specific code to use the provider's peculiarities.

Figure 6-7 shows an example of writing code in Terraform to deploy AWS resources (whatever the resources are). It will not work on another cloud provider because the Terraform API will differ.

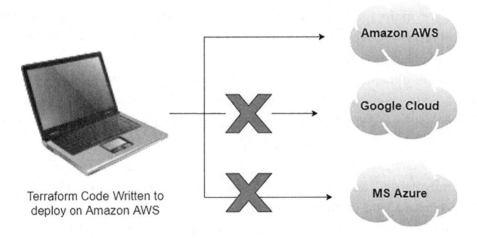

***Figure 6-7.*** *Different Terraform code for each cloud*

The Terraform provider allows you to interact with AWS resources, as follows:

```
1. provider "aws" {
2.   region = "eu-west-1"
3. }
```

I will cover the Terraform basics with AWS. It is as an excellent option for these reasons:

- Amazon AWS was the most common provider with a 32 percent market share as I wrote this book.

- AWS services are mature and include many services that focus on your needs.

- AWS offers different versions including a free tier.

# Terraform Concepts

Let's move on to the technical talk; we should start with Terraform state.

**Terraform State**

Each time you execute Terraform, it makes a Terraform state file that shows what infrastructure it built. Once you run Terraform, by default the name of the state file will be `terraformed.tfstate`. This file has a personalized JSON format that keeps track of the mapping between the Terraform assets in your system settings and how those resources look in the actual world.

The following example is a section from the `terraform.tfstate` file. You can use the following JSON every time you update the code. Terraform will read from that file and check/review these resources to ensure there are no duplicates.

```
1. {
2. "version": 4,
3.   "terraform_version": "1.2.0",
4. "serial": 222,
5. "lineage": "b697390d-f0a4-14dc-7df4-95b5b2cff75f",
6. "outputs": {},
7. "resources": [
8.     {
9. "module": "module.eks",
10. "mode": "data",
11. "type": "aws_availability_zones",
12. "name": "available",
13.       "provider": "provider[\"registry.terraform.io/hashicorp/aws\"]",
14. "instances": [
15.         {
16. "schema_version": 0,
17. "attributes": {
18. "all_availability_zones": null,
19. "exclude_names": null,
20. "exclude_zone_ids": null,
21. "filter": null,
22. "group_names": [
23. "eu-west-1"
```

```
24.                    ],
25. "id": "eu-west-1",
26. "names": [
27. "eu-west-1a",
28. "eu-west-1b",
29. "eu-west-1c"
30.                    ],
31. "state": null,
32. "timeouts": null,
33. "zone_ids": [
34.                 "euw1-az2",
35.                 "euw1-az3",
36.                 "euw1-az1"
37.               ]
38.            },
39. "sensitive_attributes": []
40.         }
41.       ]
42.     },
43.
```

When talking about the state, best practices need to be implemented; if you are using the state file for a private project, it will be saved on your local computer within the same directory as Terraform, which is acceptable. But if the project is for a company, it will not work to be local since a couple of issues will happen.

- Shared storage for state files

    - Each team member needs access to the duplicate Terraform state files because each one will need to update the infrastructure, and therefore, these changes should be saved under one state file; otherwise, it will be a messy configuration.

- State file lock

    - Without locking, data inconsistencies, lost updates, and corrupted state files might arise if more than one team member uses Terraform.

- Separate state file

  - A company will have different environments, such as production, QA, UAT, and more; when you update these environments, it is much better to keep the state file separated and not mixed.

As a remote back end, Amazon S3, Amazon's managed file store, is usually your best bet when using Terraform with AWS.

- Since it's a managed service, you don't have to set up and manage any extra hardware.

- It's made to last 99.999999999 percent of the time and be available 99.99 percent of the time, so you don't have to worry much about data loss or outages.

- You can save the state there and be supported by DynamoDB, but why?

  To secure a system and ensure its integrity, the `terraform.tfstate` file is saved in a bucket on Amazon S3. When you or a co-worker uses the `terraform plan` command, Terraform retrieves the file from that location and compares it to your Terraform settings to see if any adjustments need to be made.

  At the same time, the DynamoDB table locks its current state to prevent data corruption, lost information, and conflicts if any co-workers attempt to modify the infrastructure simultaneously.

- It enables versioning very quickly, saving the state in each change you make.

- AWS provides a different tier for S3 depending on the usage.

To use Amazon S3 for remote state storage, you must first make an S3 bucket, and you can do this in two ways, either with the console, with AWS CLI, or with some Terraform code (which should be run first).

If you choose, for example, to create the bucket using Terraform code, you should run that code first to ensure the bucket is created; otherwise, an error will be generated that the bucket will not exist.

Let's do that. The following are the best practices for creating a Terraform structure (see Figure 6-8):

- `Backend.tf` is responsible for defining the state file remote back end.

- `Main.tf` contains your module's main set of settings; if the file is not created, the state file will be on your local machine.

- `Terraform.tfvars` is used to define the variable, especially if you have a different environment so that you can call the file, for example, `prod.tfvars`, `qa.tfvars`, and so on. This is usually used to define the primary variable that can be changed all the time, and when this file used, this file has precedence over the variable file.

- `Variable.tf` is used as parameters to let us change how our deployments work by putting in values at runtime. In the `main.tf` configuration file, you can set up input variables for Terraform.

- `Version.tf` (optional) is used to define what Terraform version this code will work with. If not mentioned, it will assume you are using the latest version.

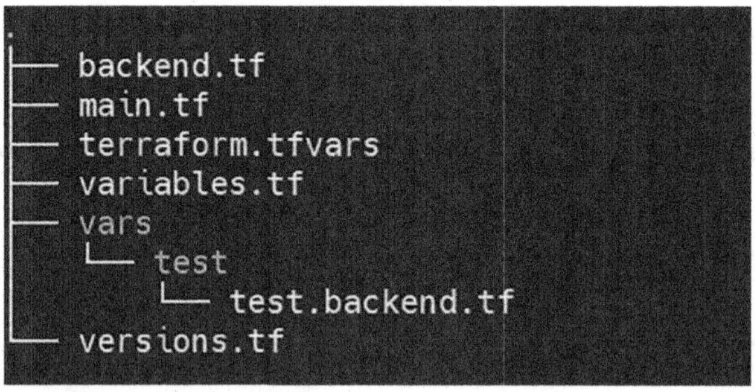

```
├── backend.tf
├── main.tf
├── terraform.tfvars
├── variables.tf
├── vars
│   └── test
│       └── test.backend.tf
└── versions.tf
```

***Figure 6-8.*** *Terraform folder structure*

Let's create our first file, which is `version.tf` or `provider.tf`.

```
1. terraform {
2.     required_version = ">= 0.13.1"
3.
4.     required_providers {
5.       aws = {
6.         source  = "hashicorp/aws"
```

```
7.          version = ">= 3.73"
8.        }
9.      }
10.  }
```

Inside `main.tf`, let's create the bucket. The code will do the following:

- Set up code changes on the S3 bucket so that each time a file in the bucket is changed, a new version of that file is created. The configuration lets you see previous models of the file and go back to them at whatever time, which can be helpful if anything goes wrong.

- Server-side encryption should be turned on for all information published to this S3 bucket. This ensures that your state files and any classified information they hold are always encrypted on an S3 disk.

- Block everyone from getting into the S3 bucket. S3 buckets are private by default.

```
1.   resource "aws_s3_bucket" "terraform_state_file" {
2.     bucket = "terraform-state-file-book-aws"
3.
4.       # Prevent accidental deletion of this S3 bucket
5.       lifecycle {
6.         prevent_destroy = true
7.       }
8.
9.     # Enable bucket versioning.
10.    resource "aws_s3_bucket_versioning" "bucket_version" {
11.      bucket = aws_s3_bucket.terraform_state_file
12.      versioning_configuration {
13.        status = "Enabled"
14.      }
15.   }
16.
17.  # Enable encryption
18. resource "aws_s3_bucket_server_side_encryption_configuration" "bucket-
    encrypt" {
19.      bucket = aws_s3_bucket. terraform_state_file
```

219

```
20.
21.     rule {
22.       apply_server_side_encryption_by_default {
23.         sse_algorithm = "AES256"
24.       }
25.     }
26.
27. # Block public access
28. resource "aws_s3_bucket_public_access_block" "bucket_public_access" {
29.     bucket                  = aws_s3_bucket.terraform_state_file
30.     block_public_acls       = true
31.     block_public_policy     = true
32.     ignore_public_acls      = true
33.     restrict_public_buckets = true
34. }
35.
```

That's it. The Terraform state file will be saved into the bucket as the remote back end. However, what if you want to ensure the lock issue is solved? Then you need to use another AWS service, called DynamoDB.

Amazon's key-value store, DynamoDB, has several copies of its data. It provides the ability to do highly consistent readings and conditional writes, which are the only two operations a distributed lock system requires. It is also inexpensive and fully managed, so you do not need to worry about the underlying infrastructure.

To utilize DynamoDB with Terraform's locking functionality, you must construct a DynamoDB table with the primary key named LockID.

```
1. resource "aws_dynamodb_table" "terraform_locks_file" {
2.     name         = "terraform-locks_table"
3.     billing_mode = "PROVISIONED"
4.     hash_key     = "LockID"
5.
6.     attribute {
7.       name = "LockID"
8.       type = "S"
9.     }
10. }
```

- Billing_mode (optional): How you are paid for read and write throughput and how capacity is managed are under your control, and there are two values: PROVISION, which is the default, or PAY_PER_REQUEST.

- Type (required): Attribute type. Valid values are S (string), N (number), and B (binary).

Now we create most of the resources needed for the bucket and DymanoDB; in case you want that, the next step is to use the Terraform commands. This is not complicated; you will use three commands here, but there are more if you want to do more.

- Terraform init

  After creating a fresh Terraform template or cloning an old one from version control, the first step is to execute this command. It is recommended that you do it immediately.

  This command will conduct multiple initialization stages to get the current working directory ready for usage with Terraform. These procedures can be found in the Terraform documentation. In most circumstances, it is not essential to worry about these specific stages, and more information on them can be found in the following sections.

  It is never dangerous to use this command more than once to bring the working directory up-to-date with modifications made to the configuration. This command will never erase your current settings or state, even though future executions may produce errors.

- Terraform plan

  This command generates an implementation strategy that previews the modifications Terraform will apply to your infrastructure.

  This command is optional as well, but it's important so the DevOps engineer can review what will be deployed or destroyed.

- Terraform apply

  The command will apply and deploy the changes of the new
  infrastructure; once you run the order, you need to confirm again
  by typing yes.

- Terraform destroy

  This eradicates all distant objects handled by a particular
  Terraform setup or state.

To run the previous code, deploy using the terraform apply command, and
then execute terraform init to get the provider code. After everything has been
deployed, you will have an S3 bucket and a DynamoDB table, but the state of your
Terraform configuration will continue to be kept locally. You must add a back-end
setting to your Terraform code to set up Terraform to save the state in your S3 bucket
(while also encrypting and locking the information). Because this is a configuration for
Terraform itself, it must be included inside a terraform block and must adhere to the
following syntax:

```
1. terraform {
2.   backend "s3" {
3.     bucket = "terraform-state-file-book-aws "
4.     key    = "chapter6/terraform-iac/terraform.tfstate"
5.     region = "eu-west-1"
6.
7. # Replace this with your DynamoDB table name!
8.     dynamodb_table = "terraform-locks_table"
9.     encrypt        = true
10.
11.   }
12. }
```

- Bucket: This is the label of the S3 bucket that will be used. Make sure
  you change the ID of the S3 bucket you established previously in the
  process.

- Key: This is the file's location inside the S3 bucket where the
  Terraform state file should be saved when created.

- Region: This is the region inside AWS where the S3 bucket is stored.

- dynamodb_table: This is the DynamoDB table that will be used for the locking operation.

- Encrypt: By setting this to true, you can be sure that the Terraform state you save in S3 will be secured on disk. Since we previously made encryption the default setting for the S3 bucket, this serves as a secondary layer of protection to guarantee that the information is always protected.

The terraform init command is responsible for downloading the provider and setting up the back end, as shown in Figure 6-9.

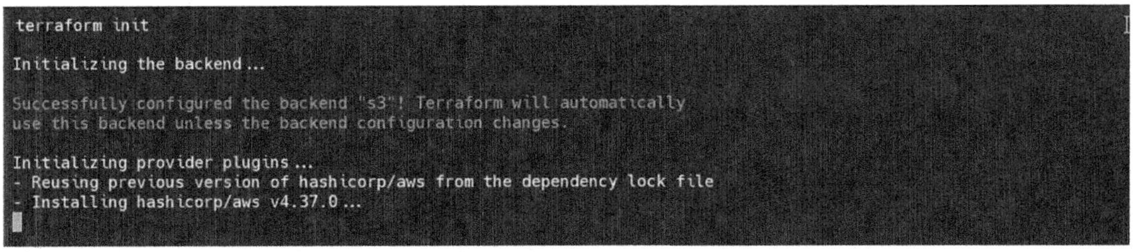

**Figure 6-9.** *Running the terraform init command to install the providers*

This command will take time, depending on how many providers you are using inside your code, but you should be able to see a message like the one in Figure 6-10.

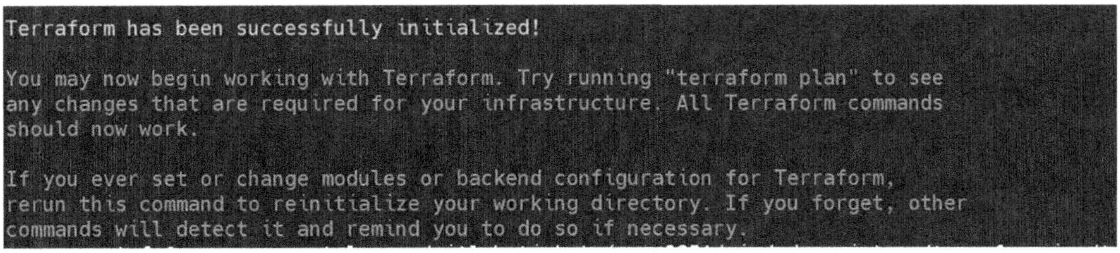

**Figure 6-10.** *Terraform init output*

If you check from the console, you will see the Terraform screen shown in Figure 6-11.

***Figure 6-11.*** *Remote back-end Terraform state*

Sometimes, you need to show some output for the resources, such as database name, public IP address, or private IP address. Terraform allows you to do that with an output, but it's better to do that and configure a file called output.tf.

For example, to show the name of the S3 bucket and DynamoDB that was created earlier, I need a file called output.tf.

```
1. output "s3_bucket_arn" {
2.    value       = aws_s3_bucket.terraform_locks_file.arn
3.    description = "The ARN of the S3 bucket"
4. }
5.
6. output "dynamodb_table_name" {
7.    value       = aws_dynamodb_table.terraform_locks_file.name
8.    description = "The name of the DynamoDB table"
9. }
10.
```

It's hard to cover everything about Terraform in one section, but I gave you the basics of how it works. I also created a different project for Terraform using another cloud provider for free and uploaded it to GitHub (https://Github.com/Osamaoracle). Plus, Chapter 11 includes some complete projects.

Let's look at a straightforward Terraform code example. I share the directory structure in Figure 6-12, which will allow you to understand how it will look at the end. The figure shows how Terraform will be set up.

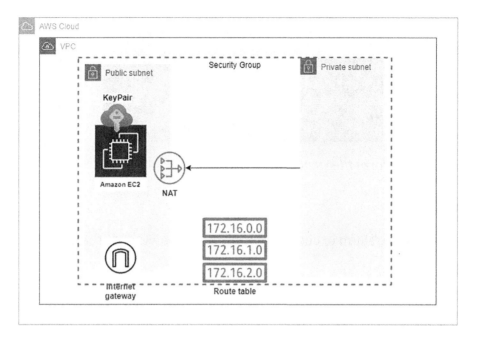

**Figure 6-12.** *Simple Terraform example to set up AWS resources*

- VPC refers to the virtual private network in AWS.

- VPC subnet, in our case, public subnet that will be expose to the Internet.

- We are creating an Internet gateway associated with the VPC.

- There is a route table inside VPC with a route that directs Internet-bound traffic to the IGW.

- Route table association with our subnet to determine where network traffic from your subnet or gateway is directed.

- Security group to provide protection at the port and protocol access levels.

- Key pair used to access the EC2.

- EC2 instance deployed inside the public subnet.

Let's look at a real-world example of Terraform to show how the structure folder works; Figure 6-13 shows the Terraform folder structure.

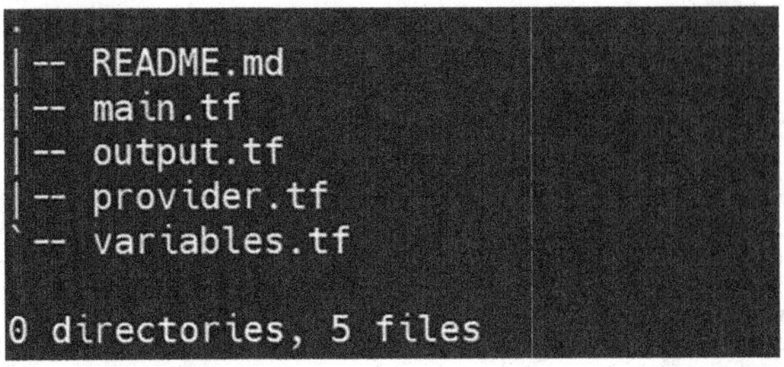

```
| -- README.md
| -- main.tf
| -- output.tf
| -- provider.tf
` -- variables.tf

0 directories, 5 files
```

***Figure 6-13.*** *Terraform file structure*

## The provider.tf

This file will allow Terraform to determine which cloud provider will be used.

```
1. provider "aws" {
2.   access_key = var.access_key
3.   secret_key = var.secret_key
4.   region = var.region
5. }
6.
```

## Variable.tf

In this file, we define the variable used inside our Terraform code to make the code more dynamic.

```
 1. variable "access_key" {
 2.   default = "ACCESS_KEY_HERE"
 3. }
 4. variable "secret_key" {
 5.   default = "SECRET_KEY_HERE"
 6. }
 7. variable "region" {
 8.   default = "us-east-2"
 9. }
10. variable "cidr_vpc" {
11.   description = "CIDR block for the VPC"
12.   default     = "10.1.0.0/16"
13. }
```

```
14. variable "cidr_subnet" {
15.    description = "CIDR block for the subnet"
16.    default     = "10.1.0.0/24"
17. }
18. variable "availability_zone" {
19.    description = "availability zone to create subnet"
20.    default     = "us-east-2a"
21. }
22. variable "public_key_location" {
23.    description = "Public key path"
24.    default     = "~/.ssh/id_rsa.pub"
25. }
26. variable "instance_ami" {
27.    description = "EC2 AMI depends on the region"
28.    default     = "ami-0cf31d971a3ca20d6"
29. }
30. variable "instance_type" {
31.    description = "EC2 Instance type"
32.    default     = "t2.micro"
33. }
34. variable "environment_tag" {
35.    description = "Resource tags"
36.    default     = "Production"
37. }
```

## Main.tf

After creating the variable needed to be used and the provider, this file will call all the necessary resources to be configured inside the AWS console.

```
1. resource "aws_vpc" "vpc" {
2.    cidr_block = var.cidr_vpc
3.    enable_dns_support    = true
4.    enable_dns_hostnames = true
5.    tags = {
```

```
 6.        "Environment" = var.environment_tag
 7.    }
 8. }
 9.
10. resource "aws_internet_gateway" "igw" {
11.    vpc_id = aws_vpc.vpc.id
12.    tags = {
13.        "Environment" = var.environment_tag
14.    }
15. }
16.
17. resource "aws_subnet" "subnet_public" {
18.    vpc_id = aws_vpc.vpc.id
19.    cidr_block = var.cidr_subnet
20.    map_public_ip_on_launch = "true"
21.    availability_zone = var.availability_zone
22.    tags = {
23.        "Environment" = var.environment_tag
24.    }
25. }
26.
27. resource "aws_route_table" "rt_public" {
28.    vpc_id = aws_vpc.vpc.id
29.
30.    route {
31.        cidr_block = "0.0.0.0/0"
32.        gateway_id = aws_internet_gateway.igw.id
33.    }
34.
35.    tags = {
36.        "Environment" = var.environment_tag
37.    }
38. }
39.
40. resource "aws_route_table_association" "rt_subnet_public" {
```

```
41.    subnet_id       = aws_subnet.subnet_public.id
42.    route_table_id = aws_route_table.rt_public.id
43. }
44.
45. resource "aws_security_group" "sg_ssh" {
46.    name = "sg_ssh"
47.    vpc_id = aws_vpc.vpc.id
48.
49.    # SSH access from the VPC
50.    ingress {
51.        from_port    = 22
52.        to_port      = 22
53.        protocol     = "tcp"
54.        cidr_blocks = ["0.0.0.0/0"]
55.    }
56.
57.    egress {
58.      from_port    = 0
59.      to_port      = 0
60.      protocol     = "-1"
61.      cidr_blocks = ["0.0.0.0/0"]
62.    }
63.
64.    tags = {
65.      "Environment" = var.environment_tag
66.    }
67. }
68.
69. resource "aws_key_pair" "ec2ssh" {
70.    key_name = "publicKey"
71.    public_key = file(var.public_key_location)
72. }
73.
74. resource "aws_instance" "test_Instance" {
75.    ami             = var.instance_ami
```

```
76.    instance_type = var.instance_type
77.    subnet_id = aws_subnet.subnet_public.id
78.    vpc_security_group_ids = [aws_security_group.sg_ssh.id]
79.    key_name = aws_key_pair.ec2ssh.key_name
80.
81.    tags = {
82.            "Environment" = var.environment_tag
83.    }
84. }
```

## Output.tf

The last file in our folder structure is output.tf; this file is responsible for showing the needed output for the user, such as the public IP address, DNS, etc.

```
1. output "vpc_id" {
2.    value = "${aws_vpc.vpc.id}"
3. }
4. output "public_subnet" {
5.    value = ["${aws_subnet.subnet_public.id}"]
6. }
7. output "public_rt_ids" {
8.    value = ["${aws_route_table.rt_public.id}"]
9. }
10. output "public_instance_ip" {
11.    value = ["${aws_instance.test_Instance.public_ip}"]
12. }
```

Figure 6-14 shows the command `terraform init` output.

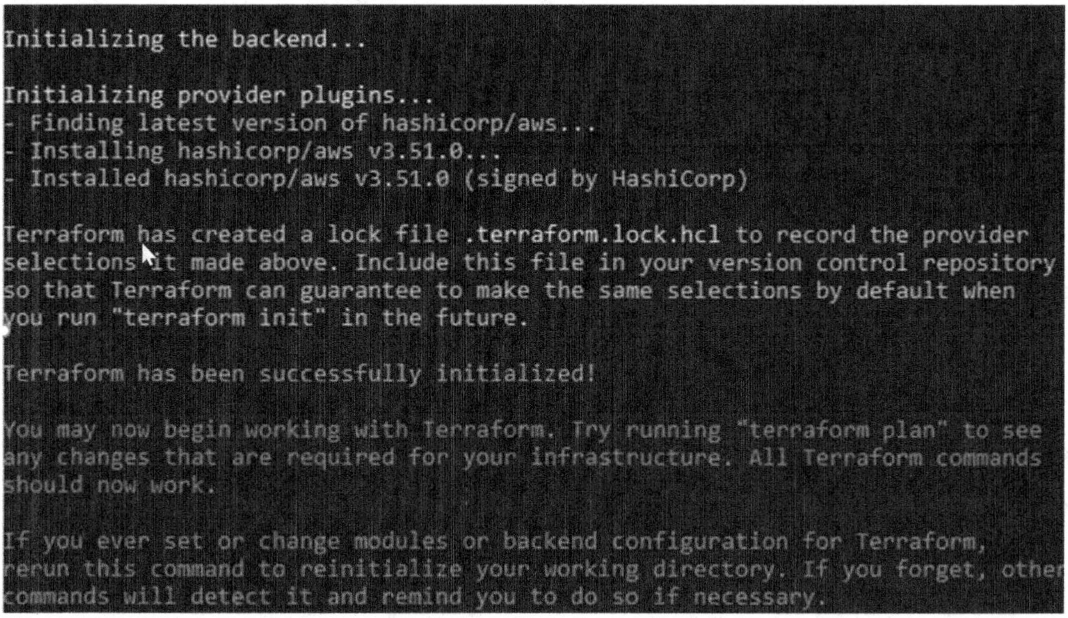

```
Initializing the backend...

Initializing provider plugins...
- Finding latest version of hashicorp/aws...
- Installing hashicorp/aws v3.51.0...
- Installed hashicorp/aws v3.51.0 (signed by HashiCorp)

Terraform has created a lock file .terraform.lock.hcl to record the provider
selections it made above. Include this file in your version control repository
so that Terraform can guarantee to make the same selections by default when
you run "terraform init" in the future.

Terraform has been successfully initialized!

You may now begin working with Terraform. Try running "terraform plan" to see
any changes that are required for your infrastructure. All Terraform commands
should now work.

If you ever set or change modules or backend configuration for Terraform,
rerun this command to reinitialize your working directory. If you forget, other
commands will detect it and remind you to do so if necessary.
```

***Figure 6-14.*** *The terraform init output*

After that, check what Terraform provision is on the AWS cloud. This is considered a critical command every time you deploy or change the configuration Terraform plan; see Figure 6-15.

```
# aws_subnet.publicsubnets will be created
+ resource "aws_subnet" "publicsubnets" {
    + arn                            = (known after apply)
    + assign_ipv6_address_on_creation = false
    + availability_zone              = (known after apply)
    + availability_zone_id           = (known after apply)
    + cidr_block                     = "10.0.0.128/26"
    + id                             = (known after apply)
    + ipv6_cidr_block_association_id = (known after apply)
    + map_public_ip_on_launch        = false
    + owner_id                       = (known after apply)
    + tags_all                       = (known after apply)
    + vpc_id                         = (known after apply)
}

# aws_vpc.Main will be created
+ resource "aws_vpc" "Main" {
    + arn                            = (known after apply)
    + assign_generated_ipv6_cidr_block = false
    + cidr_block                     = "10.0.0.0/24"
    + default_network_acl_id         = (known after apply)
    + default_route_table_id         = (known after apply)
    + default_security_group_id      = (known after apply)
    + dhcp_options_id                = (known after apply)
    + enable_classiclink             = (known after apply)
    + enable_classiclink_dns_support = (known after apply)
    + enable_dns_hostnames           = (known after apply)
    + enable_dns_support             = true
    + id                             = (known after apply)
    + instance_tenancy               = "default"
    + ipv6_association_id            = (known after apply)
    + ipv6_cidr_block                = (known after apply)
    + main_route_table_id            = (known after apply)
    + owner_id                       = (known after apply)
    + tags_all                       = (known after apply)
}
```

*Figure 6-15.*  *Terraform plan output*

# Terraform Module

A Terraform module can be anything that consists of Terraform configuration files stored in a subdirectory; in other words, a module is a pretty straightforward concept. All of the configurations you have created up to this point have, in a technical sense, been modules; however, they are not especially interesting since you deployed them directly. If you apply these configuration on a module, that module is referred to as a *root module.* It would be best if you constructed a reusable module, which is a module that is designed to be utilized inside other modules, to get a proper understanding of what the modules are capable of doing.

Figure 6-16 shows the architecture that will create the following resources using Terraform:

- VPC

    - Subnets

    - Internet gateway

    - NAT gateway

- EC2 instance

- RDS databases

- Security group

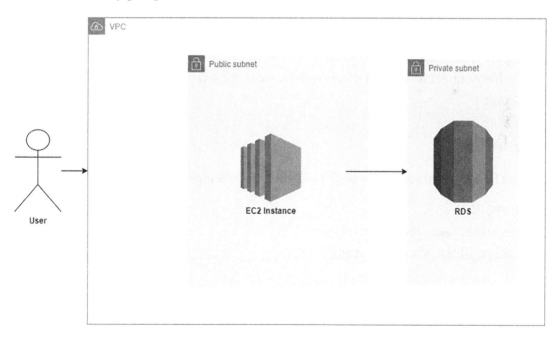

***Figure 6-16.***  *Terraform example architecture*

Figure 6-17 shows how the final folder structure will look.

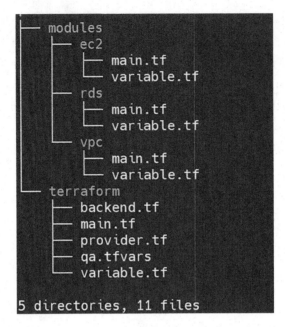

***Figure 6-17.*** *Terraform example folder structure*

VPC has only one route table that links the Internet gateway to the public subnet hosting the EC2 instance.

A private subnet is organized into a single subnet group, each hosting a single RDS server.

## VPC Code

Create a folder called vpc.tf located inside the module directory.

```
1. # VPC
2. resource "aws_vpc" "iac-chapter" {
3.   cidr_block = var.vpc_cidr
4.
5.   enable_dns_support   = var.enable_dns_support
6.   enable_dns_hostnames = var.enable_dns_hostnames
7. }
8. # Internet Gateway
9. resource "aws_internet_gateway" "iac-chapter" {
10.   vpc_id = aws_vpc.iac-chapter.id
11. }
```

234

```
12.
13. # Route Table
14. resource "aws_route_table" "iac-chapter" {
15.   vpc_id = aws_vpc.iac-chapter.id
16.
17.   dynamic "route" {
18.     for_each = var.route
19.
20.     content {
21.       cidr_block     = route.value.cidr_block
22.       gateway_id     = route.value.gateway_id
23.       instance_id    = route.value.instance_id
24.       nat_gateway_id = route.value.nat_gateway_id
25.     }
26.   }
27. }
28.
29. # associate route table with subnet.
30. resource "aws_route_table_association" "iac-chapter" {
31.   count          = length(var.subnet_ids)
32.
33.   subnet_id      = element(var.subnet_ids, count.index)
34.   route_table_id = aws_route_table.iac-chapter.id
35. }
36.
```

# EC2

To initiate the creation of the EC2 instance, all that is required is to configure the machine we want and position it inside the subnet containing our route table.

- An instance of AWS EC2

- In conjunction with an elastic IP address being attached to that instance

- A public-private key pair, also known as a PEM key, to use when connecting to the model via SSH

```
1. locals {
2.   resource_name_prefix = "${var.namespace}-${var.resource_tag_name}"
3. }
4.
5. resource "aws_instance" "iac-chapter" {
6.   ami                         = var.ami
7.   instance_type               = var.instance_type
8.   user_data                   = var.user_data
9.   subnet_id                   = var.subnet_id
10.   associate_public_ip_address = var.associate_public_ip_address
11.   key_name                    = aws_key_pair.iac-chapter.key_name
12.   vpc_security_group_ids      = var.vpc_security_group_ids
13.
14.   iam_instance_profile = var.iam_instance_profile
15. }
16.
17. resource "aws_eip" "iac-chapter" {
18.   vpc      = true
19.   instance = aws_instance.iac-chapter.id
20. }
21.
22. resource "tls_private_key" "iac-chapter" {
23.   algorithm = "RSA"
24.   rsa_bits  = 4096
25. }
26.
27. resource "aws_key_pair" "iac-chapter" {
28.   key_name   = var.key_name
29.   public_key = tls_private_key.iac-chapter.public_key_openssh
30. }
31.
```

# EC2 Security Group

A security group acts like a firewall, controlling the network that goes in (ingress) and out (egress) of your network.

*Ingress* can describe either the act of coming or an entrance. The term *egress* represents either the act of leaving or a physical door or window that allows one to do so.

We permit traffic to enter our network via ports 22 (SSH), 80 (HTTP), and 443 (HTTPS), and we let all traffic leave our network through all ports. To make this even more secure, you should profile your application's ports for outgoing traffic.

```
1.  resource "aws_security_group" "ec2" {
2.    name = "${local.resource_name_prefix}-ec2-sg"
3.
4.    description = "EC2 security group (terraform-managed)"
5.    vpc_id      = module.vpc.id
6.
7.    ingress {
8.      from_port   = var.rds_port
9.      to_port     = var.rds_port
10.     protocol    = "tcp"
11.     description = "MySQL"
12.     cidr_blocks = local.rds_cidr_blocks
13.   }
14.
15.   ingress {
16.     from_port   = 22
17.     to_port     = 22
18.     protocol    = "tcp"
19.     description = "Telnet"
20.     cidr_blocks = ["0.0.0.0/0"]
21.   }
22.
23.   ingress {
24.     from_port   = 80
25.     to_port     = 80
26.     protocol    = "tcp"
```

```
27.      description = "HTTP"
28.      cidr_blocks = ["0.0.0.0/0"]
29.    }
30.
31.    ingress {
32.      from_port   = 443
33.      to_port     = 443
34.      protocol    = "tcp"
35.      description = "HTTPS"
36.      cidr_blocks = ["0.0.0.0/0"]
37.    }
38.
39.    # Allow all outbound traffic.
40.    egress {
41.      from_port   = 0
42.      to_port     = 0
43.      protocol    = "-1"
44.      cidr_blocks = ["0.0.0.0/0"]
45.    }
46. }
47.
```

# RDS

Now, it's time to set up the database; in my case, I chose MySQL.

```
1. locals {
2.    resource_name_prefix = "${var.namespace}-${var.resource_tag_name}"
3. }
4.
5. resource "aws_db_subnet_group" "iac-chapter" {
6.    name        = "${local.resource_name_prefix}-${var.identifier}-
      subnet-group"
7.    subnet_ids = var.subnet_ids
8. }
9.
```

```
10. resource "aws_db_instance" "iac-chapter" {
11.    identifier = "${local.resource_name_prefix}-${var.identifier}"
12.
13.    allocated_storage       = var.allocated_storage
14.    backup_retention_period = var.backup_retention_period
15.    backup_window           = var.backup_window
16.    maintenance_window      = var.maintenance_window
17.    db_subnet_group_name    = aws_db_subnet_group.iac-chapter.id
18.    engine                  = var.engine
19.    engine_version          = var.engine_version
20.    instance_class          = var.instance_class
21.    multi_az                = var.multi_az
22.    name                    = var.name
23.    username                = var.username
24.    password                = var.password
25.    port                    = var.port
26.    publicly_accessible     = var.publicly_accessible
27.    storage_encrypted       = var.storage_encrypted
28.    storage_type            = var.storage_type
29.
30.    vpc_security_group_ids = ["${aws_security_group.iac-chapter.id}"]
31.
32.    allow_major_version_upgrade = var.allow_major_version_upgrade
33.    auto_minor_version_upgrade  = var.auto_minor_version_upgrade
34.
35.    final_snapshot_identifier = var.final_snapshot_identifier
36.    snapshot_identifier       = var.snapshot_identifier
37.    skip_final_snapshot       = var.skip_final_snapshot
38.
39.    performance_insights_enabled = var.performance_insights_enabled
40. }
41.
```

As you can see from the previous code, different variables need to be filled in by DevOps, such as the username, password, instance type, name of the instance, and storage.

To make our job much easier in the future, we will create `qa.tfvars`. Depending on the environment name, which contains the primary variable used by the RDS, the file will allow DevOps to change database settings easily.

```
1.  # RDS
2.  rds_identifier        = "mysql"
3.  rds_engine            = "mysql"
4.  rds_engine_version    = "8.0.15"
5.  rds_instance_class    = "db.t2.micro"
6.  rds_allocated_storage = 10
7.  rds_storage_encrypted = false
8.  rds_name              = ""
9.  rds_username          = "admin"
10. rds_port                    = 3306
11. rds_maintenance_window      = "Sun:05:00-Fri:06:00"
12. rds_backup_window           = "12:46-13:16"
13. rds_backup_retention_period = 1
14. rds_publicly_accessible     = false
15. rds_final_snapshot_identifier = "db-snapshot"
16. rds_snapshot_identifier       = null
17. rds_performance_insights_enabled  = true
```

## RDS Security Group

A security group opens the MySQL port for incoming connections.

```
1.  resource "aws_security_group" "db-sg" {
2.    name = "${local.resource_name_prefix}-rds-sg"
3.
4.    description = "RDS (terraform-managed)"
5.    vpc_id      = var.rds_vpc_id
6.
7.    ingress {
8.      from_port  = var.port
9.      to_port    = var.port
10.     protocol   = "tcp"
```

```
11.     cidr_blocks = var.sg_ingress_cidr_block
12.   }
13.
14.   # Allow all outbound traffic.
15.   egress {
16.     from_port   = 0
17.     to_port     = 0
18.     protocol    = "-1"
19.     cidr_blocks = var.sg_egress_cidr_block
20.   }
21. }
```

Now, we create the module folders, which include all our main code, but we need to call this code. We will call the module inside another directory, as mentioned in Figure 6-13.

main.tf will look like the following:

```
1. module "vpc" {
2.   source = "../../modules/vpc"
3.
4.   resource_tag_name = var.resource_tag_name
5.   namespace         = var.namespace
6.   region            = var.region
7.
8.   vpc_cidr = "10.0.0.0/16"
9.
10.   route = [
11.     {
12.       cidr_block     = "0.0.0.0/0"
13.       gateway_id     = module.vpc.gateway_id
14.       instance_id    = null
15.       nat_gateway_id = null
16.     }
17.   ]
18.
19.   subnet_ids = module.subnet_ec2.ids
20. }
```

```
21.
22.
23. module "ec2" {
24.   source = "../../modules/ec2"
25.
26.   resource_tag_name = var.resource_tag_name
27.   namespace         = var.namespace
28.   region            = var.region
29.
30.   ami           = "ami-1212sdasdas" # Choose ami depends on the region
31.   key_name      = "${local.resource_name_prefix}-ec2-key"
32.   instance_type = var.instance_type
33.   subnet_id     = module.subnet_ec2.ids[0]
34.
35.   vpc_security_group_ids = [aws_security_group.ec2.id]
36.
37.   vpc_id = module.vpc.id
38. }
```

# Terraform Tips and Tricks

As with any other language, Terraform supplies some basic building blocks to help the
DevOps engineer write the best code for the IaC; we will discuss the following in this
section:

- Loops

- Conditionals

- Zero-downtime deployment

# Loops

Terraform provides several distinct looping constructs, each of which is designed to
be used in a somewhat unique circumstance.

- Count: This parameter will be used to loop the resource; for example, if you want to create 10 EC2 instances, it does not make sense to repeat the code 10 times, so we use the `count` parameter to avoid this.

- For_each: This can be used in the same way as shown earlier.

- For: This is usually used to loop with the list and map variable.

I will give a short example to show the power of Terraform loops.

```
1. resource "aws_instance" "web-ec2" {
2.    count = 2 # generate two similar EC2 instances
3.    ami           = "ami-134324321"
4.    instance_type = "t2.medium"
5.    tags = {
6.      Name = "web-ec2-${count.index}"
7.      Owner = "Osama"
8.    }
9. }
```

This will create two similar EC2 instances, which for some resources can be an issue like the following:

```
1. resource "aws_iam_user" "count_example" {
2.    count = 2
3.    name  = "Osama" }
4.
```

All three users of IAM would have the same name, which would result in an error since the usernames are supposed to be different.

To solve this, we need to use an index, which will create a unique IAM like the following:

```
1. resource "aws_iam_user" " count_example " {
2.    count = 2
3.    name  = "Osama.${count.index}"
4. }
```

For_each works in a different way, which is usually used by mapping and listing variables, and if you don't do that, the error will be clear like the following:

The given "for_each" argument value is unsuitable: the "for_each" argument must be a map, or set of strings, and you have provided a value of type tuple.

To use the previous example with for_each, I need to define an array like the one shown here:

```
1. locals {
2.    IAM_USER_NAME = {
3.      "Osama"              = "Chapter_6"
4.      "Amazon"             = "AWS"
5.      "Test"               = "working"
6.    }
7. }
```

After that, I can create this as follows:

```
1. resource "aws_iam_user" "examples" {
2.    for_each = local.IAM_USER_NAME
3.    triggers = {
4.      name   = each.key
5.      Middle = each.value
6.    }
7. }
```

There are lots of uses for the loop conditions in Terraform. Still, to explain it entirely, I probably need another chapter to do that, so I tried to show the power of looping in Terraform and how to take advantage of it to make your code follow best practices and make it easy to understand.

## Conditionals

Terraform has several distinct options for making loops. It also provides many specific opportunities for performing conditionals; each option is designed for use in a somewhat different setting.

- Count parameter: Can be used for conditional statements

- For_each: Can be used for conditional statements and within the inline blocks

- If statement: The conditional statement

Let's assume I want to enable EC2 autoscaling, but depending on the situation and variable being set, this can be done by using a conditional statement like the following example.

In the first step, you need to define the Boolean variable.

```
1. variable "autoscaling_example" {
2.    description = "If set to true, enable auto-scaling"
3.    type        = bool
4. }
```

Inside the Terraform code, my code will look like the following one:

```
 1. resource "aws_autoscaling_schedule" "scaling-ec2-out" {
 2.    count = var.autoscaling_example ? 1 : 0
 3.
 4.    scheduled_action_name  = "${var.cluster_name}-scaling-ec2"
 5.    min_size               = 2
 6.    max_size               = 5
 7.    desired_capacity       = 5
 8.    recurrence             = "0 5 * * *"
 9.    autoscaling_group_name = aws_autoscaling_group.example.name
10. }
11.
12. resource "aws_autoscaling_schedule" "scaling-ec2-in" {
13.    count = var.enable_autoscaling ? 1 : 0
14.
15.    scheduled_action_name  = "${var.cluster_name}-scaling-ec2-in"
16.    min_size               = 2
17.    max_size               = 5
18.    desired_capacity       = 2
19.    recurrence             = "0 23 * * *"
```

```
20.    autoscaling_group_name = aws_autoscaling_group.example.name
21. }
22.
```

What is happening in the example? To explain, the count parameter for each AWS autoscaling schedule resource will have a value of 1 assigned to it if var.autoscaling_ example is configured to be true.

This will result in the creation of one instance of each resource. If var.autoscaling_ example is false, the count parameter for each AWS autoscaling schedule resource will be set to 0, meaning that none will be produced.

# AWS CloudFormation

Each cloud provider has its own built-in IaC, allowing the customer to use it if they want to deploy it to that cloud and try to make it as easy as possible.

CloudFormation is a service offered by Amazon Web Services that helps simplify constructing AWS infrastructure using template files. AWS supplies CloudFormation; you can automate the setup of workloads run on the most common AWS services using CloudFormation.

The lack of code for CloudFormation templates written in YAML is an understatement. They usually include chunks of complicated programs as well as JSON specifications. The idea of having a template is moot since they are often encoded via string processing instructions.

To understand CloudFormation more, let's see the advantage and disadvantages, starting with the advantages.

- A different template is already available from AWS and can be used.

- It is easy to use with Amazon AWS.

- If you build the AWS infrastructure manual, a tool can convert the infrastructure to CF templates.

- It can be integrated with CI/CD.

- YAML is widely used, so it's always good to learn it.

**Disadvantages**

The following are the disadvantages:

- There is a lack of instructions on maintaining a clean and clear code base for CloudFormation.

- It's not the best tool to use to avoid security threats.

- The CloudFormation community is not robust.

- It's hard to troubleshoot the broken code, especially if it's a lot of code.

- Sometimes the stack will get stuck without displaying an error, and it will continue to be stuck until it fails.

- It might be a long process to generate and update content. Sometimes the deletion operation fails, and you must do it by hand.

In my case, I prefer YAML for a different reason; as DevOps engineers, YAML is widely used, and we learn it technically by learning another tool implicitly such as Ansible or a Kubernetes manifest.

To understand it more, let's take a look at the following example, which is creating a VPC:

- Route table

- Two private subnets

```
1. Parameters:
2.   Tag:
3.     Type: String
4.
5. Resources:
6.   VPC:
7.     Type: "AWS::EC2::VPC"
8.     Properties:
9.       CidrBlock: "10.0.0.0/16"
10.      Tags:
11.      - Key: "Name"
12.        Value: !Ref "Tag"
```

```
13.
14.    privatesubnet1:
15.      Type: "AWS::EC2::Subnet"
16.      Properties:
17.        AvailabilityZone: !Select
18.          - 0
19.          - !GetAZs
20.              Ref: 'AWS::Region'
21.        VpcId: !Ref "VPC"
22.        CidrBlock: "10.0.0.0/24"
23.
24.    privatesubnet2:
25.      Type: "AWS::EC2::Subnet"
26.      Properties:
27.        AvailabilityZone: !Select
28.          - 1
29.          - !GetAZs
30.              Ref: 'AWS::Region'
31.        VpcId: !Ref "VPC"
32.        CidrBlock: "10.0.1.0/24"
33.
34.    RouteTable:
35.      Type: "AWS::EC2::RouteTable"
36.      Properties:
37.        VpcId: !Ref "VPC"
38.
39. Outputs:
40.   VpcId:
41.     Description: The VPC ID
42.     Value: !Ref VPC
```

The previous code is a sample of CloudFormation; the VPC name will depend on the tag, as you can see from the following section:

```
1. Parameters:
2.   Tag:
3.     Type: String
```

We have two different CICR sections, which will create two private subnets. The first will be 10.0.0.0/24, and the second will be 10.0.1.0/24.

Finally, to connect these to subnets, we need to define the routing table, which allows connectivity between them.

```
1.   RouteTable:
2.     Type: "AWS::EC2::RouteTable"
3.     Properties:
4.       VpcId: !Ref "VPC"
```

The last section will show the VPC ID after creation; another example of CloudFormation will show you how to create the EC2 instance. Notice that if the code gets longer, it will be hard to troubleshoot if you have an issue.

```
1.  ---
2.  AWSTemplateFormatVersion: '2022-12-16'
3.  Description: A simple example for EC2.
4.  Parameters:
5.    VpcId:
6.      Type: String
7.    SubnetId:
8.      Type: String
9.    InstanceName:
10.     Type: String
11.   allowsshcidr:
12.     Type: String
13.     Description: additional security layer to allow certain IP
        for ssh.
14.     MinLength: '7'
15.     MaxLength: '20'
```

```
16.      AllowedPattern: "(\\d{1,3})\\.(\\d{1,3})\\.(\\d{1,3})\\.
         (\\d{1,3})/(\\d{1,2})"
17.   InstanceType:
18.      Description: EC2 instance type
19.      Type: String
20.      Default: t2.micro
21.      AllowedValues:
22.      - t2.nano
23.      - t2.micro
24.      - t2.small
25.      - t2.medium
26.      - t2.large
27.      - m4.large
28.      - m4.xlarge
29.      - m4.2xlarge
30.      - m4.4xlarge
31.      - m4.10xlarge
32.      - m3.medium
33.      - m3.large
34.      - m3.xlarge
35.      - m3.2xlarge
36.      - c4.large
37.      - c4.xlarge
38.      - c4.2xlarge
39.      - c4.4xlarge
40.      - c4.8xlarge
41.      - c3.large
42.      - c3.xlarge
43.      - c3.2xlarge
44.      - c3.4xlarge
45.      - c3.8xlarge
46.      ConstraintDescription: choose from the list above
47.   KeyName:
48.      Description: SSH Key pair
49.      Type: AWS::EC2::KeyPair::KeyName
```

```
50.      ConstraintDescription: the name of the key-pair
51. Mappings:
52.   AMI2RegionMap:
53.     eu-west-1:
54.       '64': ami-1234453
55.     eu-central-1:
56.       '64': ami-1312312
57. Resources:
58.
59.   InstanceProfile:
60.     Type: AWS::IAM::InstanceProfile
61.     Properties:
62.       Path: "/"
63.       Roles:
64.       - Ref: InstanceIAMRole
65.   InstanceIAMRole:
66.     Type: AWS::IAM::Role
67.     Properties:
68.       AssumeRolePolicyDocument:
69.         Version: '2022-12-16'
70.         Statement:
71.         - Effect: Allow
72.           Principal:
73.             Service:
74.             - ec2.amazonaws.com
75.           Action:
76.           - sts:AssumeRole
77.       Path: "/"
78.       Policies:
79.       - PolicyName: s3
80.         PolicyDocument:
81.           Version: '2022-12-16'
82.           Statement:
83.           - Effect: Allow
84.             Action:
```

```
85.                - s3:*
86.             Resource:
87.             - Fn::Join:
88.                 -"
89.                 - - 'arn:aws:s3:::'
90.                     - "*"
91.    AutoScalingGroup:
92.      Type: AWS::AutoScaling::AutoScalingGroup
93.      Properties:
94.        Tags:
95.        - Key: Name
96.          Value:
97.            !Ref InstanceName
98.          PropagateAtLaunch: 'true'
99.        LaunchConfigurationName:
100.           Ref: LaunchConfiguration
101.        MinSize: 1
102.        MaxSize: 2
103.        VPCZoneIdentifier:
104.          - !Ref SubnetId
105.   LaunchConfiguration:
106.     Type: AWS::AutoScaling::LaunchConfiguration
107.     Properties:
108.       IamInstanceProfile: !Ref InstanceProfile
109.       KeyName:
110.         Ref: KeyName
111.       ImageId:
112.         Fn::FindInMap:
113.         - AMI2RegionMap
114.         - Ref: AWS::Region
115.         - '64'
116.       SecurityGroups:
117.       - Ref: InstanceSecurityGroup
118.       - Ref: SSHSecurityGroup
119.       InstanceType:
```

```
120.          Ref: InstanceType
121.        UserData:
122.          Fn::Base64:
123.            !Sub |
124.              #!/bin/bash -x
125.              apt-get update
126.              apt-get install --yes awscli
127.    InstanceSecurityGroup:
128.      Type: AWS::EC2::SecurityGroup
129.      Properties:
130.        VpcId:
131.          !Ref VpcId
132.        GroupDescription: Enable HTTP and HTTPS
133.        SecurityGroupIngress:
134.        - IpProtocol: tcp
135.          FromPort: '80'
136.          ToPort: '80'
137.          CidrIp: 0.0.0.0/0
138.        - IpProtocol: tcp
139.          FromPort: '443'
140.          ToPort: '443'
141.          CidrIp: 0.0.0.0/0
142.
143.    SSHSecurityGroup:
144.      Type: AWS::EC2::SecurityGroup
145.      Properties:
146.        VpcId:
147.          !Ref VpcId
148.        GroupDescription: SSH and HTTP enabled
149.        SecurityGroupIngress:
150.        - IpProtocol: tcp
151.          FromPort: '22'
152.          ToPort: '22'
153.          CidrIp:
154.            Ref: allowsshcidr
```

```
155. Outputs:
156.    InstanceSecurityGroup:
157.       Description: ec2-Security-group
158.       Value:
159.          Fn::GetAtt:
160.             - InstanceSecurityGroup
161.             - GroupId
162.
```

The previous code will create a security group that allows SSH, HTTP, and HTTPS plus EC2. We define the EC2 instance type so the user can choose from the list instead of guessing. This EC2 instance will be attached to the IAM role that allows the user to check the S3 services.

# Pulumi

Pulumi is a cutting-edge platform for managing infrastructure as code. Connecting with cloud resources via the Pulumi Software Development Kit (SDK) uses pre-existing programming languages and their respective native ecosystems, such as TypeScript, JavaScript, Python, Go, .NET, Java, and markup languages like YAML. A command-line interface (CLI) that can be downloaded, a runtime environment, modules, and a managed service all collaborate to provide a powerful method of creating, updating, and maintaining cloud infrastructure.

Figure 6-18 shows the purpose of Pulumi; like any other IaC tool, each project will have different resources, and the same code will be used to deploy to different environments such as production, QA, and UAT.

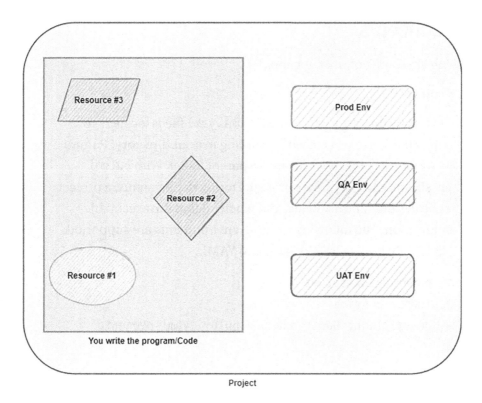

***Figure 6-18.*** *Pulumi*

Pulumi programs deployed using a programming language create and specify your desired cloud infrastructure's architecture. You are allocating resource objects whose characteristics match your infrastructure's intended state, which allows you to define new infrastructure in your application. These attributes are exposed externally to the stack and are used internally to manage dependencies between resources.

A project is a directory containing the program's source code and information about how to launch the application. To compile your code, use the `pulumi up` command from the Pulumi CLI. A stack is a stand-alone instance of your application that can be customized with the help of this command. Stacks can be considered analogous to the various deployment environments when testing and releasing software updates. For instance, you can build and test against separate stacks for development, staging, and production.

# Pulumi Concepts

The following are some Pulumi concepts:

- **Project**

  This is any directory where the `Pulumi.yaml` file is located. To detect the active project while working in a subdirectory, Pulumi looks for a `Pulumi.yaml` file in the parent folder. With `pulumi fresh`, you can start a new project. During deployments, a project indicates the runtime to use and where to find the executable application. The following runtime environments are supported: NodeJs, Python, .NET, Go, Java, and YAML.

  ```
  1. name: Nginx-server
  2. runtime: Nginx
  3. description: Basic example pulumi.yaml project.
  4.
  ```

- **Stacks**

  When you deploy anything using Pulumi, you deploy it to the stack; stacks in Pulumi are individual instances of programs that may be customized separately.

  For example, to create a stack for production, just run the following command:

```
1.  pulumi stack init staging
```

And to list the stack in Pulumi, use this:

```
1. pulumi stack ls
```

The output for the listing will be like the following one:

```
1. NAME                      LAST UPDATE      RESOURCE COUNT
2. Development               1 hour ago       70
3. production               6 hours ago      150
4. UAT                      3 weeks ago       90
```

# Resources

Any cloud resources such as compute instances, storage buckets, and Kubernetes clusters are all examples of resources, and there are two different types.

- *Custom resource*: This is a resource managed by the cloud provider such as AWS, Azure, and GCP.

- *Component resource*: For example, a VPC in AWS, with Pulumi, has a built-in module to follow the best practice.

# State and Back Ends

Like any other IaC, the state is the metadata to allow the tools to be deployed through it. The state is how Pulumi understands when and how to generate, read, delete, or update cloud resources, and each stack has its state.

Having a back end that you control yourself, just run the following command:

1. `pulumi login`

This disconnects you from the current back end.

1. `pulumi logout`

Because of this, all other stack or state operations will need a new login since all credentials data will be removed from `/.pulumi/credentials.json`.

Provide the URL for the desired back end to access it.

1. `pulumi login s3://<bucket-name> # General Syntax how to store backend in s3`
2. `pulumi login 's3://chapter6-bucket-Osama?region=eu-west-1&awssdk=v2&prof`
   `ile=AWS-book'`

# Inputs and Outputs

You can tell by the name what the files are used for. Input allows a raw value of the specified type (such as string, integer, Boolean, list, map, and so on), and output reads from another source.

### Pulumi Example

I prefer Python since it's easy to learn and has all the modules you need, so I will create an S3 bucket in this example.

Pulumi.yaml

```
1. name: aws-s3-bucket
2. runtime:
3.    name: Python
4.    options:
5.       virtualenv: venv
6. description: this is the pulumi s3 IaC
```

Save the code in __main__.py, the top-level code environment in Python. The following example will create a bucket called s3-chapter-bucket; define a policy for that bucket as read-only.

```
1. import json
2. import mimetypes
3. import os
4.
5. from pulumi import export, FileAsset
6. from pulumi_aws import s3
7.
8. web_bucket = s3.Bucket('s3-chapter-6-bucket',
9.     website=s3.BucketWebsiteArgs(
10.         index_document= "index.html",
11.     ))
12.
13. content_dir = "www"
14. for file in os.listdir(content_dir):
15.     filepath = os.path.join(content_dir, file)
16.     mime_type, _ = mimetypes.guess_type(filepath)
17.     obj = s3.BucketObject(file,
18.         bucket=web_bucket.id,
19.         source=FileAsset(filepath),
20.         content_type=mime_type)
21.
```

```
22. def public_read_policy_for_bucket(bucket_name):
23.     return json.dumps({
24. "Version": "2012-10-17",
25. "Statement": [{
26. "Effect": "Allow",
27. "Principal": "*",
28. "Action": [
29.                 "s3:GetObject"
30.             ],
31. "Resource": [
32.                 f"arn:aws:s3:::{bucket_name}/*",
33.             ]
34.         }]
35.     })
36.
37. bucket_name = web_bucket.id
38. bucket_policy = s3.BucketPolicy("bucket-policy",
39.     bucket=bucket_name,
40.     policy=bucket_name.apply(public_read_policy_for_bucket))
41.
42. # Export the name of the bucket
43. export('bucket_name', web_bucket.id)
44. export('website_url', web_bucket.website_endpoint)
45.
```

As you can see, each IaC tool has advantages and disadvantages, but in the end, they each will lead to automation and infrastructure as code.

The tools can even be mixed. Some companies don't like sticking to one IaC, so they try to combine Terraform, CloudFormation, Pulumi, or Ansible, but you decide which one you want to learn and use.

Table 6-4 compares Terraform, CloudFormation, and Pulumi to each other.

*Table 6-4.* *Comparisons*

| Factor | Terraform | CloudFormation | Pulumi |
|---|---|---|---|
| Version | Open-source and enterprise versions | Available only when you use AWS | Open-source and enterprise versions |
| Language | HCL | YAML or JSON | Python, Java, Node.js, and .NET |
| Role-based access control | No | Yes | No |
| User interface | Yes, third-party solution | Yes | No |
| Community | Massive | Not good | Not good |
| Multicloud provider | Yes | No | Yes |
| Integration with other cloud tools | Yes | No | Yes |

# Ansible

Ansible is similar to Puppet or Chef but simpler to use than any other configuration management tool.

Ansible is a tool that can be used for different purposes; imagine a scenario where you have 10 databases and have been asked to upgrade or patch them. Or say you want to install an application on a different operating system or server, create users, install packages, and more. Ansible will automate this by writing a custom playbook. Ansible is also an easy tool to learn; it already has predefined modules that will make your life easier.

Figure 6-19 shows the high-level design of how Ansible works and its benefits; the DevOps engineer has been requested to install Nginx on three servers, and they already created a playbook called, for example, `webserver-Nginx.yaml`, which will be responsible for doing the following:

1. Install NGINX.

2. Generate an NGINX configuration file.

3. Launch the service using NGINX.

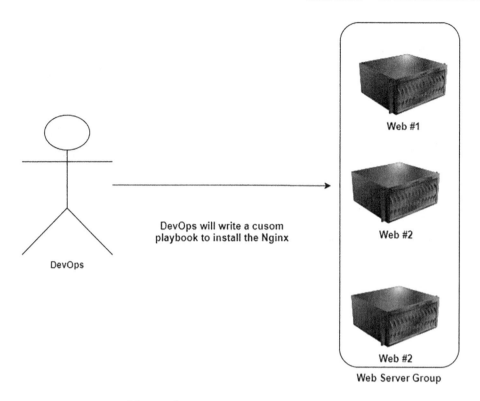

**Figure 6-19.** *How Ansible works*

Ansible will simultaneously establish SSH connections to servers in parallel. After that, it will simultaneously carry out the first job on the list across all three hosts.

Note the following:

- Each job is executed simultaneously across all hosts when using Ansible.

- Before continuing to the next job, Ansible waits until all hosts have finished the previous task.

- Ansible will perform the functions in the sequence that you specify for them.

Ansible is only one of numerous open-source configuration management technologies available; why should one use it instead of another? I will give different reasons.

- *Easy to learn and use*: Ansible's developers intended for it to be easily installed with no learning curve.

261

- *Almost nothing to install on the remote server*: Ansible server management requires SSH and Python on Linux servers and WinRM on Windows systems. Since Ansible for Windows utilizes PowerShell rather than Python, no prerequisite host software installation is required.

- *Predefined modules*: Ansible has predefined modules that make your life much easier.

- *Compatibility*: Ansible is compatible with various packaging, database, cloud, notification, monitor tools, etc.

Figure 6-20 shows how to connect to your nodes. Ansible then distributes little programs (known as *Ansible modules*) to them. After that, Ansible will run these modules (through SSH by default) and then delete them when done. You can store your modules on your computer; no servers, daemons, or databases are necessary.

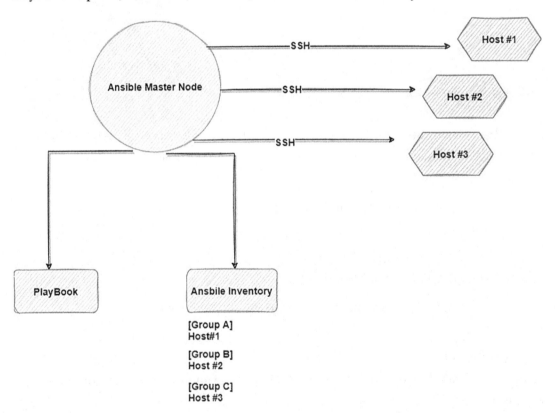

***Figure 6-20.*** *How Ansible works*

CHAPTER 6    INFRASTRUCTURE AS CODE

Python is used to develop Ansible and runs on Linux, macOS, and BSD. As long as Python is present on Linux, macOS, and BSD systems and PowerShell is present on Windows PCs, you can use it to target any method you choose. Therefore, it is recommended that you set up Ansible on your machine. You should use Python 3.8 on the computer where Ansible is installed.

Installation is pretty simple and doesn't need extra configuration from your side. You can install it in different ways.

## RHEL/CentOS Linux

1. `sudo yum install ansible`

## Debian/Ubuntu Linux

1. `sudo apt-get install software-properties-common`
2. `sudo apt-add-repository ppa:ansible/ansible`
3. `sudo apt-get update`
4. `sudo apt-get install ansible`

Install Ansible using `pip` as follows:

1. `sudo pip install ansible`

Or the last option is to install it from the source (GitHub):

1. `git clone git://github.com/ansible/ansible.git`
2. `cd ./ansible`
3. `source ./hacking/env-setup`

To work with Ansible, you need to understand these concepts:

- *Ansible inventory*: This is a file located under `/etc/ansible/hosts`, where you define the servers you want the master to communicate with. It makes your life much easier and allows a playbook's file to specify the hosts and host groups that will be used to execute the playbook's commands, modules, and tasks. According to your Ansible setup and installed plugins, the file might be in various forms.

- *Playbook*: This is a file written by YAML, and it allows you to configure and customize what you need to do with the tool, which is the instruction of what the tool will do and need to implement.

- *Facts*: This refers to the data Ansible will get from the hosts it manages throughout execution. The scripts may then make use of those variables. Data includes everything about a host you require, including its IP address, network interface card (NIC), devices, and so on.

- *Roles*: These are reusable organizational units that facilitate the distribution of automation code between users.

- *Modules*: You can store your modules on your computer; no servers, daemons, or databases are necessary. Generally, you'll need a text editor, a terminal application, and a version control system to keep track of the many iterations of your work.

- *Security*: Ansible can be used with passwords, although SSH keys and ssh-agent are among the most secure options. However, Kerberos may also be used successfully. There are multiple choices! Rather than using the root account, you can join using any other user and switch identities using su or sudo.

- *CLI*: The so-called ad hoc command-line utility is available for usage. This utility will let you manage OS users across numerous servers with a single command line.

Let's talk about the ad hoc commands and their purpose. When it comes to seldom-used tasks, ad hoc commands shine. To turn off all the lab equipment before a holiday, for instance, a simple one-liner in Ansible would suffice; no playbook would be necessary.

Here is how to reboot the server

1. `ansible group-web-server -a "/sbin/reboot"`

   - Here, `group-web-server` is a group. We defined it inside the Ansible inventory to indicate to the web server, and maybe it has 10 servers or more.

   - `/sbin/reboot` is the Linux command.

Here is how to get the uptime for a group of servers:

1. ```
ansible all -m shell -a uptime
```

Here is how to get the disk size:

1. ```
ansible all -m shell -a df -h
```

You need to understand that covering these tools in one chapter is a tough job; each one needs a book by itself. Here I am giving you a general idea of how these tools work.

Moving to the playbook and how it works, I will provide you with a simple example.

## Simple Playbook Example

Ansible installation on your local workstation and access to a remote Ubuntu server are prerequisites for this tutorial.

Installing Apache Server is one of the most straightforward examples that can be given, but be careful. YAML is an indention language; spaces are essential here, so use a good integrated development environment (IDE).

apache-installation.yaml

```
1.  ---
2.    - name: Playbook
3.      hosts: webservers #should be defined inside an inventory (/etc/
         ansible/hosts)
4.      become: yes
5.      become_user: root
6.      tasks:
7.        - name: download the latest version
8.          yum:
9.            name: httpd
10.           state: latest
11.       - name: make sure apache services are up and running
12.         service:
13.           name: httpd
14.           state: started
15.
```

Here, note the following:

- name is your playbook name.

- hosts should be defined inside an inventory (/etc/ansible/hosts).

- become tells Ansible that we will switch to a higher user.

- Become_user is our high-privilege user.

- tasks says what the playbook will do.

In our playbook, we have two tasks; the first will install Apache, and the second will ensure the Apache services are running and then run this custom playbook.

1. ansible-playbook apache-installation.yaml

We could make the previous playbook more usable by using a variable that allows you to read a different value, and you can change it when you want.

```
1.  ---
2.   - name: Playbook
3.     hosts: webservers #should be defined inside an inventory (/etc/
        ansible/hosts)
4.     become: yes
5.     become_user: root
6.     vars:
7.        key_file:  /etc/apache/ssl/DevOpsBook.key
8.        cert_file: /etc/apache/ssl/DevOpsBook.cert
9.        server_name: www.DevOpsBook.com
10.    tasks:
11.     - name: download the latest version
12.        yum:
13.         name: httpd
14.         state: latest
15.     - name: make sure apache services are up and running
16.        service:
17.         name: httpd
18.         state: started
19.     - name: copy certificate to another place, for example
```

```
20.         copy:
21.           src: {{key_file}}
22.           dest: {{cert_file}}
```

For another example, let's assume you have a group defined inside the inventory that contains, for instance, 15 servers. You need to copy files, create a user, and upgrade the packages on all the servers. What will you do? There is no time to do them one by one.

```
1. ---
2. - name: Another Custom playbook
3.   hosts: all
4.
5.   tasks:
6.   - name: Copy files and dont forget the permission
7.     ansible.builtin.copy:
8.       src: ./hosts
9.       dest: /tmp/hosts_backup
10.       mode: '0655'
11.   - name: Add the user 'Osama'
12.     ansible.builtin.user:
13.       name: Osama
14.     become: yes
15.     become_method: sudo
16.   - name: Upgrade packages
17.     apt:
18.       force_apt_get: yes
19.       upgrade: dist
20.     become: yes
21.
```

Like the earlier example, you define the name of your playbook and which servers you need to run this playbook.

- Ansible.builtin.copy is a predefined module to allow copying.

- ansible.builtin.user is a predefined module to create a user.

Ansible is one of the most common tools in use, and it has a lot of other features. Here are some examples:

- *Loops*: A loop allows you to operate repeatedly on each item in a list. In a loop, you repeat the process while changing the item's value each time.

- *Handlers*: One of the conditional forms that Ansible offers is a handler. A handler acts like a task but executes only when another job triggers it. If Ansible determines that a task has altered the system state, the task will issue the notice.

# Summary

In this chapter, you learned about IaC. Even after putting in so much time and effort on these pages, I can scarcely expect you to be able to write a complete IaC program, but at least you will have an idea of where to start.

There is no right or good tool to use; it all depends on your use case and what you feel comfortable with.

Using Terraform as the basis for your infrastructure may get you a long way and simplify management. If you don't want to invest time and learn a programing language or something so complicated, then Terraform is for you; if you already know one of the programming languages, in that case, you could use Pulumi.

CloudFormation is a valuable tool if you currently use the AWS cloud and do not intend to switch to another cloud provider or distribute your workloads over several clouds in the foreseeable future.

In the next chapter, I will cover two of the most critical aspects of DevOps and SRE, monitoring and observability; the chapter will cover the terms related to these two concepts and how you can troubleshoot them. In addition, we will discuss the Amazon AWS services that allow you to keep an eye on the application, infrastructure, and security.

# CHAPTER 7

# AWS Monitoring and Observability Tools

In this chapter, I will cover two central concepts for DevOps and SRE engineers: monitoring and observability. What does each mean? I'll explain the terms and components for each concept and why they're essential for DevOps/SRE engineers.

Moreover, this chapter will cover Amazon AWS services concerning monitoring and how to use them, such as the resource dashboard, CloudTrail, CloudWatch, X-Ray, and more.

We will dive deep into these services and show you the configuration for each one of them.

## Monitoring

One of the critical tenets of monitoring is that you cannot know whether your apps are functioning as intended, making themselves accessible, or giving a positive end-user experience if you cannot quantify what is occurring.

In computing, *monitoring* refers to the apparatus and procedures that track and control data processing and transmission networks. The process of monitoring, however, entails so much more. When your systems and apps create metrics, monitoring translates that information into something your organization can use. Your monitoring system then uses these metrics to provide quantitative user experience data. This quantifiable user experience feeds back to the company, letting you know whether its meeting the needs of its consumers. What is not functioning and what is not providing enough quality of service are both highlighted to IT by user feedback.

Once upon a time, the system was monitored by waking a developer up all night to ensure everything worked without downtime. The developer needed to generate reports

© Osama Mustafa 2023
O. Mustafa, *A Complete Guide to DevOps with AWS*, https://doi.org/10.1007/978-1-4842-9303-4_7

and fill in Excel spreadsheets for everything and then needed to hand everything over to the next person on the shift.

Sometimes the developer on the shift monitored only, meaning no experience was required to solve issues or troubleshoot, which increased the response time and downtime; therefore, DevOps/SRE solves these obsoletes and makes it much easier for the company.

Most of the company's systems should be available around the clock and work properly. You need to ensure they're running smoothly by knowing everything inside your infrastructure, recording the changes, logging in, and monitoring the application logs. This is what's meant by monitoring and observability, and they're part of the DevOps/SRE engineer's methodology.

Monitoring is all the quantitative information about a system, such as the number of queries, number of errors, amount of time it takes to execute a query, and the age of a server, which is collected, processed, aggregated, and shown in real time. It means analyzing system health to inform team decisions. Metrics and logs can be collected in advance for use in monitoring.

A system's performance may be monitored, and known flaws can be spotted with monitoring; however, monitoring is not without its drawbacks. You need to understand what indicators and logs to watch for monitoring to be effective.

You need to understand two primary monitoring types before moving on.

- White-box monitoring
- Black-box monitoring

## White-Box Monitoring

*White-box monitoring* refers to keeping an eye on server-based software programs. Everything from the volume of HTTP requests to the application's response codes might fall under this category, including the following:

- Database queries and the requests on the database server
- The user requests and users concurrently on the application and system
- HTTP requests that are included in Table 7-1

***Table 7-1.***  *HTTP Request Code Examples*

| Code | Category Description |
|---|---|
| **1xx Informational** | 100, which means continue |
| | 101, which implies protocol switching |
| **2xx Success** | 200, which means OK |
| | 201 Created |
| | 202 Accepted |
| **3xx Redirection** | 302 Found |
| | 305 Proxy |
| | 307 temp redirection |
| **4xx Client Error** | 400 Bad request |
| | 403 Forbidden |
| | 404 Not Found |
| | 444 No response |
| **5xx Server Error** | 500 Internal error |
| | 503 Services unavailable504 Timeout |

# Black-Box Monitoring

Black-box monitoring includes watching servers, paying particular attention to metrics such as free space on storage, CPU use, memory utilization, load averages, and other categories such as the following:

- Network bandwidth

- Input/output operations per second (I/Ops)

- Any alert related to storage

Whether you are a system administrator or DevOps/SRE engineer, you need to take responsibility for monitoring the application (white box) or the servers (black box) to ensure the system will function properly and know what's going on inside your infrastructure.

DevOps engineers may sometimes handle white-box monitoring, depending on company rules.

Understanding the value of both forms of monitoring is crucial. Historically, there was a con of tools for monitoring applications, which caused several issues. For example, black-box monitoring would detect system problems leading to CPU or memory issues. Nevertheless, there would not be any data from the application side to explain why this was happening there. That is why you, as an SRE or DevOps engineer, need to know and understand that both types to provide a complete picture of your system.

On the other hand, we have *observability*, where you allow the team to debug and find the issues so they can understand the system based on the external output that you get from the metrics or logs.

If a system is observable, the user may examine the data generated to determine the reason for a performance issue without resorting to further testing or coding.

The difference between monitoring and observability is the plan for dealing with inevitable difficulties and preventing unforeseen ones; therefore, we can say that monitoring is reactive, and observability is proactive.

Even for Linux performance observability tools, you can use command lines that will allow you to understand what is happening on your system, which will also be discussed in this chapter. Still, before that, we need to discuss the main factors for observability.

- *Logging*: Recording and saving information about what is happening to your application or software

- *Metrics*: A measurement level to tune the application or system

- *Traces*: Reflect the path a request or action takes as it passes through each node in a distributed system

Monitoring teams (Ops and SRE) usually use data to establish metrics and develop custom dashboards and alerting mechanisms. They also track and record connections between parts of the program, revealing how various software modules and infrastructure services are used.

An observability platform goes above and beyond. The collected information may be correlated in real time, allowing DevOps/SRE to gain a comprehensive application performance perspective. Doing so will teach them what components make up the system and its interconnections.

This will allow DevOps/SRE to debug any issue that could happen and fix it; in that way, you are avoiding a problem, a system bug, or even a performance fix by analyzing and studying your application behavior to show you what, when, and why this event is happening to your system.

Furthermore, observability will use the data proactively to find anything new to the system, for example, an API calling between two systems. Do not forget that you can also use artificial intelligence to detect any problem; this is called *artificial intelligence operation* (AIOps).

When we talk about monitoring and observability, from Amazon AWS's perspective, we have different services that will give DevOps/SRE a complete overview of what is happening in the infrastructure, such as the following:

- Resource dashboard

- AWS CloudTrail

- AWS CloudWatch

- AWS X-Ray

These service processes depend on a wide range of data collection, processing, and visualization resources. The information gained from this analysis can be used to locate security holes, forecast system behavior, and fine-tune settings.

# Resource Dashboard

When you access the AWS console and create a resource such as EC2, this resource will allow you to monitor the server status and different metrics by default.

The dashboard will give you an idea about what is happening in your server, as shown in Figure 7-1.

***Figure 7-1.*** *EC2 Dashboard*

Use this control panel to monitor your EC2 instances and other infrastructure components. The dashboard provides visibility into an instance, service health, alarm and status report management, event scheduling, and capacity and instance metric analysis.

The dashboard offers a variety of metrics that allow the SRE/DevOps engineer to understand what is happening; see Figure 7-2.

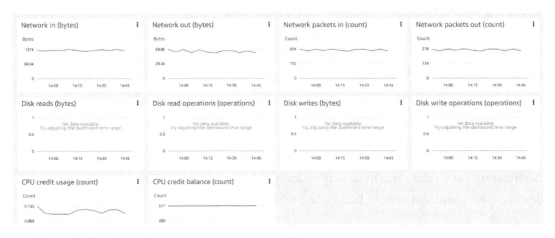

***Figure 7-2.*** *EC2 dashboard with a variety of metrics*

What happens when you click the three dots in the dashboard? You will get a new menu with the options shown in Figure 7-3.

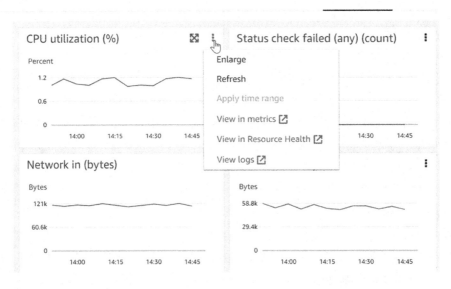

***Figure 7-3.*** *Metrics Extra menu*

The options are as follows:

- Enlarge

- Refresh

- Apply time range

- View in metrics

- View in resource health

- View logs

For instance, Enlarge is responsible for maximizing the metrics and focusing on one as an entire page; Figure 7-4 shows your CPU utilization after choosing the Enlarge option.

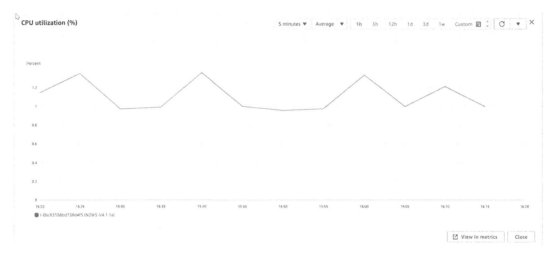

***Figure 7-4.*** *Enlargement option, EC2 dashboard*

Refresh will allow you to renew the metrics output to check if something new is happening, but this happening automatically depends on the period. Another option is to apply a time range; this is useful if you want to review what happened during a specific time.

The last three options related to CloudWatch will be discussed later in this chapter. Most AWS services allow you to monitor similarly, as shown in Figure 7-5.

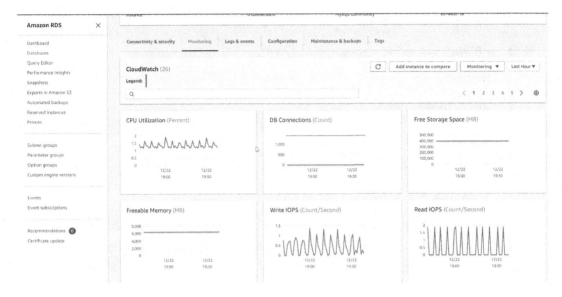

***Figure 7-5.*** *Another example of an RDS monitoring dashboard*

# AWS CloudTrail

If you want to keep tabs on what's happening in your account, you can use CloudTrail.
Your services' events and activity logs are automatically recorded and stored in S3 by
the service. The information gathered includes usernames, IP addresses of originating
traffic, and timestamps. Free access to all management activities for the last 90 days is
available. It can additionally provide data events and insights derived from your data for
an extra cost.

If you use CloudTrail to secure your accounts, the infrastructure activity will be
recorded under the CloudTrail event. Each event will be in the Event History, allowing
you to view and search for the events that happened during the last 90 days.

There are two CloudTrail types, as shown here:

- Each region will have one CloudTrail event. In this approach, any
  change made in one of the AWS regions will be recorded, and
  CloudTrail will store the event logs in the S3 bucket you choose.

- All the regions will have one CloudTrail event. CloudTrail keeps track
  of activity inside a specific area only if that region is specified in the
  trail's settings. The CloudTrail event logs are subsequently sent to an
  AWS S3 bucket of your choosing.

# Using CloudTrail

CloudTrail can be used to do the following:

- Understand and monitor infrastructure evolution

- Get instant updates on any unusual behavior

- Bring your CloudTrail data into S3 and analyze your logging activities in CloudTrail

- Make sure you've got the safest arrangement possible

You must search for the services under the AWS console to access CloudTrail; see Figure 7-6.

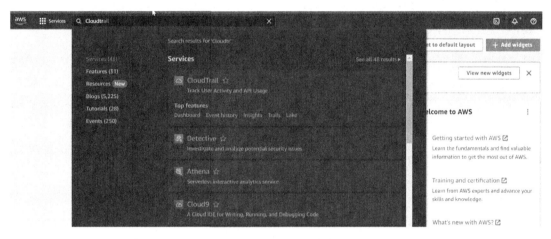

***Figure 7-6.*** *Access to CloudTrail from the AWS console*

Once you are redirected to the CloudTrail page, you will see the welcome page, allowing you to create the trail base. Let's start with the steps for how to do that and how to configure CloudTrail.

When in the CloudTrail console, go to the Trails section on the left; see Figure 7-7.

***Figure 7-7.*** *CloudTrail welcome page*

Clicking Trails will redirect you to a new page; click "Create trail," as shown in Figure 7-8.

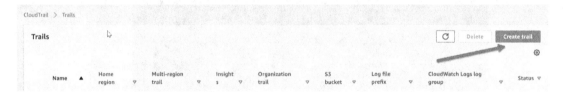

***Figure 7-8.*** *Creating the trail*

Once you click the button, you will need to fill in the following information:

- Trail attributes

- Log events

- The information you're reviewing

As you can see from Figure 7-9, this is the first configuration step.

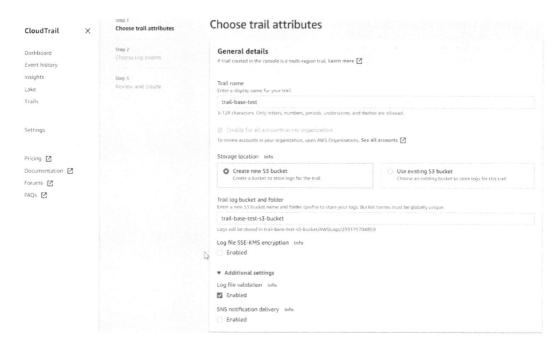

**Figure 7-9.** *Trail attributes*

Specifically, you need to configure the attributes as follows:

- *Trail name*: Choose the name for the baseline for the CloudTrail.

- *Storage location*: Set whether you will create a new bucket (I prefer not to mix old buckets with the latest event logs), or you can choose an existing bucket.

- *Log file SSE-KMS encryption*: This is set to Enabled by default; it encrypts CloudTrail log files using the AWS Key Management Service (SSE-KMS). You do not need encryption for now.

- *Log file validation*: To determine whether a log file was modified, deleted, or unchanged after AWS CloudTrail delivered it, set this to Enabled.

- *SNS notification delivery*: If you want to be alerted each time a log is sent to your bucket, choose the Enabled option.

- *CloudWatch Logs*: To transmit events to CloudWatch Logs, you must either choose an existing log group in CloudWatch Logs or establish a new one while configuring your CloudTrail trail.

We will enable this option now because we will need it later to continue the example; see Figure 7-10.

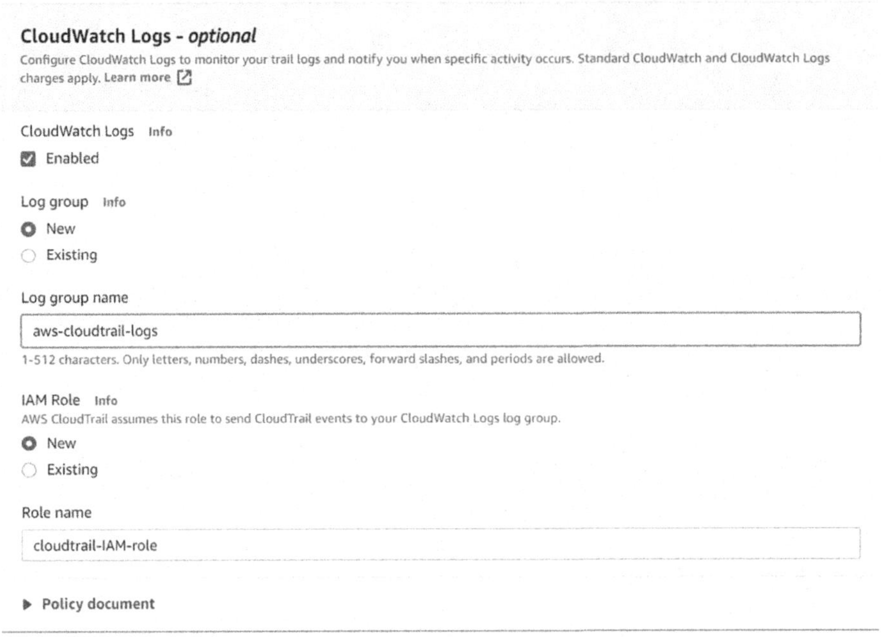

**CloudWatch Logs - *optional***

Configure CloudWatch Logs to monitor your trail logs and notify you when specific activity occurs. Standard CloudWatch and CloudWatch Logs charges apply. Learn more

CloudWatch Logs    Info

☑ Enabled

Log group    Info

⦿ New

◯ Existing

Log group name

aws-cloudtrail-logs

1-512 characters. Only letters, numbers, dashes, underscores, forward slashes, and periods are allowed.

IAM Role    Info

AWS CloudTrail assumes this role to send CloudTrail events to your CloudWatch Logs log group.

⦿ New

◯ Existing

Role name

cloudtrail-IAM-role

▶ Policy document

***Figure 7-10.*** *CloudWatch configuration, CloudTrail*

Here's more about each section on this screen:

- *Log group*: Choose a new group; if you have an existing one you want to use, just set the name here.

- *Log group name*: This is the name of the log group inside CloudWatch; choose an understandable name.

- *IAM Role*: CloudTrail sends events to the CloudWatch Logs log stream; we will choose a new one because we do not have an existing one to use.

- *Role name*: This is the new role name.

Click Next, and the screen shown in Figure 7-11 will display the event type; we need both management and data events.

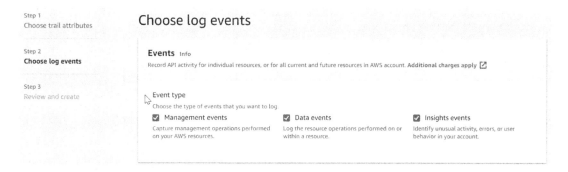

**Figure 7-11.**  *CloudTrail event type*

On the same screen, you will notice the configuration for each type you choose; as shown in Figure 7-12, you define the event you need to monitor and the log for each activity.

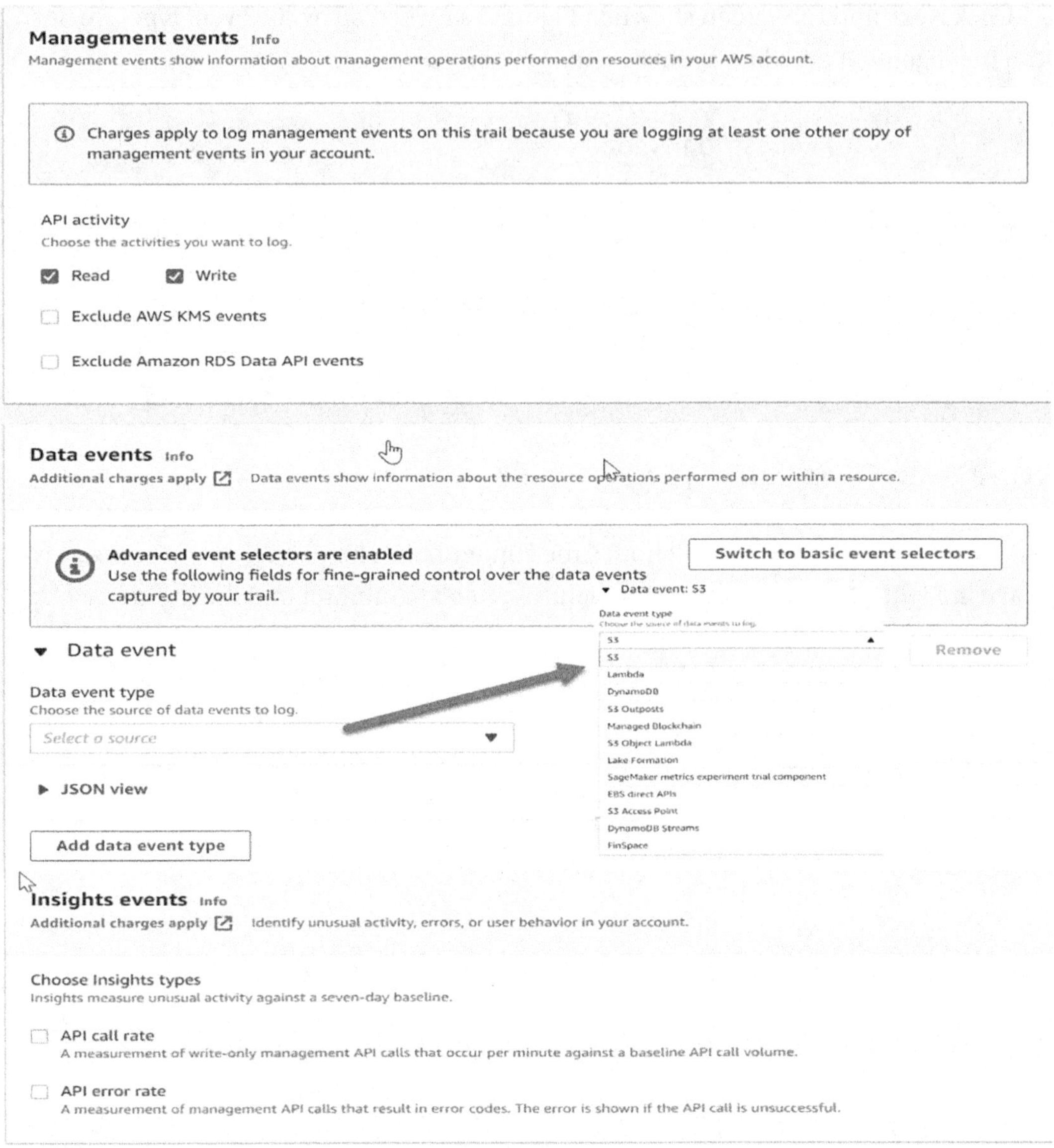

**Figure 7-12.** *CloudTrail, log event configuration screen*

Click Next and review the configuration; see Figure 7-13 for the review page. Once done reviewing, create a trail.

## Review and create

**Step 1: Choose trail attributes**                                          [ Edit ]

General details

Trail name
trail-base-test

Trail log location
trail-base-test-s3-
bucket/AWSLogs/293175704869

Log file validation
Enabled

Multi-region trail
Yes

Log file SSE-KMS encryption
Not enabled

SNS notification delivery
Disabled

Apply trail to my organization
Not enabled

*Figure 7-13.  Reviewing and creation, CloudTrail*

When the CloudTrail baseline has been created, you must wait a few minutes for
AWS to collect the event history.

After that, you can begin browsing or downloading the events based on what you
want, as shown in Figure 7-14. You can look at information based on the username, user
access key, event name, etc.

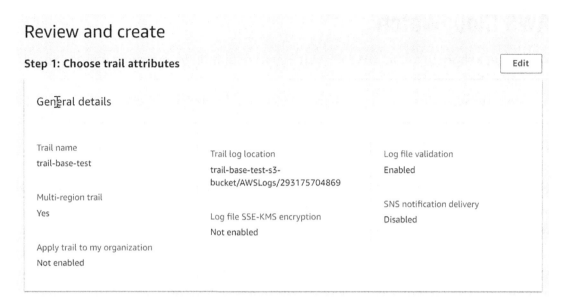

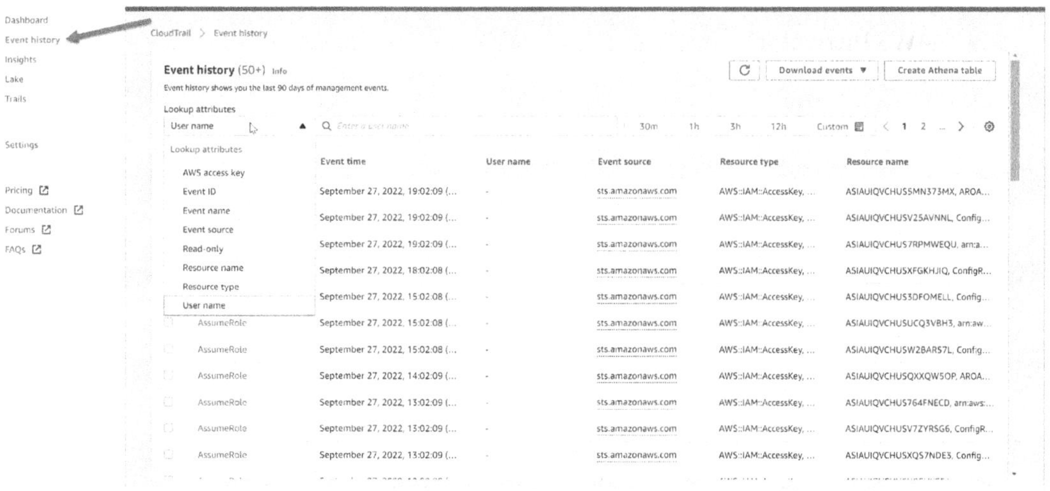

*Figure 7-14.  CloudTrail event history*

# AWS CloudWatch

We can get a shortcut to CloudWatch with a short definition of repository metrics, so you can query these metrics whenever you want.

CloudWatch allows you to configure alerts to stop or start specific actions, such as if you're going to stop/start/terminate the EC2 server based on these metrics.

To react to changes in the various AWS resources and services, CloudWatch events are built. CloudWatch events can be customized to respond in a certain way depending on the criteria used to identify the activity or action that has taken place. Not all AWS services support CloudWatch events; several different AWS services can be used in response to an event generated by CloudWatch.

With CloudWatch, DevOps/SRE engineers can centralize all their AWS infrastructure monitoring data in one place. Data gathering, monitoring, automatic actions, analysis, compliance, and security are all areas where CloudWatch excels.

The following is a list of some of the input triggers that can be used for CloudWatch events:

- AWS GameLift

- AWS Glacier

- AWS Glue

- AWS GuardDuty

- AWS Inspector

- AWS Kinesis

- AWS Elastic Container Service (ECS)

- AWS Elastic Load Balancing

- AWS Elastic MapReduce

- AWS Elastic Transcoder

- AWS Elasticsearch

- AWS Elemental MediaPackage

- AWS EventBridge

- AWS EventBridge Schema Registry

Plus, you can integrate CloudWatch with EventBridge, another serverless service, to act on your behalf in case something happens. EventBridge is responsible for receiving events from other services and responding to them appropriately. EventBridge is distinguished from CloudWatch Events by a key characteristic: it accepts input from third-party providers in addition to AWS services.

You could use a third-party solution, such as pager duty or data dog, to replace EventBridge.

Figure 7-15 shows what CloudWatch offers and how we can configure our infrastructure to be monitored and automated regarding the response.

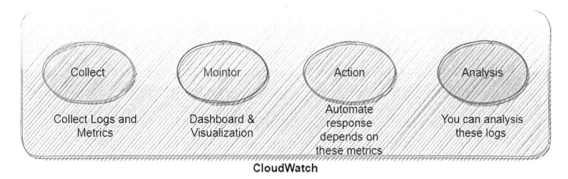

***Figure 7-15.***  *What CloudWatch offers*

CloudWatch provides different features, and each one depends on the use case that the company is trying to achieve, such as the following:

- *CloudWatch logs*: This feature will allow the DevOps/SRE engineer to receive the logs for different AWS services such as EC2, Lambda, RDS, and more, and you can write your queries to search for something specific.

- *CloudWatch metrics*: This is the same as the CloudWatch logs; you can collect them with CloudWatch and customize them depending on your needs. CloudWatch can gather metrics on-premises.

- *Microservices insights*: If you have any microservices such as containers, Kubernetes, etc., this will allow you to understand what is happening inside EKS and ECS.

- *Serverless insights*: This will allow you to collect, monitor, troubleshoot, and understand what is happening with serverless services (Lambda).

- *Contributor insights*: Data analysis depends on the time the system performance was affected; during an operational event, this aids developers and operators in swiftly isolating, diagnosing, and fixing the problem.

- *CloudWatch synthetics*: This feature consists of schedule-aware, scripted checks of your APIs and endpoints.

- *CloudWatch real user monitoring (RUM)*: RUM assists software and DevOps engineers in maximizing the end-user experience by detecting client-side performance problems and allowing a faster resolution.

- *CloudWatch Evidently*: This capability helps application developers validate new features safely across the whole application stack. It allows developers to experiment with new proposed applications, learn about unanticipated consequences, and reduce risk simultaneously.

- *Detection of anomalies*: When you enable this feature in CloudWatch, CloudWatch, by default, will use machine learning to study and analyze the past metrics and start generating the expected metrics. This will allow SRE engineers to understand what will happen to the infrastructure before doing anything.

- *Alarms*: When something happens to your infrastructure, CloudWatch dashboard will put it into a category to allow you to organize the importance of an alarm, and you could integrate this with other services to send email or an SMS.

- *Embedded metric format*: This allows you to derive relevant metrics from detailed application data stored in logs and enables you to ingest high-cardinality application data, plus build helpful customized metrics from temporary resources such as AWS Lambda and containers.

To access CloudWatch from the console, search for *CloudWatch,* as shown in Figure 7-16.

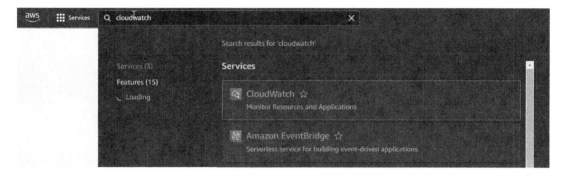

***Figure 7-16.*** *Accessing CloudWatch*

CloudWatch contains different services, and each one was described earlier. Figure 7-17 shows show what CloudWatch looks like.

***Figure 7-17.*** *CloudWatch dashboard, the first screen*

You can build many dashboards; each dashboard can be on a favorites list. Your AWS account does not restrict the total number of dashboards you can have. All dashboards are global. They are not limited to a particular region.

Creating a CloudWatch dashboard is simple; all you need to do is follow these steps:

1. Click Dashboards in the list of options in the left panel; then click the "Create dashboard" option, as shown in Figure 7-18.

***Figure 7-18.*** *Creating a CloudWatch dashboard*

2. Click "Create dashboard" after giving the dashboard a name in the "Create new dashboard" dialog box that appears after clicking the Create button; see Figure 7-19.

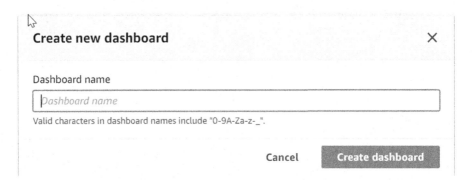

***Figure 7-19.*** *Naming the new dashboard*

Once you are done with the naming, a new screen will pop out to allow you to add the widget to your dashboard, as shown in Figure 7-20.

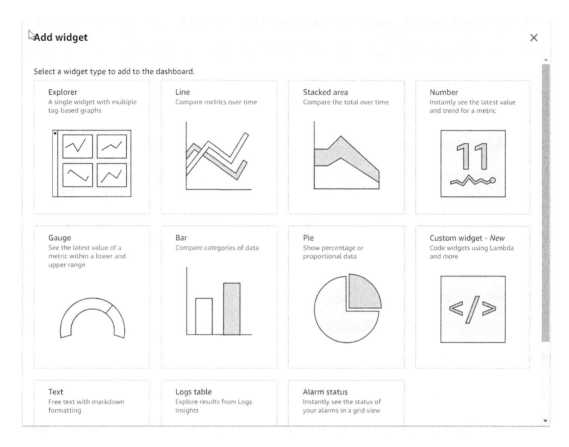

***Figure 7-20.*** *CloudWatch dashboard widget*

3.  In the next step (Figure 7-21), after choosing the widget, which is the widget template, you can use either a predefined or an empty one.

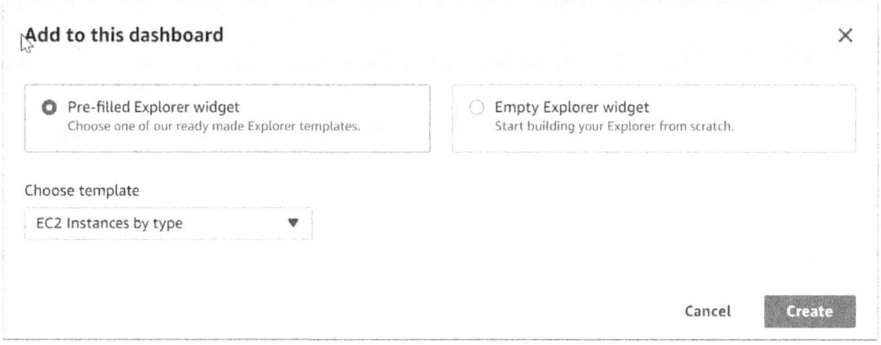

***Figure 7-21.*** *Explorer widget*

4.  Once done, the dashboard will be empty, as in Figure 7-22, because you still need to configure the CloudWatch agent for EC2 or the other resource to use CloudWatch, as shown in Figure 7-22.

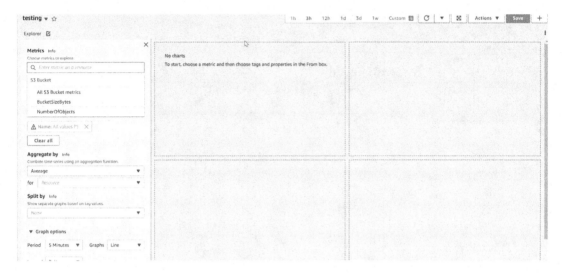

***Figure 7-22.*** *Dashboard creation*

The process of retrieving or gathering data from where it is first stored constitutes the initial state of a log. The logs are kept in a specific location, and a program sends the log's output to the path where it will be saved.

The data from the location must be read by the collector responsible for transmitting the information to the appropriate place. Within CloudWatch, the Amazon CloudWatch agent is the program that is accountable for this responsibility. A program known as the Amazon CloudWatch agent will be put into your Amazon EC2 instance. In addition, it is set up to read the specific file the logs are written to and then transmit those logs to the location where they need to be saved.

The CloudWatch agent in the background is a daemon, meaning it is not visible to the user but continues running to obtain data from the log file and transfer it to the storage destination.

The agent is equipped with all the configuration information required to identify the data source from which it retrieves data and the delivery location to which it sends data.

The Amazon CloudWatch agent was developed to be compatible with the Linux or Windows operating system. You may use it for your Amazon EC2 instance without worrying about compatibility issues.

Table 7-2 breaks down the possible setup locations for the agent.

***Table 7-2.*** *CloudWatch Logs*

| File | Linux Location | Windows Location |
|---|---|---|
| A script that will control the agent<br>• Start<br>• stop | • `/opt/aws/amazon-cloudwatch-agent/bin/amazon-cloudwatch-agent-ctl`<br>• `/usr/bin/amazon-cloudwatch-agent-ctl` | `$Programfile\Amazon\AmazonCloudWatchAgent\amazon-cloudwatch-agent-ctl.ps1` |
| Agent log file | • `/opt/aws/amazon-cloudwatch-agent/logs/amazon-cloudwatch-agent.log`<br>• `/var/log/amazon/amazon-cloudwatch-agent/amazon-cloudwatch-agent.log` | `$Programfile\Amazon\AmazonCloudWatchAgent\Logs\amazon-cloudwatch-agent.log` |
| Configuration validation | • `/opt/aws/amazon-cloudwatch-agent/logs/configuration-validation.log`<br>• `/var/log/amazon/amazon-cloudwatch-agent/configuration-validation.log` | `$ProgramData\Amazon\AmazonCloudWatchAgent\Logs\configuration-validation.log` |

The following CloudWatch agent commands are helpful to obtain more information:

- Get the CloudWatch agent version.

    1. `/usr/bin/amazon-cloudwatch-agent-ctl -a status`

- Stop the CloudWatch agent.

    1. `/usr/bin/amazon-cloudwatch-agent-ctl -m ec2 -a stop`

- Refresh the agent after updating the configuration file.

    1. `/usr/bin/amazon-cloudwatch-agent-ctl -a fetch-config -s -m ec2 -c file:configuration-location`

The CloudWatch configuration file looks like the following one:

```
1.  [general]
2.  state_file = /var/lib/awslogs/agent-state
3.  [applications_logs]
4.  region = eu-west-1
5.  datetime_format = %b %d %H:%M:%S
6.  file = /var/log/secure
7.  buffer_duration = 5000
8.  log_stream_name = Nginx_logs #you can for example database_logs or
Apache_logs.
9.  initial_position = start_of_file
10. log_group_name = server_logs
```

The configuration attributes are straightforward, but I will expand on each one a bit more here:

- *State_file*: This file will be used by a watch agent to track and follow up when pulling the logs, record where it stopped pulling, and so on.

- *Region*: This setting specifies the AWS region of Amazon CloudWatch to which the agent will deliver the logs.

- *datetime_format*: This is used to define the time and date format used to store the log data.

- *File*: With the help of this argument, you can give the path to the file from which the log should extract data.

- *buffer_duration*: This identifies the period for grouping log events in batches. Milliseconds are used as the measurement unit here. When the time is more significant, this is the amount of time it takes for the log to become available in the CloudWatch logs.

- *log_stream_name*: The name provided for the kind of log sent to CloudWatch Logs is referred to as the *log stream name*. The log stream serves as the label for determining the type of log sent to the CloudWatch Logs service.

- *initial_position*: This is the point in the file where the representative will begin reading.

- *log_group_name*: Each source of logs in CloudWatch Logs is represented by its log stream inside the service. A log group collects log streams with the same retention, monitoring, and access control settings. You can construct log groups and specify which log streams should be placed in each group; see Figure 7-23.

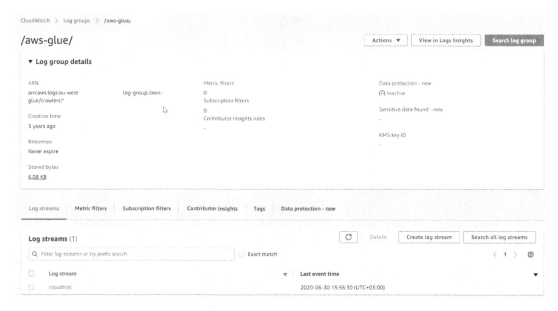

***Figure 7-23.*** *CloudWatch log group dashboard*

### Configuring an Essential CloudWatch Agent

In this section, you will understand how to install the CloudWatch Agent for AWS EC2 instances by following the steps. After the initial configuration, the agent will report certain logs to AWS CloudWatch for additional inspection after the service has started.

An EC2 instance must have an IAM role assigned to it before CloudWatch can interact with the instance. To make the CloudWatch agent work properly, we must create an IAM role that allows access to EC2.

- You need to log into your AWS account and search for IAM; from the IAM Dashboard, choose the role, as shown in Figure 7-24.

***Figure 7-24.*** *IAM Dashboard, role*

- To create a new role, go to the Roles page and click the "Create role" button at the top of the screen, as shown in Figure 7-25.

***Figure 7-25.*** *Creating a new role*

- In the next screen, we will set the entity type to AWS services. AWS service roles enable interactions between AWS resources and other kinds of resources; see Figure 7-26.

## Select trusted entity Info

**Trusted entity type**

○ **AWS service**
Allow AWS services like EC2, Lambda, or others to perform actions in this account.

○ **AWS account**
Allow entities in other AWS accounts belonging to you or a 3rd party to perform actions in this account.

○ **Web identity**
Allows users federated by the specified external web identity provider to assume this role to perform actions in this account.

○ **SAML 2.0 federation**
Allow users from a corporate directory to perform actions in this account.

○ **Custom trust policy**
Create a custom trust policy to enable others to perform actions in this account.

or from the drop down list

**Use case**
Allow an AWS service like EC2, Lambda, or others to perform actions in this account.

**Common use cases**

● **EC2**
Allows EC2 instances to call AWS services on your behalf.

**Use case**

EC2
Fleet
Auto Scaling
CapacityReservation Fleet
Image Builder

*Figure 7-26. Choosing EC2*

- Click Next. Adding permission will be the next screen; from the search bar, search for the policy name, already provided by AWS as CloudWatchAgentServerPolicy. Then click Next, as shown in Figure 7-27.

## Add permissions Info

**Permissions policies** (Selected 1/813) Info
Choose one or more policies to attach to your new role

🔍 Filter policies by property or policy name and press enter                                    1 match

"CloudWatchAgentServerPolicy" ✕    **Clear filters**

| ☑ | Policy name ☑ | ▽ | Type ▽ | Description |
|---|---|---|---|---|
| ☑ | ⊞ 🗐 CloudWatchAgentServerPolicy | | AWS ma... | Permissions required to use AmazonCloudWatchAgent on servers |

▶ **Set permissions boundary - *optional*** Info
Set a permissions boundary to control the maximum permissions this role can have. This is not a common setting, but you can use it to delegate permission management to others.

Cancel    Previous    **Next**

*Figure 7-27. Attaching permissions to a role*

This policy looks like the following one, including all the permission required to use Amazon CloudWatch on the EC2 server:

```
1.  {
2.  "Version": "2012-10-17",
3.  "Statement": [
4.          {
5.  "Effect": "Allow",
6.  "Action": [
7.  "cloudwatch:PutMetricData",
8.  "ec2:DescribeVolumes",
9.  "ec2:DescribeTags",
10.                "logs:PutLogEvents",
11. "logs:DescribeLogStreams",
12. "logs:DescribeLogGroups",
13.                "logs:CreateLogStream",
14. "logs:CreateLogGroup"
15.             ],
16. "Resource": "*"
17.         },
18.          {
19. "Effect": "Allow",
20. "Action": [
21.                "ssm:GetParameter"
22.             ],
23. "Resource": "arn:aws:ssm:*:*:parameter/AmazonCloudWatch-*"
24.         }
25.     ]
26. }
```

Click Next, choose a unique name for the role, and write a detailed description of it and its use, as shown in Figure 7-28.

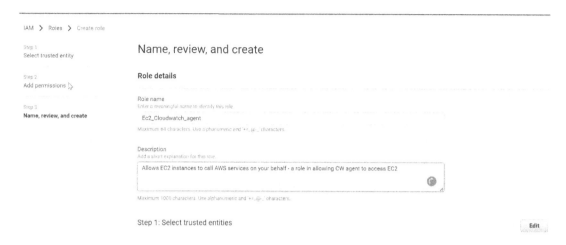

*Figure 7-28.*  *Reviewing the configuration page for the role*

Either you have an EC2 you want to monitor or you will create a new one; for both options, you need to attach the role to allow the agent to send the logs to CloudWatch; if you have an existing EC2, do the same thing, as shown in Figure 7-29.

*Figure 7-29.*  *Adding a role to EC2 to allow the CloudWatch agent to collect logs*

Once you click the Modify IAM role, a new screen will open, which allows you to choose the role we created before, as you can see in Figure 7-30, or the small box that shows you the option for creating a new EC2.

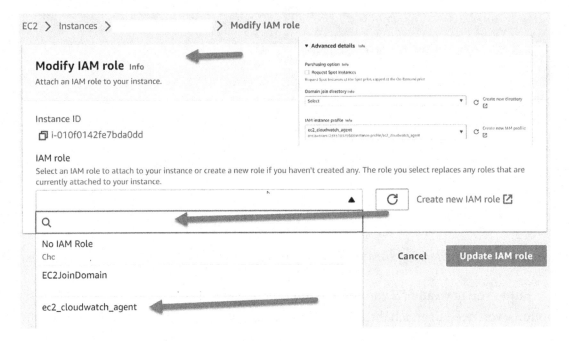

**Figure 7-30.** *Attaching a CloudWatch role to EC2*

After creating the role and assigning it to the EC2, we need to install the CloudWatch agent, which is simple. You need either SSH or a session manager, and AWS allows you also to use the command line or System Manager.

Which command you will use depends on your operating system. In my case, I'm using Red Hat, so I run the following command:

1. `sudo yum install amazon-cloudwatch-agent`

In the System Manager, click Run Command in the left panel, and search for *AWS-ConfigureAWSPackage*. From the target, select the instance manual. Select the correct box depending on your instance ID; see Figure 7-31.

***Figure 7-31.*** *Installing CloudWatch via the System Manager*

Now that the agent has been installed, the logs metrics and the logs will start appearing inside the CloudWatch dashboard depending on your configuration, as you can see in Figure 7-32. Figure 7-33 shows the CPU unitization for the EC2 instance we have.

***Figure 7-32.*** *CloudWatch logs*

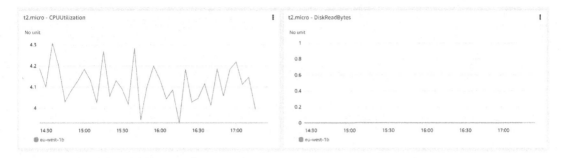

***Figure 7-33.*** *EC2 CloudWatch metrics*

# CloudWatch Metrics Concepts

This section will introduce you to the concepts and fundamental ideas necessary to comprehend before you can begin using CloudWatch.

## Namespaces

Note the following about namespaces:

- *Custom namespaces*: Namespaces established by a user from a specific log that has been produced are called *custom namespaces*. AWS namespaces are a kind of namespace created by Amazon Web Services and are used to aggregate metrics from various AWS services.

- *Metrics namespaces*: Metrics are categorized and classified using these to avoid the metrics being ungrouped. When working with metrics, grouping them into categories for convenience is helpful. Metrics do not have namespaces associated with them by default; however, namespaces may be generated while a metric is being formed or when a metric filter is being built from a log. Default settings do not include namespaces.

- *AWS namespaces*: An Amazon Web Services namespace is automatically formed for services that do not need any human setup; for instance, when an EC2 example is started up, CloudWatch will automatically begin monitoring metrics such as the percentage of CPU time being used, the number of disk reads, the number of network packets coming in, and the number of network packets going out.

## Metric Dimensions

A key and value pair describe how data is kept inside a metric, referred to as a *metric dimension*. Up to 10 sizes may be included inside a single metric. A billing metric, for instance, can be categorized according to various aspects.

## Metric Filter

This feature can be filtered through logs as they come in, and the statistics may be displayed in graphs and used to construct a CloudWatch alert when necessary. A metric filter might look for a particular phrase in the logs to see if it can find it.

Earlier in this chapter, when I discussed CloudTrail, I told you we would continue that example by using Amazon EventBridge to create notifications, known before as *CloudWatch events*.

Amazon EventBridge will track and get notifications on the attachment of an IAM policy to an IAM user.

When an event happens, the EventBridge rule that was built will look for a particular event name in CloudTrail and then send out an SNS message to tell users about the event's occurrence; the following section continues the previous example mentioned earlier.

From the console, choose Amazon EventBridge, as shown in Figure 7-34.

---

**Caution**   The following section continues our previous example in CloudTrail; you can even use the same steps to create alerts and notifications.

---

***Figure 7-34.***  *Amazon EventBridge services*

After entering the EventBridge console, go to the Rules section on the left side of the screen and click; see Figure 7-35.

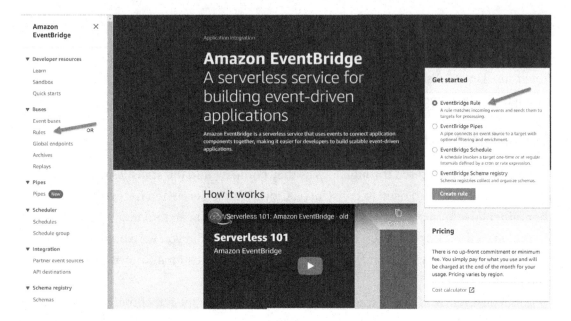

**Figure 7-35.** *Choosing Rules in Amazon Eventbridge*

Set the rule up by configuring it with the following options; see Figure 7-36:

- Enter a name for the regulation here.

- The event bus collects the events sent to them by resources known as *emitters*. These resources consist of AWS services either in your account or in other accounts, services, and apps provided by SaaS partners, as well as the applications you have developed, leaving them at their defaults.

- You have two options for the rule type; either you leave it depending on the event itself, or you will schedule when the rule will be triggered.

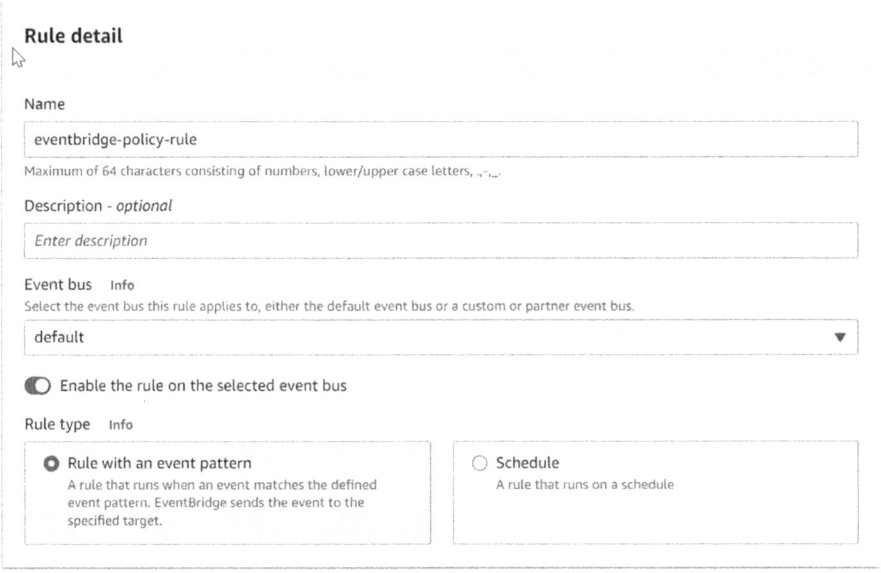

**Rule detail**

Name

eventbridge-policy-rule

Maximum of 64 characters consisting of numbers, lower/upper case letters, .,-,_.

Description - *optional*

Enter description

Event bus    Info

Select the event bus this rule applies to, either the default event bus or a custom or partner event bus.

default                                                                                      ▼

🔘 Enable the rule on the selected event bus

Rule type    Info

🔘 **Rule with an event pattern**
A rule that runs when an event matches the defined
event pattern. EventBridge sends the event to the
specified target.

⭘ Schedule
A rule that runs on a schedule

***Figure 7-36.*** *Sets a rule name for the Amazon EventBridge*

The next step will be to build an event pattern; we will choose "AWS event or EventBridge partner events," depending on the use case the source will be. In our case, we do not need to get everything, and we need only one basis, so we will go with first option, as shown in Figure 7-37.

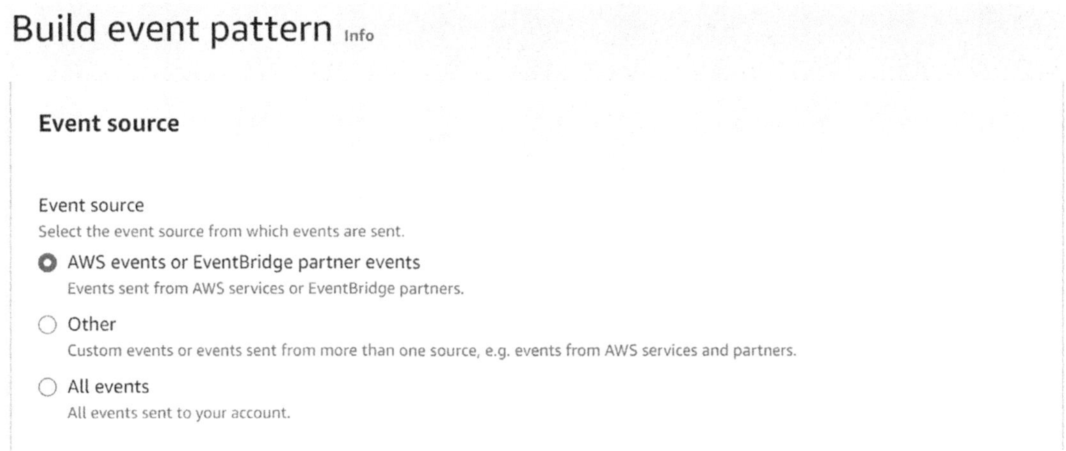

# Build event pattern Info

**Event source**

Event source

Select the event source from which events are sent.

🔘 AWS events or EventBridge partner events
Events sent from AWS services or EventBridge partners.

⭘ Other
Custom events or events sent from more than one source, e.g. events from AWS services and partners.

⭘ All events
All events sent to your account.

***Figure 7-37.*** *Event source configuration*

The event sample is optional, and usually, it is used when you are writing and testing the event pattern with Amazon AWS; there are three options for that.

- *AWS event*: Used for any resource within the AWS

- *EventBridge partner events*: Usually, as a third-party solution

- *Enter my own*: Custom one created by DevOps

For example, Figure 7-38 shows the event sample options.

**Sample event - *optional***

You don't have to select or enter a sample event, but it's recommended so you can reference it when writing and testing the event pattern, or filter criteria.

You can reference the sample event when you write the event pattern, or use the sample event to test if it matches the event pattern. Find a sample event, enter your own, or edit a sample event below. Learn more about the required fields in a sample event. ☑

Sample event type

◉ AWS events    ○ EventBridge partner events    ○ Enter my own

Sample events
Filter by event source and type or by keyword.

AWS API Call via CloudTrail ▼

```
13      "type": "AssumedRole",
14      "principalId": "AAOAAA555CCC6AAAADD55:test",
15      "arn": "arn:aws:sts::123456789012:root/test",
16      "accountId": "123456789012",
17      "accessKeyId": "AAOAAA555CCC6AAAADD55",
18      "sessionContext": {
19        "sessionIssuer": {
20          "type": "Role",
21          "principalId": "AAOAAA555CCC6AAAADD55",
22          "arn": "arn:aws:iam::123456789012:role/Test",
23          "accountId": "123456789012",
24          "userName": "Test"
25        },
26        "webIdFederationData": {},
27        "attributes": {
28          "creationDate": "2022-04-01T00:00:00Z",
29          "mfaAuthenticated": "false"
30        }
31
```

Copy

***Figure 7-38.*** *Event sample configuration example*

Finally, on the same screen, the event pattern, which means which AWS services I will send notifications about in this case, will be IAM, and the event name will be IAM-Policy-Attach. See Figure 7-39.

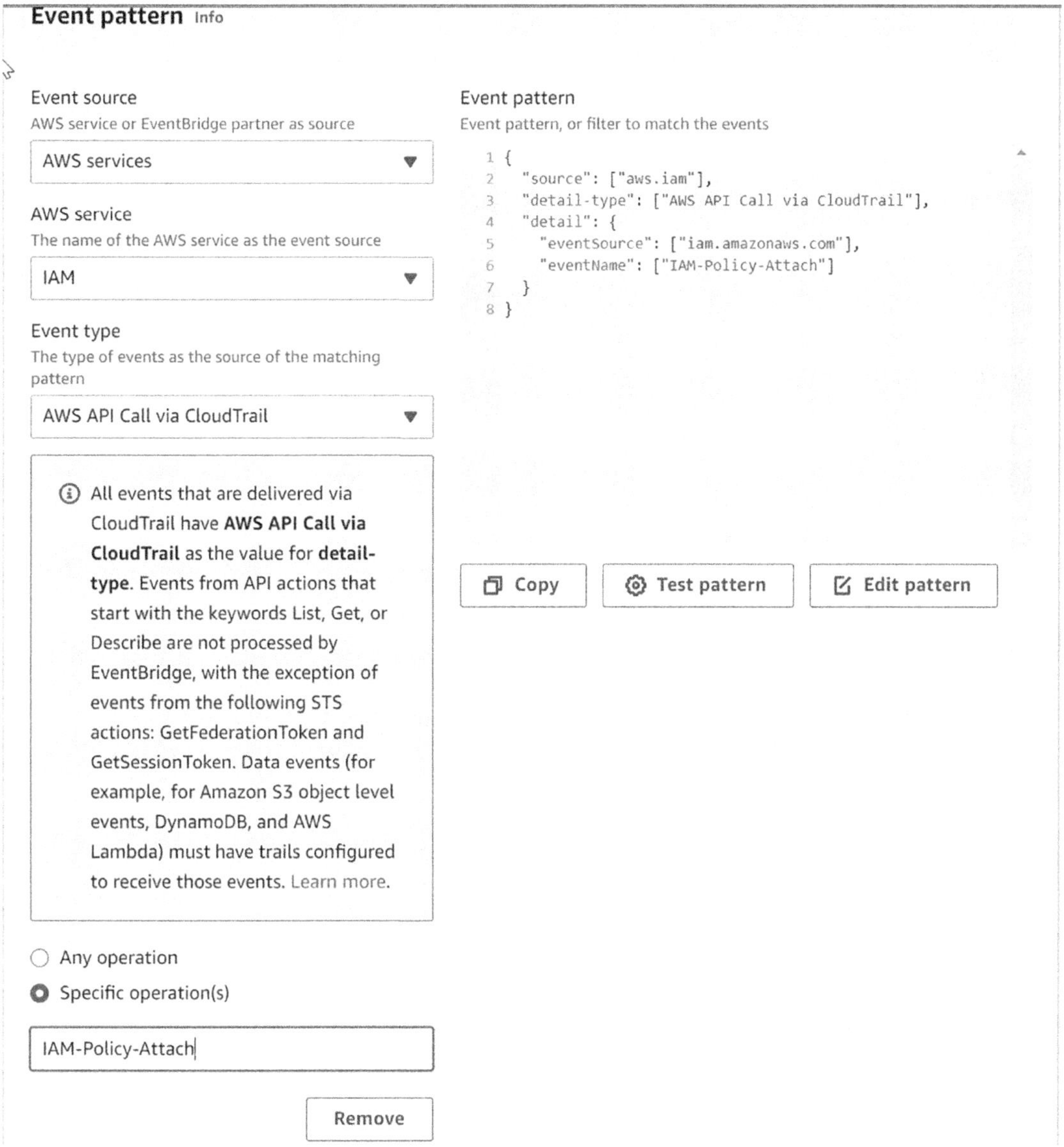

## Event pattern  Info

**Event source**
AWS service or EventBridge partner as source

```
AWS services                                  ▼
```

**AWS service**
The name of the AWS service as the event source

```
IAM                                           ▼
```

**Event type**
The type of events as the source of the matching pattern

```
AWS API Call via CloudTrail                   ▼
```

> ⓘ All events that are delivered via CloudTrail have **AWS API Call via CloudTrail** as the value for **detail-type**. Events from API actions that start with the keywords List, Get, or Describe are not processed by EventBridge, with the exception of events from the following STS actions: GetFederationToken and GetSessionToken. Data events (for example, for Amazon S3 object level events, DynamoDB, and AWS Lambda) must have trails configured to receive those events. Learn more.

○ Any operation
◉ Specific operation(s)

```
IAM-Policy-Attach|
```

[ Remove ]

**Event pattern**
Event pattern, or filter to match the events

```
1  {
2    "source": ["aws.iam"],
3    "detail-type": ["AWS API Call via CloudTrail"],
4    "detail": {
5      "eventSource": ["iam.amazonaws.com"],
6      "eventName": ["IAM-Policy-Attach"]
7    }
8  }
```

[ 🗗 Copy ]   [ ⚙ Test pattern ]   [ ✓ Edit pattern ]

***Figure 7-39.*** *Event pattern configuration*

Click Next. On the next screen, we need to define the target for our case. SNS and SNS work based on topics, so either you will create one before or you can add one later, as shown in Figure 7-40.

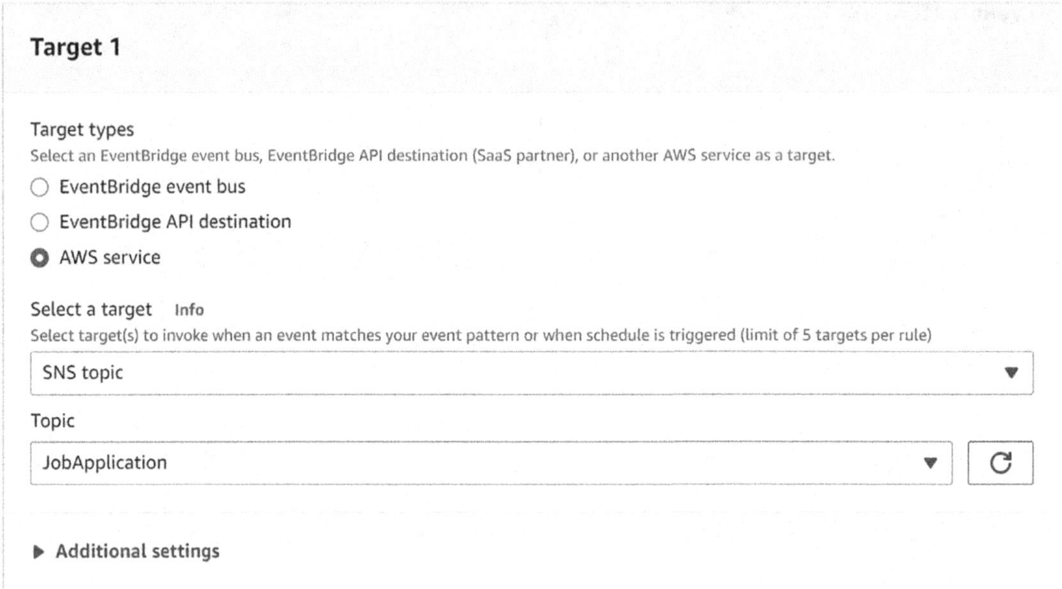

**Target 1**

Target types
Select an EventBridge event bus, EventBridge API destination (SaaS partner), or another AWS service as a target.
○ EventBridge event bus
○ EventBridge API destination
● AWS service

Select a target    Info
Select target(s) to invoke when an event matches your event pattern or when schedule is triggered (limit of 5 targets per rule)

| SNS topic | ▼ |

Topic

| JobApplication | ▼ | ⟳ |

▶ Additional settings

***Figure 7-40.*** *Target, SNS topic*

Click Next, tag your resource, and review and create, as shown in Figure 7-41.

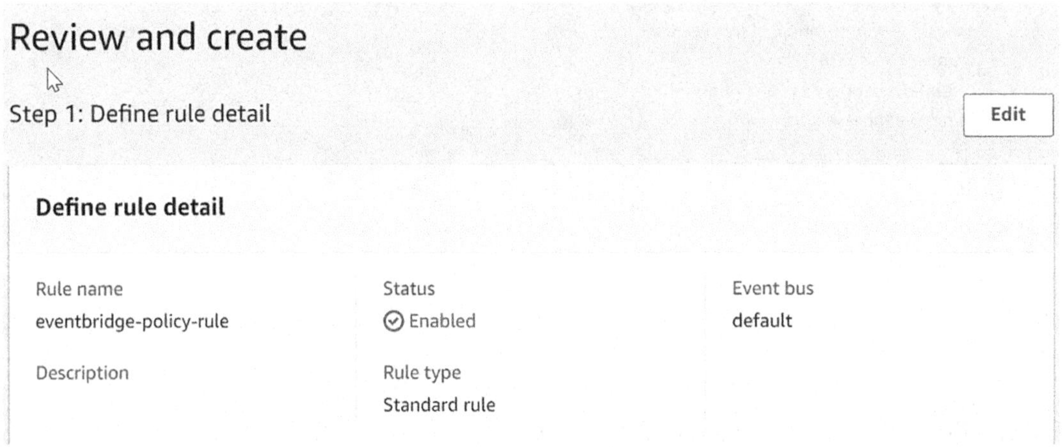

# Review and create

Step 1: Define rule detail                                                    Edit

**Define rule detail**

| Rule name | Status | Event bus |
|---|---|---|
| eventbridge-policy-rule | ⊘ Enabled | default |

| Description | Rule type | |
| | Standard rule | |

***Figure 7-41.*** *Reviewing and creation*

CloudWatch is considered one of the most common monitoring tools for Amazon AWS, and there are many things to cover when it comes to CloudWatch.

For example, you are configuring metric monitoring in RDS, logging in DynamoDB, and monitoring events in Elasticache, Redshift, DocumentDB, and more.

Monitoring is often an afterthought during application creation and deployment. Even though it is an effective procedure and a significant component of the responsibility of the SRE/DevOps, one of the primary goals of this function is to guarantee that the system continues to have a high level of availability and dependability.

To guarantee that the system is highly available and dependable, one of the most important things that must be done is to ensure that it can be monitored and observed appropriately.

SRE/DevOps brings significant automation to the work, and programming language knowledge is always beneficial when automating things.

# AWS X-Ray

The AWS X-Ray application is tracked and debugged by another Amazon AWS service, which does so by gathering various data from the application side.

For instance, X-Ray will be able to utilize the data associated with requests to characterize the problem and determine whether there is room for improvement.

From the console, search for *X-Ray*, as shown in Figure 7-42.

***Figure 7-42.*** *Console X-Ray*

The next screen will be the welcome screen, allowing you to configure X-Ray for your application quickly, or you can do it by clicking Cancel. See Figure 7-43.

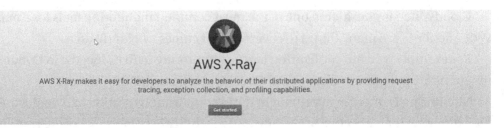

***Figure 7-43.*** *X-Ray welcome screen*

Before moving to work with X-Ray, we need to explain the following concepts:

- *Segments*: This provides information about the request and the task that has been completed. Take, for instance, the case when your application receives an HTTP request, and the information will be, for example, the host, response status, etc.

- *Subsegments*: Supply additional precise time information and specifics about calls made downstream by your application to satisfy the first request.

- *Service graph*: A document written in JSON details the many services and resources included in your application.

- *Traces*: This assembles all the segments produced by a single request. This request is often an HTTP GET or POST request that goes via a load balancer, reaches your application code, and creates downstream calls to other AWS services or external web APIs.

- *Sampling*: The default sample rate is set to a low value to protect you from paying any service costs while you are getting started. You may configure X-Ray to change the default sample rule and set other rules that apply to the sample depending on the service's or request's characteristics. The X-Ray also allows you to create additional sample rules based on the attributes of the request.

- *Tracing header*: This will include different information that helps X-Ray to retrieve the data.

- *Filter expressions*: This allow you to filter depending on the term you need.

- *Groups*: This can be extended for the previous filter expression and will enable the developer to create a group using the term he set.

- *Annotations and metadata*:

  - *Annotation*: These are straightforward key-value pairs that have been indexed and are available for use in filter expressions. Record the data you want to use to group traces in the console by making annotations and recording them there.

  - *Metadata*: These are key-value pairs that do not have their corresponding values indexed may include values of any kind, including objects and lists. You may record data that you want to keep in the trace but do not need to utilize while searching traces using metadata.

- *Errors, faults, and exceptions*: This monitors problems generated by your application code and errors sent back by further downstream services. Errors will be

  - *Error*: Client errors (400 series errors)

  - *Fault*: Server faults (500 series errors)

  - *Throttle*: Throttling errors (429 Too Many Requests)

To use X-Ray, we need to deploy an application that allows us to collect data. Fortunately, AWS provides you with a sample application built on Node.js; to do that, follow the steps here.

Choose the X-Ray services from the console, and click "Getting started." Once you do that, the screen in Figure 7-44 will appear.

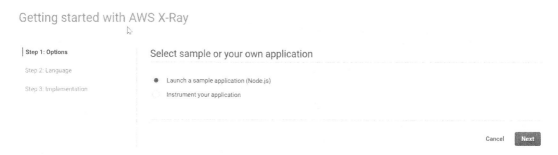

*Figure 7-44.* *Deploying the sample Node.js application*

The next screen will give you information on what will happen and how this application will be deployed; this will be done using CloudFormation.

Clicking the Launch Sample application button will open a new CloudFormation tab; see Figure 7-45.

**Figure 7-45.**  *Review sample application deployment*

For the new tab, leave all the settings with no changes unless you need to do some custom configuration from your side; see Figure 7-46, which shows the CloudFormation template will be used to deploy the Node.js application.

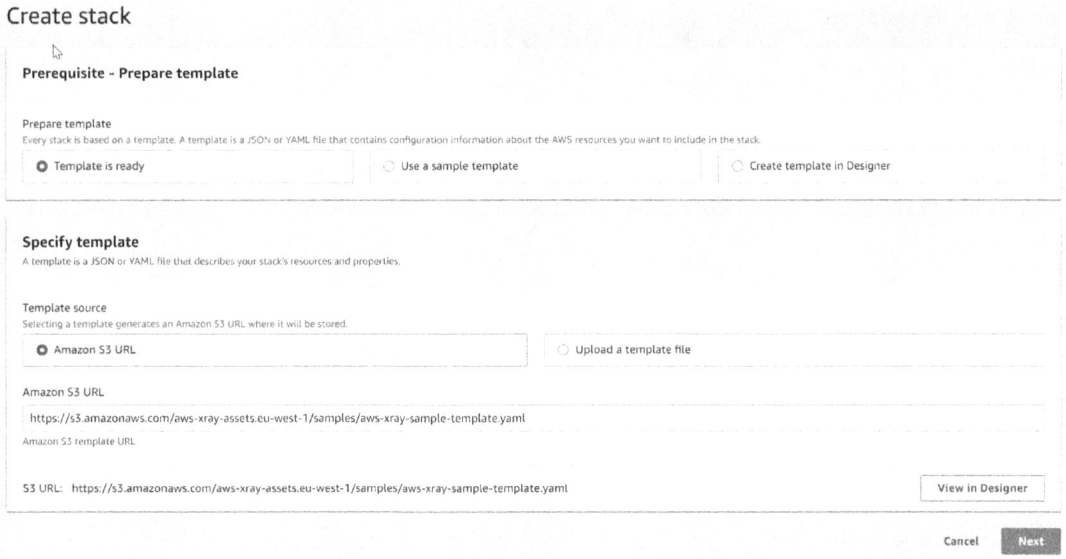

## Create stack

**Prerequisite - Prepare template**

**Prepare template**
Every stack is based on a template. A template is a JSON or YAML file that contains configuration information about the AWS resources you want to include in the stack.

- ● Template is ready
- ○ Use a sample template
- ○ Create template in Designer

**Specify template**
A template is a JSON or YAML file that describes your stack's resources and properties.

**Template source**
Selecting a template generates an Amazon S3 URL where it will be stored.

- ● Amazon S3 URL
- ○ Upload a template file

**Amazon S3 URL**

https://s3.amazonaws.com/aws-xray-assets.eu-west-1/samples/aws-xray-sample-template.yaml

Amazon S3 template URL

S3 URL:  https://s3.amazonaws.com/aws-xray-assets.eu-west-1/samples/aws-xray-sample-template.yaml          View in Designer

Cancel    Next

***Figure 7-46.*** *CloudFormation: the template that will deploy NodeJS*

On the next screen, you will see the setting for the stack name and what VPC you need to deploy; the CloudFormation template will create a new one for you unless you use an existing one. See Figure 7-47.

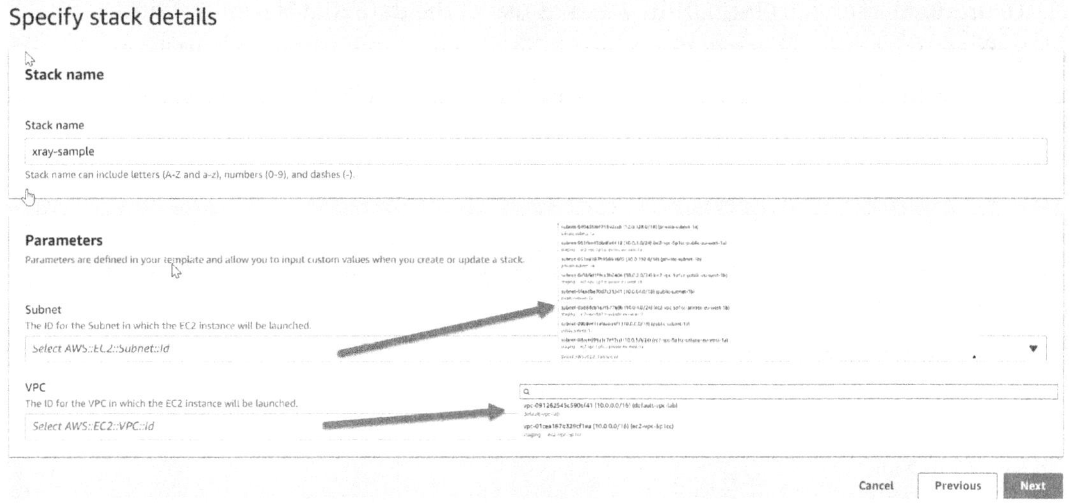

## Specify stack details

**Stack name**

Stack name

xray-sample

Stack name can include letters (A-Z and a-z), numbers (0-9), and dashes (-).

**Parameters**
Parameters are defined in your template and allow you to input custom values when you create or update a stack.

**Subnet**
The ID for the Subnet in which the EC2 instance will be launched.

Select AWS::EC2::Subnet::Id

**VPC**
The ID for the VPC in which the EC2 instance will be launched.

Select AWS::EC2::VPC::id

Cancel    Previous    Next

***Figure 7-47.*** *CloudFormation template, stack details screen*

The next screen is for stack options, tagging the resource, the permission for the CloudFormation, and stack failure; see Figure 7-48.

311

**Configure stack options**

**Tags**

You can specify tags (key-value pairs) to apply to resources in your stack. You can add up to 50 unique tags for each stack.

No tags associated with the stack.

Add new tag

You can add 50 more tag(s)

**Permissions**

IAM role - optional

Choose the IAM role for CloudFormation to use for all operations performed on the stack.

| IAM role name ▼ | Sample-role-name | ▼ | Remove |

**Stack failure options**

Behavior on provisioning failure

Specify the roll back behavior for a stack failure. Learn more ⧉

○ Roll back all stack resources
   Roll back the stack to the last known stable state.

○ Preserve successfully provisioned resources
   Preserves the state of successfully provisioned resources, while rolling back failed resources to the last known stable state. Resources without a last known stable state
   will be deleted upon the next stack operation.

***Figure 7-48.*** *CloudFormation, stack option*

Review the configuration, click Create, and the application will be deployed. X-Ray will start getting the data for you.

To produce a service graph, X-Ray makes use of the data that is sent by your application. Each Amazon Web Services resource that transfers data to X-Ray is represented in the chart as a separate service. Edges are the connecting points between the many benefits that collaborate to fulfill requests. Edges are the connection points between your application and its customers and between your application and the downstream services and resources it uses.

Your application comprises various services and resources, detailed in a document known as a *service graph,* a JSON file. The X-Ray console will build a depiction of the service, also known as the *service map,* using the service graph; see Figure 7-49.

**Figure 7-49.** *X-Ray service map*

The movement of a request via your application can be followed using a trace ID.
A single request will produce many segments, all of which will be collected in a trace; see
Figure 7-50.

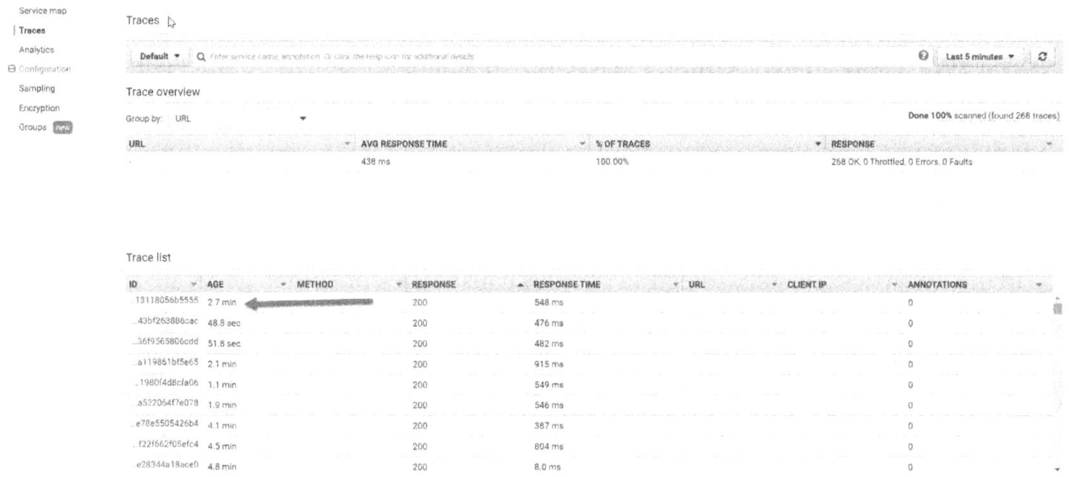

**Figure 7-50.** *X-Ray, Traces section*

Clicking one of the trace IDs will give you more information about it; see Figure 7-51.

**Figure 7-51.** *X-Ray, trace details*

The AWS X-Ray analytics interface is a tool that allows users to interact with trace data to rapidly obtain a better understanding of how their application and the underlying services it uses are functioning. Through interactive reaction time and time-series graphs, the console allows you to investigate, analyze, and see traces in graphical form.

In the Analytics console, selecting choices causes the console to generate filters that reflect the specified subset of all traces. By clicking the graphs and the panels of metrics and variables linked with the current trace set, you can adjust the active dataset using progressively more specific filters; see Figure 7-52.

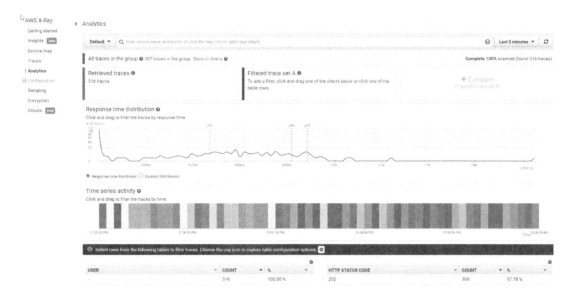

***Figure 7-52.*** *X-Ray analytics*

# Summary

In this chapter, we discussed settings and administration and safeguarding your workloads operating on AWS.

In addition, to understand infrastructure monitoring from AWS's perspective, we explained different services, starting with the basic services: the resource dashboard, CloudTrail, CloudWatch, and, finally, AWS X-Ray.

In the next chapter, we will discuss a new concept, security, and how it is crucial in the DevOps life cycle; we will define new terms called DevSecOps and how to use it daily to ensure that the environment is secured.

We will go through different Amazon AWS services that can be used to secure your environment; moreover, the next chapter will discuss code analysis and tools that can be used as well as show some examples.

# CHAPTER 8

# DevOps Security (DevSecOps)

In this chapter, I will cover the importance of security in DevOps as well as tools and strategies you can employ to ensure your company's assets remain secure, including the following:

- AWS Certificate Manager

- Web Application Firewall

- Enabling security

- Policy as code

To succeed in a highly competitive market, businesses need to act quickly, be willing to take risks, and maintain operations at affordable costs. The purpose of security teams in these types of companies is to serve as a safety net that protects the firm's assets while also contributing to the company's overall success. The engineers and managers responsible for constructing the company's goods must collaborate closely with the security teams. When a business uses DevOps, the security department must modify its culture to be compatible with DevOps, which must begin with an emphasis on the company's end users.

Everyone involved in the development pipeline must maintain a customer-centric mindset in DevOps.

- Product managers measure the engagement and retention rates of customers.

- The developers evaluate the product's ergonomics and its usefulness.

- The operators also measure uptime and response times.

But first, let's talk about why security is so important.

© Osama Mustafa 2023
O. Mustafa, *A Complete Guide to DevOps with AWS*, https://doi.org/10.1007/978-1-4842-9303-4_8

# Why Is Security Crucial for DevOps?

Security is often lacking in DevOps, which is quite concerning to any company. Pipelines that support continuous integration/ continuous deployment (CI/CD) and infrastructure as code (IaC) make it possible to deploy infrastructure and applications more quickly. The challenge, however, is that to deploy more rapidly, some companies do not involve security teams, which results in the following issues:

- Security usually slows down the process, which leads to delays.

- Security flaws are discovered in the infrastructure and the apps very late in the game.

- Discovering security flaws late means changing the whole process for CI/CD.

Therefore, a development-security-operations (DevSecOps) culture has emerged, where there is nothing outside the scope of the security measures. Because of the quick pace at which we generate new products, it makes great sense to include security measures in the process rather than keep them separate.

Table 8-1 shows the difference between DevOps and DevSecOps.

***Table 8-1.*** *DevOps vs. DevSecOps*

|  | **DevOps** | **DevSecOps** |
|---|---|---|
| Purpose | DevOps' primary goal is to enhance the efficiency and reliability of software creation and distribution. | DevSecOps is a movement that tries to protect software development by including security early and maintaining it across the whole software development life cycle (SDLC). |
| Involved teams | Developers and operation. | Developers, operation, and security. |
| Used tools | Different tools, such as IaC and CI/CD. | CI/CD tools and security process tools. |
| Threats | Seldom attended to throughout the whole software development process. | Discovered and addressed. |

The lessons we learn from DevOps show that for a plan to be effective, the operational side must be brought closer to the development side, and the communication barrier between different developers and operators must be broken down. Similarly, safeguarding DevOps requires establishing a deep connection between security teams and the engineers with whom they collaborate. Security has to be a function of the service to provide value to the client, and the internal objectives of security teams and DevOps teams need to be aligned to achieve this.

By bringing together engineers and operational staff, the DevSecOps culture or approach ensures that security is included in projects from the outset and that it takes place as early as feasible in the creation procedure. Compliance and security verification processes in CI/CD pipelines are also automated as part of the DevSecOps approach to keep security standards high without impeding the speed with which applications can be deployed.

When security is included in DevOps, the security team can incorporate security controls into the product from the beginning rather than adding them as an afterthought. Everyone's primary focus is on the company's overall success. As a result, everyone is on the same page, lines of communication are more transparent, and sensitive information is better protected. Integrating security into DevOps is predicated on the premise that security teams will embrace DevOps practices and shift their attention from safeguarding simply the infrastructure to securing the whole enterprise via continuous improvement.

Security teams and all other security processes for tools, infrastructure, and applications must be fully included in the modern DevOps culture. The goal is to produce software that is both higher quality and more secure.

# Security and the Cloud

To reap the benefits of DevOps, you need not host your systems on the cloud, although it is highly recommended that you do so; cloud computing plays an essential part in many businesses.

Amazon Web Services (AWS), Microsoft Azure, and Google Cloud Platform are just a few of the popular cloud computing environments that can handle your infrastructure as a service (IaaS) and platform as a service (PaaS) needs.

They provide elastic capacity on demand to accommodate expansion without waiting for hardware to be deployed, and they reduce the up-front costs associated with purchasing hardware and establishing a data center.

These services are all hidden under the hood by data center and network management, server and storage provisioning, configuration, management, and monitoring.

When using a cloud infrastructure like AWS, you can access various application programming interfaces (APIs) for managing accounts; dividing data; auditing, encrypting; facilitating failover; storing; monitoring; and more. In addition, they provide templates for quickly establishing template settings.

However, you must be familiar with the correct methods of accessing and using this information. And under the shared responsibility model for cloud operations, you need to understand where the cloud provider's obligations stop and yours begin and how to ensure your cloud provider is doing what you need them to do.

Figure 8-1 points out some of the most pressing security issues for cloud users; these are well-known and mentioned by Sangfor, a cybersecurity company specializing in computing and network security.

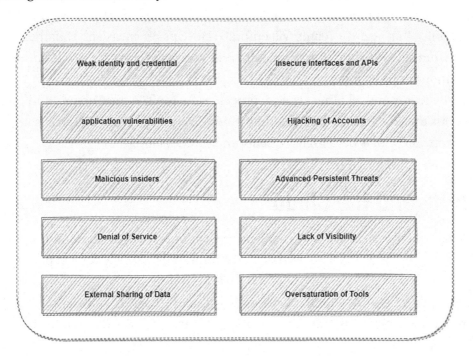

***Figure 8-1.***  *Major cloud security issues*

Let's go through each of these issues to gain a better understanding of what we need to focus on from a security perspective.

# Weak Identity and Credentials

Organizations may control who has access to sensitive data and other resources with the help of identity, credentials, and access management solutions. Digital data, computer networks, and even physical facilities like data centers are all potential examples.

The use of cloud computing brings about several modifications to the conventional internal system management procedures connected to the administration of identities and access (IAM). It's not like these are brand-new problems by any stretch of the imagination. Because cloud computing profoundly influences identity, credential management, and access control, these concerns are much more critical when dealing with public or private cloud computing.

Credentials and cryptographic keys should never be included in source code or published in public-facing repositories like version control (GitHub, GitLab); doing so puts them at risk. For key management actions to be carried out, it is necessary to guarantee that keys are correctly protected using an adequately protected public key infrastructure (PKI).

Another way is to enable multifactor authentication (MFA) so every identity or user will have another security layer. This authentication method assists in preventing password theft, which occurs when an individual fraudulently gains access to a system using another person's stolen login credentials.

# Application Vulnerabilities

There is often a lack of implementation or incorrect implementation of critical security parameters. Cloud misconfiguration refers to any technical flaws in your cloud infrastructure that might potentially expose your business to harm.

Application misconfiguration can lead to many issues and allow hackers to easily access your infrastructure and data.

# Malicious Insider

One of the most common threats a company needs to be aware of is an insider threat. Insider threats usually are employees who could inadvertently or maliciously use their access privileges to provide outsiders access to a company's network. When there is an absence of infrastructure management and increased accessibility, it is considerably more challenging to identify a hostile insider in cloud-based applications.

Any employee with access to sensitive information and who knows the company's security measures might be considered a malevolent insider. The four basic types of insider threats are sabotage, fraud, IP theft, and espionage. It's important to note that carelessness isn't necessarily the root cause of these dangers, despite popular belief.

# Denial-of-Service Attacks

Denial-of-service (DoS) attacks, also known as *distributed denial-of-service attacks*, are aimed at bringing down a network and making it unavailable to the people for whom it was created.

They are accomplished by overwhelming the targeted system with traffic or feeding it information that causes it to crash. A successful distributed DoS assault might compromise the network's data, which can subsequently be used to gain financial advantage at the expense of the targeted firm. Most businesses now store and operate mission-critical applications in the cloud.

# External Sharing of Data

The advent of cloud computing has changed file sharing and collaboration by making data more readily available. However, this external access poses a serious security risk to your cloud system. The problem stems from the simplicity with which one can distribute a link to resources and get access to several databases, jeopardizing the confidentiality of those resources. We have uncovered exploitable weaknesses in the infrastructure in our haste to make cloud sharing more accessible and inventive.

# Insecure APIs

Cloud service providers present a collection of UIs and APIs to facilitate client management and interaction with cloud services. The safety and reliability of all cloud services depend on the integrity of these application programming interfaces.

These interfaces must be developed to defend against accidental and malicious efforts to get around the security policy. This protection should include authentication, access control, encryption, and activity monitoring. APIs that are not developed well may result in their abuse or, even worse, a data breach. APIs that have been hacked, broken, or left exposed have been the root cause of many significant data breaches; understanding the security standards that must be met while building and delivering these interfaces on the Internet is essential for organizations.

Typically, a system's APIs and UIs are the most visible elements to outsiders, and they can be the only assets with a public IP address that need to be secured.

# Hijacking the Accounts

There is a risk of account hijacking, which occurs when hostile attackers obtain access to extraordinarily privileged or sensitive accounts and then misuse those accounts.

Accounts for cloud services or subscriptions pose the most risk in cloud settings because of the nature of the services they provide. These accounts are vulnerable to being compromised by phishing, exploitation of cloud-based services, or stolen credentials.

Although distinct and potentially devastating, these dangers may pose significant problems in the cloud, such as the loss of data and assets or the interruption of services; these risks come from how cloud services are organized, run, and delivered. Data and applications live in cloud services.

# Advanced Persistent Threats

Advanced persistent threats (APTs) are sophisticated forms of network assault that include numerous phases and a variety of various attack methods. An advanced persistent threat is not an assault that is dreamed of or carried out on the spur of the moment. Instead, attackers actively plan their assault plans against specific targets, and then they attack the course of an extended period.

APT is a cyberattack that has been planned and executed by a group of threat actors that are highly experienced and knowledgeable; the attackers meticulously prepare their campaign to take place over an extended period targeting key targets, and they then carry it out.

## Lack of Visibility

Implementing a suitable security architecture that can survive cyberattacks is one of the most challenging difficulties that must be overcome by moving to the cloud. Sadly, the steps involved in this procedure remain a mystery to many organizations.

When companies think migrating data to the cloud is just lifting and shifting their current information technology stack and security controls to a cloud environment, they leave their data vulnerable to various potential risks. Insufficient comprehension of shared responsibility for security contributes to the problem.

## An Abundance of Available Tools

As the demand for cloud technology continues to rise, tools have also been developed to meet these demands. Each tool has pros and cons; more tools can lead to misconfiguration, allowing an attacker to use these threats to access the company's data.

Now we have explained security and DevOps in general, let's do this. Still, from the Amazon AWS side, Amazon AWS provides different security services that allow clients to understand what is happening on their accounts and correctly protect them; Figure 8-2 shows you the security services inside Amazon AWS.

***Figure 8-2.*** *Amazon AWS security services*

We also have other services in AWS that can be considered helpful for security purposes and guide you to secure the company account, as you can see in Figure 8-3.

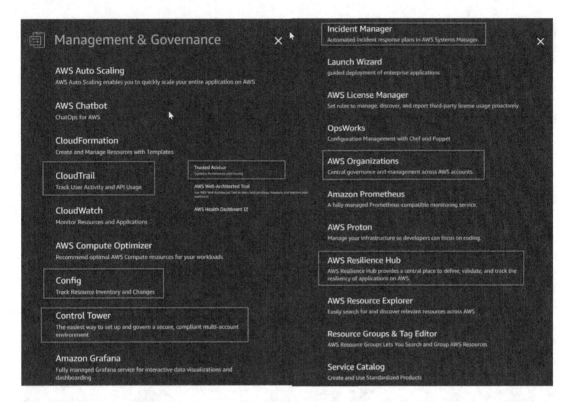

***Figure 8-3.*** *AWS helpful security services*

I will highlight some of these services. After that, I will cover how you can integrate DevSecOps with your pipeline and show you an example of the SonarCloud and Checkov tools that allow you to check threats into your IaC.

# AWS Artifact

AWS Artifact is a free service provided by Amazon AWS. It is a self-service portal that allows on-demand access to compliance reports and entry into certain online agreements.

Figure 8-4 shows the welcome screen for AWS Artifact.

***Figure 8-4.*** *Amazon AWS Artifact*

Click "View reports" and you will see a different security report issued by Amazon or a third party; see Figure 8-5.

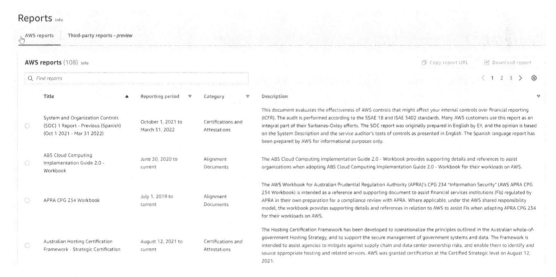

***Figure 8-5.*** *AWS Artifact report*

# AWS Certificate Manager

The AWS Certificate Manager (ACM) simplifies managing SSL/TLS X.509 certificates and keys for your AWS-hosted websites and apps, including their generation, storage, and renewal.

# Request a Public Certificate Using the Console

From the console, under Certificate Manager in the left panel, click "Request certificate"; see Figure 8-6.

***Figure 8-6.***  *Certificate Manager, request certificate*

The next screen will be information for the certification, such as the domain name, which can be on Route 53 or any other third-party solution.

We have a validation method, which is either by DNS if you have permission to modify the DNS or via email; AWS recommends using DNS by adding a CNAME record after creating the certificate to your domain.

Note for the domain setup on Route 53, the validation will take a few minutes, but the third-party solution will take 24 to 28 hours.

Figure 8-7 shows the certificate configuration needed on AWS.

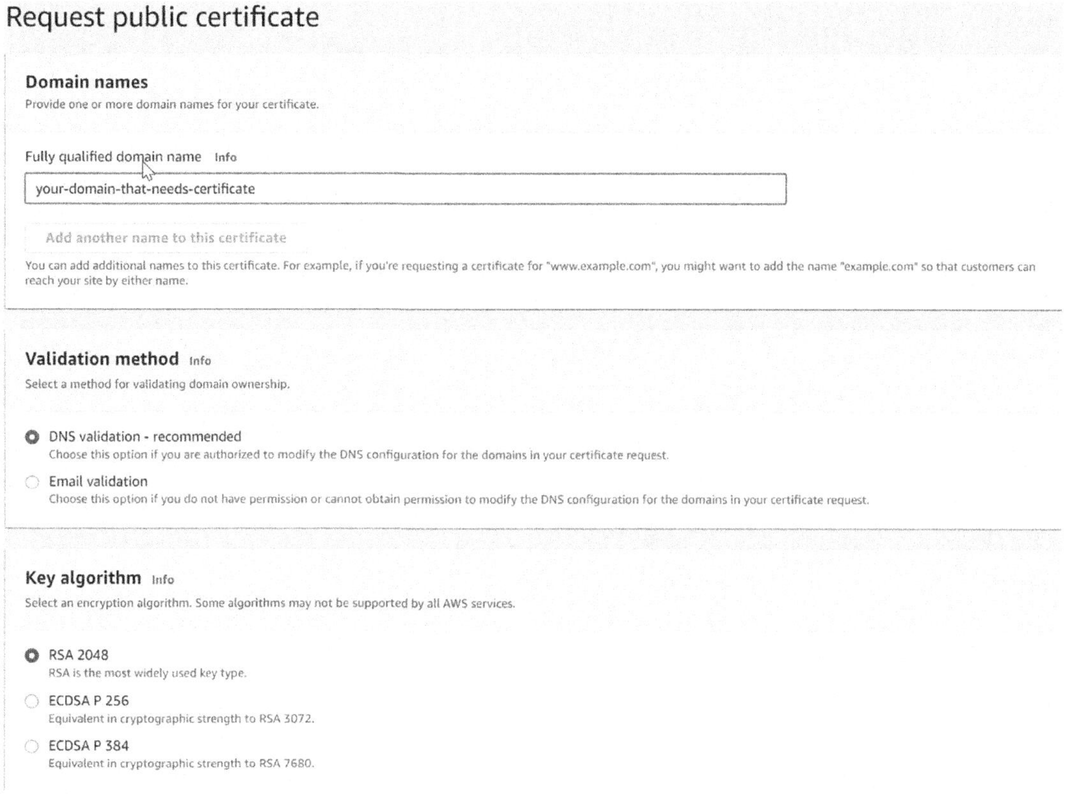

## Request public certificate

**Domain names**

Provide one or more domain names for your certificate.

Fully qualified domain name   Info

```
your-domain-that-needs-certificate
```

Add another name to this certificate

You can add additional names to this certificate. For example, if you're requesting a certificate for "www.example.com", you might want to add the name "example.com" so that customers can reach your site by either name.

---

**Validation method**   Info

Select a method for validating domain ownership.

⦿ DNS validation - recommended
  Choose this option if you are authorized to modify the DNS configuration for the domains in your certificate request.

○ Email validation
  Choose this option if you do not have permission or cannot obtain permission to modify the DNS configuration for the domains in your certificate request.

---

**Key algorithm**   Info

Select an encryption algorithm. Some algorithms may not be supported by all AWS services.

⦿ RSA 2048
  RSA is the most widely used key type.

○ ECDSA P 256
  Equivalent in cryptographic strength to RSA 3072.

○ ECDSA P 384
  Equivalent in cryptographic strength to RSA 7680.

***Figure 8-7.*** *AWS Certificate Manager, request certificate configuration*

Click the Request button, and the status of the certificate will be pending validation until you add the CNAME to your domain; see Figure 8-8.

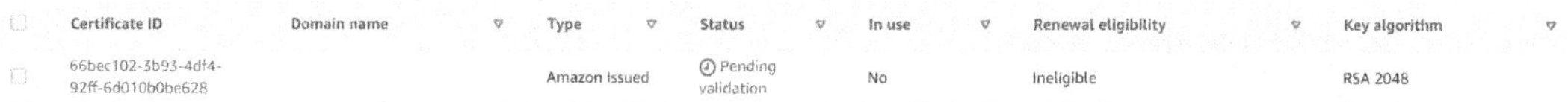

| | Certificate ID | Domain name | ▽ | Type | ▽ | Status | ▽ | In use | ▽ | Renewal eligibility | ▽ | Key algorithm | ▽ |
|---|---|---|---|---|---|---|---|---|---|---|---|---|---|
| ☐ | 66bec102-5b93-4df4-92ff-6d010b0be628 | | | Amazon Issued | | ⏱ Pending validation | | No | | Ineligible | | RSA 2048 | |

***Figure 8-8.*** *AWS Certificate Manager, pending validation*

If you click the generated certificate, you will see the CNAME that should be added to your domain; either you will do it manually or by clicking the "Create records" button, as shown in Figure 8-9.

**Figure 8-9.** *Certificate Manager, certificate validation in Route 53*

You can list your certificate from the right panel, as shown in Figure 8-10.

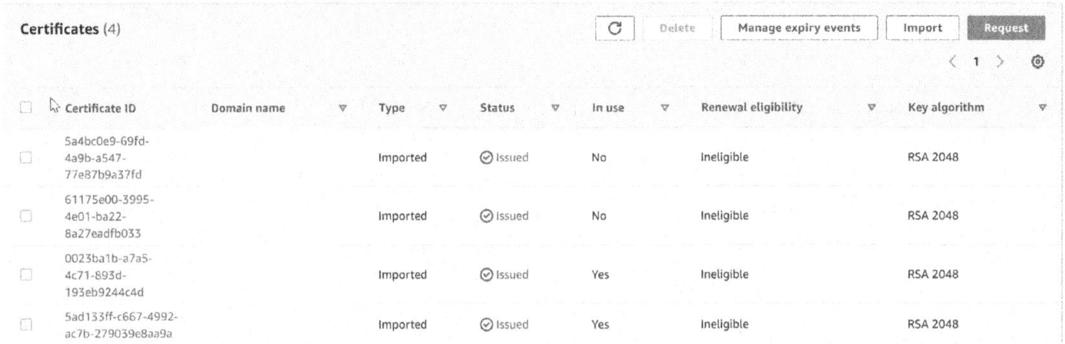

| | Certificate ID | Domain name | Type | Status | In use | Renewal eligibility | Key algorithm |
|---|---|---|---|---|---|---|---|
| ☐ | 5a4bc0e9-69fd-4a9b-a547-77e87b9a37fd | | Imported | ⊘ Issued | No | Ineligible | RSA 2048 |
| ☐ | 61175e00-3995-4e01-ba22-8a27eadfb033 | | Imported | ⊘ Issued | No | Ineligible | RSA 2048 |
| ☐ | 0023ba1b-a7a5-4c71-893d-193eb9244c4d | | Imported | ⊘ Issued | Yes | Ineligible | RSA 2048 |
| ☐ | 5ad133ff-c667-4992-ac7b-279039e8aa9a | | Imported | ⊘ Issued | Yes | Ineligible | RSA 2048 |

**Figure 8-10.** *AWS Certificate Manager services, list certificate*

# Web Application Firewall

You can keep tabs on all the HTTP(S) traffic sent to your secure web app resources with the help of AWS Web Application Firewall (WAF) (Figure 8-11), a web application firewall. The following resources, such as Load Balancer, CloudFront, API Gateway, and more, can be shielded from harm.

**Figure 8-11.** *WAF services, main page*

You can also manage who can access what is inside your site using AWS WAF; whenever access is blocked, the WAF-connected service will verify and respond with HTTP status code 403.

Or it will send a response you have customized based on the criteria specified, such as the IP addresses from which the requests originated or the values of query strings.

Let's talk about the central components of AWS WAF.

# Web ACLs

You can create an ACL in a web browser to restrict access to sensitive Amazon Web Services data. To establish a security policy for your website, you must create a web ACL and add rules. Web requests can be inspected according to the criteria defined by the regulations. The action to be taken based on recommendations that meet the requirements is also specified in the rules. Any requests not explicitly denied or granted by the rules can be banned or granted access based on the web ACL's default action, which you specify.

# Rules

Each rule has a statement describing the inspection criteria and an action to take if a web request fulfills the rule's requirements. A match occurs whenever the conditions are satisfied by a web request. You can configure rules to reject requests that match, to let those requests through, or to count them, and you have two options: the custom rule or the rule managed by AWS.

# Rules Group

The rules for a web access control list can be organized into groups for easy reuse.

In the next section, I will show you how to set up the WAF using Terraform. Using IaC will demonstrate the power of using it.

The Terraform module to configure WAF Web ACL V2 for Application Load Balancer; the module accepts Load Balancer ARNs and will support the following:

- AWS managed rule sets

- Associating with Application Load Balancers (ALBs)

- Blocking IP sets

Terraform will be structured within two files only.

- `Main.tf`
- `Variable.tf`

## Variable.tf

First, we need to define the variable file, which will contain the changeable things inside the code, such as the ARN or name, so deploying the code to a different environment will work fine.

```
1. variable "name_prefix" {
2.     type        = string
3.     description = "Name prefix used to create resources."
4. }
5.
6. variable "create_alb_association" {
7.     type        = bool
8.     description = "Whether to create alb association with WAF web acl"
9.     default     = true
10. }
11.
12. variable "alb_arn" {
13.     type        = string
14.     description = "Application Load Balancer ARN"
15.     default     = ""
16. }
17.
18. variable "tags" {
19.     description = "A map of tags (key-value pairs) passed to resources."
20.     type        = map(string)
21.     default     = {}
22. }
23.
24. variable "rules" {
25.     description = "List of WAF rules."
26.     type        = any
```

```
27.    default     = []
28.  }
29.
30.  variable "visibility_config" {
31.    description = "Visibility config for WAFv2 web acl. https://www.
         terraform.io/docs/providers/aws/r/wafv2_web_acl.html#visibility-
         configuration"
32.    type        = map(string)
33.    default     = {}
34.  }
35.
36.  variable "add_blacklist_rule" {
37.    type        = bool
38.    description = "Add blacklist rule?"
39.  }
40.
41.  variable "blacklist_ips" {
42.    type        = list(string)
43.    description = "Black list IPs to add, required when add_blacklist_
rule = true"
44.  }
45.
46.  variable "scope" {
47.    type        = string
48.    description = "Specifies whether this is for an AWS CloudFront
         distribution or a regional application. Valid values are CloudFront
         or REGIONAL. To work with CloudFront, you must also specify the
         region us-east-1 (N. Virginia) on the AWS provider."
49.    default     = "REGIONAL"
50.  }
51.
```

# main.tf

The main file will have the WAF configuration.

```
1.  resource "aws_wafv2_ip_set" "blacklist" {
2.     count               = var.add_blacklist_rule ? 1 : 0
3.     name                = "blacklist"
4.     description         = "IPs to blacklist"
5.     scope               = "REGIONAL"
6.     ip_address_version  = "IPV4"
7.     addresses           = var.blacklist_ips
8.  }
9.
10. #####
11. # WAFv2 web ACL
12. #####
13. resource "aws_wafv2_web_acl" "main" {
14.    name  = var.name_prefix
15.    scope = var.scope
16.    /* depends_on = [
17.     aws_wafv2_ip_set.blacklist
18.    ] */
19.    default_action {
20.      allow {}
21.    }
22.
23.    dynamic "rule" {
24.      for_each = var.rules
25.      content {
26.        name     = lookup(rule.value, "name")
27.        priority = lookup(rule.value, "priority")
28.
29.        # Action block is required for ip_set
30.        dynamic "action" {
31.          for_each = length(lookup(rule.value, "action", {})) == 0 ?
                 [] : [1]
```

```
32.          content {
33.            dynamic "allow" {
34.              for_each = lookup(rule.value, "action", {}) == "allow" ?
                 [1] : []
35.              content {}
36.            }
37.
38.            dynamic "count" {
39.              for_each = lookup(rule.value, "action", {}) == "count" ?
                 [1] : []
40.              content {}
41.            }
42.
43.            dynamic "block" {
44.              for_each = lookup(rule.value, "action", {}) == "block" ?
                 [1] : []
45.              content {}
46.            }
47.          }
48.        }
49.
50.
51.      # Required for managed_rule_group_statements. Set to none,
         otherwise count to override the default action
52.      dynamic "override_action" {
53.        for_each = length(lookup(rule.value, "override_action", {}))
           == 0 ? [] : [1]
54.        content {
55.          dynamic "none" {
56.            for_each = lookup(rule.value, "override_action", {}) ==
               "none" ? [1] : []
57.            content {}
58.          }
59.
```

```
60.              dynamic "count" {
61.                for_each = lookup(rule.value, "override_action", {}) ==
                   "count" ? [1] : []
62.                content {}
63.              }
64.            }
65.          }
66.
67.      statement {
68.
69.        dynamic "ip_set_reference_statement" {
70.          for_each = length(lookup(rule.value, "ip_set_reference_
             statement", {})) == 0 ? [] : [lookup(rule.value, "ip_set_
             reference_statement", {})]
71.          content {
72.            arn = var.add_blacklist_rule ? aws_wafv2_ip_set.
               blacklist[0].arn : null //lookup(ip_set_reference_
               statement.value, "arn")
73.          }
74.        }
75.
76.        dynamic "managed_rule_group_statement" {
77.          for_each = length(lookup(rule.value, "managed_rule_group_
             statement", {})) == 0 ? [] : [lookup(rule.value, "managed_
             rule_group_statement", {})]
78.          content {
79.            name        = lookup(managed_rule_group_statement.
               value, "name")
80.            vendor_name = lookup(managed_rule_group_statement.value,
               "vendor_name", "AWS")
81.
82.            dynamic "excluded_rule" {
83.              for_each = length(lookup(managed_rule_group_
               statement.value, "excluded_rule", {})) == 0 ? [] :
               toset(lookup(managed_rule_group_statement.value,
               "excluded_rule"))
```

```
84.              content {
85.                  name = excluded_rule.value
86.                }
87.              }
88.            }
89.          }
90.        }
91.
92.      dynamic "visibility_config" {
93.        for_each = length(lookup(rule.value, "visibility_config")) ==
           0 ? [] : [lookup(rule.value, "visibility_config", {})]
94.        content {
95.          cloudwatch_metrics_enabled = lookup(visibility_config.
             value, "cloudwatch_metrics_enabled", true)
96.          metric_name                = lookup(visibility_config.
             value, "metric_name", "${var.name_prefix}-default-rule-
             metric-name")
97.          sampled_requests_enabled   = lookup(visibility_config.
             value, "sampled_requests_enabled", true)
98.        }
99.      }
100.    }
101.  }
102.
103.  tags = var.tags
104.
105.  dynamic "visibility_config" {
106.    for_each = length(var.visibility_config) == 0 ? [] : [var.
         visibility_config]
107.    content {
108.      cloudwatch_metrics_enabled = lookup(visibility_config.value,
           "cloudwatch_metrics_enabled", true)
109.      metric_name                = lookup(visibility_config.
           value, "metric_name", "${var.name_prefix}-default-web-acl-
           metric-name")
```

```
110.          sampled_requests_enabled   = lookup(visibility_config.value,
              "sampled_requests_enabled", true)
111.      }
112.    }
113.  }
114.
115.  #####
116.  # WAFv2 web acl association with ALB
117.  #####
118.  resource "aws_wafv2_web_acl_association" "main" {
119.    count = var.create_alb_association ? 1 : 0
120.
121.    resource_arn = var.alb_arn
122.    web_acl_arn  = aws_wafv2_web_acl.main.arn
123.
124.    depends_on = [aws_wafv2_web_acl.main]
125.  }
```

Check what kind of input you need to use and deploy the code in Table 8-2.

***Table 8-2.*** *WAF Terraform Input Needed*

| Variable | Description |
| --- | --- |
| **Region** | The geographic area where the WAF will be deployed |
| **blacklist_ips** | The list of the IP will be blocked |
| **name_prefix** | WAF name |
| **alb_arn** | Load balancer ARN that will be attached with the WAF |
| **Tags** | A map of tags (key-value pairs) passed to resources. |
| **create_alb_association** | Whether to create an ALB association with the WAF web ACL |
| **visibility_config** | Visibility config for WAFv2 web ACL |
| **add_blacklist_rule** | Add blacklist rule |
| **blacklist_ips** | Blacklist IPs to add, required when add_blacklist_rule = true |

One of the benefits of creating a code like this is that you can use it as a module in another repo in case you would like to do that by calling the repo itself like the following example:

```
1. module "waf" {
2.    source                 = "git@github.com:osamaoracle/aws_waf.git"
3.    name_prefix            = var.name_prefix
4.    tags                   = var.tags
5.    rules                  = var.rules
6.    visibility_config      = var.visibility_config
7.    create_alb_association = var.create_alb_association
8.    alb_arn                = var.alb_arn
9.    add_blacklist_rule     = var.add_blacklist_rule
10.   blacklist_ips          = var.blacklist_ips
11. }
```

# Security Hub

The AWS Security Hub gives you a complete picture of your security status in AWS. It assists you in evaluating the condition of your environment in comparison to the standards and best practices used in the security sector. It collects information on security incidents involving all AWS accounts, services, and compatible third-party partner products.

The data is then used to assist you in analyzing your security patterns and determining which security concerns should be given the most attention.

**AWS Security Hub's Advantages**

- Less work is required to gather and sort data. Security Hub decreases the labor required to gather and prioritize security finds across accounts. It also analyzes finding data via a standard finding format, removing the need to handle finding data. After that, Security Hub will assist you in selecting the most significant providers by correlating the results from all the other providers.

- It has the ability to remediate findings automatically. Amazon EventBridge can be integrated with Security Hub. When a discovery is received, you can set a custom action to automate the remediation of that finding.

- It compares current security measures to industry standards and best practices. The AWS recommended practices and industry standards are the foundation for the continual installation and security checks carried out automatically by Security Hub at the account level.

# Enabling Security Hub

You can activate the supported security standards when you enable Security Hub from the console.

To activate the Security Hub, follow these steps:

1. You will need the IAM credentials with permission.

2. Choose to activate AWS Security Hub when you launch the Security Hub interface for the first time.

3. The security requirements that Security Hub adheres to are detailed on the welcome page under the heading "Security standards."

   a. Simply checking the box next to a standard will turn it on.

   b. Remove the check mark from the box next to the standard you want to deactivate.

4. Finally, Select the check box Enable Security Hub.

If you want to enable multiple accounts, follow the steps in this repo: `https://github.com/awslabs/aws-securityhub-multiaccount-scripts`.

# Security Standards

Compliance with regulatory frameworks, industry best practices, or business rules can be determined using a set of associated controls provided by security standards; see Figure 8-12.

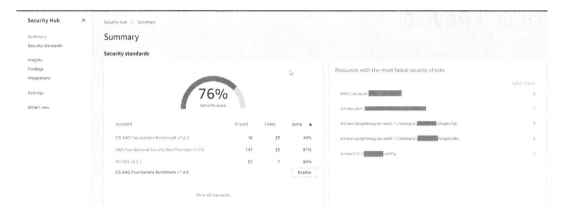

**Figure 8-12.** *Security Hub, security standard section*

The following information can be found in this section of the Security Hub:

- The kind of security protocol to which the control was assigned

- The AWS resource that applied any rules or control

- Whenever it is relevant, the AWS Config rule that is applied to exercise control

- All of the control's parameters, if there are any

Plus, you can find the current security issues based on the region and categorize them by level, as shown in Figure 8-13.

**Figure 8-13.** *Security Hub, finding by region*

# Trusted Advisor

The idea of a Trusted Advisor service incorporates the best practices that AWS has discovered in catering to hundreds of thousands of users. The Trusted Advisor will analyze your AWS setup, after which suggestions will be provided if there are any changes to reduce costs, increase system availability and performance, or assist in closing security vulnerabilities.

You may see the message "Check findings for your AWS account" on the Recommendation page of the Trusted Advisor interface. After reviewing the results, you can take the suggested actions to resolve any problems. For instance, to lower your monthly price, Trusted Advisor may indicate that you can eliminate underutilized resources, such as Lambda and EC2; Figure 8-14, shows the Trusted Advisor dashboard.

If you have Security Hub enabled for your AWS account, the Trusted Advisor dashboard will allow you to examine any findings that have been generated.

The Trusted Advisor checks the following seven core things:

- Permission, S3 bucket

- Security group

- IAM usage

- Root account, MFA

- Public snapshot for EBS

- Public snapshot for RDS

- Services limits

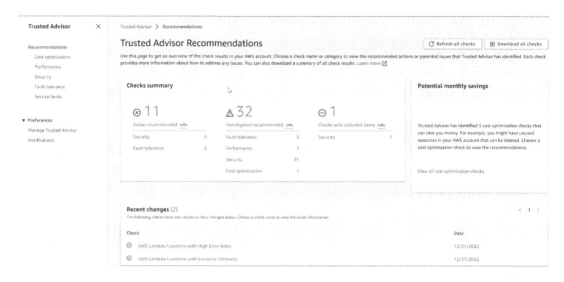

***Figure 8-14.*** *Trusted Advisor dashboard*

Clicking Security will give the AWS services you use and the security recommendation you need to apply or reconfigure, as shown in Figure 8-15.

**Overview**

⊗ 9

Action recommended  Info

⚠ 25

Investigation recommended  Info

⊘ 43

No problems detected  Info

⊖ 1

Checks with excluded items  Info

**Security checks**

Filter by tag  Learn more about using tags ☑

| Tag Key | Tag Value | Reset | Apply filter |

Search by keyword  Info

| Filter checks | Source | View |

| | All sources ▼ | Action recommended ▼ |

▶ ⊗  **AWS Lambda Functions Using Deprecated Runtimes**    Last updated: an hour ago  ↻  ⊞
    Checks for Lambda functions that are configured to use a runtime that is approaching deprecation or is deprecated.

▶ ⊗  **EC2 instances should not have a public IPv4 address**    Last updated: an hour ago  ↻  ⊞
    Checks if EC2 instances have a public IP address.
    1 of 1 resources failed this Security Hub control.

▶ ⊗  **EC2 instances should use Instance Metadata Service Version 2 (IMDSv2)**    Last updated: an hour ago  ↻  ⊞
    Checks if your Amazon Elastic Compute Cloud (Amazon EC2) instance metadata version is configured with Instance Metadata Service Version 2 (IMDSv2).

***Figure 8-15.*** *Trusted Advisor security recommendation*

After discussing some security services in Amazon AWS, it's time to explain policy as code, how it can benefit security and compliance, and how it works.

# Policy as Code

The policy can be considered a collection of rules or strategies for particular circumstances. It is a method for enforcing specific rules and limitations prohibiting illegal access to resources such as services and environments. There are three distinct categories of insurance plans, namely:

- Security policies are organizational policies that an organization implements to ensure the safety of its infrastructure resources.

- Compliance policies ensure that the system or resources comply with PCI-DSS, GDPR, or HIPAA standards. The guidelines ensure compliance.

- Policies for operational excellence prioritize ensuring that all services and resources have elements that simplify day-to-day operations, for example, labeling all available resources.

Policy as code automates and manages these rules or plans by expressing them in a high-level language such as JSON. Infrastructure as code (IaC) involves writing infrastructure resources as code. HashiCorp Sentinel, OPA, and CloudFormation Guard are popular policy-as-code technologies.

Policy as code is an outgrowth of DevSecOps, a culture that supports the shift-left mentality. If we adopt security measures at each level of the process, we can detect and resolve problems sooner, saving us time, effort, and money.

## Policy as Code Benefits

The following are the benefits:

- *Integration with automation*: Since the policy is written down as code in a text file, we can utilize it in the tools we use for automation. For instance, before providing your infrastructure, you may build up a pipeline stage that runs before to verify whether the infrastructure resources fulfill all of the requirements indicated in the policy file; this can be done before applying your infrastructure.

- *Version control*: The most significant benefit of defining policy in code is that it is much simpler to use and administer under a version control system (VCS); it enables you to use all of the current capabilities of the version control system.

- *Accessibility*: The policy's information and logic are stated directly in the code, and the code can be commented on for more clarification; this makes the policies more accessible than just being told about them.

As part of your CI/CD strategy, you may use policy as code in several ways, as mentioned in Figure 8-16.

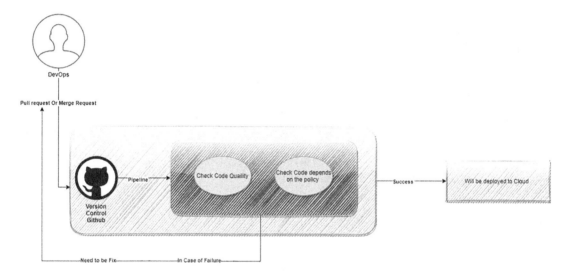

***Figure 8-16.*** *How policy as code works, one of the methods*

The following is what happens in the cycle:

1. DevOps will upload the code/new code to version control (GitHub, GitLab).

2. Depending on the stages built, the pipeline will start automatically once the PR/MR is created.

3. One of the stages will validate the code, for example, IaC, against the policy code.

4. Pipeline termination occurs if validation fails; in this case, the DevOps engineer must modify the infrastructure code to ensure it satisfies the policy; we'll send it to the cloud provider if everything checks out.

5. The code for the infrastructure has already been verified to work so that it can be automatically deployed.

Another method for the policy as code, called a *pre-approved template*, will be locked based on the procedure. Usually, the policy will disable changing the variable of the IaC and will not allow any changes to the code.

For example, it is forbidden for programmers to utilize the template with some minor configuration changes, such as instance type.

Otherwise, developers are free to utilize whichever high-end VM instance type they choose, which can be prohibited due to cost considerations; Figure 8-17 explains this cycle.

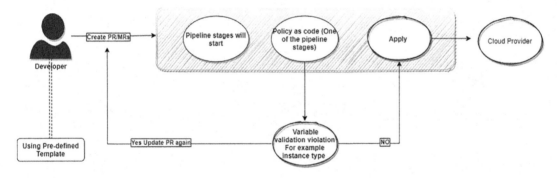

***Figure 8-17.*** *Policy as code, predefined template*

As the figure shows, I aim to allow developers to apply/modify the infrastructure resources. However, based on specific rules, I reduce wait times by eliminating the need for tickets and saving DevOps time.

A pipeline failure signals a policy violation if developers use a value in the infrastructure code that violates the policy.

1. The developer will use the template, change the code depending on their needs, and then create a pull/merge request to allow team review.

2. The pipeline will automatically start and be integrated with the policy as code to check whether the code meets the policy.

3. The pipeline checks out the application and the underlying infrastructure code.

4. After everything has been checked and verified, the pipeline system will run the infrastructure code to set up the necessary conditions for the application. If the validation fails, then the pipeline will fail too.

Now we know about the policy as code, but how will I use it with Amazon AWS? The following section will explain how to use it.

# CloudFormation Guard

The CloudFormation Guard tool is a policy-as-code validation solution that is a free source; It is compatible with technologies for configuring the infrastructure, such as Terraform and CloudFormation.

It allows developers to design rules and evaluate structured data in YAML or JSON format; the good thing about it is that it supports Kubernetes.

Refer to this repo for more information about it: `https://github.com/aws-cloudformation/cloudformation-guard`.

# How to Install CloudFormation Guard

Open the terminal, whether Mac, Linux, or PowerShell.

1. `$ curl --proto '=https' --tlsv1.2 -sSf https://raw.githubusercontent.com/aws-cloudformation/cloudformation-guard/main/install-guard.sh | sh`

Depending on your operating system, remember to add `~/.guard/bin/` to your `$PATH`.

Or the easier way is to use Homebrew. You can configure Brew on Ubuntu, for example, efficiently and use it to install the package.

1. `brew install cloud formation-guard`

To validate the CloudFormation template with CloudFormation Gurard, all you have to do is run the following command:

```
1. cfn-guard validate -d cloud formation-template-name -r guard-rule-file
```

How do you write the Guard policy against the CloudFormation template you wrote?

Assuming that we have a CloudFormation template that will define the Amazon EBS, use this:

```
1. ---
2. AWSTemplateFormatVersion: '2023-01-28'
3. Description: EBS template
4. Resources:
5.   SampleVolume:
6.     Type: AWS::EC2::Volume
7.     Properties:
8.       AvailabilityZone: eu-west-1a
9.       Size: 25
10.      VolumeType: gp3
```

On the other hand, the policy as code or Guard, in this case, protects from deploying or setting up any other EBS with a particular rule that we are using.

```
1. AWS::EC2::Volume {
2.     Properties {
3.         Encrypted == true
4.         Size >= 30
5.         VolumeType == 'ssd'
6.         AvailabilityZone == 'eu-west-1b'
7.     }
8. }
```

We need to execute the previous command to determine whether the CloudFormation file we wrote corresponds to the EBS disk that complies with the policy.

```
1. cfn-guard validate -d mycloudformation-template.yaml -r
mypolicy-template
```

The output will look like the following:

```
1. FAILED rules
2.
3. cfntestrule/default    FAIL
4.
5. ---
6.
7. Evaluation of rules cfntestrule against data cfntest.yaml
8.
9. --
10.
11. Property traversed until [/Resources/SampleVolume/Properties] in data
[cfntest.yaml] is not compliant with [cfntestrule/default] due to retrieval
error. Error Message [Attempting to retrieve array index or key from map at
path = /Resources/SampleVolume/Properties , Type was not an array/object
map, Remaining Query = Encrypted]
12.
13. Property [/Resources/SampleVolume/Properties/Size] in data [cfntest.
yaml] is not compliant with [cfntestrule/default] because provided value
[25] did not match expected value [30]. Error Message []
14.
15. Property [/Resources/SampleVolume/Properties/AvailabilityZone] in data
[cfntest.yaml] is not compliant with [cfntestrule/default] because provided
value ["us-west-2a"] did not match expected value ["eu-west-2b"]. Error
Message []
16.
```

But on the other hand, we can change the CloudFormation template to meet the policy like the following:

```
1. ---
2.  AWSTemplateFormatVersion: '2023-01-28'
3. Description: EBS template
4. Resources:
5.    SampleVolume:
6.       Type: AWS::EC2::Volume
```

```
7.        Properties:
8.          Encrypted: true
9.          AvailabilityZone: eu-west-1b
10.         Size: 30
11.         VolumeType: ssd
```

Run the same command as shown previously against the policy; the output will look like this:

```
1. PASS rules
2. cfntestrule/default     PASS
3. ---
4. Evaluation of rules cfntestrule against data cfntest.yaml
5. --
6. Rule [cfntestrule/default] is compliant for Template [mycloudformation-
template.yaml]
7.
```

After learning about the CloudFormation Guard, it's time to move on to the following service.

# Amazon AWS Service Catalog

AWS Service Catalog is a managed service offered by AWS that enables businesses to provide catalogs that the team will already approve; any AWS resources, including EC2, RDS, applications, and many more, are included in AWS IT services. See Figure 8-18.

*Figure 8-18.* *Service Catalog dashboard*

This service offers the ability to construct a service catalog and grant access to other teams via a centralized interface.

IT administrators or teams working in DevOps can use this method to guarantee that other groups are correctly applying compliant infrastructure resources.

Since we are talking about the Service Catalog, it will be good for you to understand some concepts.

**Users:** Two types of catalogs are supported:

- *Administrator catalog*: From the name, you can understand that catalog is for the IT administrator, which will be a template for the CloudFormation, access, and policies.

- *End-user catalog*: This is responsible for a team member interested in provisioning the resources via the catalog.

**Products:** You have an IT service that you want to let people use on AWS. A product comprises one or more AWS resources, such as EC2 instances, storage volumes, databases, monitoring configurations, networking components, or packaged AWS Marketplace products. A product can be anything from a single compute instance running AWS Linux to a fully configured, multitier web application running in its environment.

**Portfolios:** These are collections of products with details on their setup and provide better control over which customers can utilize certain products and under what conditions. The Service Catalog allows you to construct a unique portfolio for each user role within your business and selectively offer them access to the right portfolio based on their specific needs.

**Constraints:** The last concept is how you will deploy AWS resources for the product; you need to know there are different types of AWS Service Catalog constraints, shown here:

- Launch constraints

- Notification constraints

- Template constraints

**The first step is to set up the Service Catalog.**

To set up and provision the products and portfolios, you can use a CloudFormation template as an example provided by AWS. You can change settings depending on what you need.

Here is the template link:

1. https://awsdocs.s3.amazonaws.com/servicecatalog/development-environment.template

This template will allow you to launch a new Amazon EC2 machine using the Amazon Linux AMI; the template will enable you to change the region and determines which AMI is used.

For this purpose, an EC2 security group is created, and SSH access is allowed.

**The second step is to create a portfolio.**

- Launch the Service Catalog admin panel.

- Select Portfolios from the sidebar, as shown in Figure 8-19.

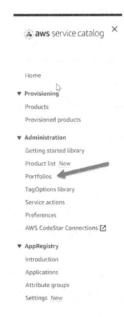

***Figure 8-19.*** *Creating portfolios*

Once you click, you will be redirected to a new screen; click "Create portfolio," as shown in Figure 8-20.

***Figure 8-20.*** *Portfolios screen*

Fill in the information based on your setup, as shown in Figure 8-21.

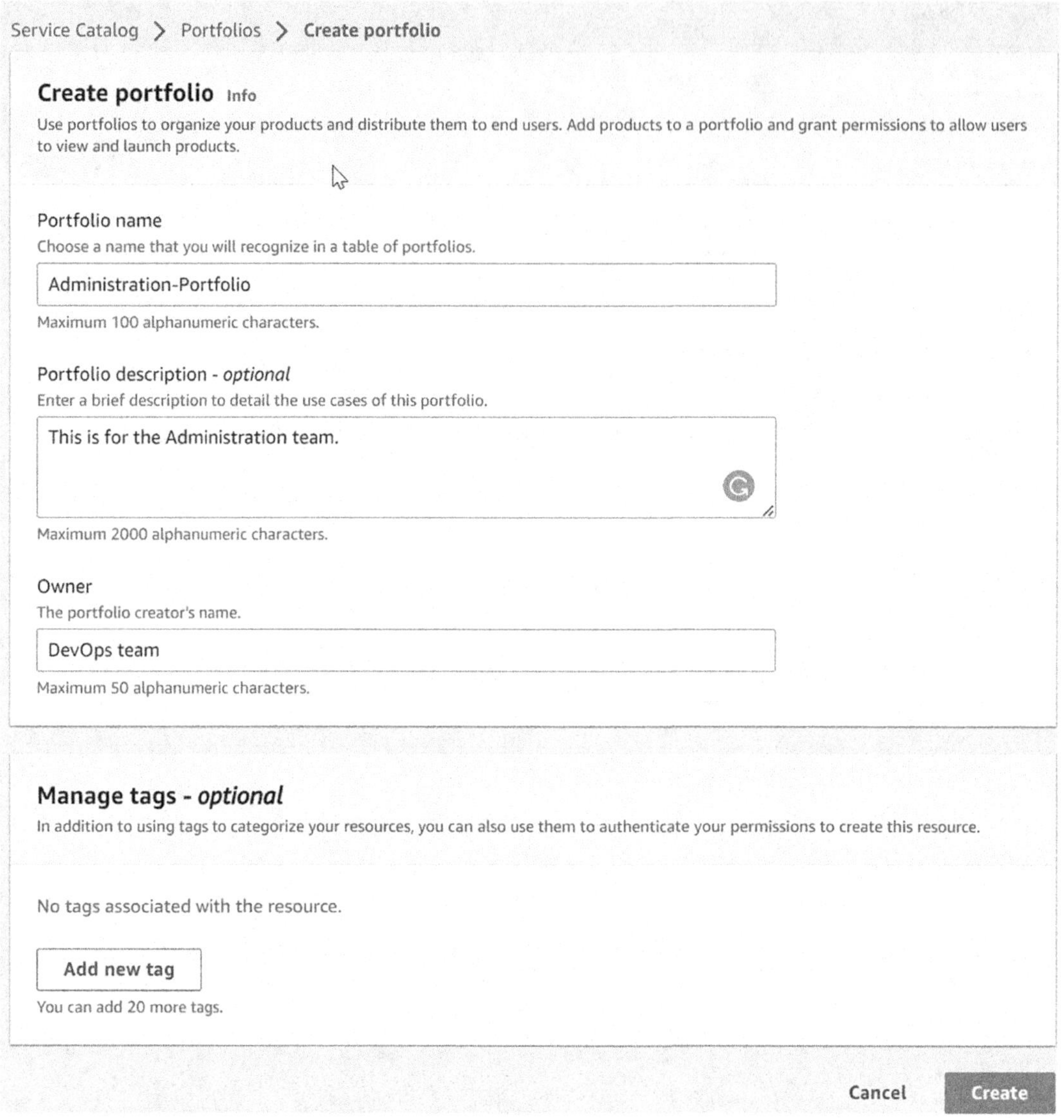

Service Catalog  >  Portfolios  >  **Create portfolio**

## Create portfolio  Info

Use portfolios to organize your products and distribute them to end users. Add products to a portfolio and grant permissions to allow users to view and launch products.

### Portfolio name

Choose a name that you will recognize in a table of portfolios.

```
Administration-Portfolio
```

Maximum 100 alphanumeric characters.

### Portfolio description - *optional*

Enter a brief description to detail the use cases of this portfolio.

```
This is for the Administration team.
```

Maximum 2000 alphanumeric characters.

### Owner

The portfolio creator's name.

```
DevOps team
```

Maximum 50 alphanumeric characters.

## Manage tags - *optional*

In addition to using tags to categorize your resources, you can also use them to authenticate your permissions to create this resource.

No tags associated with the resource.

```
Add new tag
```

You can add 20 more tags.

Cancel          Create

***Figure 8-21.*** *Portfolio configuration screen*

Click Create, and the portfolio will be created; confirm the creation and click it again, as shown in Figure 8-22.

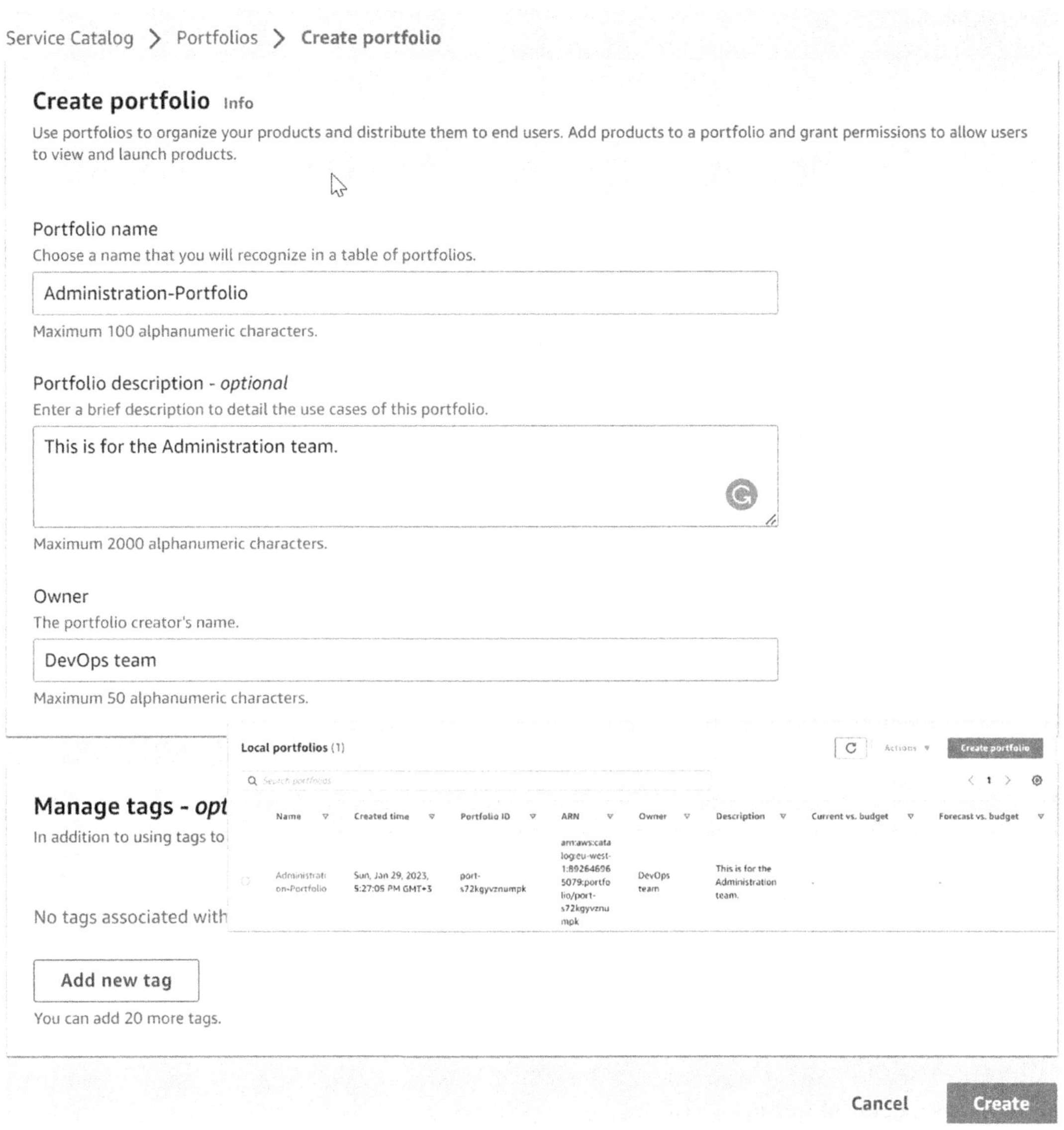

***Figure 8-22.*** *Portfolio configuration and creation*

Once you have created a portfolio, click the administration portfolio (that we created earlier) to add the product, as you can see in Figure 8-23.

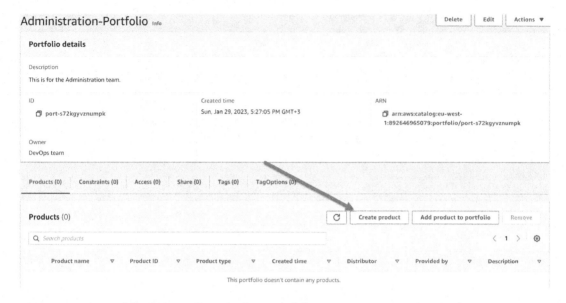

**Figure 8-23.**  *Adding a product to the portfolio*

Enter the following information about your product into the corresponding field on the "Create product" page:

- Set the product name to EC2-Linux.

- Fill in Product Description as **for DevOps Team – EC2 Products**.

- Set Owner to DevOps.

- Leave Distributor empty.

- For the version, we will use the cloud formation template provided by Amazon AWS.

- Set version name to v1.0.

The support details will depend on the company.

- *Email contact*: Team-email@company.com

- *Support Link*: http://company.zendesk.com/

- Support description

Figure 8-24 shows this configuration.

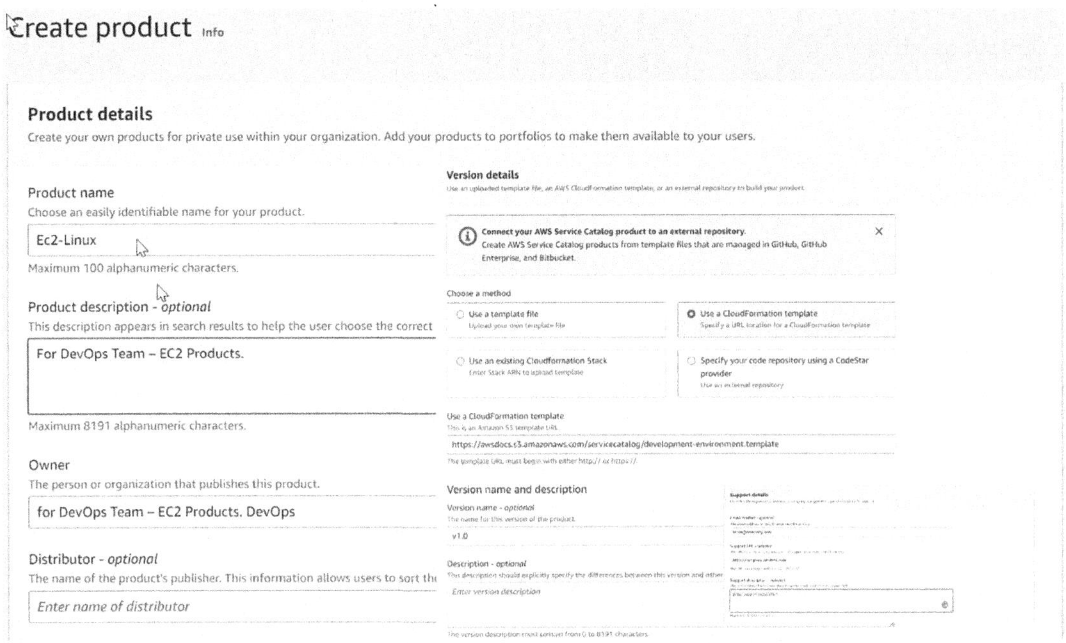

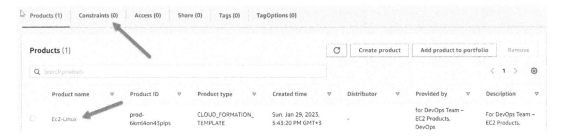

*Figure 8-24.  Product configuration*

The next step is to make the constraints now that the products have been created. As shown in Figure 8-25, choose the second tab inside the portfolio.

*Figure 8-25.  Creating a constraint*

Use the "Create constraint" page to specify Ec2-Linux as the product we created earlier; finally, choose Template as the constraint type; see Figure 8-26.

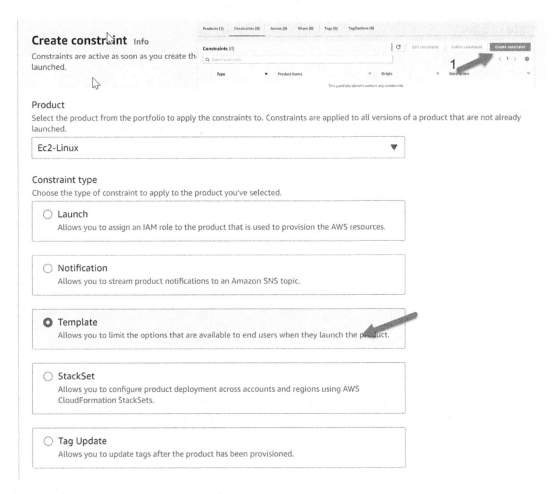

***Figure 8-26.*** *Creating constraints for products*

Choose the text editor option under "Template constraint"; we will use the following rule:

```
1.  {
2.    "Rules": {
3.      "Rule1": {
4.        "Assertions": [
5.          {
6.            "Assert" : {"Fn::Contains": [["t2.medium", "t2.small"],
                {"Ref": "InstanceType"}]},
7.            "AssertDescription": "Instance type should be t2.medium or
                t2.small"
```

```
 8.          }
 9.       ]
10.    }
11.  }
12. }
```

You can understand from the rule mentioned earlier that the EC2 has to be only t2.small or t2.medium; see Figure 8-27.

**Template constraint**  Info

Apply template constraints to ensure that end users can use products while adhering to the compliance requirements of your organization. Template constraints consist of a rule or set of rules.

**Method**

You can create a constraint by adding rules using the interactive editor or manually by using the text editor if you want to write your own rules. Or, use the text editor to view the output of the interactive editor.

○ Interactive editor
Build a constraint with existing parameters and values.

● Text editor
Use the text editor to view the output of the interactive editor or write your own constraint JSON.

▼ Text editor

The text editor shows the output of rules you have added using the interactive editor. You can also write or edit your own constraint, or use a sample constraint for inspiration.

Samples

```
 1 ▼ {
 2 ▼     "Rules": {
 3 ▼         "Rule1": {
 4 ▼             "Assertions": [
 5 ▼                 {
 6                       "Assert" : {"Fn::Contains": [["t2.medium", "t2.small"]
                            , {"Ref": "InstanceType"}]},
 7                       "AssertDescription": "Instance type should be t2
                            .medium or t2.small"
 8                   }
 9               ]
10           }
11       }
12   }
```

*Figure 8-27.* *Template constraint*

We will need to set up the access to allow users to use this portfolio, as shown in Figure 8-28; by clicking "Grant access," you will have three different options under AWS IAM.

- Groups

- Roles

- Users

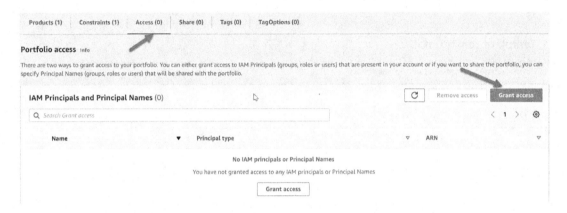

***Figure 8-28.*** *Granting access to allow users to use a portfolio*

You can let others see your portfolio in one of two ways. Your portfolio can be shared with other accounts in two ways: by granting access to IAM principals (groups, roles, or users) already existent in your account or by specifying principal names (groups, roles, or users); see Figure 8-29.

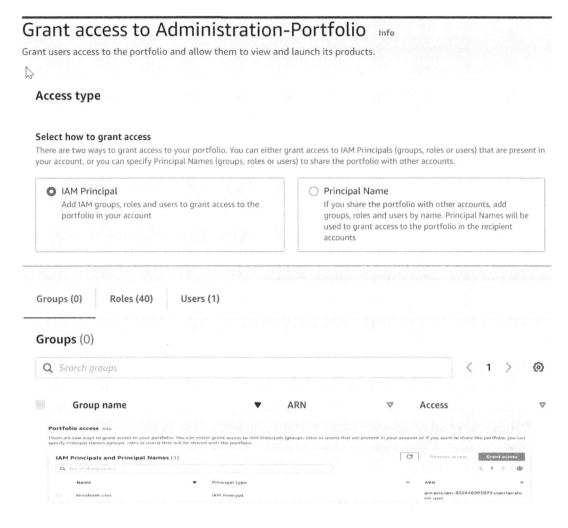

**Figure 8-29.** *Granting access to a portfolio*

After that, you should attempt to log in as the authorized user you assigned, go to the AWS Service Catalog, click Products, and click Launch.

Try to set any instance type other than the one mentioned in the previous role (t2.meduim or t2.small); se Figure 8-30. The error will look like the following:

**The instance type should be either t2.meduim or t2.small (Same as we set before).**

**Figure 8-30.** *Launching a new product*

Service catalogs ensure that the end user can offer legally permissible resources.

# Static Code Analysis

Static code analysis is a process that analyzes the code primarily independent of the programming language and the computing environment in which it is executed. It is possible to do this without running the software.

This strategy is a tried-and-true method that can identify vulnerabilities and flaws in any code, regardless of the programming language it was built since the program is not run while the analysis is taking place.

Even before a program is launched for the first time, static analysis may help uncover bugs. Not only can finding a mistake lower the cost of repairing the problem, but the short feedback loop may assist in steering a programmer's work. Sometimes, a coder can fix bugs they had no idea were possible. A static analysis tool facilitates knowledge transfer by providing attack scenarios and details on code structures.

Moreover, static analysis tools simplify the process of revisiting a large body of code once a security researcher has discovered a new kind of attack to look for potential entry points. Analyzing historical code for newly found types of faults is crucial since certain security flaws in software might linger for years before they are uncovered.

Although both are undesirable, false negatives pose a considerably more significant threat to security; in other words, a false negative occurs when a tool should detect a flaw in a program but does not.

False positives and negatives are an inevitable byproduct of any static analysis technique. The vast majority of factories make both.

Different tools can be used for static code analysis, the most common one is covered next.

# Checkov

Within DevOps, many options can be used to secure your code, and you can add an extra layer of security to your code to scan it and ensure there are no threats.

One of the famous wells known tools and open source is Checkov.

Whether using Terraform, CloudFormation, Kubernetes, Helm, ARM Templates, or the Serverless framework, Checkov's unified command-line interface makes it easy to manage and evaluate IaC scan results from any of these and other platforms.

The installation for this tool is simple; I am using Ubuntu. To install it, follow these steps:

```
1. sudo apt update
2. sudo apt install software-properties-common
3. sudo add-apt-repository ppa:deadsnakes/ppa
4. sudo apt install python3.7
5. sudo apt install python3-pip
6. sudo python3.7 -m pip install -U checkov
```

To set up the Checkov tool inside your pipeline, first you have to define which CI/CD tools you are using and what configuration inside the company; the second step will be to write the pipeline stage that will call the tool to check IaC code based on a file called .checkov.check.yaml.

You can call the file whatever you want.

Check the following pipeline stage, which calls the Checkov tool based on the previous file; I will also share the file configuration:

```
1. .terraform:test: &terraform_test
2.   stage: security-check
3.   image:
4.     name: bridgecrew/checkov:2-pyston
5.     entrypoint:
6.       - '/usr/bin/env'
7.       - 'PATH=/usr/local/sbin:/usr/local/bin:/usr/sbin:/usr/bin:/
          sbin:/bin'
```

```
8.    script:
9.        - (if [ -f "${TF_STATE_NAME}.cache" ]; then  checkov -f ${TF_
          STATE_NAME}.cache; checkov -d . --config-file $CHECKOV_CONFIG_
          FILE;  checkov -d .terraform --config-file
10.           $CHECKOV_CONFIG_FILE; else exit 0; fi );
```

Note this variable:

```
1. CHECKOV_CONFIG_FILE = ${CI_PROJECT_DIR}/.checkov.check.yaml
```

The file checkov.check.yaml configuration will look like this:

```
1. compact: true
2. directory:
3.    - modules
4. download-external-modules: false
5. evaluate-variables: true
6. external-modules-download-path: .external_modules
7. framework: all
8. no-guide: false
9. output: cli
10. quiet: false
11. skip-fixes: true
12. skip-check: [CKV_AWS_18,CKV_AWS_144]
13. skip-suppressions: true
14. soft-fail: false
```

Once the pipeline runs, Checkov will start running based on the previous file; if the code meets the check, it will be deployed and will give you a summary of the code, the same as the following example:

```
Passed checks: 4, Failed checks: 0, Skipped checks: 0

Check: "Ensure all data stored in the S3 bucket is securely encrypted
at rest."
 PASSED for resource: aws_s3_bucket.aws-bucket
 File: /s3.tf:1-25

Check: "Ensure the S3 bucket has access logging enabled."
```

```
PASSED for resource: aws_s3_bucket.aws-bucket
File: /s3.tf:1-25
```

Check: "Ensure all data stored in the S3 bucket have versioning enabled."
```
 PASSED for resource: aws_s3_bucket.aws-bucket
 File: /s3.tf:1-25
```

Check: "S3 Bucket has an ACL defined which allows public access."
```
 PASSED for resource: aws_s3_bucket.aws-bucket
 File: /s3.tf:1-25
```

Otherwise, you need to fix the issues inside the code, the same as in the following example:

```
Passed checks: 3, Failed checks: 1, Skipped checks: 0
```

Check: "Ensure all data stored in the S3 bucket is securely encrypted at rest"
```
 PASSED for resource: aws_s3_bucket.aws-bucket
 File: /s3.tf:1-25
```

Check: "Ensure the S3 bucket has access logging enabled"
```
 PASSED for resource: aws_s3_bucket.aws-bucket
 File: /s3.tf:1-25
```

Check: "Ensure all data stored in the S3 bucket have versioning enabled"
```
 PASSED for resource: aws_s3_bucket.aws-bucket
 File: /s3.tf:1-25
```

Check: "S3 Bucket has an ACL defined which allows public access."
```
 FAILED for resource: aws_s3_bucket.aws-bucket
 File: /s3.tf:1-25
```

If you need more information about this tool, refer to `https://www.checkov.io/`.

# SonarQube

Java-based SonarQube is a free and open-source program developed by SonarSource (`https://www.sonarsource.com/`) and is a cloud-based and on-premises solution.

The ability to do static code analysis is a huge step toward ensuring that all of the code in an application is of a high standard and is safe to use; developer teams can showcase the quality of their code with SonarQube's help.

It is possible to automate code analysis on developer contributions with SonarQube thanks to its seamless integration with CI/CD pipelines; it lowers the possibility of releasing an app with flaws such as poor security or too complicated code.

## Installing SonarQube

Both manual and automated Docker container installations of SonarQube using the Sonar image are supported. Another option is to deploy a SonarQube VM from the Azure Marketplace if you have an Azure subscription.

## Manual Installation

I will not go through the manual installation steps because SonarQube needs the following prerequisites:

- Java, or you can use Oracle JRE or OpenJDK

- PostgreSQL database, Oracle, or MS SQL Server

- Web browser

    - Install the SonarQube CE (Community Edition).

    - From the $SONARQUBE-HOME/conf/sonar.properties file, configure access to the database.

    - Start the web browser.

## Docker Installation

The Docker engine and the official Docker image for the SonarQube Community Edition can be downloaded from Docker Hub at https://hub.docker.com/sonarqube/ if you need to set it up for testing or demonstration reasons.

Or you can even install it using Helm and deploy it on Kubernetes from this GitHub repo:

https://github.com/SonarSource/helm-chart-sonarqube/tree/master/charts/sonarqube

It's easy to install it via Helm. All you have to do is the following:

1. `helm repo add sonarqube https://SonarSource.github.io/helm-chart-sonarqube`

2. `helm repo update`

3. `kubectl create namespace sonarqube`

4. `helm upgrade --install -n sonarqube sonarqube/sonarqube`

Also, you can install SonarCube from the AWS Marketplace provided by the cloud provider, as shown in Figure 8-31.

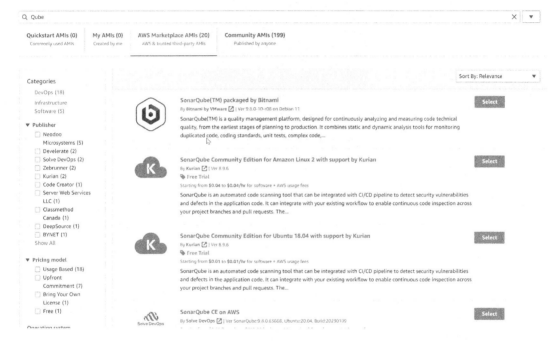

***Figure 8-31.*** *AWS Marketplace, SonarQube*

When using SonarQube in a continuous integration setting, developers typically have to wait a long time for the analysis findings. Before seeing the code analysis results, users must commit their changes and wait for the CI process to complete; SonarCube can be integrated into your CI/CD pipeline easily.

To solve this issue, you need to use another tool called SonarLint, which allows real-time code analysis, and the good thing about this tool is that you can integrate it with VS Code and use it while writing your code, as shown in Figure 8-32.

**Figure 8-32.**  *VS Code SonarLint*

In addition, you can use Terraform to configure SonarCube using the following. A URL and credentials (username and password or token) must be entered when setting up the provider.

```
1. terraform {
2.   required_providers {
3.     sonarqube = {
4.       source = "jdamata/sonarqube"
5.     }
6.   }
7. }
8.
9. provider "sonarqube" {
10.    user  = "admin"
11.    pass  = "admin"
12.    host  = "http://127.0.0.1:9000"
13. }
14.
```

# SonarCloud

Another tool that can be integrated into the CI/CD pipeline and add an extra layer of security is SonarCloud (Figure 8-33).

### Welcome to SonarCloud

Let us help you get started in your journey to code quality

***Figure 8-33.*** *SonarCloud dashboard*

This is a cloud-based service for analyzing code to find bugs and improve quality. SonarCloud's algorithms are deliberately cautious while searching for problems. These tools aim to reduce the occurrence of false positives.

There are three distinct categories of problems.

- Code smells are issues in the code that don't directly impair the program's functionality but might lead to larger, more difficult-to-fix matters down the line and make it harder to maintain. If these problems are found early on, technical debt in the application can be reduced.

- Bugs are programming mistakes that prevent a program from functioning as intended. The trustworthiness of the code is impacted.

- Security flaws, also known as vulnerabilities, are flaws in the program that attackers might use to gain unauthorized access to the system.

SonarCloud was built to be included in the software development life cycle to intervene and stop problems before they reach production; it occurs in the editor, the pull request, and the actual code. See Figure 8-34.

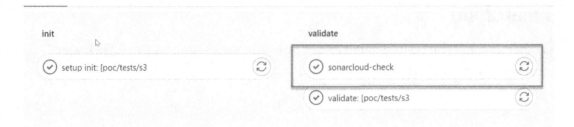

***Figure 8-34.*** *Adding SonarCloud to the pipeline*

We need to mention that SonarCloud is still new to scanning IaC, which was added in 2021; the documentation says the following kind of security threats will be discovered and examined:

- Allowing public ACLs or policies on an S3 bucket is security sensitive.

- Authorizing HTTP communications with S3 buckets is security sensitive.

- Disabling S3 server access logging is security sensitive.

- Disabling server-side encryption of S3 buckets is security-sensitive.

- Granting access to S3 buckets to all our authenticated users is security sensitive.

- Having policies granting anonymous access to S3 buckets is security sensitive.

- Unversioned or suspended versioned S3 bucket is security sensitive.

In my opinion, SonarCloud, so far in writing this chapter, will not be your first option when scanning the IaC, such as Terraform; there have been other tools in the market for a long time.

As shown in Figure 8-35, you can add the version control repo to the SonarCloud to ensure it's free of bugs and security issues.

***Figure 8-35.*** *SonarCloud with one repo*

Click the repo.

SonarCloud will give all the information and insight on what has been done and scan for that repo; see Figure 8-36.

***Figure 8-36.*** *SonarCloud inside the repo*

If you click one of the branches, you will see complete information on scanning the desired repo, as shown in Figure 8-37.

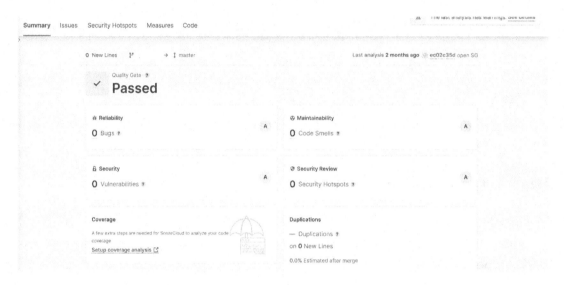

***Figure 8-37.*** *Complete information for the repo*

If you need to check the code and the quality of your code, SonarCloud will allow you to do that by choosing the Code tab; see Figure 8-38, which shows the Terraform structure and the points that SonarCloud checks.

| | Lines | Bugs | Vulnerabilities | Code Smells | Security Hotspots | Coverage | Duplications |
|---|---|---|---|---|---|---|---|
| | 0 | 0 | 0 | 0 | 0 | — | — |
| backend.tf | 0 | 0 | 0 | 0 | 0 | — | — |
| main.tf | 0 | 0 | 0 | 0 | 0 | — | — |
| variables.tf | 0 | 0 | 0 | 0 | 0 | — | — |
| versions.tf | 0 | 0 | 0 | 0 | 0 | — | — |
| vpc.tf | 0 | 0 | 0 | 0 | 0 | — | — |

***Figure 8-38.*** *SonarCloud code tab*

So far, DevSecOps is one of the primary important things to consider when talking about DevOps.

Moreover, AWS provides different services that can be used for this purpose; another tool that can be used for this is called Amazon CodeGuru.

# Amazon CodeGuru

The code review process will begin when all the developers have finished writing their code and have submitted a pull request to merge it to an upstream branch. It is common practice for the project's team leader to review the code; but visually examining the whole code can be time-consuming.

The code review process is essential, but it must not increase the burden of reviewers or constitute a stumbling block in the development process. We can automate the process of examining the code by using several tools for code review. Some well-known products now available on the market, such as SonarQube, do this for us.

In addition, Amazon has just introduced a new service called Amazon CodeGuru (Figure 8-40), which can undertake code evaluations and provide information about application performance. It helps improve the program's stability, enables us to delve deep, and reduces the time we spend discovering challenging problems. Such issues include sensitive data, race situations, undefined functions, and sluggish resource leaks. See Figure 8-39.

***Figure 8-39.***  *Amazon CodeGuru Dashboard*

The following are some of the functions that CodeGuru offers:

- The reviewer provides automated code inspection and review for static code.

- The profiler provides visibility and suggestions on the program's performance while running.

To understand more about CodeGuru, let's go through the following example: integrating CodeGuru with CodeCommit will analyze the pull request.

1.  The first step is creating a CodeCommit repository inside Amazon AWS; see Figure 8-40.

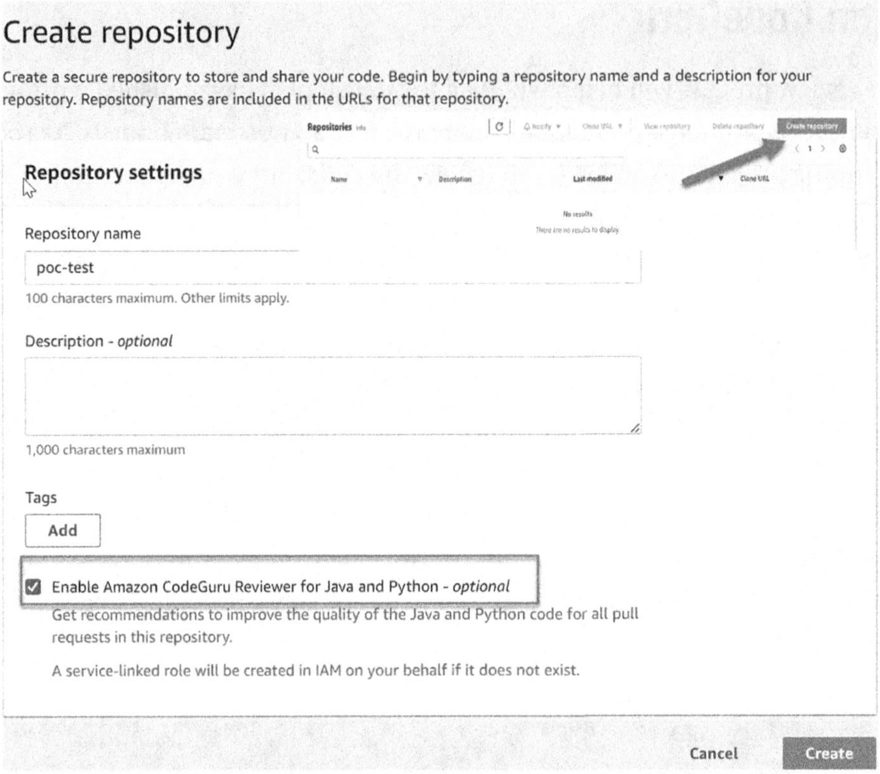

*Figure 8-40. Creating a CodeCommit repository and enabling CodeGuru*

2. To upload the code, go to `https://github.com/OsamaOracle` and upload the code from there, but before doing that, go to CodeGuru and check the associated repo.

   See Figure 8-41.

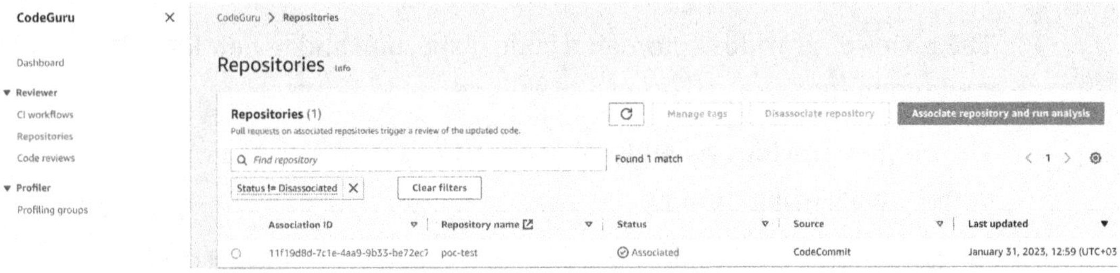

*Figure 8-41. CodeGuru associated repo that we created earlier*

You can upload the code by using the following:

```
1. git clone ssh://git-codecommit.eu-west-1.amazonaws.com/v1/
repos/poc-test
2. cp Python-new-file-devops poc-test
3. git add .
4. git commit -m "First draft."
5. git push origin master
```

3. Create a new branch named test, make some changes to the code, and then push the updated version back to the repository. After that, we will submit a pull request to the main/master branch from the test branch. See Figure 8-42.

***Figure 8-42.***  *Creating a pull request inside the code commit*

4. Once you have done this, under Code Guru, the details section will provide suggestions whenever you submit a pull request. See Figure 8-43.

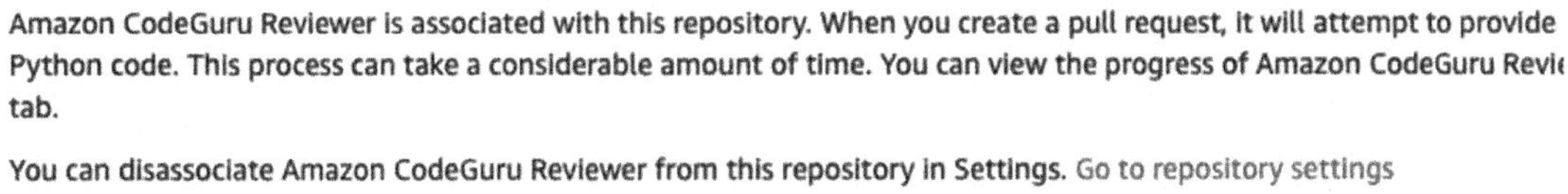

Amazon CodeGuru Reviewer is associated with this repository. When you create a pull request, it will attempt to provide Python code. This process can take a considerable amount of time. You can view the progress of Amazon CodeGuru Revie tab.

You can disassociate Amazon CodeGuru Reviewer from this repository in Settings. Go to repository settings

***Figure 8-43.***  *The details section*

5. Code Guru Dashboard will provide information on what is pending or completed for review (review status); it will take 10 minutes to complete the analysis for the code and give you the recommendation needed; see Figure 8-44.

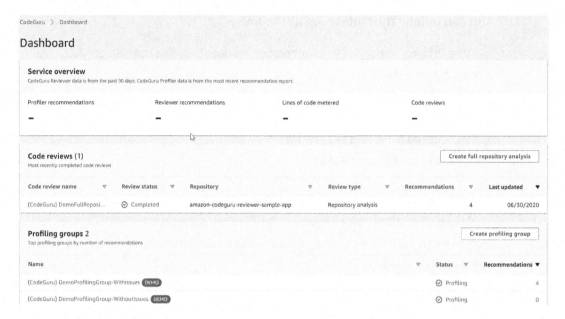

***Figure 8-44.*** *CodeGuru dashboard*

6.  Click the pull request once the status shows it's completed, and
    you will see the recommendation related to the code, as shown in
    Figure 8-45.

**Recommendations** (4)

| 🔍 Find recommendation | | Found 4 matches | ‹ 1 › ⚙ |
|---|---|---|---|

| Type = Secrets  ✕ | Clear filters |
|---|---|

src/resources/application.conf Line: 1 ⬏  `Security`  `Secrets`

It appears your code contains a hardcoded URI-formatted Database Connection String. Hardcoded secrets or credentials can allow attackers to bypass authentication methods and perform malicious actions. We recommend revoking access to resources using this credential and storing future credentials in a management service such as AWS Secrets Manager ⬏.

Learn more about the use of hardcoded credentials ⬏

Hardcoded credentials can be intercepted by malicious actors. Even after removing them from the code they may still pose a risk because an attacker might have recorded them to use them at a later point in time.

Source
CodeGuru

src/resources/application.conf Line: 5 ⬏  `Security`  `Secrets`

It appears your code contains a hardcoded Stripe Live Secret Key. Hardcoded secrets or credentials can allow attackers to bypass authentication methods and perform malicious actions. We recommend revoking access to resources using this credential and storing future credentials in a management service such as AWS Secrets Manager ⬏.

Learn more about the use of hardcoded credentials ⬏

Hardcoded credentials can be intercepted by malicious actors. Even after removing them from the code they may still pose a risk because an attacker might have recorded them to use them at a later point in time.

Source
CodeGuru

***Figure 8-45.*** *CodeGuru recommendations*

# Summary

In this chapter, I focused on the relationship between DevOps and security under one concept called DevSecOps; I mentioned different tools provided by Amazon AWS and third parties.

I provided an example for a real case scenario using these tools. You learned the difference between SonarQube and SonarCloud and how to integrate Amazon AWS services to provide a complete DevOps solution included with a security layer.

Again, there is no good or bad tool, and it's all up to the company's configuration, budget, and use case; you can see that the continuous integration and delivery pipeline is automated, except for the human reviews at certain stages.

The next chapter will cover one of the most commonly used tools by DevOps engineers: Kubernetes. The chapter will detail what Kubernetes is, as well as Kubernetes architecture, Kubernetes objects, and how to create Kubernetes in different ways.

Since we are talking about Amazon AWS, we will cover Amazon EKS and real-life examples of how to manage the EKS.

# CHAPTER 9

# Microservices vs. Monolithic

In this chapter, we will compare two popular application architectures: microservices and monolith.

In addition, I will walk you through containers of the most common tools used for microservices.

I will also demonstrate the containerization solution from Amazon AWS's side, including how to configure it and how to use it to deploy an application.

## Monolithic

A standard method for creating server and client applications is to use a monolithic architecture, wherein one huge codebase is used to create these applications. It is necessary to rebuild and redeploy the whole application to make any code modifications or updates. If something goes wrong, this process could cause the entire program to crash.

Application components are merged into one massive whole in monolithic programs, which are single-tiered. This results in huge codebases that can be difficult to maintain over time; Figure 9-1 shows the classic application architecture and how a monolithic application is deployed.

379

O. Mustafa, *A Complete Guide to DevOps with AWS*, https://doi.org/10.1007/978-1-4842-9303-4_9

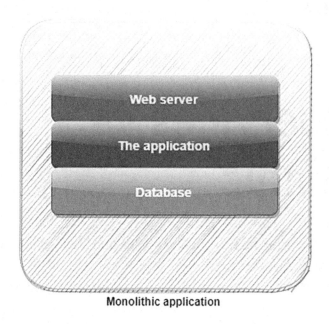

Monolithic application

**Figure 9-1.** *Monolithic architecture*

The fact that all of a monolith's components are housed in a single location makes it possible for the development process to be kept to a minimum, which in turn helps speed up the product's time to market. Creating a monolith enables a single developer or a small development team to design, test, and launch apps in less time. Since there is just one code repository to keep track of for testing and debugging monoliths, rather than the several code repositories required by microservices-based systems, monoliths are often much simpler to test. When there are fewer elements to a monolithic program, the program is easier to maintain and troubleshoot.

The simplicity of a monolithic app's deployment, management, and maintenance over a microservices solution is due to its streamlined lack of moving parts.

Suppose we have a simple application that uses this approach. In that case, it will be necessary to reserve three servers: one for a web application that the public will face, one to deploy the application, and one for the database. Each of these servers would, in turn, require expertise.

You *can* install all the monolithic on one server, but it is not a best practice for production. Adding another feature to the application will cause extra headaches, complexity, and downtime. Moreover, if a company deploys to the server once or twice a year, more planning, operations, and weekends are required.

While a monolithic approach may involve fewer moving parts at the outset, it becomes more challenging to install, administer, and keep the overall system working smoothly as the number of deployable components grows and as data centers grow. It is far more challenging to pinpoint precisely where to place each part to maximize resource efficiency and save hardware expenses. Regularly deploying new software versions is so great that it may make or break many businesses.

## Modular Monolith

The modular monolith is a subset of the single-process monolith, consisting of independently workable parts that must be combined for deployment. Modules are a tried and true method of organizing software; see Figure 9-2.

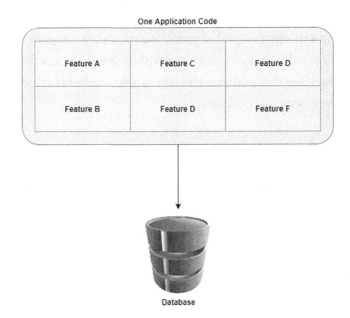

*Figure 9-2.* *Monolith but deployed as modular*

A modular monolith is indeed a good option for many businesses. It can facilitate a high degree of parallel work if the module borders are specified. It avoids the difficulties of the more distributed microservice design and has far fewer complicated deployment considerations; one of the companies that applied a modular monolithic is Shopify.

# The Challenge

The monolith, whether a single process monolith or a distributed monolith, is typically more susceptible to the dangers of coupling, particularly implementation and deployment coupling, which we will examine in further depth in the following sections.

There is a more significant potential for disruption when more people are confined to a small space. Several developers will want to change the same piece of code simultaneously, and several groups will want to release new features at various intervals. Questions of ownership and decision-making authority remain unanswered. The problems caused by muddled ownership lines have been the subject of numerous studies.

In my opinion, this is a case of delivery contention. A pertinent query to ask is, how long does it takes your team to deploy a hotfix to a live environment? In an outage, users will immediately notice whether your pipeline delivers updates slowly.

Neither adopting a microservice design nor maintaining a monolith ensures that you will never encounter the difficulties associated with delivery contention. Still, you have a lot more leeway in tackling this issue when you employ a microservice design because of the more explicit boundaries it provides.

# Coupling and Cohesion

Other concepts you will hear when you work with microservices and monolithics are coupling and cohesion. *Coupling* describes how modifying one element impacts another, while *cohesiveness* describes how related pieces of code are grouped. Conversely, coding cohesion describes how we pile together similar pieces of software. You can draw a straight line between these ideas.

Cohesion is low if the same functionality is dispersed over two unrelated parts of code. Also, there is tight coupling, because when this code is modified, it is necessary to adjust both it and the linked object.

The high cost of modification across service borders in distributed systems means dealing with a shifting code structure will be costly. Making changes across several decoupled services while potentially addressing the fallout from service contract breaks is a significant hassle.

The monolith is flawed because it frequently fails to be either of these. We accumulate and affix together all kinds of unrelated code instead of leaning toward cohesiveness and keeping things together that tend to change together.

Similarly, loose coupling is nonexistent; modifying a single line of code may be straightforward, but deploying the resulting change may have far-reaching consequences for the rest of the monolith, necessitating yet another round of deployments.

# Monolithic Advantages and Disadvantages

Like anything else, monoliths present both advantages and disadvantages. The following are some reasons you might opt for a monolithic architecture:

- *Cost-effective at the first phases of the application*: The source code may be found in a single location and then distributed as a single deployment unit. What could be simpler? There are no overhead costs associated with the infrastructure or product creation.

- *Easy to deploy*: As shown in Figure 9-1, monolithic is less complex; the deployment should include only a single deployment item (such as a JAR file, for example). There are no dependencies. You will not encounter breaking changes when the user interface (UI) is bundled with the back-end code. At one location, everything both persists and changes.

- *Easy to test*: Since a monolithic is built as a single application, you can do the testing for one application and automation as one; moreover, you test only a single service independent of any others. In most cases, everything is quite apparent.

- *Easy to manage*: It's easy because you are working with one application and one database as one stack.

Let's not forget the disadvantages of the monolithic approach:

- Scaling the application is not easy; you must plan when to mount the application or add new features.

- Want to apply new technology to the infrastructure? Different obstacles will be in your way.

- Development and operation work are separated without any collaboration; the gap between the two teams is considered an issue, and the operation team is not aware of any development work, and it's the same for development.

- When you employ a monolithic architecture, you are restricted to using the technologies already inside your monolith. You are not allowed to utilize any other tools, even if those other tools might be more effective in solving the situation at hand.

The software business has changed to accommodate the growing number of users by releasing new versions of existing programs at a higher frequency and with fewer bugs.

Because of the rise in the number of deployments, it was necessary to conceive an architecture that would handle frequent deployments and tighter update cycles while lowering the risk of the application being generally unavailable—and thus, microservices were born.

# Microservices

The idea behind the microservices architecture is to build your program as a collection of smaller apps. The term *microservice* is used to describe each of these programs.

It is versioned, has a life cycle, operates in its environment, and is independent of other components. It also has the option of its deployment life cycle; your application comprises a collection of microservices, each responsible for a small set of business rules; Figure 9-3 shows the high-level architecture.

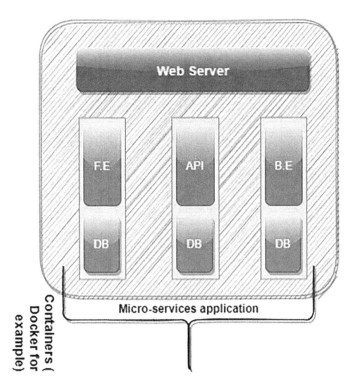

***Figure 9-3.*** *Microservices high-level architecture*

A microservice is similar to a stand-alone piece of full-featured software with its development cycle and versioning mechanism.

Decoupling microservices is another essential component of the microservice architecture; each microservice must be able to be provisioned, scaled, started, updated, or stopped separately from the others. This way, if any of these microservices becomes unavailable or unstable, it must not affect the availability or stability of the other microservices or the program.

Microservices support different protocols, such as HTTP (Rest API) or AMQP, and in general, each of the services completes each other, so we need to access each other.

Figure 9-4 shows an example of different microservices communicating.

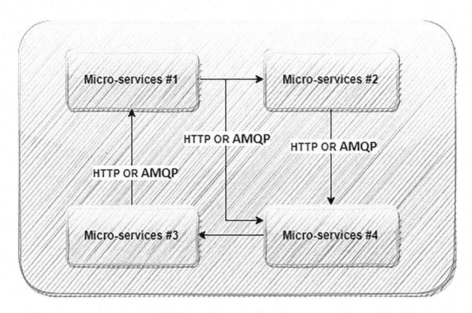

***Figure 9-4.*** *Microservices and how they communicate with each other*

Now, if I have many internal microservices, when would it make sense to use the REST API instead of AMQP for interservice communication? The simple answer is that it depends on the company's business.

Note that with the REST API, the debugging process for an HTTP request is relatively straightforward and straightforward; however, the debugging process for an AMQP message is more complicated.

Since HTTP is a technology the developers are already aware of, there is no need to provide further training for a new developer who joins the project. Sharing your application programming interfaces (APIs) as HTTP APIs is a recommended best practice since HTTP is the Internet protocol that receives the most significant support.

On the other hand, using AMQP to send messages provides you with dependability, and the fact that AMQP is asynchronous frees you from worrying about when messages will be sent. It is unnecessary to know the host or IP address of the cluster of AMQP brokers to send or receive notifications; this is in contrast to the situation with HTTP, in which you can have various hosts and IP addresses for each area.

Microservices cannot share resources such as databases; thus, they require the resource to be separate, even though some companies share the microservices for ease of management.

For example, if microservice A's database goes down, microservice B will keep running as usual; Figure 9-5 explains how microservices architecture is meant to function.

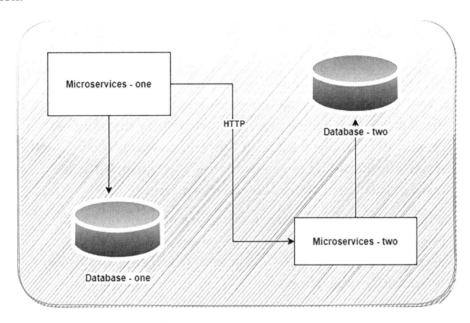

***Figure 9-5.*** *Microservices architecture*

The standard way for developing applications is known as a *monolithic architecture,* which is an approach to application development. This design builds applications from their component elements, each treated as an independent entity. When we say this, we are referring to consolidating all relevant functions into a single location where they can be managed and controlled.

On the other hand, the microservices methodology makes it possible to construct application architecture using specialized services that each serves a particular function and is independent regarding their database and business logic. The microservice architecture operates as a decentralized system in which the individual components communicate independently using predefined protocols, explained earlier, called APIs.

# Microservices Advantages and Disadvantages

Each service uses its unique set of access restrictions in a microservice architecture. You need to ensure that only authorized users cam access each service from inside the environment and through third-party apps that use the environment's APIs. To understand it more, we need to discuss the advantages of this approach.

- With better scaling than monolithic scaling, new features can be added without affecting the current features; in an architecture that utilizes microservices, every service is individually conceived, created, and put into operation. If one of the software's components requires an update, we can update the microservice that manages that particular capability and continue to utilize it.

- With improved fault tolerance, each application component will be deployed as a microservice, which means no downtime, the development process will be accelerated, and developers can focus on enhancing the application.

Even if one of the services fails, the applications contained inside the microservices might continue to function normally.

- *Resiliency*: When microservices face an issue or a bug, it is not mandatory to have downtime to fix the problem; it can be fixed without affecting the users.

- *Migrate*: It's easy to move to the new technology and use the latest with microservices.

Like any other technology, there are disadvantages:

- Using microservices means for some companies you will add complexity because you are working with different tools and layers; the communication overhead of an application is increased when it is broken up into several smaller components. While transferring requests across the various modules, developers have to exercise an increased level of caution.

- Your team needs to be up-to-date with technology and what they are doing; the idea of these kinds of architecture is to adopt the new technology and keep the system up-to-date and the technology moving fast, which means the team needs to stay up-to-date.

- Troubleshooting will not be like before because the developer needs to inspect different logs and services to find the root cause of the issue. It would be best if you combined another solution for logging (mentioned in Chapter 7).

Table 9-1 summarizes the differences between microservices and monolithic depending on various aspects.

***Table 9-1.***  *Difference Between Microservices and Monolithic*

| Factor | Monolithic | Microservices |
| --- | --- | --- |
| Scaling | Hard to scale up or down the system. | Easy to implement, and each microservices can be scaled up or down depending on the needs. |
| Security | Since you are maintaining one application as one stack, the security is increased, and the communication is done as a single unit. | We need to increase the focus on security and try to secure the API by providing a token, which needs implementation. |
| Agile methodology | The development team and operation work as two separate teams. | With implementation services, you increase automation, which means more collaboration between the development and operation. |
| Agility | Hard to adopt new technology. | Easy to adopt new technology. |
| deployment | Done as one single deployment makes it easy; perhaps you will need downtime. | Done depends on which stack or features need to be deployed; there is no need for downtime. |
| Testing | Usually, done as one stack application. | It can be done on a different level, and each microservice must be tested separately. |
| Rollback | Sometimes, rollback will affect the downtime if the deployment fails. | Deployment failure can be rolled back easily without affecting the users. |

# Which Architecture Is the Best for You?

Based on the factors in Table 9-1, you can choose between these two architectures based on different factors; the next section will explain these factors.

Monoliths are best suited for small solutions that don't require extensive business logic, high scalability, or much flexibility.

Also, if you want to build your app and start using it immediately, a monolithic model is the way to go. It's helpful if you want to preserve your legacy system but don't have any immediate plans to modernize it or if you want to pay less up front to test your company's idea. Plus, if you are looking for lower latency, all interactions in monolith-based solutions occur inside a single instance of a running program. The time it takes for a data packet to go from one place on the network to another has been reduced to a minimum due to the decreased network communications.

There is no need to move to microservices if your code is well-organized and observable within a monolith. But when will you go for the microservices architecture, and based on what?

Including new features and growing your app will be a breeze using the microservices design. A microservice paradigm is a way to go if you want to build a complex application with many different parts and paths for users.

One of the most common reasons to choose microservices is if you plan to deploy often and release new features; when using microservices, you can drastically cut down your time to market. By focusing on individual services, development teams can add new features without reworking the entire architecture.

If you want to apply the latest technology to your application or integration, microservices are the best solution, and that means using containers.

# Containerization

Increasing the demand for automation and deployment frequently requires adopting a solution that will feature automated setup, monitoring, and failure handling, as well as automatic scheduling of these components to our servers, and this solution will be Kubernetes.

With Kubernetes, the development team may independently and often deploy their apps without involving the operation/system administrators team. Kubernetes will help the operation team by letting them focus on enhancing the infrastructure because it has built features that allow self-healing in case of failure. You can deploy and operate your applications without worrying about the underlying infrastructure. Kubernetes picks a server for each component, deploys it, and makes it easy to identify and interact with all the other parts of your program when delivering a multicomponent application.

As Kubernetes relies on Linux container technologies such as Docker to isolate running programs, you should be acquainted with the fundamentals of containers before delving into Kubernetes.

Before moving to Kubernetes in detail, we need to understand containers such as Docker.

## Why Containerization?

When I have one extensive application and need to move into microservices, I can deploy each application component on a specific virtual machine (VM). Nevertheless, it will not make any sense, and the hardware waste will be huge.

In addition, to increase the strain on system administrators, the expanding number of VMs also leads to demolishing human resources because of the need to configure and manage each VM. Individually, we must find another way to implement the solution.

The VM approach has its own advantages. This solution can be implemented to meet many companies' needs; it is now simpler to access and share data and back it up and restore it. This facilitates greater flexibility and mobility in company operations. Not only does this add to the benefits of cooperation and enhanced productivity, but it also contributes to preserving company continuity.

On the other hand, when we are talking about microservices, we need to find a solution for them; as DevOps engineers, you use something called a *container*. They function similarly to VMs but with significantly less overhead, allowing you to run many services on the same host computer while providing a different environment to each of them and isolating them from each other.

Like any other process, one executed in a container does so inside the host operating system. The containerized process, however, retains its segregation from other processes. The process seems only to use the hardware and operating system.

Unlike containers, which all call the same Linux kernel, each virtual machine runs its kernel, providing complete isolation.

Figure 9-6 shows the virtual machine types.

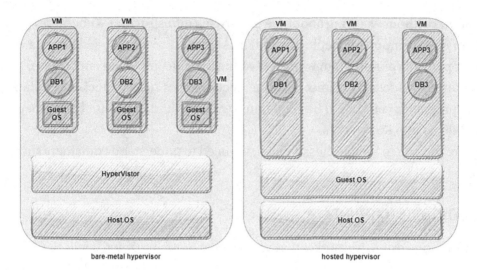

***Figure 9-6.*** *VM architecture type*

As you can see, virtual machines have two types.

- *Bare-metal hypervisor*: This type operates directly on the existing host system (server) and accesses its hardware. The bare-metal class runs on servers and is more efficient and faster than Type 2 hypervisors, used mainly by companies, and there are different solutions, such as VMware ESXi or KVM.

- *Hosted hypervisor*: If you have a laptop and need to use another operating system, you will probably install a solution such as a VM player or virtual box, which allows you to do what you need from testing or another operating system.

On the other hand, containers all make system calls to the same kernel operating in the host operating system. Only this kernel runs x86 instructions on the host computer's central processing unit (CPU). In contrast to the case with virtual machines, the central processing unit is not required to perform any virtualization; see Figure 9-7.

If your hardware resources are restricted, you may be able to use virtual machines only for isolating a few critical activities. Containers, with little impact on performance, are the superior option when many processes must be isolated on a single host computer.

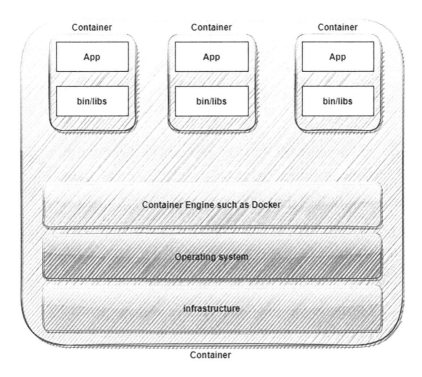

*Figure 9-7.* *Container architecture*

After comparing a monolithic design and a microservice architecture, you should now be aware that the microservice architecture is the one that combines Agility and DevOps the best.

# Docker

Kubernetes is a software solution that allows you to deploy and manage containerized apps on top of it rapidly and straightforwardly. It uses the capabilities of containers to run various apps without knowing any of the technical characteristics of these applications or manually installing them on each host; it also eliminates the need for manual deployment of these applications.

One of the most well-known container tools is Docker; Docker allows you to manage containers, which are, in reality, separate namespaces running Linux. Docker is responsible for making available a user-friendly application programming interface (API) for managing containers. Containers are analogous to tiny virtual machines operating on top of the Linux kernel rather than at the hypervisor level.

As a result of the isolation provided by containers, you are free to run an unlimited number of containers, each of which may execute programs written in a different language without any interference from the others. The process of relocating a microservice is simplified to the point where it only requires halting a container that is already operating and starting a new container from the same image on a different computer.

Docker's integration with microservices results in the following three primary benefits:

- It decreases the load on the host computer.

- The host system is synchronized without any fighting between the many microservices.

- Decoupling the microservice from the host system.

Docker is an ecosystem built around containers. Its network management and container-to-container communication capabilities are especially well suited to the characteristics of the microservice architecture we discussed previously.

Cloud computing and Docker provide a robust platform to host your microservice. You can access as many computers as you need over the cloud. After installing Docker, you can use each machine to run several containerized microservices.

Using Docker, you can control containers, which are just separate Linux namespaces. Docker aims to provide an easy-to-use interface for managing containers, basically lightweight virtual machines that operate on top of the Linux kernel rather than the hypervisor. So, you can add still another layer of virtualization to your host computer by installing Docker on top of your Linux system.

To avoid putting unnecessary strain on the host machine, which exists to execute Docker, your microservices will be deployed on top of this layer. As a result of the isolation provided by containers, you are free to run an unlimited number of containers, each of which may execute programs written in a different language without any interference from the others. The process of relocating a microservice is simplified to the point where it just requires halting a container that is already operating and starting a new container from the same image on a different computer.

Docker's use with microservices has three significant advantages.

- It lightens the load on the host computer.

- The host system is synchronized without any fighting between the many microservices.

- It decouples the microservice from the host system.

Docker is also compatible with the DevOps approach. Build and deploy a Docker container locally before releasing it to production, and you can be confident that you're working in the same environment where the application will ultimately operate.

Docker is often used to refer to the underlying technology used to power containerization. At the same time, there are at least three caveats to keep in mind while discussing Docker as a technology.

- The runtime

- Daemon

- The orchestrator

Figure 9-8 shows the Docker three-layer architecture.

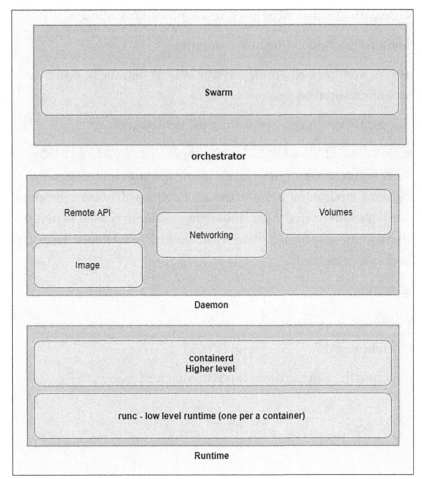

Docker architecture.

***Figure 9-8.*** *Docker architecture*

The runtime is the lowest level of operation. It is in charge of initiating and terminating container processes (this includes building all of the OS constructs, such as namespaces and cgroups). Docker employs a multilevel runtime structure, with high-level and low-level runtimes communicating.

Runc is the Open Containers Initiative (OCI) runtime-spec reference implementation. Docker nodes run runc instances for every container.

Containerd is the name of the runtime environment at the upper level. When compared to runc, containerd has much more functionality. It handles everything from obtaining images to setting up network connections and running instances of runc at lower levels, the complete container life cycle.

The Docker daemon (dockerd) is a higher-level process that sits atop containerd. It handles more complex responsibilities such as providing the Docker remote API, managing images, managing volumes, managing networks, and more.

## Docker Installation

Dockers can be set up in a wide variety of environments. Several operating systems are available, including Windows, macOS, and Linux. Installing is possible in the cloud, on-premise, or on a laptop. There are also programmed installations, wizard-based setups, and manual setups. You may set up Docker in a wide variety of environments.

Docker installation is simple. Assuming you use Ubuntu, the steps are shown here.

To use a repository that is accessible only over HTTPS, it is necessary to update the apt package index and install the required packages.

```
sudo apt-get update
sudo apt-get install \
    ca-certificates \
    curl \
    gnupg \
    lsb-release
```

Next, you need to add GPG key (which enables data to be sent safely between parties and can be used to confirm a message came from a trusted source).

```
sudo mkdir -m 0755 -p /etc/apt/keyrings
curl -fsSL https://download.docker.com/linux/ubuntu/gpg | sudo gpg
--dearmor -o /etc/apt/keyrings/docker.gpg
```

To start the repository, use the following command:

```
echo \
  "deb [arch=$(dpkg --print-architecture) signed-by=/etc/apt/keyrings/
docker.gpg] https://download.docker.com/linux/ubuntu \
  $(lsb_release -cs) stable" | sudo tee /etc/apt/sources.list.d/docker.list
> /dev/null
```

Next, Install Docker Engine, containerd, and Docker Compose.

```
sudo apt-get install docker-ce docker-ce-cli containerd.io docker-buildx-
plugin docker-compose-plugin
```

By executing the hello-world image, you can ensure that Docker Engine was installed correctly.

```
sudo docker run hello-world
```

If you don't want to install it at all, you still can use https://labs.play-with-docker.com/, which is a website that allows you to play with Docker.

# Images

Docker images may be objects with a complete operating system's filesystem, a program, and all of the necessary dependencies, akin to a virtual machine template from someone working in operations. A virtual machine template is the same as a virtual machine that has been shut down. An image in Docker terminology is just a dormant container. As a programmer, you can compare a picture to a type.

Or you can say a Docker image is a prepackaged bundle that includes the software and data needed to launch an application. It encompasses the OS, the application code, and any dependencies. You need a PC with Docker installed and the image for your desired application to execute it.

Docker images can be obtained by downloading them from an image repository. Docker Hub is the most popular registry, although others are out there. The image is pulled down to the local Docker host, which may be used to launch containers.

Layers of information are superimposed on one another to form a single image. The image contains a minimal operating system (OS), all the application files, and their dependencies. Containers are designed to be quick and light; thus, the pictures within them are often minimal (Microsoft images tend to be huge).

Type docker image ls into the Docker host's terminal to see the available Docker images.

```
$ docker image ls
REPOSITORY     TAG          IMAGE ID        CREATED        SIZE
```

You'd see the previous output if you were working from a newly installed Docker host or using Play With Docker, neither of which comes with any images.

*Pulling* refers to transferring images to your Docker host. Use the ubuntu: latest image if you want to keep up with Linux.

```
$ docker image pull ubuntu: latest
latest: Pulling from library/ubuntu
50aff78429b1: Pull complete
f6d82e297bce: Pull complete
275abb2c8a6f: Pull complete
9f15a39356d6: Pull complete
fc0342a94c89: Pull complete
```

To see the newly downloaded image, do another docker image ls command.

```
$ docker images
REPOSITORY      TAG       IMAGE ID      CREATED       SIZE
ubuntu          latest    2d33efk222    3 hours ago   76.9MB
```

Supplying the repository's name and the picture's tag, separated by a colon, is enough to reference an image from an official repository (:). Docker image pull follows this pattern when using an image from the official repository.

```
$ docker image pull <repository>:<tag>
```

## Image Commands

Here are some Docker commands:

- The docker's image pull command is what you use to get files to work with. To get an image, we search external registries' image archives.

- docker image ls returns a list of all the images currently available on the local Docker host.

- docker manifest inspect shows the whole manifest for any image hosted on Docker Hub.

- docker image rm is used to delete the image.

- docker buildx is an add-on to the Docker command-line interface, enabling the CLI to handle many architectures simultaneously.

# Containers

During runtime, a picture is contained inside a container. Similar to how a VM can be launched from a VM template, containers can be found from a single image.

Containers are much more efficient and lightweight than virtual machines (VMs) because, unlike VMs, they do not need to run their operating system (OS) but instead share the OS and kernel of the host computer. Commonly used container images provide the essential software and dependencies for the specific use case.

Figure 9-9 shows the image and how it will be responsible for running either one container or two containers.

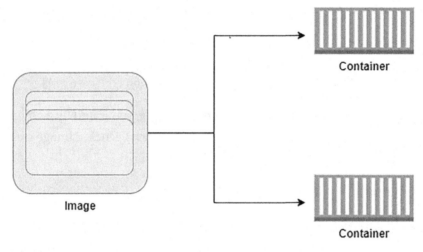

***Figure 9-9.***  *Images and container*

The docker container run command is the most straightforward container launch method. The command has several options, but the simplest form is as follows:

```
docker container run --name [container_name] [docker_image]
```

Docker supports interactive container execution. It also implies that you may provide commands inside the container while executing. You can get a command prompt within a running container if you use it interactively. The following command will do this:

```
docker container run -it [docker_image] /bin/bash
```

The following is a list of different containers commands and what they do:

- `docker container run` is the new container creation command s. It may be as easy as taking a picture and a command as input. It is the image used to create the container, and the command specifies the software to launch within the container.

- The Ctrl+PQ command will disconnect your shell from the container's terminal while leaving the container.

- `docker container ls` enumerates all containers that are currently operational. The `-a` option also displays containers in the halted (Exited) state.

- `docker container exec` deploys a new process into an already active container. It helps extend your Docker host's shell into a container's internal terminal.

- `docker container insecpt` will show the container and Docker configuration.

- `docker container stop` will exit a container that is currently operating.

- `docker container start` will begin running again a container that was previously stopped (exited). When using `docker container start`, you may provide a container by name or ID.

## Dockerfile

To make any application run as a Docker or container, you will need a Dockerfile, and you can define it as a text file but with instructions on how the Docker engine will build this image.

After reading the instructions from a Dockerfile, Docker can automatically construct image bundles. A Dockerfile is a text file containing instructions for building an image using the command line. The Dockerfile instructions are described in Table 9-2.

***Table 9-2.*** *docker file instructions*

| Dockerfile Instruction | Purpose |
|---|---|
| ADD | Adds the contents of src> (which could be a local file, directory, or URL), together with any additional files or external file URLs, to the image's filesystem at the location dest>. |
| COPY | Adds the contents of src> to the image's filesystem at the specified destination. |
| ENV | Sets the environment variable |
| EXPOSE | Signals to the Docker that the container listens on the specified network port(s) at runtime. |
| FROM | required must be the first noncomment instruction in the Dockerfile. It can be repeated several times in a single Dockerfile to generate several different images. When issuing a new FROM command, remember the last image ID that was output by the commit. |
| LABEL | Adds metadata to an image. |
| STOPSIGNAL | Configuration of the system call signal that will be used to terminate the container. This signal can be an unsigned integer, such as 9, corresponding to an entry in the kernel's syscall table, or a signal name, such as SIGKILL, following the format SIGNAME. |
| USER | Sets the user ID to use when running the image and any RUN, CMD, or ENTRYPOINT commands that follow it in the Dockerfile. |
| VOLUME | It makes a mount point you provide visible on the filesystem and indicates that it can store volumes mounted from a host computer or another container. |
| WORKDIR | Makes the directory specified after it the current working directory for subsequent RUN, CMD, ENTRYPOINT, COPY, and ADD commands, working as a cd command in Linux. |
| ONBUILD | It puts a trigger instruction into the picture that will be run when the image is used as a starting point for another construction. The trigger will run as part of the downstream build, just as if it had been placed after the FROM instruction in the Dockerfile for that build. |

(*continued*)

***Table 9-2.*** (*continued*)

| Dockerfile Instruction | Purpose |
|---|---|
| RUN | The command's shell form is executed in a shell, often /bin/sh -c on Linux or cmd /S /C on Windows. |
| CMD | A CMD's primary function is to specify the default values for the running container. If an executable is not included by default, an ENTRYPOINT instruction must also be limited.<br>A Dockerfile is limited to a single CMD instruction. If you list multiple CMD, only the last one will take effect. |
| ENTRYPOINT | It makes it possible to set up a container as an executable.<br>It's unable to utilize CMD or run command-line arguments with the shell form. However, the ENTRYPOINT will launch in a shell. This action prevents the executable from being PID 1 and receiving UNIX signals. To get around this shortcoming, prepend exec. |
| HEALTHCHECK | Provides instructions for Docker to run to verify the container is working. |
| SHELL | Allow you to use a different shell such as csh, zsh, or PowerShell. |
| MAINTAINER | The author who created the Dockerfile is working as LABEL. |

There is nothing better to understand the technical stuff than to look ay an example; in the next section, a simple application will print "hello world" using Nginx.

The first thing we need is a Dockerfile like the following one so it can tell the Docker engine what to do, but before working with the Dockerfile, we need to make sure all the files are located under one directory. Figure 9-10 shows the folder structure.

```
|-- Dockerfile
|-- index.html
|-- nginx.conf
`-- simple-bash.sh
```

***Figure 9-10.***  *Folder structure*

As mentioned, the Dockerfile will be a set of instructions to tell the Docker Engine what to do.

### Dockerfile

```
FROM ubuntu
# Install Nginx
# Update the repository
RUN apt-get update

# Install necessary tools
RUN apt-get install -y vim wget dialog net-tools
RUN apt-get install -y nginx

# Remove the default Nginx configuration file
RUN rm -v /etc/nginx/nginx.conf

# Copy a configuration file from the current directory
ADD nginx.conf /etc/nginx/

# Add a the HELLO WORLD index file
ADD index.html /www/data/

RUN echo "daemon off;" >> /etc/nginx/nginx.conf
COPY simple-bash.sh /simple-bash.sh
RUN chmod +x /simple-bash.sh

EXPOSE 80
ENTRYPOINT ["/simple-bash.sh"]
CMD ["nginx"]
```

The index.html file contains an HTML tag that will print only what we need.

```
<!DOCTYPE html>
<html>
    <head>
        <title>DOCKER</title>
    </head>
    <body>
        <p>HELLO DOCKER WORLD.</p>
    </body>
</html>
```

For the next file, since we will set up our custom page and we need to expose it, we need to use Nginx as the web server, but the default configuration will not work because we need to print the previous message.

```
worker_processes 1;

events { worker_connections 1024; }

http {
    access_log /dev/stdout;
  sendfile on;
    access_log /dev/stdout;
    error_log /etc/nginx/logs/nginx-error.log;

  server {
      root /www/data;

    listen 80;

    location / {
    }
  }
}
```

This is a simple bash script that will just replace the Docker hostname and execute the file inside Docker.

```
#!/bin/sh

# Replace the hostname in the container
sed -i.bak 's/HOSTNAME/'"$HOSTNAME"'/g' /www/data/index.html

# Startup the cmd
exec "$@"
```

We are ready to build the image by running the following command inside our folder:

```
docker build -t helloworld:1.0 .
```

Figure 9-11 shows the output.

```
Sending build context to Docker daemon  101.9kB
Step 1/15 : FROM ubuntu
latest: Pulling from library/ubuntu
2ab09b027e7f: Pull complete
Digest: sha256:67211c14fa74f070d27cc59d69a7fa9aeff8e28ea118ef3babc295a0428a6d21
Status: Downloaded newer image for ubuntu:latest
 ---> 08d22c0ceb15
Step 2/15 : MAINTAINER Karthik Gaekwad
 ---> Running in 39c82f40384a
Removing intermediate container 39c82f40384a
 ---> 2051fd4ba6e9
Step 3/15 : RUN apt-get update
 ---> Running in 90e033789720
Get:1 http://archive.ubuntu.com/ubuntu jammy InRelease [270 kB]
Get:2 http://security.ubuntu.com/ubuntu jammy-security InRelease [110 kB]
Get:3 http://archive.ubuntu.com/ubuntu jammy-updates InRelease [119 kB]
Get:4 http://archive.ubuntu.com/ubuntu jammy-backports InRelease [107 kB]
Get:5 http://archive.ubuntu.com/ubuntu jammy/universe amd64 Packages [17.5 MB]
Get:6 http://security.ubuntu.com/ubuntu jammy-security/universe amd64 Packages [900 kB]
```

***Figure 9-11.*** *Docker build output*

Now after waiting around two minutes, the image will be built, and if you run, your screen will look like Figure 9-12.

```
docker images
```

```
REPOSITORY    TAG         IMAGE ID         CREATED         SIZE
helloworld    1.0         1be2c9e3302d     4 minutes ago   239MB
```

***Figure 9-12.*** *Docker image command output*

Now, let's run the container from this image by running the following command:

```
docker run -d -p 9090:80 --name aws-book helloworld:1.0
```

The output for the previous command should be a generated hash like the following:

```
03063e592fac9a8eefeb413ea6e9a5557473aef69e6de623f3d876895e5ae668
```

See Figure 9-13.

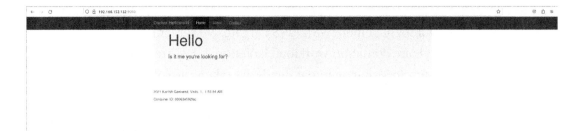

***Figure 9-13.***  *Our website running inside Docker*

We covered the Docker basics and now understand how it works, but what about Amazon AWS? What do I need to do if I want to run Docker inside AWS? The following section will cover this.

When you delete a container, its associated volumes will be removed.

```
docker rm -vf $(docker ps -aq)
```

Delete all images:

```
docker rmi -f $(docker images -aq)
```

Or you can use the `docker cleanup` command to eliminate disconnected images and close down containers that have been shut down.

```
docker system prune -a --volumes
```

If you're looking for a simple way to deploy, manage, and scale containerized applications, look no further than Amazon Elastic Container Service.

## Amazon Elastic Container Service

Amazon Elastic Container Service (Amazon ECS) is a fully managed container orchestration service that includes AWS configuration and operational best practices by default. Because of this, you won't have to worry about the control plane, nodes, or extensions. It works with AWS and third-party tools like Docker and the Amazon Elastic Container Registry. Before discussing these services, you need to know, as a DevOps engineer, that you can create your EC2 instance and run Docker there.

Running Docker on EC2 will not be different from creating EC2 (discussed in Chapter 3 and Chapter 4) and installing Docker inside the EC2 instance. Just follow the Docker installation steps, which leads us to the next question, why do you need to use

ECS? ECS has many features that could be used, such as one of the most prominent features, optional server management with AWS Fargate. No server management, capacity planning, or secure container workload isolation is required with AWS Fargate. Your workload's infrastructure management needs are taken care of by Fargate.

With planning, you can distribute containers across your cluster according to your needs regarding resources, isolation policies, and availability guarantees. ECS Anywhere now supports running instances outside its infrastructure. If you use ECS Anywhere, you can control your containerized workloads locally from the same Amazon ECS console and AWS CLI you use in the cloud or possibly use Amazon's EC2 cloud service. You can control your EC2 instances through the AWS CLI or the Amazon Elastic Compute Cloud console.

Another feature of ECS is integration with AWS Identity and Access Management Integration (IAM). Permissions for containers can be set at a finer level. As a result, your application development can take place in complete secrecy.

That is to say, you can deploy containers with the same high safety and regulation compliance standards expected from Amazon Web Services.

If you're looking for a way to manage your containers using ECS, here are two examples:

- Fargate launch is a serverless, pay-as-you-go service. Containers remove the need to manage server hardware and software, and it's suitable for massive tasks that must be optimized for minimum overhead and intermittently large amounts of work from a small number of workers.

- Use the EC2 launch type to set up and deploy EC2 instances in your cluster, where your containers will be run. This can be used for a lot of work that needs cost optimization or if your application requires access to long-term storage.

You need to understand the ECS components, which we will cover in the next section.

## ECS Components

ECS has different components that, as a DevOps engineer, you need to understand to allow you to know how this service is working; the first principal component is called a *cluster*.

Amazon Elastic Compute Cloud (ECS) clusters are collections of related jobs or services. Applications can be partitioned using clusters. It separates them so that they don't share the same underlying system. When you use Fargate to run your tasks, it will also manage the resources in your cluster.

It is required that your application's components be set up to run in containers before you can deploy them to Amazon ECS.

A container stores all the components your app needs to function. All necessary code, runtime, system tools, and libraries are included. Images are used as a blank, readable template to build containers.

So, you can consider images and containers as types components of ECS; in most cases, a Dockerfile is used to construct an image. A container's contents are described in a plain-text file called a Dockerfile; after the images have been created, they are added to a registry from which they can be retrieved at any time.

The next component, a task definition, is a text file that details the containers that make up your application. The file is a JSON document. Up to 10 storage units can be described using this term. The job description is like a plan for your submission. It lays out all the particulars of your application. It can define various aspects of a given task, such as the OS parameters and the containers to be used; your task definition options will vary based on the requirements of your application.

Standardizing all of your application components on a single task definition is unnecessary. Indeed, we advise distributing your application across several different task definitions. To achieve this, you can merge related containers into new task definitions, with each definition standing in for another part of the whole.

Another ECS component in a cluster is a task. A task is the concrete realization of a task definition. In Amazon Elastic Compute Cloud, you can control how many instances of your application run on a cluster by defining individual tasks. Both independent tasks and those that are integrated into services can be executed.

The Amazon Elastic Compute Cloud (ECS) allows you to launch and manage as many Amazon ECS clusters as needed to handle your workload. The `Amazon ECS service` scheduler will start a new instance according to your task definition if a running task fails or is terminated. It does this as a replacement, keeping the service's workload at your set level.

Finally, we need a container agent that uses the Amazon Elastic Container Service (ECS), which runs on each container instance in the cluster. With the agent's help, Amazon ECS receives updates on the tasks and resources your containers are using.

Figure 9-14 shows the ECS component architecture discussed earlier.

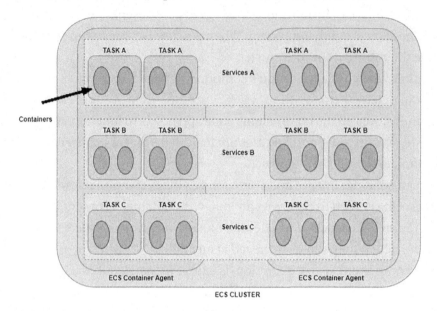

***Figure 9-14.*** *ECS component architecture*

## Create an ECS Cluster via Console

In this section, we will create an ECS cluster using a console and use Terraform to create an ECS cluster. The Amazon Elastic Container Service (ECS) cluster resources can be quickly and easily generated via the console cluster creation wizard by generating an AWS CloudFormation stack.

Amazon AWS provided a quick CloudFormation template that allows you to launch ECS to your account using this GitHub repository `https://github.com/aws-samples/ecs-refarch-cloudformation`.

You can change the CloudFormation template based on what you need, and based on the region, you can click "Launch stack," as mentioned in the README file inside this repository. From the console, search for ECS, and you will be redirected to the ECS welcome screen, as shown in Figure 9-15; go to the `https://console.aws.amazon.com/ecs/` to access the Amazon ECS management interface.

***Figure 9-15.*** *ECS welcome screen*

Select Clusters in the sidebar menu, and then create a cluster, as shown in Figure 9-16.

***Figure 9-16.*** *Creating an ECS cluster*

You can give your cluster a unique identity by giving it a name on the "Configure cluster" page. Upper and lowercase letters, numbers, hyphens, and underscores (up to 255 total) are acceptable; your cluster's virtual private cloud settings can be found under Networking. See Figure 9-17.

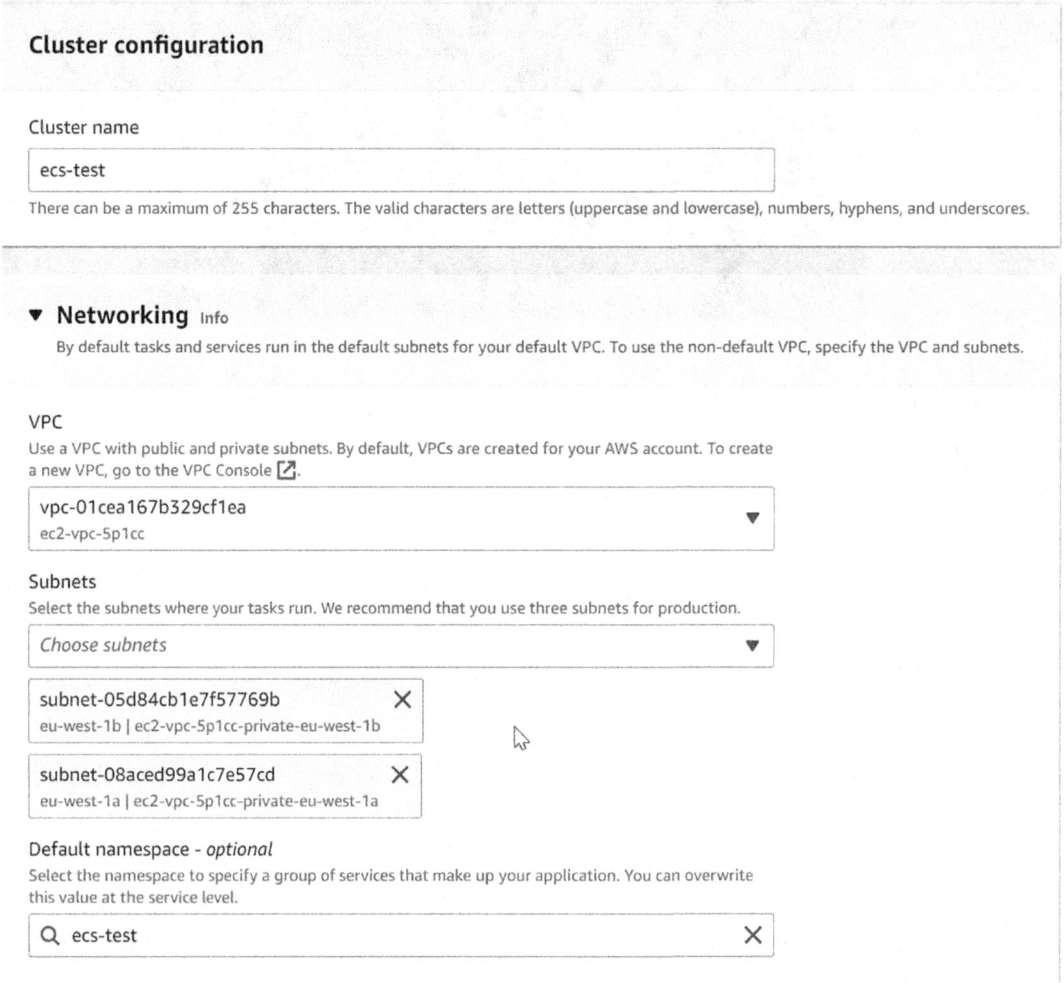

**Cluster configuration**

Cluster name

```
ecs-test
```

There can be a maximum of 255 characters. The valid characters are letters (uppercase and lowercase), numbers, hyphens, and underscores.

▼ **Networking**  Info

By default tasks and services run in the default subnets for your default VPC. To use the non-default VPC, specify the VPC and subnets.

VPC

Use a VPC with public and private subnets. By default, VPCs are created for your AWS account. To create a new VPC, go to the VPC Console ↗.

```
vpc-01cea167b329cf1ea                                        ▼
ec2-vpc-5p1cc
```

Subnets

Select the subnets where your tasks run. We recommend that you use three subnets for production.

```
Choose subnets                                               ▼
```

```
subnet-05d84cb1e7f57769b                    ✕
eu-west-1b | ec2-vpc-5p1cc-private-eu-west-1b
```

```
subnet-08aced99a1c7e57cd                    ✕
eu-west-1a | ec2-vpc-5p1cc-private-eu-west-1a
```

Default namespace - *optional*

Select the namespace to specify a group of services that make up your application. You can overwrite this value at the service level.

```
Q  ecs-test                                                  ✕
```

***Figure 9-17.*** *ECS creating the cluster*

As mentioned, the following section will allow you to choose which method to launch your ECS; see Figure 9-18.

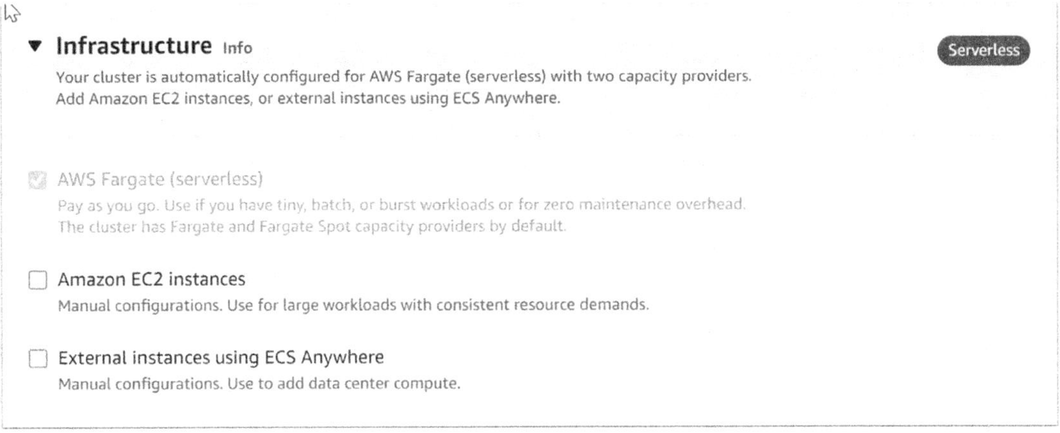
Infrastructure Info
Serverless
Your cluster is automatically configured for AWS Fargate (serverless) with two capacity providers.
Add Amazon EC2 instances, or external instances using ECS Anywhere.
AWS Fargate (serverless)
Pay as you go. Use if you have tiny, batch, or burst workloads or for zero maintenance overhead.
The cluster has Fargate and Fargate Spot capacity providers by default.
Amazon EC2 instances
Manual configurations. Use for large workloads with consistent resource demands.
External instances using ECS Anywhere
Manual configurations. Use to add data center compute.

***Figure 9-18.*** *ECS launch method*

Click On to enable CloudWatch for the ECS instances and see Figure 9-19.

Many resource metrics, including a central processing unit, memory, disk, and network usage, are automatically collected by CloudWatch.

You can use the diagnostic data provided by Container Insights to quickly pinpoint the source of any problems and implement a solution. Metrics collected by Container Insights can also be used as the basis for CloudWatch alerts.

Monitoring - optional Info
Container Insights is off by default. When you use Container Insights, there is a cost associated with it.
Use Container Insights

***Figure 9-19.*** *Enabling the CloudWatch option*

Once the cluster configuration is done, you will see it under the cluster; see Figure 9-20.

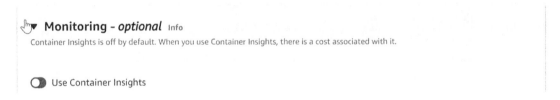

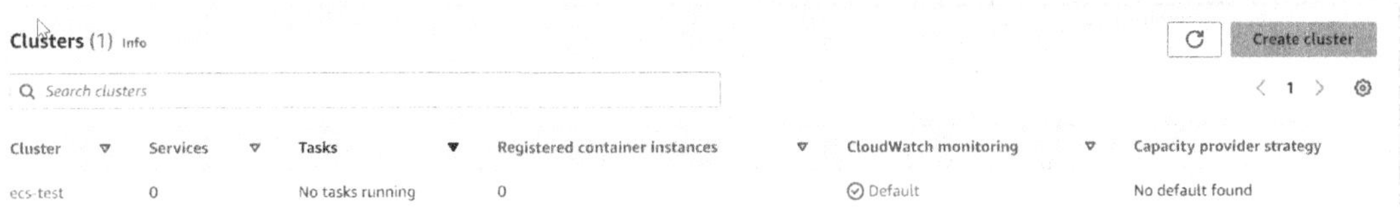
Clusters (1) Info
Create cluster
Search clusters
Cluster
Services
Tasks
Registered container instances
CloudWatch monitoring
Capacity provider strategy
ecs-test
0
No tasks running
0
Default
No default found

***Figure 9-20.*** *Creation completed, ECS test*

A task definition is needed for Docker containers with Amazon Elastic Container Service. Multiple containers can be defined within a single task definition. Which launch type you use determines which parameters you set.

To do that, in the left panel, click "Task definitions"; you have two options: create it via the console or provide JSON.

It should look like the following file if you provide it via JSON:

```
{
  "executionRoleArn": "$TASK_EXECUTION_ROLE_ARN",
  "taskRoleArn": "$TASK_EXECUTION_ROLE_ARN",
  "containerDefinitions": [
    {
      "logConfiguration": {
        "logDriver": "awslogs",
        "secretOptions": [],
        "options": {
          "awslogs-group": "$LOG_GROUP",
          "awslogs-region": "$AWS_DEFAULT_REGION",
          "awslogs-stream-prefix": "awslogs-tripmgmtdemo-ecstask"
        }
      },
      "entryPoint": [],
      "portMappings": [
        {
          "hostPort": 8080,
          "protocol": "tcp",
          "containerPort": 8080
        }
```

```
      ],
      "environment": [
        {
          "name": "JAVA_OPTS",
          "value": "-Djava.net.preferIPv4Stack=true -Djava.net.
          preferIPv4Addresses"
        },
        {
          "name": "JHIPSTER_SLEEP",
          "value": "0"
        },
        {
          "name": "SPRING_DATASOURCE_URL",
          "value": "jdbc:mysql://$AURORA_MYSQL_RDS_URL:3306/tripmgmt?useUni
          code=true&characterEncoding=utf8&useSSL=false&useLegacyDatetimeCo
          de=false&serverTimezone=UTC"
        },
        {
          "name": "SPRING_DATASOURCE_USERNAME",
          "value": "$DB_USERNAME"
        },
        {
          "name": "SPRING_DATASOURCE_PASSWORD",
          "value": "$DB_PASSWORD"
        },
        {
          "name": "SPRING_PROFILES_ACTIVE",
          "value": "prod,swagger"
        }
      ],
      "image": "$ECR_LATEST_IMAGE_URL",
      "essential": true,
      "name": "cntr-img-tripmgmt"
    }
  ],
```

```
"requiresCompatibilities": [
  "EC2"
],
"networkMode": "awsvpc",
"family": "task-tripmgmt-demo",
"cpu": "2048",
"memory": "4096"
}
```

We must ensure that our image has been uploaded to an Elastic Container Registry (ECR) or any other option you prefer.

If you don't want to create one, go to `https://gallery.ecr.aws/`.

After that there is a link should be provided to you; see Figure 9-21.

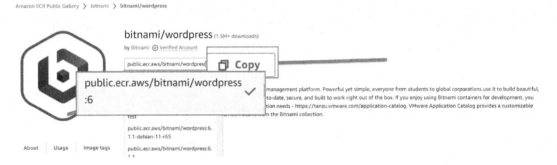

***Figure 9-21.*** *AWS ECR repo, WordPress image*

You have a different image and application deployed as a container, so feel free to choose what you want to run inside your ECS; see Figure 9-22.

***Figure 9-22.*** *ECR public repo main page*

If you create a task definition without JSON, you will get the screen shown in Figure 9-23; the image URL will have the copied URL shown in Figure 9-21.

You must insert the container's name, ports, and protocol.

# Configure task definition and containers

## Task definition configuration

Task definition family   Info

Specify a unique task definition family name.

```
ecs-td-test
```

Up to 255 letters (uppercase and lowercase), numbers, hyphens, and underscores are allowed.

---

**Container - 1** Info                                    Essential container    Remove

Container details

Specify a name, container image, and whether the container should be marked as essential. Each task definition must have at least one essential container.

Name                        Image URI                                          Essential container

```
wordpress
```          `public.ecr.aws/bitnami/wordpress:6`                    Yes ▼

Port mappings   Info

Add port mappings to allow the container to access ports on the host to send or receive traffic. Any changes to port mappings configuration impacts the associated service connect settings.

Container port    Protocol        Port name              App protocol

`80`              TCP ▼           `wordpress-80-tcp`      HTTP ▼         Remove

**Add more port mappings**

▼ Environment variables - *optional* Info

Add individually

Add a key-value pair to specify an environment variable.

**Add environment variable**

***Figure 9-23.*** *Task definition option setting without JSON*

Click Next, and you will need to configure how to manage the ECS, using either Fargate or EC2, based on the use case mentioned earlier in this chapter. Figure 9-24 shows the resource assigned to this task definition.

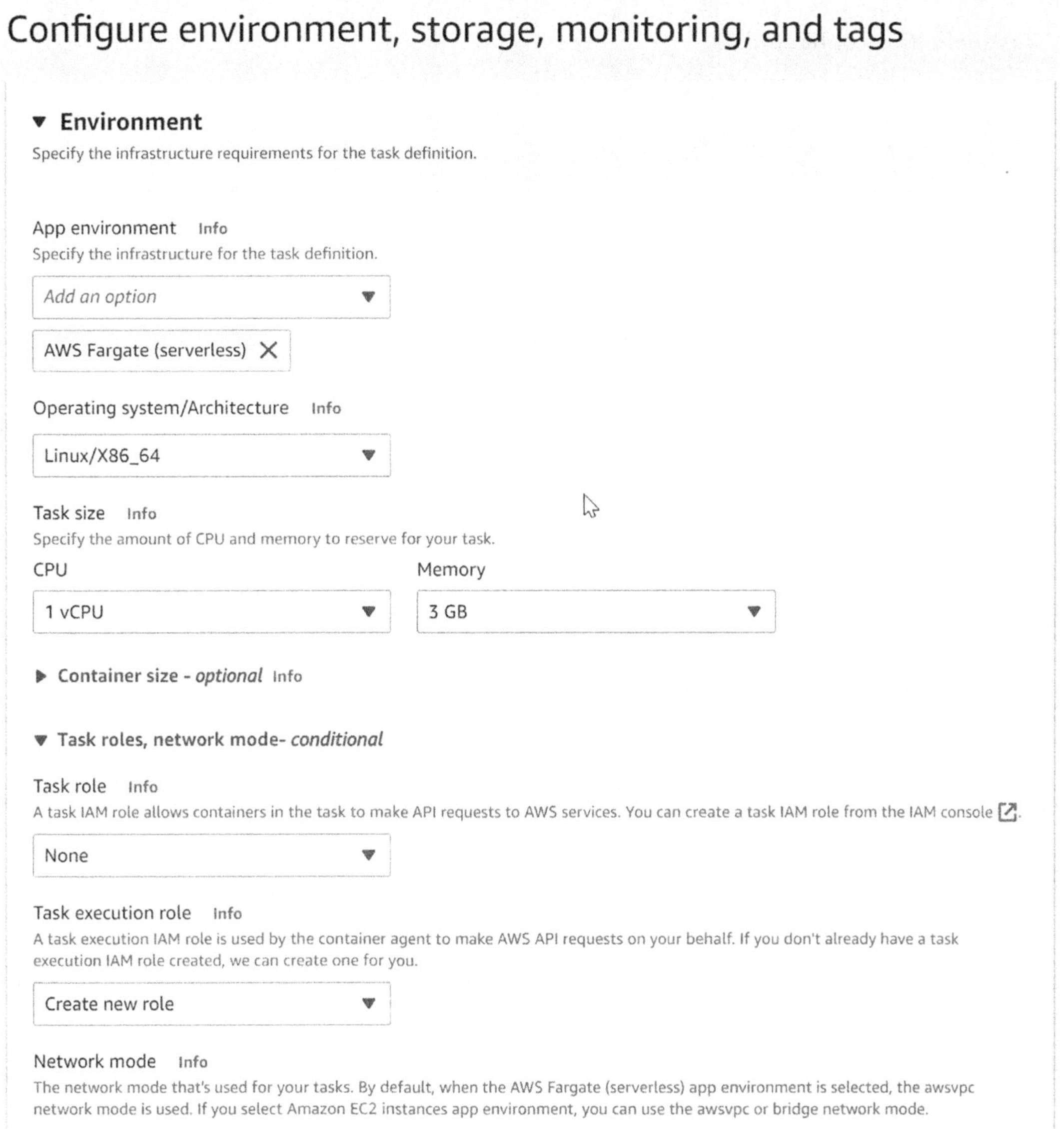

# Configure environment, storage, monitoring, and tags

**▼ Environment**

Specify the infrastructure requirements for the task definition.

App environment   Info

Specify the infrastructure for the task definition.

| Add an option ▼ |

| AWS Fargate (serverless)  ✕ |

Operating system/Architecture   Info

| Linux/X86_64 ▼ |

Task size   Info

Specify the amount of CPU and memory to reserve for your task.

| CPU | | Memory | |
|---|---|---|---|
| 1 vCPU | ▼ | 3 GB | ▼ |

▶ Container size - *optional*  Info

**▼ Task roles, network mode- *conditional***

Task role   Info

A task IAM role allows containers in the task to make API requests to AWS services. You can create a task IAM role from the IAM console ⬈.

| None ▼ |

Task execution role   Info

A task execution IAM role is used by the container agent to make AWS API requests on your behalf. If you don't already have a task execution IAM role created, we can create one for you.

| Create new role ▼ |

Network mode   Info

The network mode that's used for your tasks. By default, when the AWS Fargate (serverless) app environment is selected, the awsvpc network mode is used. If you select Amazon EC2 instances app environment, you can use the awsvpc or bridge network mode.

***Figure 9-24.*** *Configuring the environment, storage, monitoring, and tags*

Click Next and review the setting before clicking Create; see Figure 9-25.

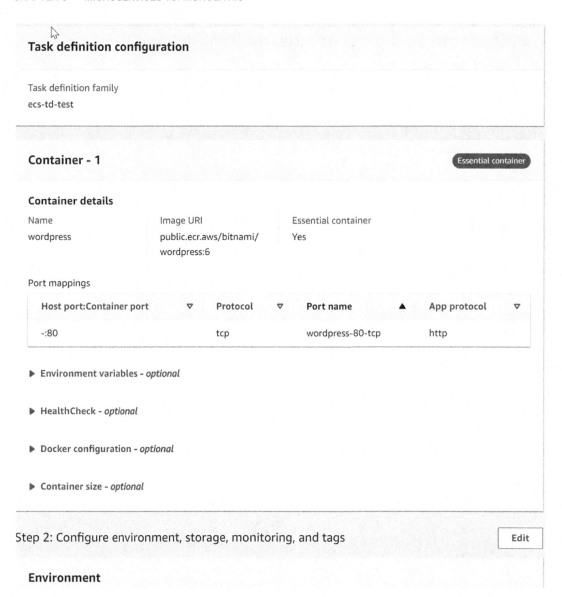

**Figure 9-25.** *Review and create a screen*

Once the task definition is created, you should see it under the task definition in the left panel; see Figure 9-26.

**Figure 9-26.** *Task definition creation completed successfully*

Amazon ECS allows you to run and maintain a specified number of instances of a task definition simultaneously in an Amazon ECS cluster. You can create one by clicking the task definition itself, as shown in Figure 9-27.

**Figure 9-27.** *Creating ECS services*

Once you click "Create service," you will be redirected to the next screen, and you must configure the services with the options needed for the first section, which is the cluster that needs to be assigned, as shown in Figure 9-28.

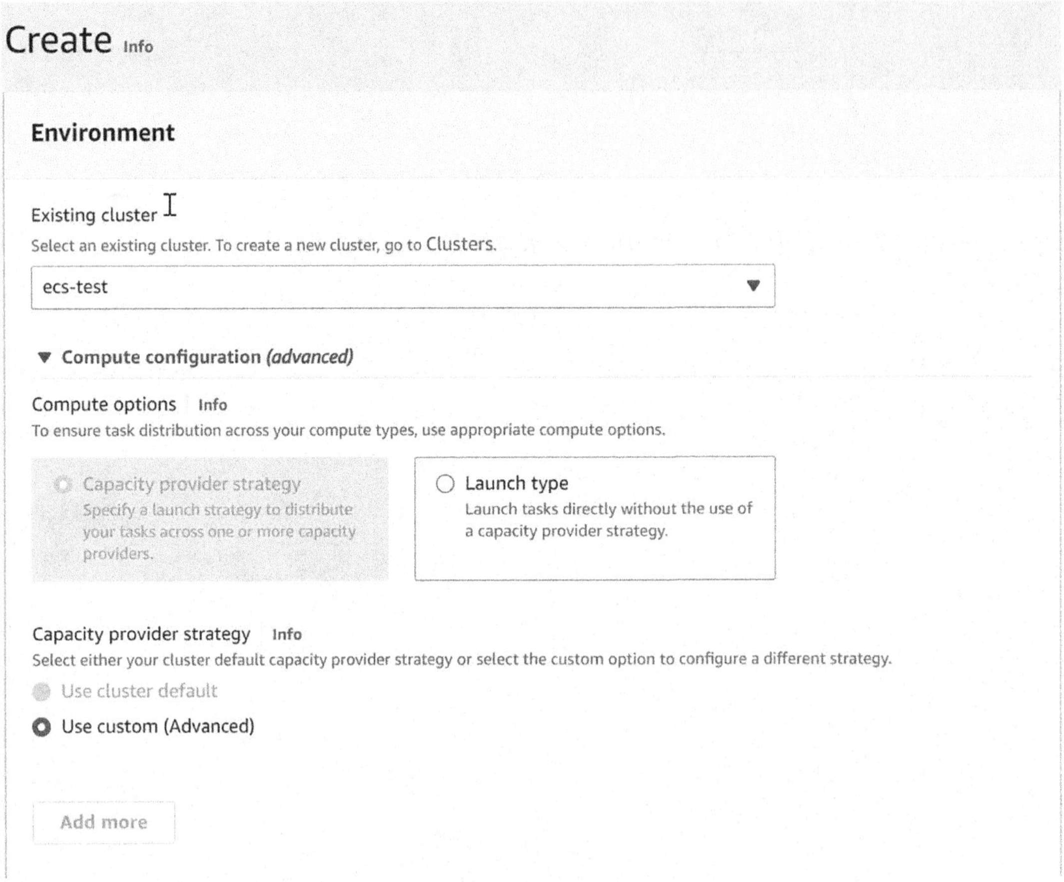

**Figure 9-28.**  *Service configuration, cluster*

On the same screen, you can choose how many replicas you need and a load balancer to expose your ECS to the world or internally, as shown in Figure 9-29.

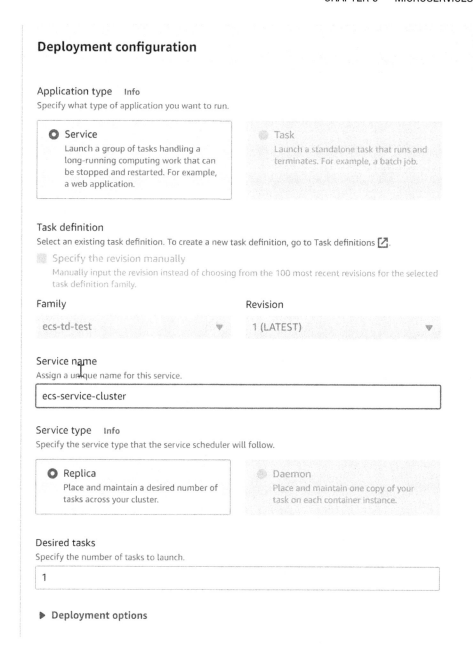

**Figure 9-29.** *Services configuration, replica number*

Also, you need to configure the load balancer, which type you need, and the health check for the load balancer, the ports, and the target group; see Figure 9-30.

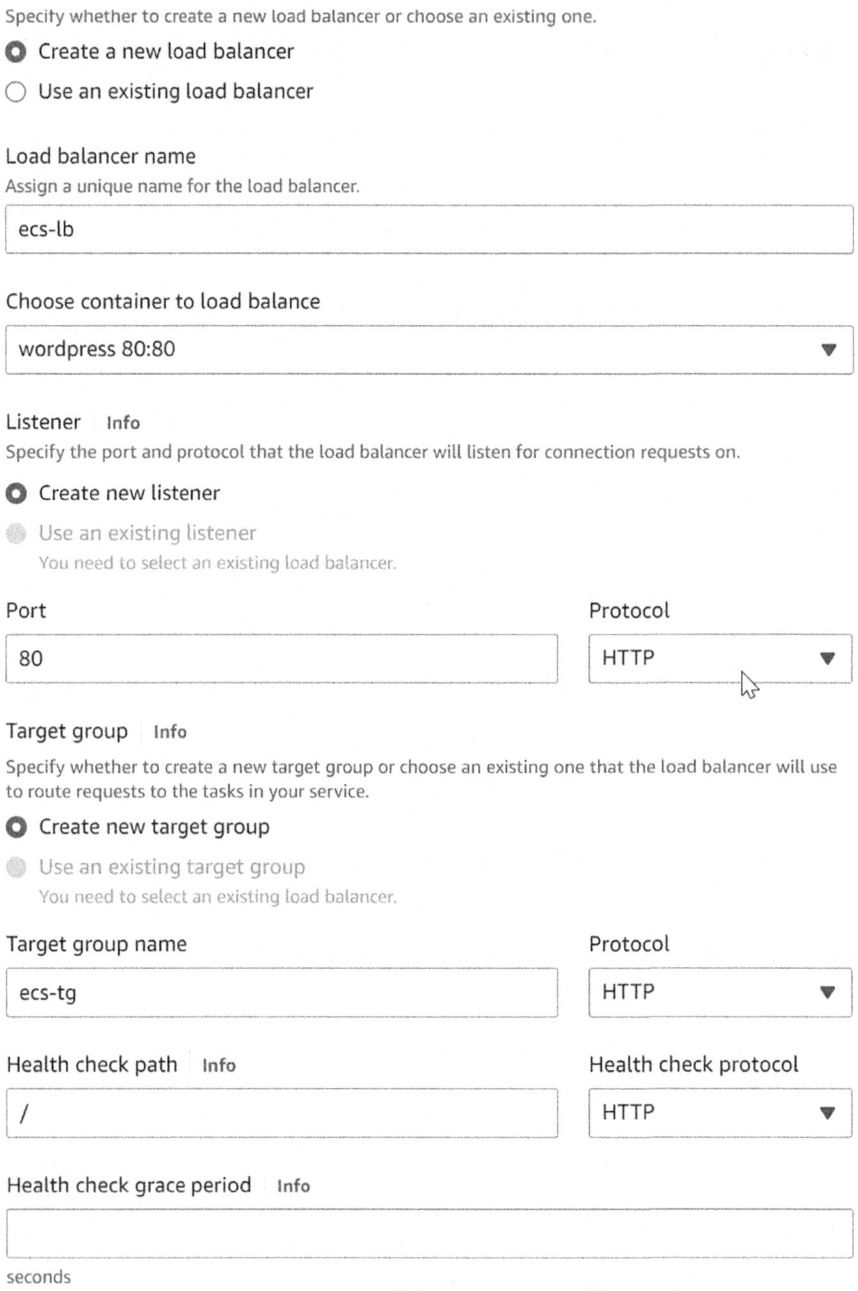

Specify whether to create a new load balancer or choose an existing one.

● Create a new load balancer

○ Use an existing load balancer

**Load balancer name**
Assign a unique name for the load balancer.

```
ecs-lb
```

**Choose container to load balance**

```
wordpress 80:80                                              ▼
```

**Listener**  |  Info
Specify the port and protocol that the load balancer will listen for connection requests on.

● Create new listener

◉ Use an existing listener
    You need to select an existing load balancer.

Port                                    Protocol

```
80
```
```
HTTP                    ▼
```

**Target group**  |  Info
Specify whether to create a new target group or choose an existing one that the load balancer will use to route requests to the tasks in your service.

● Create new target group

◉ Use an existing target group
    You need to select an existing load balancer.

Target group name                       Protocol

```
ecs-tg
```
```
HTTP                    ▼
```

Health check path  |  Info                Health check protocol

```
/
```
```
HTTP                    ▼
```

Health check grace period  |  Info

```

```
seconds

***Figure 9-30.*** *Service configuration, load balancer*

Once you click Create, the services will start deploying, and the load balancer will be deployed; see Figure 9-31.

**Figure 9-31.** *Services in progress to deploy*

If you go to the Load Balancer section under EC2, you will see the load balancer there, as shown in Figure 9-32.

**Figure 9-32.** *Load balancer created*

Copy the Load Balancer DNS name and an open new tab in the browser, paste the DNS name there, and WordPress will open.

The previous are steps to create the ECS using the console. The next section will show how to complete the ECS, but this time using IaC as well as Terraform.

## Create an ECS Cluster via Terraform

Terraform is one of the most potent IaC tools, and as a DevOps engineer, you will probably review or write Terraform code daily. This section will explain how to create an ECS instance using Terraform; the folder structure should look like what is shown in Figure 9-33.

```
|-- main.tf
|-- outputs.tf
|-- providers.tf
|-- terraform.tfvars
|-- variables.tf
`-- vpc.tf
```

**Figure 9-33.** *ECS Terraform folder structure*

The Terraform code will be able to create a new VPC, ECS cluster, task definition, and services that will provision load balancer and target group.

Let's start.

In your project's root folder, make the changes to the following files.

425

## main.tf

The data in this file can be used to build an AWS Elastic Container Service cluster.

```
# Create ECS cluster

resource "aws_ecs_cluster" "cluster" {
  name = "ecs-cluster"
}

resource "aws_ecs_cluster_capacity_providers" "cluster" {
  cluster_name            = aws_ecs_cluster.cluster.name
  capacity_providers      = ["FARGATE"]

  default_capacity_provider_strategy {
    base                  = 1
    weight                = 100
    capacity_provider     = "FARGATE"
  }
}

# ECS Service
resource "aws_ecs_service" "ecs_service" {
  name               = "ecs-service"
  cluster            = aws_ecs_cluster.cluster.id
  task_definition    = aws_ecs_task_definition.ecs_task.arn
  launch_type        = "FARGATE"
  desired_count      = 1

  network_configuration {
    subnets = [aws_subnet.private_east_a.id, aws_subnet.private_east_b.id]
  }
}

# Tasks definitions
resource "aws_ecs_task_definition" "ecs_task" {
  family                    = "service"
  network_mode              = "awsvpc"
  requires_compatibilities  = ["FARGATE", "EC2"]
```

```
  cpu                      = 512
  memory                   = 2048
  container_definitions    = <<DEFINITION
  [
    {
      "name"               : "centos",
      "image"              : "centos:7",
      "cpu"                : 512,
      "memory"             : 2048,
      "essential"          : true,
      "portMappings" : [
        {
          "containerPort"  : 80,
          "hostPort"       : 80
        }
      ]
    }
  ]
  DEFINITION
}
```

## variables.tf

The file will contain a variable that will be used across the code.

```
variable "region" {
  description   = "region to use for AWS resources"
  type          = string
  default       = "us-east-1"
}

variable "region_a" {
  description   = "The region the environment is going to be
installed into"
  type          = string
  default       = "us-east-1a"
}
```

```
variable "region_b" {
  description  = "The region the environment is going to be
installed into"
  type         = string
  default      = "us-east-1b"
}

variable "cidr" {
  description  = "CIDR range for created VPC"
  type         = string
  default      = "10.0.0.0/16"
}

variable "private_cidr_a" {
  description  = "CIDR range for created VPC"
  type         = string
  default      = "10.0.1.0/24"
}

variable "private_cidr_b" {
  description  = "CIDR range for created VPC"
  type         = string
  default      = "10.0.2.0/24"
}

variable "access_key" {
  type         = string
  sensitive    = true
}

variable "secret_access_key" {
  type         = string
  sensitive    = true
}
```

## vpc.tf

A virtual private network, such as subnets, an Internet gateway, and a NAT gateway, will create the network.

```
# Create VPC for ECS

resource "aws_vpc" "vpc_ecs" {
  cidr_block   = var.cidr

  tags = {
    Name  = "Project ECS"
  }
}

# Create Private subnets for ECS

resource "aws_subnet" "private_east_a" {
  vpc_id              = aws_vpc.vpc_ecs.id
  cidr_block          = var.private_cidr_a
  availability_zone   = var.region_a

  tags = {
    Name  = "You can set tags here"
  }
}

resource "aws_subnet" "private_east_b" {
  vpc_id              = aws_vpc.vpc_ecs.id
  cidr_block          = var.private_cidr_b
  availability_zone   = var.region_a

  tags = {
    Name  = "You can set tags here"
  }
}
```

## Provider.tf

Here we will define the Terraform version, which cloud provider Terraform will use, and the version.

```
terraform {
  required_providers {
    docker = {
      source   = "kreuzwerker/docker"
      version  = "~> 2.20.0"
    }
    aws = {
      source   = "hashicorp/aws"
      version  = "~> 4.16"
    }
  }
}

provider "docker" {}
```

Run the Terraform code using the following command.

```
terraform init
```

The output will look like Figure 9-34.

```
Initializing the backend...

Initializing provider plugins...
- Reusing previous version of kreuzwerker/docker from the dependency lock file
- Reusing previous version of hashicorp/aws from the dependency lock file
- Using previously-installed kreuzwerker/docker v2.20.3
- Using previously-installed hashicorp/aws v4.59.0

Terraform has been successfully initialized!

You may now begin working with Terraform. Try running "terraform plan" to see
any changes that are required for your infrastructure. All Terraform commands
should now work.

If you ever set or change modules or backend configuration for Terraform,
rerun this command to reinitialize your working directory. If you forget, other
commands will detect it and remind you to do so if necessary.
```

***Figure 9-34.*** *Terraform init output*

You can validate the configuration by running this command:

```
terraform validate
```

This in turn should give you output like this:

```
Success!  The configuration is valid.
```

`output.tf` and `terraform.tfvars` are optional files, but they give users more visibility when they deploy the code. For example, `output.tf` will present the main deployment output based on our configuration; on the other hand, `terraform.tfvars` is used to set the primary variable in one file.

## Output.tf

The following will show the ECS cluster name once the deployment is finished, and as mentioned, it's an optional file.

```
output "aws_ecs_cluster" {
  value         = aws_ecs_cluster.cluster.name
  description   = "ECS Cluster name"
}
```

## Terraform.tfvars

Inside this file, you can set the primary variable that will probably change based on the environment; you can add the VPC CIDR or cluster name.

```
access_key          = <"AWS access key">
secret_access_key   = <"AWS Secret key">
```

The code will be able to run without these two files usually and without any issues.

# Summary

In this chapter, we discussed two of the most crucial concepts for DevOps to understand: the microservices and monolithic application architectures. We explained the cons and pros of these two architectures and their guidelines; after that, we discussed one separately.

After reviewing Docker's core concepts, we deployed an application using Docker and learned how to write a Dockerfile and the Docker commands.

Then we covered the container services inside Amazon AWS, which is ECS, and the concepts of this service; we learned a different method to deploy it, either using the console or IaC/Terraform.

In the next chapter, you will continue your learning journey and learn about one of the most potent DevOps tools, Kubernetes, and you will learn about EKS.

# CHAPTER 10

# Kubernetes

In the previous chapter, we discussed what containers are and why they are used. In this chapter, I will cover one of the most potent tools in the DevOps world. Kubernetes is a container orchestration automation tool used to deploy microservices applications. We'll review Kubernetes concepts and the architecture of the tool. We will then look at different configurations, how to deploy Kubernetes, and how to create CI/CD. We'll also explore Kubernetes architecture and Kubernetes objects and how to create them using different methods.

## What Is Kubernetes?

Figure 10-1 shows the official website for Kubernetes.

***Figure 10-1.*** *Kubernetes website*

Kubernetes can be defined in just a few words: a production-ready container orchestration platform. Kubernetes is not meant to replace Docker or any of its functionality; rather, it is intended to facilitate the management of clusters of servers running Docker. Kubernetes requires the basic Docker installation and the full-featured Docker image to function correctly.

With Kubernetes, your program can be deployed over a cluster of thousands of computers and operate as if they were a single supercomputer. By hiding the specifics of the underlying infrastructure, it makes life easier for programmers and IT administrators.

O. Mustafa, *A Complete Guide to DevOps with AWS*, https://doi.org/10.1007/978-1-4842-9303-4_10

We can refer to Kubernetes as "K8S". *Kubernetes* is a Greek vocabulary word that means "poilt," and the 8 is the letter count between the *K* and *S*. Kubernetes application deployment is consistent whether your cluster has two nodes or two thousand. The cluster's size is irrelevant. More nodes in a cluster mean more computing power for programs already in use.

Figure 10-2 shows how much effort the company made to maintain the data center from servers, storage, and networking.

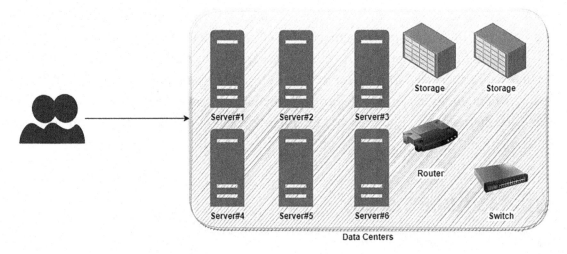

***Figure 10-2.*** *Company that built a complete data center to deploy their application*

## Kubernetes Benefits

Kubernetes simplifies application management by automating operational tasks associated with container management and providing built-in commands for deploying and distributing updates to applications, scaling them up or down to meet fluctuating demand, keeping an eye on them, and more.

### Facilitating a Focus on Essential App Features for Developers

When talking about Kubernetes, it is helpful to consider it as the cluster's operating system. Kubernetes takes the burden off of app developers to include infrastructure-related services in their applications by handling them independently.

This includes finding new services, increasing their capacity, distributing the load, fixing problems as they arise, and choosing a new server to redeploy the services. Instead of worrying about how to connect their apps to the network, developers can concentrate on creating the applications themselves.

## Improving Operational Teams' Ability to Make Effective Use of Available Resources

Kubernetes will deploy your containerized software to a node in the cluster, tell its parts where to locate one another, and keep everything up and running. Kubernetes can achieve far better resource usage than is feasible with manual scheduling since your application does not care whose node it is running on and can be moved at any moment.

## High Availability Solution and Ensure It

Production is based on the notion of maximum availability. Therefore, ensure your app is constantly running. However, remember that this is the end game. With a microservice design, the possibility of catastrophic failure is reduced. It incorporates microservices.

An individual microservice's failure will not affect the application's overall stability. Using Kubernetes, you can make your Docker containers highly accessible by replicating them over many host computers and often checking their status.

## Management of Release and Deployment of Containers

Kubernetes's ability to handle Docker container deployments and rollbacks will significantly simplify your response to this issue. Kubernetes quickly updates container images across several hosts with a single command.

## Scaling

When a traffic surge hits your production machines and a single container cannot handle it, you need the means to pinpoint which one it is. Decide whether you want to scale it vertically or horizontally; otherwise, your container may fail if the load is not reduced.

The scale has two types; see Figure 10-3.

- *Vertical scale*: This refers to scale by adding more resources such as CPU and RAM; the container will allow the use of the more powerful machine.

- *Horizontal scale*: This approach means adding more servers to the current one (more nodes); in that case, the container will run on different machines.

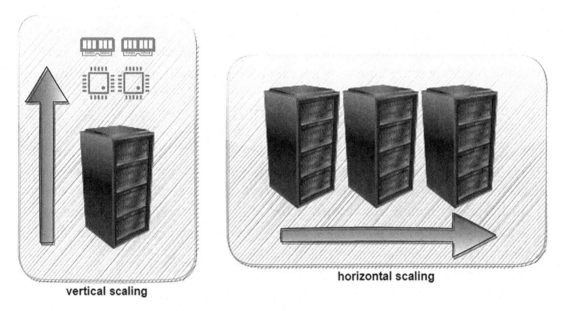

vertical scaling                    horizontal scaling

***Figure 10-3.*** *Vertical scales vs. horizontal scale*

Sometimes, using K8S will not be the best option for the company, because it will add complexity to your application and infrastructure; these cases could differ from one setup to another, depending on the use case.

In general, it will be similar to the following:

- Monolithic application

- Kubernetes can be used to deploy container-based monoliths, but it shines when it manages many containers. When a monolithic program is containerized, it often uses only a few containers. With so little to handle, Kubernetes is not the best option, and you may discover something more suitable.

- If you do not use a container, Kubernetes is not the best option.

- If your application has been deployed on a single EC2 instance, moving to Kubernetes will make it complex.

- The application does not support containerization solutions or is not configured as a container solution.

Let's understand how Kubernetes architecture works, which is the first step of everything; Figure 10-4 shows the architecture but not the details, which can be split into two types.

- The master node, where everything is managed and controlled by Kubernetes

- Applications that are deployed and executed on worker nodes

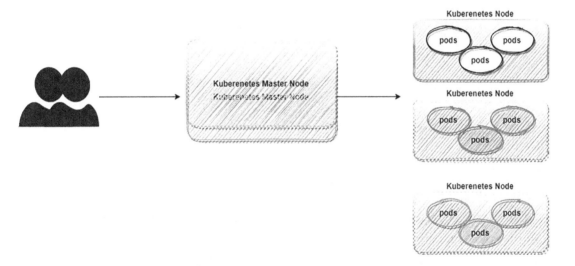

***Figure 10-4.*** *How Kubernetes architecture compares to traditional datacenters*

Whether the master node or the worker node, each has its components, which will be discussed next.

# Kubernetes Components

The section covers the components of the master and worker nodes.

# Master Node Components

It is the master node's job to oversee the Kubernetes cluster and provide the application programming interface (API) that controls everything from resource configuration to deployment. Components of the Kubernetes master node can be operated within Kubernetes as a pod, with each container handling a specific task.

Figure 10-5 explains the components of a master node.

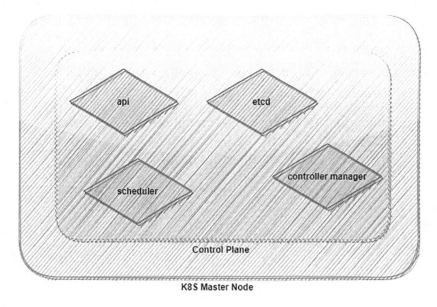

***Figure 10-5.***  *Kubernetes master node components*

The cluster's control and functionality are provided through the control plane. It comprises several parts that can either share a single node as a master and operate in tandem or be run independently on other nodes and duplicated to guarantee availability. The elements are covered next.

## API

Alternatively, we can call the API the Kube-API server, one of the main components that allows you to communicate to K8S and the control plane parts.

## Scheduler (kube-scheduler)

The scheduler (also called the *kube-scheduler*) is responsible for selecting and scheduling nodes to run the newly created pods. The factors for choosing the nodes are as follows:

- Resource requirements
- Affinity and anti-affinity specifications
- Workload
- Constraints

## Controller Manager

Several different types of controllers handle cluster-level tasks, such as component replication, worker node tracking, and node failures.

The Job controller detects and reacts to node failures, while the Node controller keeps an eye out for job objects representing one-time activities and spins up pods to carry them out.

As is probably apparent from its name, the Services-Account controller is responsible for the services account for new namespaces, while the EndpointSlice controller links the services account to pods.

## Etcd

Etcd is a trustworthy distributed data store that always keeps a copy of the cluster's configuration as Kubernetes' backup store for all the cluster data.

It's essential to ensure you have a backup strategy for Ectd; otherwise, you could lose the Kubernetes setup and may need to reinstall again.

But possibly all currently running workloads will keep running. The Etcd role prevents Kubernetes from modifying the existing configuration. Pods that have already been planned can continue to operate, but no new pods can be scheduled.

This section will cover how you can back up Etcd if you run K8S locally, but if you use a cloud provider such as EKS, it will manage this part for you, and you don't have to worry about it.

Cloud services such as Amazon EKS and Google GKE will install and configure a pool of servers running Etcd on your behalf, but they will not provide much information on the machines. They provide you with an operational Kubernetes cluster but do not provide too much information about the resources behind the scenes.

You should be aware that Etcd is a component of the Kubernetes control plane. Operating on a primary node is recommended if you want to administer an Etcd datastore on-premises or if you plan to run an Etcd datastore on your own. You have the option of choosing between the following:

- You can install Etcd on the primary node.

- You can install as a group that will be running with the other components.

The first option is preferable since it lowers the likelihood that your cluster will be inaccessible if there is an interruption in service. Having a collection of servers devoted to running Etcd helps eliminate potential security threats.

The issue is that it will constantly cost more than the first method because it includes more machinery, planning, and maintenance; the problem is that it will always cost more. Even though it is perfectly OK to operate Etcd on the same machines as the kube-apiserver, you should not be reluctant to utilize dedicated servers for Etcd if you have the financial means.

If you plan to manage Etcd locally, you need to back up frequently; you can follow these following steps:

1. Look up the value for the critical cluster.name in the Etcd cluster.

   ```
   ETCDCTL_API=3 etcdctl get cluster.name \
   --endpoints=https://192.169.1.102:2379 \
    --cacert=/home/cloud_user/etcd-certs/etcd-ca.pem \
   --cert=/home/cloud_user/etcd-certs/etcd-server.crt \
   --key=/home/cloud_user/etcd-certs/etcd-server.key
   ```

2. Back up Etcd using etcdctl and the provided Etcd certificates.

   ```
   ETCDCTL_API=3 etcdctl snapshot save/home/cloud_user/etcd_
   backup.db \
   --endpoints=https://192.169.1.102:2379 \
   --cacert=/home/cloud_user/etcd-certs/etcd-ca.pem \
   ```

```
--cert=/home/cloud_user/etcd-certs/etcd-server.crt \
--key=/home/cloud_user/etcd-certs/etcd-server.key
```

Figure 10-6 illustrates what the previous commands will do, namely, back up Etcd and restore it. Everything will be done on the primary node, assuming the primary private node IP address is 192.169.1.102.

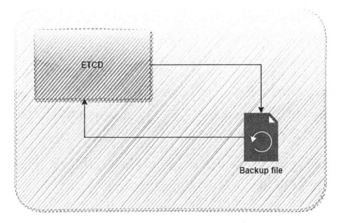

***Figure 10-6.*** *Backups and restoration process for Etcd*

To restore Etcd, follow these steps:

Restore the Etcd data using the backup (the following command will spin up a temporary Etcd cluster and save the data from the backup file to a new data directory in the same place as the previous data directory):

```
sudo ETCDCTL_API=3 etcdctl snapshot restore/home/cloud_user/etcd_
backup.db \
--initial-cluster etcd-restore=https://192.169.1.102:2380 \
--initial-advertise-peer-urls https://192.169.1.102:2380 \
--name etcd-restore \ --data-dir/var/lib/etcd
```

3. Change who owns the newly created data directory.

```
sudo chown -R etcd:etcd/var/lib/etcd
```

4.  Start Etcd.

    ```
    sudo systemctl start etcd
    ```

5.  Check to see whether the data that was restored is still there by
    checking up the value for the key cluster name again.

    ```
    ETCDCTL_API=3 etcdctl get cluster.name \
    --endpoints=https://192.169.1.102:2379 \
    --cacert=/home/cloud_user/etcd-certs/etcd-ca.pem \
    --cert=/home/cloud_user/etcd-certs/etcd-server.crt \
    --key=/home/cloud_user/etcd-certs/etcd-server.key
    ```

    If you create Kubernetes on the cloud, you don't have to manage Etcd
    by yourself, but it's a good idea to show you how it will be backed up
    and restored in case of failure.

    Before moving to the cloud part, I would like to show you how to set
    up Kubernetes locally or on a virtual machine.

## Worker Node Components

The host that carries out your containerized apps is the worker node. The job of keeping
your apps up and running, monitoring them, and delivering services has completed;
Figure 10-7 shows the components of the worker node.

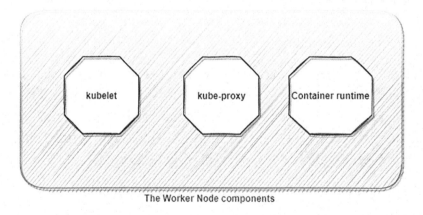

Figure 10-7. *Kubernetes worker node components*

Kubelet is an agent executable on every node part of the cluster. It ensures that containers are operating inside a pod at all times.

It ensures that the containers specified in the PodSpecs run in good health. It does this by taking a collection of PodSpecs that are delivered via a variety of techniques. The kubelet service does not manage containers not initially produced by Kubernetes.

Kube-Proxy distributes the strain of the network traffic across the many application components and controls how network rules are applied to nodes; the rules allow sessions inside or outside your cluster to send data to your pods across the network.

We have the container runtime, and we also have Docker or RKT, the software responsible for running the container.

There are several alternatives to Kubernetes, and some are also open-source. Others are restricted to using a single cloud service provider. The following are some examples of containers as services:

- Amazon ECS/Amazon Fargate

- Mirantis Kubernetes Engine

- G2 Deal

- Apache Mesos

- Docker Swarm

- Hashicorp Nomad

And we have the cloud Kubernetes solution offered by a different cloud provider, which can assist you in getting a Kubernetes cluster up and operating with the click of a few buttons.

- Amazon Elastic Kubernetes Service (Amazon EKS)

- Google Kubernetes Engine (GKE)

- Azure Kubernetes Service (Azure AKS)

To get Kubernetes up and running, you will need Linux computers, called *nodes* in Kubernetes. A node could be a real computer or a virtual machine hosted by a cloud provider, such as an EC2 instance.

# Building a Kubernetes Cluster

This section will walk you through creating Kubernetes on-premises or on local machines, and during the process, I will use kubeadm.

Kubeadm is a tool that simplifies setting up the Kubernetes cluster; I will use the following three servers:

- One server acts as the master node.

- Two servers act as worker nodes.

Assuming you are using the Ubuntu operating system, Table 10-1 will guide you about the specification.

***Table 10-1.*** *Kubernetes Installation Server Information*

| Server Name | Operating System | IP |
|---|---|---|
| k8s-master | Ubuntu 22 | 192.168.1.2 |
| k8s-worker1 | Ubuntu 22 | 192.168.1.3 |
| k8s-worker2 | Ubuntu 22 | 192.168.1.4 |

**Note**   You must run the commands and install the package on all three nodes through step 16.

1. Configure the host file on each node so all nodes can communicate using the following hostnames:

   sudo vi/etc./hosts

2. Put the hosts on every node. You will be responsible for providing each node's private IP address.

   1. <master node private IP> k8s-master
   2. <worker node 1 private IP> k8s-worker1
   3. <worker node 2 private IP> k8s-worker2

3. On all nodes, set up containerd. This procedure requires loading specific kernel modules and modifying certain system settings.

```
cat <<EOF | sudo tee/etc./modules-load.d/containerd.conf
Overlay
br_netfilter
EOF
```

4. Load the modules.

```
sudo modprobe overlay
sudo modprobe br_netfilter
```

5. Create the necessary network settings for Kubernetes.

```
1. cat <<EOF | sudo tee/etc./sysctl.d/99-kubernetes-cri.conf
Net.bridge.bridge-nf-call-iptables = 1
3. net.ipv4.ip_forward = 1
Net.bridge.bridge-nf-call-ip6tables = 1
5. EOF
6.
```

6. Apply the previous settings.

```
sudo system
```

7. Install containerd.

```
sudo apt-get update && sudo apt-get install -y containerd.io
```

8. Make a new, blank configuration file for containerd.

```
sudo mkdir -p/etc./containerd
```

9. Create a template for containerd and save the settings there.

```
sudo containerd config default | sudo tee/etc./containerd/
config.toml
```

10. To apply the modifications made to the configuration file, restart containerd.

```
Sudo systemctl restart containerd
```

11. First, make sure the containerd is up and running.

```
Sudo systemctl status containerd
```

12. Disable swap.

```
sudo swapoff -a
```

13. Install the dependency packages.

```
sudo apt-get update && sudo apt-get install -y apt-transport-
https curl
```

14. Download and add the GPG key.

```
curl -s https://packages.cloud.google.com/apt/doc/apt-key.gpg |
sudo apt-key add -
```

15. Add Kubernetes to the repository in Linux.

```
1. cat <<EOF | sudo tee/etc./apt/sources.list.d/kubernetes.list
2. deb https://apt.kubernetes.io/Kubernetes-xenial main
3. EOF
```

16. Update the package and install the Kubernetes packages; we will install version 1.24, the latest version at the time this book was written.

```
1. sudo apt-get update
2. sudo apt-get install -y kubelet=1.24.0-00 kubeadm=1.24.0-00
kubectl=1.24.0-00
```

After finishing the prerequisites to install Kubernetes, you must set up the master node.

## The Master Node Setup

The first step to start with Kubernetes is to set up the master/primary node; after that, the worker node can join it by running one command; the section will show the steps to set up the master node.

- Start the Kubernetes cluster initialization using kubeadm on the control plane node.

```
sudo kubeadm init --pod-network-cidr 192.168.0.0/16
--kubernetes-version 1.24.0
```

- Set the access for kubectl.

```
1. mkdir -p $HOME/.kube
2. sudo cp -i/etc./kubernetes/admin.conf $HOME/.kube/config
3. sudo chown $(id -u):$(id -g) $HOME/.kube/config
```

- To check if you can access the cluster, just run the following command:

```
kubectl get nodes
```

Kubernetes' present network architecture and pod support depend on plugins for other networking frameworks. Explore the details of CNI's integration with Kubernetes and evaluate the many network plugins for Kubernetes, such as Calico, Flannel, Weave Net, Cilium, and Multus.

1. Calico's Network Extension can be set up like so:

```
Kubectl apply -f https://docs.projectcalico.org/manifests/
calico.yaml
```

2. Verify the node's health on the control plane.

```
kubectl get nodes
```

The master node is ready to welcome any joining the worker node; each master node generates a token that will enable the worker to join.

```
kubeadm token create --print-join-command
```

The previous command will generate a complete command, copy it, and paste it one by one from worker node one and worker node two, but do not run it in parallel; see Figure 10-8.

```
Then you can join any number of worker nodes by running the following on each as root:

kubeadm join                      --token i55tp0.2pbex252ygp6lkcl \
        --discovery-token-ca-cert-hash sha256:88036a8f40bfe92538d17e5f6c89c9567ba25ec7940c5b70030f8f676c9a051c
```

***Figure 10-8.*** *Kubeadm join command for the worker node*

Kubernetes will now be working with one master node and two workers; another way to set up and test Kubernetes is to use the following (just for testing, not in production):

- Minikube (`https://minikube.sigs.k8s.io/`)

  Whether using macOS, Linux, or Windows, minikube makes deploying a local Kubernetes cluster easy. Proudly, we have made it our mission to aid Kubernetes beginners and application developers.

- Microk8s (`https://microk8s.io/`)

  To get Kubernetes up and running quickly and easily, you should use MicroK8s. Explore new upstream capabilities and promptly turn on/off services.

## Minikube Installation for a Single-Node Cluster

Minikube does not cost anything to use and is very user-friendly. In addition to configuring Kubernetes, it will install all its necessary components on your local PC. If you ever want to delete your local cluster completely, Minikube makes it simple to uninstall all the required components.

Never use it in production because it is not designed for it.

Minikube's main benefit is that it is an excellent tool for rapidly testing different Kubernetes implementations. The biggest issue is that it will not let you set up a Kubernetes cluster with many nodes, making it impossible to try any multimode situations we will cover later.

Minikube's primary function is to bring together your local Kubernetes components and get them talking to one another. Minikube offers two options for accomplishing this goal.

- Virtual machine

- Docker

The first involves running a hypervisor on top of the existing system. Minikube will launch a virtual machine with all Kubernetes preinstalled, such as a hypervisor or KVM.

That alternative approach is far less complicated. Minikube eliminates the need for a virtual machine by launching Kubernetes components within a single, massive Docker container using a local Docker daemon. You needs to run Docker on their computer to benefit from this strategy. That is the plan we will implement here.

The following instructions will guide you on how to install Minikube on Ubuntu; see Figure 10-9.

**1**    Installation

Click on the buttons that describe your target platform. For other architectures, see the release page for a complete list of minikube binaries.

| | | | | | |
|---|---|---|---|---|---|
| Operating system | **Linux** | macOS | Windows | | |
| Architecture | **x86-64** | ARM64 | ARMv7 | ppc64 | S390x |
| Release type | **Stable** | Beta | | | |
| Installer type | **Binary download** | Debian package | RPM package | | |

***Figure 10-9.*** *Minikube documentation depends on the operating system*

1. `curl -LO https://storage.googleapis.com/minikube/releases/latest/minikube-linux-amd64`
2. `sudo install minikube-linux-amd64/usr/local/bin/minikube`

After package installation, start the cluster by running the following command:

1. `minikube start`

After starting the cluster, you can deploy the application and test Kubernetes.

```
$ minikube status
host: Running
kubelet: Running
apiserver: Running
kubeconfig: Configured
```

Your Minikube installation may need to be terminated or removed. Instead of terminating the Docker container manually, you should utilize the Minikube CLI. The two necessary commands are as follows:

```
$ minikube stop
Stopping "minikube" in docker...
Node "aws-node" stopped.
```

Check again if all the processes have been stopped.

```
$ minikube status
host: Stopped
kubelet: Stopped
apiserver: Stopped
kubeconfig: Stopped
```

Use this command to delete the cluster permanently.

```
$ minikube delete
```

## Using Kubernetes and Kind to Create a Cluster with Several Nodes

As an alternative to Minikube, we will talk about a tool called Kind (https://kind.sigs. k8s.io/), which has a lot in common with Minikube but is far less well-known. Like Minikube, Kind is meant to host a Kubernetes cluster on a local machine. The critical distinction between Kind and Minikube is that Kind can initiate Kubernetes clusters with many nodes, whereas Minikube can only create a cluster with a single node.

The Docker-in-Docker (DIND) concept allows Kubernetes worker nodes to run within Docker containers. You can get them to act as Kubernetes worker nodes by deploying Docker containers, which include the Docker daemon and the Kubelet.

To install Kind, all you have to do is follow the steps; these are for Linux:

```
curl -Lo./kind https://kind.sigs.k8s.io/dl/v0.17.0/kind-linux-amd64
chmod +x./kind
sudo mv./kind/usr/local/bin/kind
```

Immediately after Kind has been installed, a new Kubernetes cluster can be created with the following command:

```
kind create cluster # Default cluster context name is `kind.`
```

This is an example of what you will see when listing your clusters of the same Kind:

```
kind get clusters
kind
AWS Test
```

We discussed installing Kubernetes using different tools on your local laptop or virtual machine; if you do not want to install Kubernetes on your local device, you can always create the cluster on any cloud provider.

The following section will show you how to set up a Kubernetes cluster on Amazon Elastic Kubernetes Service (EKS).

## Amazon EKS Kubernetes Installation

EKS is a commercial offering that rivals the Google Cloud Platform or Azure AKS. See Figure 10-10.

***Figure 10-10.***  *Amazon EKS dashboard*

If you use EKS, Amazon AWS will take care of your Kubernetes control plane. Rather than letting you directly interact with the servers that make up the control plane, the service will set up a few nodes to operate everything needed.

Note that this service is not free. You can estimate the cost using the AWS calculator, as shown in Figure 10-11; I am using one cluster and one worker node.

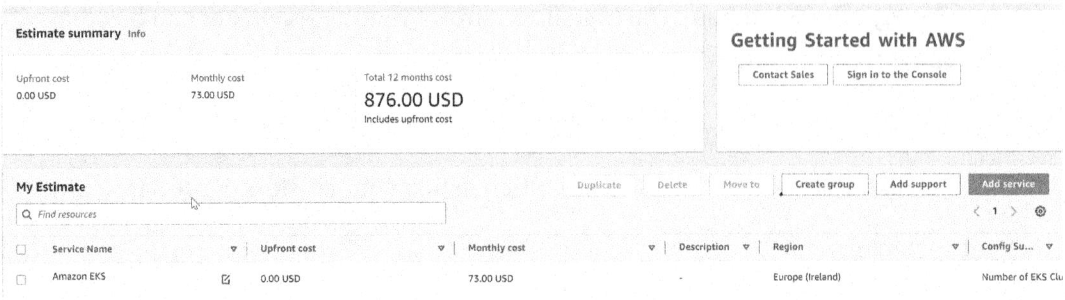

*Figure 10-11.  AWS calculator pricing for EKS*

With Amazon EKS, you can create a cluster in several different ways. You can utilize the AWS command-line interface (CLI), CloudFormation, Terraform, or the AWS Management Console.

Using the command-line interface tool `eksctl,` which AWS provides, you can create Kubernetes clusters on Amazon EKS with as few as two commands.

# EKSCTL

A straightforward CLI for working with Amazon's EKS-managed Kubernetes service for EC2. It is built on CloudFormation and written in Go.

The easiest way to set up EKS is using `eksctl,` and you can do that with the following steps:

1. Install eksctl depending on your operating system.

2. The following command will download and extract the most recent version of `eksctl`:

```
curl --silent --location "https://github.com/weaveworks/eksctl/
releases/latest/download/eksctl_$(uname -s)_amd64.tar.gz" | tar
xz -C/tmp
```

3. Copy the executable to the `/usr/local/bin` directory.

```
sudo mv/tmp/eksctl/usr/local/bin
```

4. Check and test the `eksctl` by running the following

```
eksctl version.
```

The AWS documentation has clear steps depending on your operating system to install the tool; see https://docs.aws.amazon.com/eks/latest/userguide/eksctl.html.

After installing eksctl, you can use the tool to provision the EKS cluster. Note that you must configure the AWS CLI command and provide the access and secret keys; otherwise, eksctl cannot communicate with the account.

You can also use AWS CloudShell and install eksctl there. See Figure 10-12.

***Figure 10-12.***  *AWS CloudShell*

The following YAML file will make it much easier to install and set up the cluster with what you need. The comments are written in the YAML file; it is changeable depending on the setup and configuration needs and can save time over a manual installation.

You can assign a policy to the cluster depending on the needs of the cluster.

```
cat << EOF > book.yaml
apiVersion: eksctl.io/v1alpha4
kind: ClusterConfig

metadata:
  name: aws-eks
  region: eu-west-1

nodeGroups:
  - name: node-group-1
    instanceType: t2.small
    desiredCapacity: 2
EOF
```

Next run the following:

```
1. eksctl create cluster -f book.yaml
```

Or, without the YAML file, you can provision the EKS cluster using a different parameter in eksctl, as shown here:

```
eksctl create cluster \
  --name= aws-eks \
  --region=eu-west-1 \
  --nodes=2 \
 --tags environment=develop \
  --node-type=t2.small \
 --ssh-access \
  --ssh-public-key=public-key-value \
  --node-private-networking \
  --vpc-private-subnets=your-private-subnet-az1, your-private-subnet-az2 \
  --vpc-public-subnets= your-public-subnet-az1, your-public-subnet-az2
```

## Terraform

In this section, I will show you how to create an EKS instance using Terraform; you already learned what Terraform is and how to use it to provision different resources on Amazon AWS.

I will not dive deep into how to create EKS; a complete project will be provided to you in next chapter.

## CloudFormation

Another way to create an EKS instance is with CloudFormation; no AWS service, including Amazon EKS, can be installed outside a virtual private cloud. Two potential solutions are as follows:

- The EKS cluster is set up on top of an existing virtual private network.

- Create a new VPC to house your EKS cluster.

AWS provides a complete CloudFormation template to set up EKS. Follow these steps:

1.  A key pair must be created; see Figure 10-13.

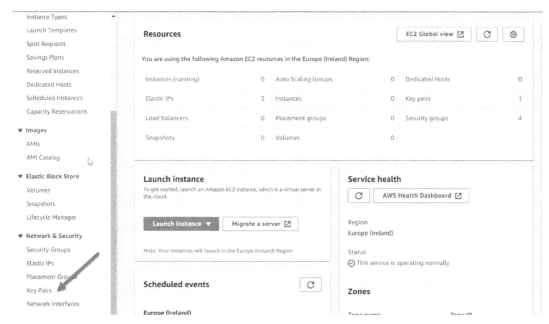

***Figure 10-13.*** *Key pair AWS creation*

2.  After creating the key pair, in the CloudFormation dashboard, click "Create stack." See Figure 10-14.

***Figure 10-14.*** *CloudFormation creating a stack*

3.  Enter the following URL: `https://s3.amazonaws.com/aws-quickstart/quickstart-amazon-eks/templates/amazon-eks-entrypoint-new-vpc.template.yaml`.

    Then click Next. See Figure 10-15.

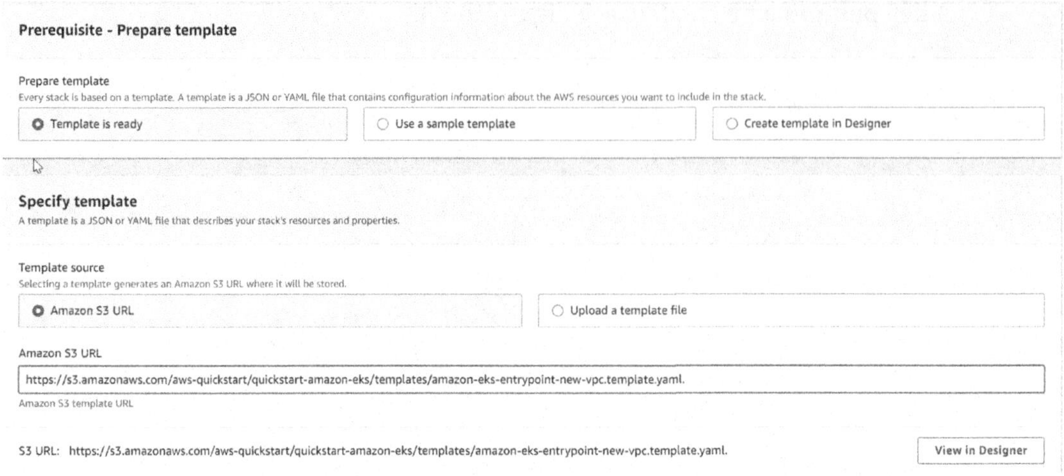

**Prerequisite - Prepare template**

Prepare template
Every stack is based on a template. A template is a JSON or YAML file that contains configuration information about the AWS resources you want to include in the stack.

| ⦿ Template is ready | ○ Use a sample template | ○ Create template in Designer |

**Specify template**
A template is a JSON or YAML file that describes your stack's resources and properties.

Template source
Selecting a template generates an Amazon S3 URL where it will be stored.

| ⦿ Amazon S3 URL | ○ Upload a template file |

Amazon S3 URL

https://s3.amazonaws.com/aws-quickstart/quickstart-amazon-eks/templates/amazon-eks-entrypoint-new-vpc.template.yaml

Amazon S3 template URL

S3 URL:  https://s3.amazonaws.com/aws-quickstart/quickstart-amazon-eks/templates/amazon-eks-entrypoint-new-vpc.template.yaml   [ View in Designer ]

***Figure 10-15.*** *Using the AWS template to create EKS*

4. CloudFormation requires you to provide a few variables and parameters before it can deploy your Amazon EKS cluster.

You can do so on the following screen. Enter the following variables:

- *Stack name*: Choose a meaningful name for your CloudFormation stack so you can identify the resources it generates.

- *Availability zone*: Choose two, at a minimum, from those in your AWS region.

- *CIDR*: Define the IP address where EKS will be set up and allow a remote connection using the correct security group.

- *The number of availability zones*: The best practice is to choose at least two availability zones.

- *Bastion host*: This will allow you to access the EKS; by default AWS allows only the EKS creator to access the EKS unless they give your permission.

- *SSH key name*: Choose the key pair name we created earlier. See Figure 10-16.

**Bastion host on-demand percentage**
Set the percentage of on-demand instances and spot instances. With a default of 100, the percentages are 100% for on-demand instances and 0% for spot instances

```
100
```

**Amazon EKS configuration**

**EKS cluster name**
(Optional) Name for the EKS cluster. If left blank, one is auto-generated. This must be unique within the Region.

```
Book-EKS
```

**Kubernetes version**
(Optional) Kubernetes control plane version. If ConfigSetName is set, this value will be ignored and the Kubernetes version specified in the advanced configuration template (including the default) will be used.

```
1.24                                                                              ▼
```

**EKS public access endpoint**
Configure access to the Kubernetes API server endpoint from outside of your VPC

```
Enabled                                                                           ▼
```

**Additional EKS admin ARN (IAM user)**
(Optional) IAM user ARN to be granted administrative access to the EKS cluster.

```
Enter String
```

**Additional EKS admin ARN (IAM role)**
(Optional) IAM role ARN to be granted administrative access to the EKS cluster.

```
Enter String
```

**Fargate namespaces**
(Optional) Comma-separated list of namespaces for which Fargate should be enabled.

```
Enter String
```

**Fargate labels**
Requires at least one Fargate namespace to be specified. This is a comma-separated list of key-value pod labels. For a pod to run on Fargate, all of the labels must match, and it must run in a namespace defined by "Fargate namespaces."

```
Enter String
```

***Figure 10-16.*** *CloudFormation template variable*

- The new clusters will be fully operational after some time. To communicate with the Amazon EKS cluster, you must create a new Kubeconfig file on your local workstation by doing the following:

  - You first need to be an IAM user with access and secret keys; see Figure 10-17.

457

# :ess key best practices & alternatives

using long-term credentials like access keys to improve your security. Consider the following use cases and ;

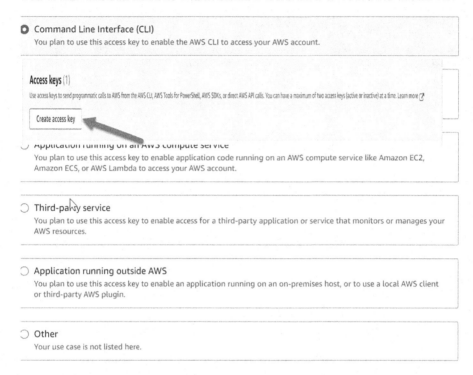

**⦿ Command Line Interface (CLI)**
You plan to use this access key to enable the AWS CLI to access your AWS account.

**Access keys** (1)

Use access keys to send programmatic calls to AWS from the AWS CLI, AWS Tools for PowerShell, AWS SDKs, or direct AWS API calls. You can have a maximum of two access keys (active or inactive) at a time. Learn more ☐

Create access key

○ Application running on an AWS compute service
You plan to use this access key to enable application code running on an AWS compute service like Amazon EC2, Amazon ECS, or AWS Lambda to access your AWS account.

○ Third-party service
You plan to use this access key to enable access for a third-party application or service that monitors or manages your AWS resources.

○ Application running outside AWS
You plan to use this access key to enable an application running on an on-premises host, or to use a local AWS client or third-party AWS plugin.

○ Other
Your use case is not listed here.

***Figure 10-17.*** *Creating access key and secret key*

- The next step will be to install AWS CLI, and to do that, define which operating system you have; I am using Ubuntu.

```
curl "https://awscli.amazonaws.com/awscli-exe-
linux-x86_64.zip" -o "awscliv2.zip"
unzip awscliv2.zip
sudo./aws/install
```

- We will need access and secret keys, so note them. The AWS CLI setup procedure begins with the following command:

```
$ aws configure -profile book-aws
AWS Access Key ID [None]: [Access Key ID]
AWS Secret Access Key [None]: [Secret access key]
Default region name [None]: [Your current AWS region]
Default output format [None]: json
```

- The kubeconfig file can be generated using the AWS CLI now that it has been set up correctly. Run this command. The cluster's name is the value returned by the preceding command:

```
aws eks update-kubeconfig --name [depend-on-name-you-
set-in-cloud-formation]
Added new context arn:aws:eks:eu-west-1:XXX:cluster/
book-aws to/root/.kube/config
```

You need to know that once the EKS cluster is created, you cannot stop it from being out of charge, but you either delete or use it.

If it is destroyed, there will be no way to put the cluster back in the same condition as before it was deleted.

If you create the cluster using IaC, destroying the cluster is pretty straightforward; there is no need to do extra work. What you have to do depends on whether you used Terraform or CloudFormation.

Removing the cluster is as simple as selecting the stack from the list in the CloudFormation web dashboard and clicking the "Remove stack" button. This will cause CloudFormation to delete all of the newly generated resources.

For Terraform, the Terraform instance is destroyed, and the cluster is gone.

It would be best to remember to delete the cluster when you are not using it, such as at night. Disabling unused resources is the best strategy to reduce cloud service costs.

# Diving into Kubernetes

The next topic in this chapter is talking about Kubernetes in detail, as well as the Kubernetes objects.

Kubernetes can control a group of computing nodes and allocate them to containers depending on their resource needs and the computing power available in the cluster.

One or more containers can be grouped into logical units (or *pods*) and run/scaled as a single unit, which we will discuss in this section.

# Pods

Earlier in this chapter, I showed how to install Kubernetes and the components. Now I will show you how to deal with the Kubernetes objects.

Kubernetes pods are where all the container management happens; you will never have to modify, deploy, or remove containers manually. Launching many containers on the same host under the same user namespace creates a *pod*. Figure 10-18 shows how pods work.

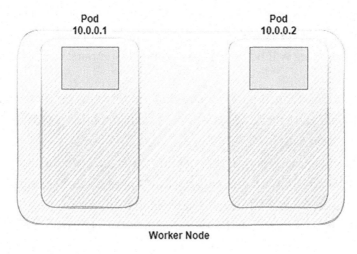

**Figure 10-18.**  *How pods work*

Not only can containers within the same pod talk to one another via local hosts, but pods can communicate. Each pod will be assigned to a private IP address at boot time.

Without requiring a NAT device, Kubernetes networking models allow pods to connect directly with one another. Remember that they are not NAT gateways for communication between pods in your cluster.

However, then, why do we need pods? To put it another way, why can't we utilize containers? There seems to be no need to use numerous containers at once. We need a way to centralize our operations; why can't we use one big box? Now is the time for us to respond to your inquiries.

A container can host only a single process at a time; the onus of keeping numerous unrelated methods alive inside a single container, managing their logs, and so on falls on the user. You'd need features such as an automated process that resumes when there is a process crash. In addition, everything would be reported to the same standard output, making it impossible to tell which method was responsible for which logs.

Pods are designed to be readily deleted and regenerated; nevertheless, if a worker node hosting two pods were to die, all the containers they were running would become unreachable. Because of this, you may safely delete and regenerate your pods without worrying about your app crashing.

The kubectl run command creates a pod on your Kubernetes cluster. Getting a pod up and operating on your Kubernetes cluster could not be easier or quicker than that.

```
kubectl run my-nginx --image=nginx
```

The previous command will run a pod inside the cluster; the pod name is my-nginx based on the official image for Nginx.

What if I create a pod based on specs that I define, for example, declarative syntax, based on YAML?

```
apiVersion: v1
kind: Pod
metadata:
  name: nginx
  labels:
    env: test
spec:
  containers:
  - name: nginx
    image: nginx
```

This YAML is easy to understand; as you can see, the YAML depends on the key/value.

- apiVersion: Which version of the Kubernetes API you're using to create this object

- Kind: What kind of object do you want to create

- Metadata: Data that helps uniquely identify the thing, including a name string, a UID, and an optional namespace

- spec: What state you desire for the object

Save the previous YAML as a file called `K8s-first-example.yaml` and then run the following command to deploy it on the cluster:

```
$ kubectl create -f K8s-first-example.yaml
Pod/nginx-Pod created
```

There are many components of a pod. The Kubernetes API version and resource type are the first things to consider while working with YAML files. Third, all Kubernetes materials share the following three sections:

- The metadata of a pod consists of its name, namespace, labels, and other data.

- The pod's contents, including its containers, volumes, and other information, are described in its Spec file.

- The pod's current status, the containers' descriptions, respective states, internal IP address, and other pertinent data can all be found in the status field.

After deploying the pods, how can you check the information on the pods you have on the cluster? To achieve this, you can use two commands.

- `kubectl gets` lists items; it is used to generate a list of things. To use the command, you must specify the kind of item you want to display. Therefore, the `kubectl get Pods` command will be what we use.

- `kubectl` describes that its primary goal is to obtain all the details about a single item that its kind and name can recognize. Using the command `kubectl describe Pods my-nginx,` we can get the details of the pod we just created; the command will return a complete set of information about that specific pod, such as its IP address.

The `kubectl` command can be used in different ways, and you can format the output depending on your needs; a beneficial `kubectl` command-line option is the `-o` option. It would be best if you did not ignore this one's advantages. You can modify the `kubectl` command line's output by selecting this option.

```
$ kubectl get pods my-nginx -o yaml # In YAML format
$ kubectl get pods my-nginx -o json # In JSON format
```

These settings can also be used to back up your Kubernetes cluster. Let's say you're in a position where you do not have the YAML declaration because you imperatively built a pod; check the following command:

```
kubectl get my-nginx -o yaml > my-nginx.yaml
```

Or run the following command:

```
kubectl run my-nginx --image=nginx:latest \
 --labels type=test \
 --dry-run=client -o yaml > mypod.yaml
```

The -o wide format is useful. You can get additional information than is shown in the standard output by selecting this option.

```
$ kubectl get Pods -o wide
```

According to Kubectl get and your application's log, the pod has started and is now operating. OK, but what does it look like in practice?

Because services get their, you can connect to a pod in numerous ways for testing and debugging. Using port forwarding is one of them, as shown here:

```
$ kubectl port-forward my-nginx 8080:80
Forwarding from 127.0.0.1:8080 -> 80
Forwarding from [::1]:8080 -> 80
```

You can easily deduce what this command does: forward port 8080 to my local PC to port 80 on the pod identified by my-nginx, as shown in Figure 10-19.

# Welcome to nginx!

If you see this page, the nginx web server is successfully installed and working. Further configuration is required.

For online documentation and support please refer to nginx.org. Commercial support is available at nginx.com.

*Thank you for using nginx.*

***Figure 10-19.*** *Redirecting Nginx pods to my local PC*

Try to run a `curl` command; you will get an Nginx page. Figures 10-20 show what occurs when you make the request. The kubectl procedure is not the only thing standing between you and your pod; however, those other pieces are not important now.

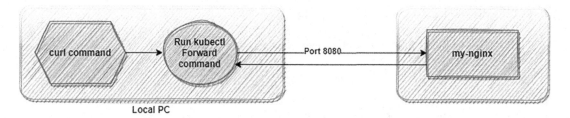

***Figure 10-20.*** *How the Kubectl forward command works*

The pod can be accessed after it has been launched. Docker's `docker exec` command runs external code within a container; Kubernetes mimics this functionality with the help of the `kubectl exec` command. The following command will allow you to connect to your NGINX container inside the nginx pod that was created earlier:

```
$ kubectl exec -ti pods my-Nginx bash
```

There should still be active pods that you've built. Assume you have two pods, one in the default namespace and one in the custom namespace (we will discuss the namespace later).

Now that you no longer need their services, you want to terminate them.

```
$ kubectl delete po my-nginx
pod "my-nginx" deleted
```

## Labels and Annotations

We will move on to another fundamental idea of Kubernetes: labels and annotations. Labels allow you to associate a key with your Kubernetes objects; Figure 10-21 shows what label is used in Kubernetes.

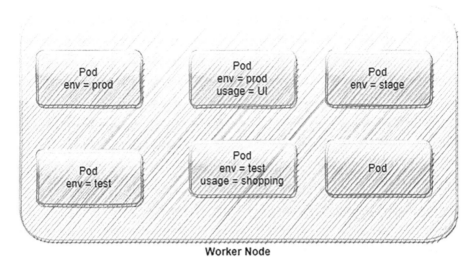

**Figure 10-21.** *What is the label in K8S*

Labels in Kubernetes are used to assign a custom key to objects. To obtain certain Kubernetes things based on their labels, you must first label those objects.

Labels allow you to associate a key with objects you build, such as pods. There is no hard and fast rule on what you must use as an object's label.

Once your objects have been labeled, you can use those labels to list and query them in your Kubernetes cluster.

To illustrate this, let's say you wanted to see all the pods running in the production environment so you labeled some of them with the label env = prod and then ran the kubectl get pods command.

```
$ kubectl get pods my-nginx --label env = prod
```

Or, you can even use the new command shown here:

```
kubectl label pods my-nginx env = prod
```

You can add a label when creating a pod.

```
$ kubectl run my-nginx --image nginx --label "usage=web-server"
```

It is also worth noting that labels can be specified using a declarative syntax.

```
apiVersion: v1
kind: Pod
```

```
metadata:
name: my-nginx
Labels:
    env: prod
    usage: web-server
spec:
containers:
    - name: my-nginx
      image: nginx:latest
```

To list the label using kubectl, use this:

```
$ kubectl get Pods --show-labels -o wide
```

The output will be as follows:

```
$ kubectl get po --show-labels
NAME           READY     STATUS    RESTARTS   AGE                 LABELS
aws-book       1/1       Running   0          16 m      <none>    env = prod
devops-pod     1/1       Running   0           2 m                usage = test
```

Here's how you update the labels:

```
kubectl label --overwrite pods my-nginx status=unhealthy
```

Imagine you want to launch a new pod to a specific node by including a node selector in the pod's YAML, as follows:

```
apiVersion: v1
kind: Pod
metadata:
  name: my-nginx
spec:
  nodeSelector: <worker-node-name>
  containers:
  - image: Nginx
    name: my-nginx
```

Annotations are an additional kind of information used by Kubernetes. Since both labels and annotations are made up of a key and a value, they have many similarities.

Annotations are utilized in place of fields. After the necessary API modifications become evident and are agreed upon by the Kubernetes developers, new labels are created, and the associated annotations are deprecated.

Adding descriptions for each pod or API item is an excellent way to utilize annotations since this allows all cluster users to quickly seek information about a specific pod or API object.

However, annotations are not as helpful as labels. Labels are used to classify items and establish connections between them.

On the other hand, annotations provide background data about the resource upon which they are defined.

Similar to labels, annotations are key/value maps.

```
"metadata": {
  "annotations": {
    "key1" : "value1",
    "key2" : "value2"
  }
}
```

Here's how to use annotations with declarative syntax within Kubernetes:

```
apiVersion: v1
kind: Pod
metadata:
  annotations:
    kubernetes.io/created by: |
      {"kind": "SerializedReference", "apiVersion": "v1",
      "reference" :{ "kind": "ReplicationController", "namespace":
      "default",...
```

Or you can, for example, use them like the following example:

```
apiVersion: v1
kind: Pod
metadata:
  name: annotations-usage
  annotations:
    image: "https://registry.Gitlab.com/"
```

You will utilize what you know about label selectors instead of naming each pod to be deleted, another benefit of labels.

```
$ kubectl delete po -l env=prod
pod "my-nginx" deleted
pod "app-1" deleted
```

## Namespaces

Namespaces (Figure 10-22) allow you to partition your cluster's resources into manageable chunks. The name of a resource must be unique inside a namespace but not between them; I will compare this object with a tablespace in the database.

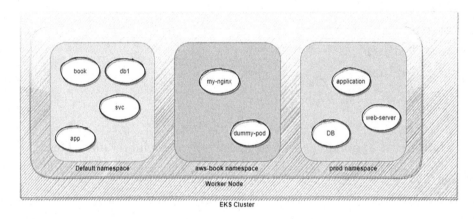

***Figure 10-22.*** *How namespaces look in Kubernetes*

Using several namespaces enables you to partition large systems into more manageable chunks. They can also divide resources for usage in different settings, such as production, development, and quality assurance.

Resource names are solely required to be unique inside a given namespace. Resources with identical names but in separate namespaces are possible. Many different resources have their namespaces; however, a few exceptions exist.

A node is a resource that can be used anywhere in the system and is not associated with any specific namespace.

Here's how to check the current namespaces in your cluster:

```
$ kubectl get ns #or namespaces
NAME            LABELS      STATUS    AGE
default         <none>      Active    1 h
kube-public     <none>      Active    1 h
kube-system     <none>      Active    1 h
```

By default, kubectl only displays items located in the default namespace. The list also shows the existence of the kube-public and kube-system namespaces. Let's check out the kube-system namespace's pods.

```
$ kubectl get po --namespace kube-system
NAME                            READY     STATUS     RESTARTS    AGE
fluentd-cloud-kubia             1/1       Running    0           1 h
kube-dns-v9-udsa                1/4       Running    0           1 h
lb-controller-v1                2/2       Running    92          1 h
```

As a namespace is just another Kubernetes object, it can be created by a YAML file to the Kubernetes. Therefore, let's check out the procedure.

```
apiVersion: v1
kind: Namespace
metadata:
  name: aws-book
```

To apply the previous YAML, use this:

```
$ kubectl create -f aws-book-ns.yaml
```

Instead of manually crafting a YAML file, use the specialized kubectl create namespace command. Developing a namespace manifest in YAML requires your attention, and usually, I prefer to learn things in a complex way and then use the easy way so you can be aware of both methods.

```
$ kubectl create namespace aws-book
namespace "aws-book" created
```

Adding an object for a namespace we created earlier can be done differently, either by using the YAML or by providing the namespace when creating the resource using the kubectl create command to create resources in the namespace you have established.

```
$ kubectl create -f My-Nginx.yaml -n aws-book
pod "My-Nginx" created
```

If the namespace and associated pods are no longer needed, you can safely delete them. It is possible to remove the whole namespace with the following command (the pods will be removed automatically):

```
$ kubectl delete ns aws-book
namespace "aws-book" deleted
```

To remove everything from the current namespace, including the pods and services, use the following command. I do not recommend using this command, especially if you are unsure if these pods are in use.

```
$ kubectl delete all --all
pod "my-nginx" deleted
service "my-nginx-svc" deleted
```

# Jobs

The Kubernetes API makes jobs available to users with another resource object. Last, a task will spin up a few pods to carry out an order you provide.

A job may launch several pods, each executed repeatedly until some threshold is reached. The task keeps a tally of how many pods have finished without incident.

The job is considered finished after some threshold number of completed iterations. When a job is deleted, the associated pods are also removed. When a job is suspended, any running pods are terminated until the job is restarted.

A primary use case is creating a single job object to consistently execute a single pod to completion. If the first pod fails or is removed, the Job object will initiate a new pod.

Several common scenarios using Kubernetes jobs are listed here:

- Creating a database copy for safekeeping

- Indicating one's interest through electronic mail

- Removing messages from a queue

Because of the potential complexity of the settings involved in establishing a task or job, this section will emphasize declarative syntax. Here is a Kubernetes YAML job creation example:

```
apiVersion: batch/v1
kind: Job
metadata:
name: hello-world-job-example
spec:
template:
    metadata:
      name: hello-world-job-example
    spec:
      restartPolicy: Never
      containers:
      name: hello-world-example
        image: busybox
        command: ["/bin/sh", "-c"]
        args: ["echo 'Hello world'"]
```

This task will produce a pod from the busybox Docker image, and the command echo Hello World will be executed.

The restart policy option is set to Never, which tells Kubernetes to restart the pod or the container if it fails. A new pod will be started if the current pod is lost.

The restart policy parameter has two options.

- Never

- OnFailure

If you set this to Never, the job will never try to restart the pods, and this option is useful when trying to troubleshoot; otherwise, the logs will keep updated every time the pod attempts to launch.

Check the logs by running the following:

```
$ kubectl logs
```

The job has five options; we need to talk about them to allow you to understand the power of the job and how to be helpful.

- backoffLimit
- completions
- parallelism
- activeDeadlineSeconds
- ttlSecondsAfterFinished

## backoffLimit

After a failed launch, if the Kubernetes job is left alone for six minutes, it will automatically attempt to restart the failed pod six times. By adjusting the backoffLimit setting, you can alter this restriction.

```
apiVersion: batch/v1
kind: Job
metadata:
name: hello-world-job-example
spec:
  backoffLimit: 4
template:

    metadata:
      name: hello-world-job-example
    spec:
      restartPolicy: Never
      containers:
      name: hello-world-example
        image: busybox
        command: ["/bin/sh", "-c"]
        args: ["echo 'Hello world'"]
```

## completions

This option will allow Kubernetes to understand how often you need to run the job even after finished or completed.

```
apiVersion: batch/v1
kind: Job
metadata:
name: hello-world-job-example
spec:
  completions: 5
template:

    metadata:
      name: hello-world-job-example
    spec:
      restartPolicy: Never
      containers:
      name: hello-world-example
        image: busybox
        command: ["/bin/sh", "-c"]
        args: ["echo 'Hello world'"]
```

The previous code will create five different pods for each job, which will wait until it is finished and rerun the new job, leading us to the following parameter.

## parallelism

Using the completions feature guarantees that the pods will be built sequentially. The parallelism switch can be used to compel simultaneous processing.

```
apiVersion: batch/v1
kind: Job
metadata:
name: hello-world-job-example
spec:
 parallelism: 5
template:

    metadata:
      name: hello-world-job-example
    spec:
      restartPolicy: Never
```

```
  containers:
  name: hello-world-example
    image: busybox
    command: ["/bin/sh", "-c"]
    args: ["echo 'Hello world'"]
```

## activeDeadlineSeconds

You can set a pod to expire after a certain length of time if you so want. When a job's purpose is to consume a queue, this can be pretty helpful, and it should be seconds.

```
apiVersion: batch/v1
kind: Job
metadata:
name: hello-world-job-example
spec:
  backoffLimit: 4
  activeDeadlineSeconds: 120
template:

    metadata:
      name: hello-world-job-example
    spec:
      restartPolicy: Never
      containers:
      name: hello-world-example
        image: busybox
        command: ["/bin/sh", "-c"]
        args: ["echo 'Hello world'"]
```

## ttlSecondsAfterFinished

Even after your task has finished, Kubernetes will keep it around if you need to rerun it later. This is because its logs will be interesting to read even years after the project has been finished.

Jobs and pods can be removed from the system in an automated manner by using this parameter.

```
apiVersion: batch/v1
kind: Job
metadata:
name: hello-world-job-example
spec:
  ttlSecondsAfterFinished: 60
template:

    metadata:
      name: hello-world-job-example
    spec:
      restartPolicy: Never
      containers:
      name: hello-world-example
        image: busybox
        command: ["/bin/sh", "-c"]
        args: ["echo 'Hello world'"]
```

Now, you can delete a job like usual using the kubectl command.

```
$ kubectl delete jobs hello-world-job-example
```

However, what you want to delete the job and keep the pods that the job has created? Use this:

```
$ kubectl delete jobs hello-world-job-example --cascade=false
```

## Kubernetes and CronJob

If you are a Linux user, you should know what crontab is, but if you use Windows, let me explain.

Scheduled tasks in Linux can be executed using the a cron job. By using cron jobs, you can program your server to run a series of commands or scripts automatically, such as a backup or maybe a server check script.

However, why do you need to use a cron job with Kubernetes?

- Some databases can be run on Kubernetes, so you may need to create a backup.

- You can clear caching data.

- You can send a report email to the team at 3 a.m.

Let's create a cron tab on Kubernetes.

A cron expression typically has five items, each separated by whitespace. These numbers, from left to right, mean the following:

- Minutes

- Hour

- Day of the month

- Month

- Day of the week

Here is the syntax:

```
<Minute> <Hour> <Day_of_the_Month> <Month_of_the_Year> <Day_of_the_Week>
<command>
```

Here are examples of a cronjob:

- Schedule a cron to execute at 3 a.m. daily.

  ```
  0 2 * * */bin/sh backup.sh
  ```

- Schedule a cron to execute every minute.

  ```
  * * * * * /scripts/script.sh
  ```

You can see many other examples to understand how the cron job works at `https://crontab.guru/examples.html`.

Make your first cronjob now within Kubernetes; using declarative syntax will make this easier.

```
apiVersion: batch/v1
kind: CronJob
```

```
metadata:
  name: hello-world-cronjob
spec:
 schedule: "* * * * *"
jobTemplate:
    spec:
      template:
        spec:
          containers:
          - name: hello-world
            image: busybox:1.28
            command: # or you can use this format command: ["/bin/
            sh", "-c"]
            -/bin/sh
            - -c
            - date; echo Hello world # or you can use this format args:
              ["echo 'Hello world'"]
          restartPolicy: Never
```

A cronjob can be removed from Kubernetes using the kubectl delete command, similar to any other resource.

```
$ kubectl delete -f  <path-to-your-yaml/name-of-the-yaml.yaml
cronjob/hello-world-cronjob deleted
```

## Kubernetes Trick and Tips

Kubernetes' primary strength is that it can be fed a list of containers and left to maintain their stateful execution in the background, distributed throughout the cluster. To do this, you must create a pod resource and have Kubernetes assign a worker node to operate the containers inside the pod.

However, what if the container dies? What will happen?

The Kubelet that is running on a node, will start running the pod's containers as soon as the pod is scheduled to run on that node, and it will continue to keep those containers running for as long as the pod continues to exist. The Kubelet will restart the container if the container's primary process terminates unexpectedly.

Even if your app sometimes crashes due to a problem, running it on Kubernetes will immediately restart it, giving it the capacity to self-heal without any further code changes on your part.

## Liveness Probe

Using liveness probes, Kubernetes can determine whether a container is still functioning. Each pod container's specification may include a liveness probe. Once the probe fails, Kubernetes will restart the container and try again.

One of the three methods through which Kubernetes may investigate a container is as follows:

- A TCP socket probe attempts to establish a TCP connection to the container's designated port.

- A container's IP address and the port and route you choose are sent in an HTTP GET probe; if the diagnostic returned a code between 200 and 399, it was successful.

- To test a container, an Exec probe can run any command within the container and examine the resultant exit status code.

Let's look at an example of HTTP and how to use it; I will use a Docker image called `luksa/kubia-unhealthy` to see what an unhealthy probe is.

The Docker image is here: `https://hub.Docker.com/r/luksa/kubia-unhealthy`.

```
apiVersion: v1
kind: Pod
metadata:
  name: liveness-http-example
spec:
  containers:
  - image: luksa/kubia-unhealthy
    name: liveness-http-example
    livenessProbe:
      httpGet:
        path:/ᵥ
        port: 8080
```

This image is based on a broken application and will work as a load balancer healthy check for the path and which port will be used.

```
$ kubectl get po liveness-http-example
NAME                     READY   STATUS    RESTARTS   AGE
liveness-http-example 1/1      Running   2          5 m
```

The RESTARTS column shows that the pod's container has been restarted once.

The time and computing power required for liveliness should be minimal. The probes are run often and are given a one-second time limit by default. You should expect a significant decrease in container speed if you equip it with a probe designed to handle the heavy lifting.

# Replication Controllers

A Kubernetes resource called a *replication controller* guarantees the continuous operation of its pods; a replication controller will detect a missing pod and generate a new one if it is lost for any reason.

Figure 10-23 shows when a node is removed from the cluster or the pod is forcibly removed from the node.

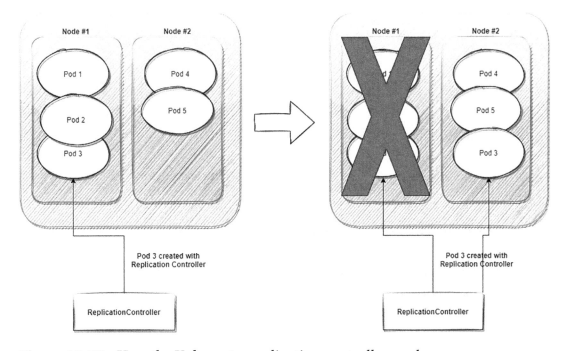

***Figure 10-23.*** *How the Kubernetes replication controller works*

The results of a node #1 failure take three pods down. Pods 1 and 2 are unmanaged since they were generated without a replication controller, whereas pod 3 is managed by one.

When a node fails, a replication controller immediately spins up a replacement pod (pod 3) to take its place, but pods 1 and 2 are irretrievably erased.

A replication controller closely monitors the number of active pods to ensure that a particular type's target number of pods is consistently met.

It will duplicate an existing pod if there are not enough active pods. If there are too many copies in operation, it will shut down the extra pods.

The following are three components of a replication controller:

- A replication controller's scope selector uses a label selector to narrow down which pods it will manage.

- A replica defines how many instances of the pod system are supposed to be active.

- A pod template is used when creating a new pod.

Figure 10-24 shows the three parts of a replication controller.

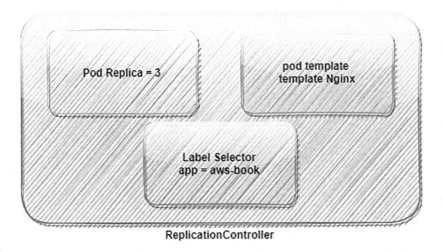

*Figure 10-24.  The three parts of a replication controller*

A replication controller, like many things in Kubernetes, is a deceptively basic notion that delivers or allows significant functionalities.

- It ensures that a pod continually operates by spawning a new pod whenever the previous pod disappears.

- When a node in a cluster fails, its pod copies are automatically replicated on other nodes.

- The pods scale horizontally

The following is a replication controller defined in this manifest that uses a replica of three pods, and the selector will be tested:

```
apiVersion: v1
kind: ReplicationController
metadata:
  name: replication-example
spec:
 replicas: 3
  selector:
    app: Test
 template:
    metadata:
      labels:
        app: Test
    spec:
      containers:
      - name: replication-example
        image: luksa/kubia
        ports:
        - containerPort: 8080
```

Here is a look at the data available about replication controllers using the kubectl get command:

```
$ kubectl get rc
NAME                    DESIRED   CURRENT   READY    AGE
replication-example  3         3         2        3 m
```

The previous has a replication replica of three pods; if you want to change or edit the replica, either you edit the YAML or you can run the following command:

```
kubectl scale rc replication-example  --replicas=10
```

However, if you want to scale down, you can run the following command:

```
kubectl scale rc replication-example  --replicas=3
```

## Replica Set

A *replica set* is functionally identical to a replication controller, except its pod selectors are more granular, unlike the label selector of a replication controller, which restricts matching pods to those with a given label. See Figure 10-25.

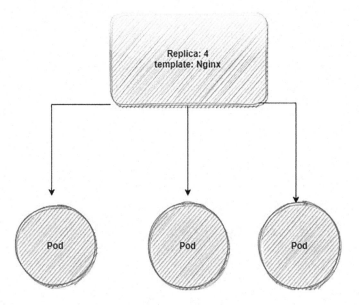

***Figure 10-25.***  *A replica set and how it works*

A replica set can also be used to find pods with the same set of labels but differ in their values; a single replication controller cannot match pods marked with labels, for example, env=prod and usage=test.

Now that your replication controller has generated and abandoned several pods, you will establish a replica set to see how these pods might be brought into a larger group.

Check the following example, which shows you how to use the replica set; you're using the more straightforward `matchLabels` selection, which is analogous to the selector used by a replication controller.

```
apiVersion: apps/v1
kind: ReplicaSet
metadata:
  name: replication-example
spec:
 replicas: 3
  selector:
    matchLabels:
      app: Test
 template:
    metadata:
      labels:
        app: Test
    spec:
      containers:
      - name: replication-example
        image: luksa/kubia
```

## DaemonSets

When you want to operate a certain number of pods deployed anywhere in the Kubernetes cluster, you must employ replication controllers and replica sets. On the other hand, there are circumstances where you would want a pod to operate on each node in the cluster.

Figure 10-26 shows the difference between how a daemon set works versus a replica set; a daemon set ensures that one pod of each container will run on the worker node.

If you have three worker nodes, then daemon sets will ensure that the pod will run on three of them.

On the other hand, a replica set replicates the pod on any of the worker's nodes.

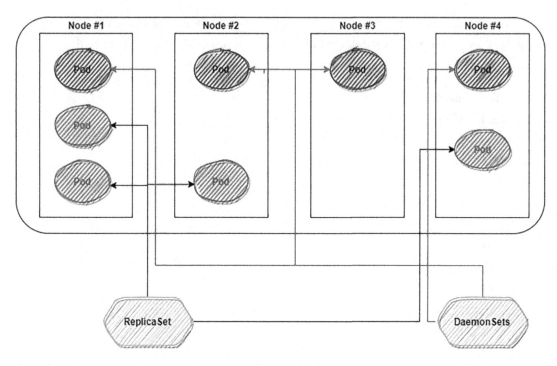

**Figure 10-26.** *Daemon set versus replica set*

```
apiVersion: apps/v1
kind: DaemonSet
metadata:
name: daemon-example
spec:
selector:
   matchLabels:
name: daemon-example
 template:
   metadata:
 labels:
name: daemon-example
   spec:
 containers:
   - image: nginx
     name: daemon-example
```

You can check the daemon set like so:

```
$ kubectl get ds
NAME              DESIRED CURRENT READY UP-TO-DATE AVAILABLE
daemon-example O        O       O     O          O
```

# Logs

Like any other tech tool, Kubernetes has its log to allow you to debug and troubleshoot.

The kubectl logs command can obtain application logs from the container and can stream the stdout property of a dedicated container in a dedicated pod.

To access a particular container, as we did when we used kubectl exec, you will need to know the individual container's name and the pod's name.

```
kubectl logs <pod-name>
```

In the pod nginx console, if you want to get the most recent lines of output from a log, you can do so by using the --tail option.

```
kubectl logs --tail=20 <pod-name>
```

See all logs from pod nginx that were generated in the last hour with the following:

```
kubectl logs --since=1 h <pod-name>
```

# Volumes

When you create a pod, you can build volumes and connect them to the containers contained inside the pods. Volumes are storage-bound to the pod's life cycle.

Volumes are simply a kind of storage tied to the pod's life cycle. The volumes produced with the pod will be erased as soon as the pod is removed from the system.

You might think of volumes as an excellent method to share a directory and files among containers operating in the same pod. However, they are not restricted to this use case, which is not always true. This is because volumes are not limited to this use case.

When Docker first introduced the idea of volumes, it consisted of more than shared folders and containers that could be mounted. Moreover, the Kubernetes volume functionality was designed around this concept, and volumes were utilized instead of shared directories.

Within Kubernetes, you need to understand different types of volumes.

- emptyDir volumes

- Persistent volumes

- Ephemeral volumes

- hostPath volumes

- ConfigMap

## emptyDir

The first example will be an empty volume.

The emptyDir volume type is the most commonly used. You can mount it to the location of each container executing in the pod. As the name indicates, it is merely an empty directory initialized when the pod is created.

The following section will demonstrate how to create a pod to launch two containers. These containers will be a nginx container and a busybox container.

To stop the busybox container from doing its task, I will interfere with the command it executes at the beginning of the process.

In this manner, we will be able to get it going endlessly as a long process, and we will be able to execute further commands to verify whether our emptyDir has been initialized appropriately.

The emptyDir is the volume type generated whenever a pod is trying to run, and while a pod is starting to run, it will exist in an emptyDir, which can be used for temporary storage. If we delete a pod, the data from an emptyDir will also be deleted permanently.

```
apiVersion: v1
kind: Pod
metadata:
  name: myvolumes-example
spec:
  containers:
  - image: alpine
    imagePullPolicy: IfNotPresent
```

```
Name: myvolumes-container

    command: [   'sh', '-c', 'echo The Bench Container 1 is Running ;
    sleep 3600']

    volumeMounts:
    - mountPath:/aws-book
      name: example-volume
  volumes:
  - name: example-volume
    emptyDir: {}
```

We define a directory volume with the name example-volume that is empty. The braces that are placed at the end indicate that we do not give any more information for the emptyDir.

The emptyDir requirement makes it accessible to all of the containers that are contained inside the pod.

The pod is empty when formed, but the container can read and write the same file in the emptyDir volume such that each container can mount it at a different path.

The emptyDir can be used for scratch space for disk-based merge sorting, checkpoints for each crash, and files the website fetches to manage content.

## awsElasticBlockStore

This volume type has been described but still can be used; from the name, you can tell it is related to AWS. Amazon AWS has storage called Elastic Block Storage (EBS), which can be attached to EC2.

When a pod mounts an AWS EBS volume, EBS volumes still exist even when unmounted, unlike emptyDir, which is destroyed when a pod is removed.

To use EBS within Kubernetes, use the following:

```
apiVersion: v1
kind: Pod
metadata:
  name: test-ebs
```

```
spec:
  containers:
  - image: Nginx
    name: test container
    volumeMounts:
    - mountPath:/test-ebs
      name: test volume
  volumes:
  - name: test volume
    # You must create the EBS before use it here.
    awsElasticBlockStore:
      volumeID: "<volume id in AWS>"
      fsType: ext3
```

## Persistent Volumes

A persistent volume is storage inside a cluster that has been provided statically or dynamically using storage classes after being provisioned by an administrator. It is a resource inside the cluster, like a node is a resource within the cluster.

Another concept called PersistentVolumeClaim (PVC) is like a request for that storage; compare this concept to pods; when you deploy pods, you are consuming that node's resources and writing YAML to do the PVC work like with pods.

Usually, you use a PV for different reasons.

- Sometimes you need a volume to ensure the logs will be saved there.

- Database storage and data are always essential; a backup will need a volume to ensure that it will be saved and can be restored at any time.

- Keep the files after a cluster is destroyed.

The following example will create a PV.

```
apiVersion: v1
kind: PersistentVolume
metadata:
  name: example-pv
spec:
  accessModes:
```

```
- ReadOnlyMany #you can change this
capacity:
storage: 10Gi
storageClassName: standard
volumeMode: Filesystem
```

The following are the different access modes:

- `ReadWriteOnce`: Even when using the `ReadWriteOnce` access mode, it is possible for many pods that are operating on the same node to have access to the disk; you can use `ReadWriteOnce`.

- `ReadOnlyMany`: Many pods can mount the disk in read-only mode, referred to as ROX.

- `ReadWriteMany`: This can be mounted as read-write by different nodes and is referred to as RWX.

- `ReadWriteOncePod`: This is a new feature in K8S 1.22, in which read-write access can be granted to a single pod running on a single node, referred to as RWOP.

For volume mode, we also have two different options:

- *File system*: A volume will be mounted into pods such that it appears as a directory in the file system of each pod.

- *Block*: This is a volume as a raw block storage device that does not already have a file system preconfigured.

After creating the PV, you need to link it with the pod; to do that, we need to make the persistent volume claim or PVC.

```
apiVersion: v1
kind: PersistentVolumeClaim
metadata:
  name: example-pvc
spec:
  storageClassName: ""
  volumeName: example-pv
```

This will link the PV and the pod and allow the pod access to that storage.

However, this is considered a static PVC for a different reason since we did not leave the storage class name empty. To make it dynamic, control it, and change it to be more usable, use the following:

```
apiVersion: v1
kind: PersistentVolumeClaim
metadata:
  name: example-pvc
spec:
  accessModes:
 - ReadWriteOnce
  resources:
 requests:
    storage: 10Gi
  storageClassName: standard
```

The next step is to create a pod manifest that will be able to use the persistent volume, as shown here:

```
apiVersion: v1
kind: Pod
metadata:
  name: my-nginx
spec:
  containers:
 - name: my-nginx
   image: nginx:latest
   volumeMounts:
    - mountPath:/Nginx-mount
      name: pv
  volumes:
 - name: pv
   persistentVolumeClaim:
     claimName: example-pvc
```

Like any other Kubernetes resource, this can be managed by kubectl, which means listing the persistent volume.

```
$ kubectl get pv
```

Likewise, you can examine all of your persistent volume claims by using this:

```
$ kubectl get pvc
```

The pending state of a volume or claim indicates that the storage class has not yet finished supplying space for the volume.

Troubleshoot and understand what is happening; to do that, you must run the following command:

```
$ kubectl describe pvc example-pvc
```

## ConfigMaps

A ConfigMap can be used as an API object to organize nonsensitive information, such as settings. Pods can use ConfigMaps in many different ways: as environment variables, as command-line arguments, or as configuration files in a volume.

Both ConfigMap and secrets can act as volume mounts. When a ConfigMap is mounted as a volume, all the values it stores in a given directory can be injected into the running container. This functionality makes replacing a configuration directory a breeze if you have the configuration files in your ConfigMap.

It is simple to list the ConfigMaps in your cluster.

```
$ kubectl get configmap #, or you can use cm
```

There are two ways to generate a ConfigMap: declaratively or imperatively. Similar to how we created pods using the command line, declarative techniques include writing a YAML file and then applying it to the cluster to build the resource. The status quo is unchanged.

```
$ kubectl create configmap configmap-example
configmap/configmap-example created
```

The previous will create an empty ConfigMap; let's use a declarative method.

```
apiVersion: v1
kind: ConfigMap
```

```
metadata:
name: configmap-example
```

Having an empty ConfigMap is pointless; in this sample ConfigMap, some keys have single-valued values, while others have values that resemble configuration format fragments.

```
apiVersion: v1
kind: ConfigMap
metadata:
  name: example-configmap
data:
  color: "black"
  version: "1.5"
  environment: "prod"
```

Several lines can be used in the YAML format by simply separating them with the | character. As part of our declaration file, we use the following syntax:

```
apiVersion: v1
kind: ConfigMap
metadata:
  name: example-configmap
data:
  color: "blue"
  configfile.txt: |
    However, another example in this book
```

However, using the ConfigMap within the pods can be done in two different ways.

- All the values in a ConfigMap can be injected into an environment.

- Set the value of an environment variable using the parameters in one or more ConfigMaps, each of which may have a single value.

Although the first approach allows you more leeway, maintaining and staying structured over time might be more challenging.

For situations where you want to have a separate ConfigMap for each pod specification or application before deploying them, the second method is recommended.

```
apiVersion: v1
kind: Pod
metadata:
  name: nginx-example-with-configmap
spec:
  containers:
    - name: nginx-example-with-configmap
      image: nginx:latest
      env:
        - name: COLOR
          valueFrom:
            configMapKeyRef:
              name: example-configmap
              key: color
```

However, how will ConfigMap be helpful, and what is the point of it? It will allow you to load the variable with the pods.

To understand the point of using ConfigMap, run the following command:

```
$ kubectl exec Pods/nginx-example-with-configmap -- env
PATH=/usr/local/sbin:/usr/local/bin:/usr/sbin:/usr/bin:/sbin:/bin
HOSTNAME=nginx-example-with-configmap
COLOR=black
KUBERNETES_PORT_443_TCP_PROTO=tcp
KUBERNETES_PORT_443_TCP_PORT=443
KUBERNETES_PORT_443_TCP_ADDR=192.168.0.1
KUBERNETES_SERVICE_HOST=1192.168.0.1
KUBERNETES_SERVICE_PORT=443
KUBERNETES_SERVICE_PORT_HTTPS=443
KUBERNETES_PORT=tcp://192.168.0.1:443
KUBERNETES_PORT_443_TCP=tcp://192.168.0.1:443
NGINX_VERSION=1.22.1
NJS_VERSION=0.4.3
PKG_RELEASE=1~buster
HOME=/root
```

Since the `ConfigMap` is considered one of the volume types, how can we use it as a volume or even mount it?

```
apiVersion: v1
kind: Pod
metadata:
  name: nginx-with-configmap
spec:
  volumes:
    - name: configuration-volume
      configMap:
        name: example-configmap
  containers:
   - name: nginx-with-configmap
     image: nginx:latest
     volumeMounts:
       - name: configmap-volume # you need to configure the volume to match
       this name
         mountPath:/opt/configmap
```

If you want to double-check that the directory has been mounted in the container, type ls and see what comes up.

```
$ kubectl exec Pods/nginx-with-configmap -- ls/opt/configmap
color
testfile.txt
book.txt
```

## Kubernetes Secrets

Earlier, we covered the `ConfigMap` and how to use it to save nonsensitive data, but what about protecting the password and sensitive information? Another object in Kubernetes is called `Secret`.

Configuring Kubernetes apps is done with the help of the `Secret` object. Both `ConfigMaps` and `Secrets` serve the same purpose and are thus compatible with one another.

`ConfigMaps` are designed to store nonsensitive configuration data, whereas Secrets are designed to store sensitive data such as passwords, tokens, and secret API keys. Apart from that, the functionality of Secrets and `ConfigMaps` are the same.

The `kubectl get` command may list secrets just as it lists any other Kubernetes resource.

```
$ kubectl get secret
```

As with `ConfigMaps`, the hashed parameters of your secret can be seen in the data column, and both imperative and declarative techniques for generating a secret are supported. Both the imperative and declarative methods of developing a secret are supported.

You can create a secret using this:

```
kubectl create secret generic app-secret --from-literal=username=aws
--from-literal=password=book
```

In addition, you can create a secret from a file; if this file already contains a value, you could do the same as `ConfigMap` earlier and create a Secret.

Assume that we already have a file named `sensitive-info.txt`.

```
$ kubectl create secret generic app-password –from-file=./
sensitive-info.txt
```

---

**Note**   Your shell will read special characters such as $, *, =, and ! as commands; therefore, you must use the escape character before entering them.

---

This is the same with the following example:

```
kubectl create secret generic prod-db-secret --from-literal=username=aws
--from-literal=password= 'BC$pS$2/8wpyXEH8'
```

In addition, a YAML file can be used for declarative secret creation; you will need to take an extra step and convert your secret argument into a Base64 string. If we were to hard-code your secret value into a YAML file, it would be a security risk since these values are meant to be confidential.

```
$ echo 'awsdevopsbyosama' | base64
YXdzZGV2b3BzYnlvc2FtYQ==
```

After encoding the password, you can write the YAML based on the following:

```
apiVersion: v1
kind: Secret
metadata:
name: app-password
type: Opaque
data:
    app_password: YXdzZGV2b3BzYnlvc2FtYQ==
```

What if we insert a secret but as a variable like as we did before with the `ConfigMap`? As a test, I want to inject a variable inside an Nginx pod that will have the password.

```
apiVersion: v1
metadata:
name: nginx-example
namespace: aws-book
spec:
containers:
   - name: nginx-example
     image: nginx:latest
     env:
     - name: APP-PASSWORD # set the name of the variable here
       valueFrom:
         secretKeyRef:
           name: app-secret  # Name of secret object we created earlier.
           key: username # Name of key we created earlier
```

Another example of something you should be familiar with when reading a secret from a pod is the envFrom YAML key; read all of the values inside a Secret and get them all at once as environment variables within the pod.

```
apiVersion: v1
metadata:
  name: nginx-example
  namespace: aws-book
spec:
```

```
containers:
  - name: nginx-example
    image: nginx:latest
    envFrom:
    - secretRef:
      name: app-secret # Name of the secret
```

Because ConfigMaps and secret work together, you can mount the secret as a volume, as in an earlier example.

```
apiVersion: v1
metadata:
  name: nginx-example
  namespace: aws-book
spec:
  containers:
    - name: nginx-example
      image: nginx:latest
      VolumeMounts:
      - name: voume-example-with-secrets # Name of the volume you choose.
          MountPath:/opt/test
    Volumes:
    - name: volume-example-with-secrets # Name of the volume
      Secret:
        SecretName: app-secret # name of the secret
```

# Services

A Kubernetes service is a resource you can establish to provide a single, consistent point of access to a set of pods that all offer the same service. Each service has a fixed IP address and port number that will not shift as long as the service is in operation.

The services dentition is easy to create and will look like the following:

```
apiVersion: v1
kind: Service
metadata:
  name: serivces-definition
```

```
spec:
  selector:
    app.kubernetes.io/name: prod
  ports:
    - protocol: TCP
      port: 80
      targetPort: 8080
```

Clients can establish connections to that IP address and port, which are subsequently routed to one of the pods supporting that service. Clients of service do not have to be aware of the location of the individual pods delivering the service in this manner, making it possible for those pods to be relocated anywhere within the cluster at any moment.

We have four different types of Kubernetes services.

1. ClusterIP

   - This is considered to be the default service and the most common one.

   - The service will not be reachable from the outside.

   - Kubernetes will assign an internal IP address to the services.

   - We can use it to communicate between the different services operating inside the cluster. For example, consider the communication between the app's front-end and back-end components.

   Figure 10-27 shows how ClusterIP works, and the traffic will be internal.

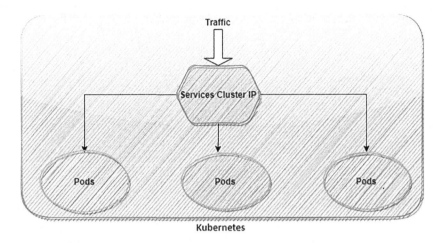

***Figure 10-27.*** *ClusterIP services and how they work*

The following is how you configure the ClusterIP service:
apiVersion: v1

```
kind: Service
metadata:
  name: clusterip-example
spec:
type: ClusterIP
  clusterIP: 192.168.0.1
  ports:
  - name: http
    protocol: TCP
    port: 80
    targetPort: 8080
```

    2.  NodePort

- This allows the services to be exposed outside.

- The port range for NodePort should be in the specific scope of 30000–32767.

- Provide a connection to your service from the outside world.

- When you use a NodePort, you have the flexibility to build up your load-balancing solution.

Figure 10-28 shows how NodePort works, and the traffic will be external.

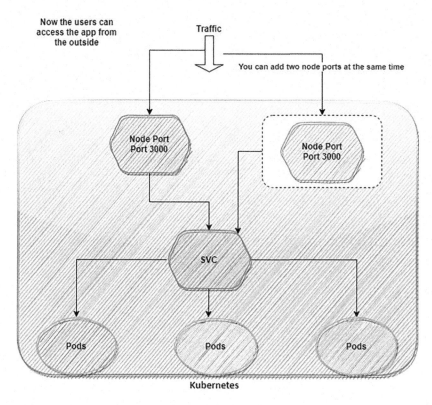

**Figure 10-28.** *NodePort services and how they work*

Here's an example of node port configuration:

```
apiVersion: v1
kind: Service
metadata:
  name: nodeport-example
spec:
type: NodePort
  selector:
    app: web
  ports:
  - name: http
    protocol: TCP
```

```
port: 80
targetPort: 8080
nodePort: 30000 # 30000-32767, Optional field
```

3. LoadBalancer

4. This is considered an extension for load balancing.

- Each cloud provider, such as Amazon Web Services, Microsoft Azure, Google Cloud Platform, and so on, has its native load balancer technology.

- The back-end pods receive traffic that is routed by the external load balancer. The cloud provider determines the load-balancing strategy.

- The LoadBalancer service will be created with no manual human intervention once you make the services.

- Use these services when running your Kubernetes cluster on a server provided by a cloud provider. See Figure 10-29.

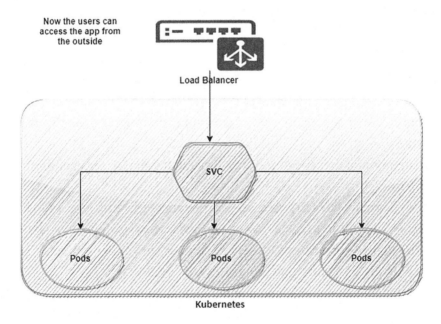

***Figure 10-29.*** *LoadBalancer and how it works*

You can configure LoadBalancer with the following:

```
apiVersion: v1
kind: Service
metadata:
  name: LoadBalancer
spec:
type: LoadBalancer
  # clusterIP: 192.168.1.100
  loadBalancerIP: 192.168.1.1
  selector:
    app: web
  ports:
  - name: http
    protocol: TCP
    port: 80
    targetPort: 8080
```

You can list all of the service's resources, as shown here:

```
$ kubectl get svc
```

Accessing services from the outside world is possible using tools such as ClusterIP, NodePort, and LoadBalancer. Kubernetes provides several networking alternatives, but their shortcomings are a significant reason why many developers of applications seek other substitutes.

Since we mentioned the type of services, let's not forget the most common one used by most companies: Ingress.

Why is it so popular? For starters, each LoadBalancer service needs its load balancer with its public IP address, but Ingress needs one, even when giving access to hundreds of services. The Ingress service forwards HTTP requests from clients to appropriate services based on the host and route provided in the request.

See Figure 10-30. Ingress, which functions at the network stack's application layer of HTTP, can provide benefits such as cookie-based session affinity and more that other services do not.

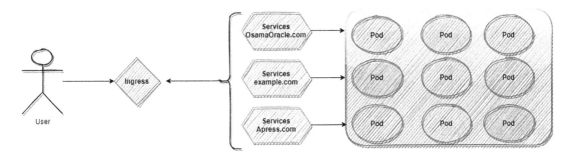

**Figure 10-30.**  *How Ingress works*

An Ingress controller mediates between Kubernetes and external services, hiding the complexities of application traffic routing.

Ingress controllers for Kubernetes do the following:

- Incoming traffic is load balanced to operating pods within the Kubernetes cluster.

- Services that need to connect with services outside the cluster may have their outbound traffic inside the cluster managed.

- Keep an eye on the Kubernetes pods and have the load balancing rules adjusted if any pods are added or withdrawn from service.

Many ingress controllers are often kept on hand inside a Kubernetes cluster, ready to be picked and deployed as needed; the following are some well-known ingress controllers:

- *Traefik*: The Traefik project is an open-source Kubernetes ingress controller that aims to make integrating Kubernetes with third-party applications easier.

- *Amazon Application Load Balancers (ALB)*: This widely used ingress controller uses AWS ALBs to process incoming resource requests.

- *Nginx*: The Nginx web server is used by this controller as the ingress server.

The following is an example of Ingress and how it forwards to the multiple back ends simultaneously; you can path section as much as you have.

```
apiVersion: networking.k8s.io/v1
kind: Ingress
metadata:
  name: prod-ingress
  annotations:
    kubernetes.io/ingress.class: alb
    alb.ingress.kubernetes.io/scheme: internet-facing
    alb.ingress.kubernetes.io/target-type: instance
spec:
tls:
    - hosts:
        - https://osamaoracle.com
      secretName: tls-secret
  rules:
- host: https://osamaoracle.com
      http:
        paths:
          - path:/cloud
            pathType: Exact
            backend:
              service:
                name: cloud-book
                port:
                  number: 443
          - path:/devOps
            backend:
              service:
                name: DevOps-Apress
                port:
                  number: 443
```

As you can see, the path type from the previous took a value exactly, and we have another three different options, each used for another purpose.

- *Exact*: This is used to find a URL with the same path, case-insensitively.

- *Prefix*: URL prefixes are separated by/are matched.

- *ImplementationSpecific*: The `IngressClass` is responsible for matching this sort of route. An implementation can regard this as its path type or the same as the prefix and exact route types.

Using services differs from company to company; what allows you to define what you want in your application and how to expose it online?

To avoid the hassle of manually managing services and load balancing, Kubernetes Ingress offers a centralized resource.

# Deployment

The following types of workloads are often required for cloud-based application deployment:

- **Stateless**

  By definition, stateless applications and services do not save any client data (state) that can be modified and then used in subsequent actions or sessions.

  When discussing containers or pods being stateless in containerization, we imply that they do not persist in any data related to the running application inside the container or any associated volumes.

  Let me give you an example; imagine you have two pods for the same app, the first one storing the request or access into JSON file and the second one the same app but storing the access or request that is coming into a database.

  We can call the first pod stateless because it does not depend on anything, but the second one is stateful.

- **Stateful**

  We refer to containers and pods as stateful if they keep any
  mutable data inside them; managing this kind of application
  is complex and you need to be careful, especially with rollouts,
  rollbacks, and scalability.

  We talked about most of the Kubernetes objects, but the question
  is, what if you need to update the pods? What will you need to do?
  This is the purpose of Kubernetes.

There are two options for upgrading all of those pods. The following are options:

- You must terminate the old ones to make room for the new pods.

- Begin a new one and remove the old one once the new one is ready.
  One option is adding all the new pods at once and then deleting the
  old pods; another is adding new pods and progressively deleting
  old pods.

There are advantages and disadvantages to each of these approaches. If you choose
the first option, your app could be inaccessible.

For another one, your app must support concurrently executing two different app
versions. The new version of your app should not change the data store's structure or
data in a manner that causes incompatibilities with older versions.

Instead of using a replication controller or a replica set, both considered lower-level
notions, a deployment can be used to deploy apps and update them declaratively.

Newer, more advanced replica sets have replaced the older replication controllers;
replica sets can also control and oversee pods. When using a deployment, the actual
pods are created and managed by the deployment's replica sets, not by the deployment
directly; see Figure 10-31.

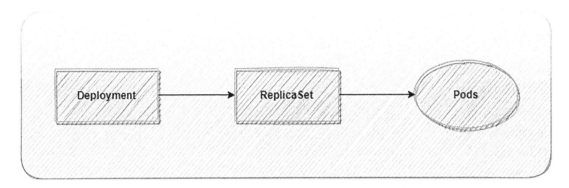

***Figure 10-31.***  *Deployment using a replica set*

Why would adding another object on top of a replication controller or a replica set be a good idea?

- By using deployments, we can automatically generate fresh pods and replica sets. Kubernetes may replicate pods and replica sets according to the parameters specified in the definition file.

- With deployments, you can use declarative language to define the intended configuration of your pods and replica sets.

- If the current state of a cluster in deployment is unstable, it can be returned to a former state with the aid of a deployment.

- When extra capacity is needed, deployments are helpful. They aid in the production of more pods and replica sets. Adding different pods to your deployment allows you to increase the pod workload as demand grows automatically.

The following are the benefits of using deployment:

- Applications that are containerized benefit from deployments since the process of deploying, updating, and scaling such apps is fully automated.

- As pod instances are immediately created during deployments, the process is often quicker and more error-proof than manually establishing your pods.

In Chapter 4, we discussed the deployment type and each of them; here, we can use them and control how our pods will be deployed to the cluster.

The deployment definition is the same as any other Kubernetes object and can be done as follows:

```
apiVersion: apps/v1
kind: Deployment
metadata:
  name: my-nginx
  labels:
    app: nginx
spec:
  replicas: 1 # you can change depending on the number of pods needed.
  selector:
    matchLabels:
      app: nginx
  template:
    metadata:
      labels:
        app: nginx
    spec:
      containers:
      - name: my-nginx
        image: nginx:1.14.2
        ports:
        - containerPort: 80
```

You can see the deployment's specifics using the standard `kubectl get` deployment and `kubectl describe` deployment commands; we need to learn another concept within the deployment.

Rolling deployment is a method of deploying new software that gradually replaces older versions by upgrading the underlying infrastructure.

```
kubectl rollout undo deployment/my-nginx
```

You can check the status of this rollout by running the following command:

```
$ kubectl rollout status deployment/my-nginx
deployment my-nginx successfully rolled out
```

The output is similar to this:

```
Waiting for rollout to finish: 2 out of 3 new replicas have been updated...
```

Let me explain the deployment dentition structure by showing the following YAML:

```
apiVersion: apps/v1
```

```
apiVersion: apps/v1
kind: Deployment
metadata:
  name: nginx-deployment-example
spec:
 replicas: 3
  selector:
    matchLabels:
      app: nginx
      environment: test
  minReadySeconds: 10
  strategy:
    type: RollingUpdate
    rollingUpdate:
      maxUnavailable: 1
      maxSurge: 1
 template:
    metadata:
      labels:
        app: nginx
        environment: test
    spec:
      containers:
      - name: nginx
        image: nginx:1.17
        ports:
        - containerPort: 80
```

- `Replica:` This defines the pod number that needs to be running using the template selector.

- `Selector:` The pods that belong to the underlying replica set can be located using a selector labeled with this set of instructions.

- `Template:` This sets the parameters for making pods. Tags in the metadata must be compatible with our filter.

- `Strategy:` This clarifies the plan for upgrading to new pods; we discussed the strategy in Chapter 4.

# Kubernetes and Helm

Providing people with the YAML manifest files for your Kubernetes objects is the quickest method to get your application into the hands of those who can deploy it on their cluster, and you share these YAML files on version control.

`https://artifacthub.io/` will provide you with all the available charts.

This method is often used as an example of executing a specific application in a container on Kubernetes. There are several drawbacks, however, to distributing YAML manifests in their raw form.

- Hard-coded values are used for all possible fields in the YAML templates. You must modify the manifest files directly to modify the `ConfigMap` object's value or the number of Service object copies.

- Each application can have a unique deployment procedure. Unfortunately, there is no rule on which YAML manifests the author should provide and which components you should deploy.

- Dependency management, which can be there, is not.

Helm is the go-to package management for Kubernetes services and apps, and it is available in the Kubernetes ecosystem. Helm's fundamentals are straightforward if you've used other popular package managers like APT or yum.

Helm contains three concepts you need to understand.

- *Chart*: This is what gets set up with your command-line interface with Helm. Each Kubernetes YAML manifest needed to deploy the app to the cluster is stored in a Helm chart.

- *Repository*: This is a place where Helm charts can be kept and shared by chart collectors and chart users. You have the option of making them open or closed to the general public.

- *Release*: This is a Helm chart that has been deployed to a Kubernetes cluster and is actively serving requests. While working with the Helm CLI, you may do tasks like these and install and remove Helm.

Helm, in general, is familiar to anyone using Kubernetes, but what is the use case for Helm?

- Use Helm to make the development on Kubernetes much more accessible; if you have multiple YAML files and want to speed up the deployment process, you can use Helm.

- Use Helm to make sure the software is updated correctly. The system to update Helm versions is unique.

- Dependency is easier to use within Helm; by default, Helm can manage this.

Installing Helm is easy and can be done on most operating systems, but you can refer to the documentation at `https://helm.sh/docs/`.

There is now a local installation script for Helm that can automatically download and install the most recent version of Helm.

You can download the script and run it on your computer. Before launching, you can read the documentation to understand the app's purpose.

```
$ curl -fsSL -o get_helm.sh https://raw.githubusercontent.com/helm/helm/
main/scripts/get-helm-3
$ chmod 700 get_helm.sh
$./get_helm.sh
```

When you've added Helm to your system, you can double-check that it is working by running the following:

```
helm version.
```

After entering this command, you will see the results.

```
$ helm version
version.BuildInfo{Version:"v3.7.1", GitCommit:"1d11fcb5d3f3bf00dbe6fe3
1b8412839a96b3dc4", GitTreeState:"clean", GoVersion:"go1.16.9"}
```

No repositories are set up in Helm by default; let's try to deploy our first application to Kubernetes. Let's get NGINX up and running on your local Kubernetes cluster by deploying a preconfigured Helm chart. To locate this chart in your local repository, use this:

```
$ helm repo add nginx-stable https://helm.nginx.com/stable
$ helm repo update
```

Once you add the repo, you can update it by running the following command:

```
$ helm repo update
```

After that, you can install the Nginx to the Kubernetes cluster by running only one command.

```
$ helm install nginx bitnami/nginx
NAME: nginx
LAST DEPLOYED: Mon Feb 20 11:29:33 2023
NAMESPACE: default
STATUS: deployed
REVISION: 1
TEST SUITE: None
NOTES:
** Please be patient while the chart is being deployed **
```

```
NGINX can be accessed through the following DNS name from within your
cluster.
```

You can verify the installation by running kubectl get pods.

Another example of how Helm will simplify the work is by installing WordPress; visit https://github.com/bitnami/charts/tree/main/bitnami/wordpress.

1. To add a trusted Helm repository, use the following command:

   ```
   helm repo add bitnami https://charts.bitnami.com/bitnami
   ```

2.  If you want to install WordPress, you can do it using the following command:

```
helm install wordpress bitnami/wordpress
```

The output will be something like this:

```
NAME: WordPress
LAST DEPLOYED: Mon Feb 20 02:12:10 2023
NAMESPACE: default
STATUS: deployed
REVISION: 1
NOTES:
** Please be patient while the chart is being deployed **
```

3.  Once the deployment is finished, you can access the WordPress URL by checking the Kubernetes services.

```
kubectl get svc --namespace default wordpress --template
"{{ range (index.status.loadBalancer.ingress 0) }}{{. }}
{{ end }}"
```

The command output will be the load balancer IP, which you can insert inside the browser and configure WordPress.

This is how all files in the chart folder are organized:

- Chart.yaml is the chart metadata YAML file, which includes information such as the chart's version, keywords, and references to other charts required for installation.

- Values.Schema.JSON is a JSON structure describing the values is acceptable. Please use the YAML format, which is optional.

- The chart folder contains supplementary diagrams that rely on the principal diagrams (optional).

- The template folder is the primary location for Kubernetes YAML manifest file generation templates.

- Values.Yaml is the default chart setup settings will be utilized as template parameters in the YAML file.

I will provide three examples that show you the power of the Helm chart and how easy it is to use it and allow you to install and configure the stack you need.

# Kubernetes Dashboard

A Kubernetes dashboard is a web UI that provides an overview of the cluster, which will be easy for the administrator to monitor and update Kubernetes settings.

The first step is to add the Kubernetes dashboard repo to Helm.

```
$ helm repo add kubernetes-dashboard
```

The Helm chart can be deployed to the cluster as a Kubernetes dashboard.

```
helm install kubernetes-dashboard kubernetes-dashboard/kubernetes-dashboard
```

An authentication token allows users to log into the Kubernetes UI (RBAC). We will have to create a new user account using the service account mechanism of Kubernetes, grant the user admin permissions, and log in to the dashboard using the bearer token tied to the user. Each person has a unique token.

The first step is to establish a Kubernetes dashboard service account and give it a name.

```
apiVersion: v1
kind: ServiceAccount
metadata:
  name: aws-book #or any other name you want.
  namespace: kubernetes-dashboard
```

The second step will be to create `ClusterRoleBinding`.

```
apiVersion: rbac.authorization.k8s.io/v1
kind: ClusterRoleBinding
metadata:
  name: admin-user
roleRef:
apiGroup: rbac.authorization.k8s.io
  kind: ClusterRole
  name: cluster-admin
subjects:
```

514

```
- kind: ServiceAccount
  name: admin-user
  namespace: kubernetes-dashboard
```

Once you deploy the previous code, you will need to generate a token by running the following command:

```
kubectl -n kubernetes-dashboard create token admin
```

Choose the token, copy it, and then paste it into the Enter token form when prompted, as shown in Figure 10-32.

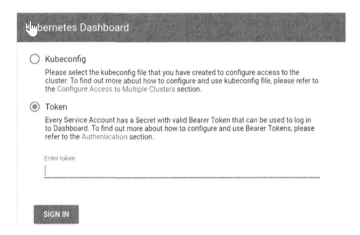

***Figure 10-32.*** *Kubernetes dashboard token*

## Elasticsearch with Kibana

Elasticsearch is a distributed, freely available, and open analytics and search engine that can be used with any data, whether textual, numerical, geographic, structured, or unstructured.

Kibana is an open-source front-end application that works with Elastic Stack to provide search and data visualization for information stored in Elasticsearch.

Elasticsearch can be set up in Helm by adding the repository.

```
helm repo add elastic https://helm.elastic.co
```

Then, you can define the namespace or the custom value by running the following
.yaml file:

```
helm install elasticsearch elastic/elasticsearch -n aws-book
```

Or if you want to use the custom values.yaml, use this:

```
helm install elasticsearch elastic/elasticsearch -n aws-book -f./
values.yaml
```

The helm test command is another way to determine the state of the cluster.

```
helm test elasticsearch
```

We are done with the first part, which is installing Elasticsearch; let's install Kibana,
which requires almost the same steps.

```
helm install kibana elastic/kibana
```

Figure 10-33 shows the Kibana dashboard once it's installed.

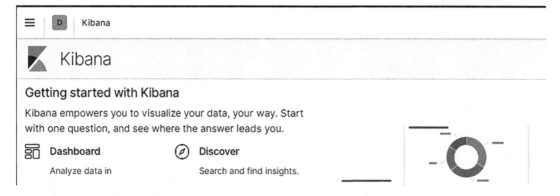

***Figure 10-33.***  *Access after the installation*

## Prometheus with Grafana

Metrics and other time-series data can be stored and monitored using Prometheus. If
your data is being saved in Prometheus, you can use Grafana to examine it (and other
sources). This example shows you how to collect data from NServiceBus, put it into
Prometheus, and then use Grafana to explore it.

Like any other example for the helm, the first step is to add the repo.

```
helm repo add prometheus-community https://prometheus-community.github.io/
helm-charts
```

Plus, you need to add a Grafana repo.

```
helm repo add grafana https://grafana.github.io/helm-charts
```

The next step is to install the tools individually, starting with Prometheus.

```
helm install prometheus prometheus-community/prometheus
```

I don't recommend exposing the Prometheus to the Internet because this tool's GUI is not that good, but if you want to do that, just run the following command:

```
kubectl expose service prometheus-server – type=NodePort – target-
port=9090 – name=prometheus-server-example
```

Use this command to set up Grafana.

```
helm install grafana grafana/grafana
```

Like the previous command, you can expose Grafana using the following command:

```
kubectl expose service grafana – type=NodePort – target-port=3000 –
name=grafana-example
```

## RBAC in Kubernetes

Role-based access control (RBAC) system access control, often known as *role-based security*, is a technique that limits user privileges. Authorizing users and giving them access requires providing appropriate permissions and privileges.

There are two distinct kinds of RBAC. Authorization API resources are required for RBAC to work in Kubernetes. API for K8s.io

- Both Role and ClusterRole serve to specify a group's access privileges. A role determines which actions are authorized by rules for each API resource. The only distinction between Role and ClusterRole is that the former is namespace specific, while the latter is global.

- RoleBinding and ClusterRoleBinding assign a particular role to a person or set of users (alternatively, groups of users or ServiceAccounts). Similarly, RoleBinding is limited to a specific namespace, but ClusterRoleBinding applies to the whole cluster. It is important to note that ClusterRoleBinding is compatible only with ClusterRole, while RoleBinding is consistent with ClusterRole and Role.

Figure 10-34 shows how RBAC works.

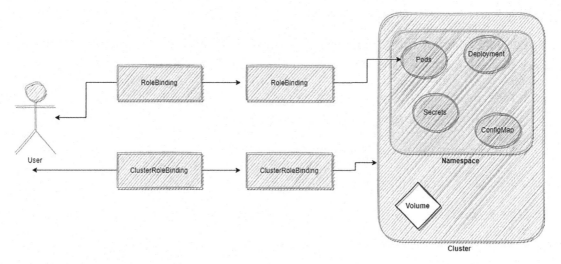

***Figure 10-34.*** *How role binding works*

There are several applications for ClusterRoles. You can do the following with a ClusterRole:

- Rights can be defined on namespace resources, and access can be given to each unique namespace.

- Permissions can be limited on namespace-specific resources, and access can be allowed across all namespaces.

- Permissions on cluster-scoped resources need to be defined.

The process of creating a role is relatively straightforward to understand. To clarify, you should first declare a namespace and then the rules. The following rules are an example of allowing GET and LIST operations to be performed on pods located in the default namespace.

```
apiVersion: rbac.authorization.k8s.io/v1
kind: Role
metadata:
  namespace: default                       # Namespace
  name: role-example
rules:
- apiGroups: [""]
  resources: ["pods"]                       # The pod can be accessed.
  verbs: ["get", "list"]                    # operations can be
performed.
```

- *Resources*: These are resources that have the potential to be used. Support is provided for pods, deployments, ConfigMaps, and other Kubernetes resources.

- *Verbs*: These identify the different operations that can be carried out. The GET method is used to query a particular object, whereas the LIST method lists all objects of a specific type. Create, update, and remove are other possible value alternatives.

- *apiGroups*: This displays the name of the API group of which the resource is a member.

When a role has been created, assigning that role to a particular user is called *role binding*. Here's an example:

```
apiVersion: rbac.authorization.k8s.io/v1
kind: RoleBinding
metadata:
  name: RoleBinding-example
  namespace: default
roleRef:
  kind: Role
name: role-example   #the one we created above.
  apiGroup: rbac.authorization.k8s.io
```

```
subjects:
- kind: User
  name: <user-id> # User ID of the user-example
  apiGroup: rbac.authorization.k8s.io
```

What if you need to provide full access to the namespace and allow users to do what they want to the specified namespace?

```
apiVersion: rbac.authorization.k8s.io/v1
kind: Role
metadata:
  name: full-access-namespace
  namespace: aws-book
rules:
- apiGroups:
  - '*'
  resources:
  - '*'
  verbs:
  - get
  - list
  - watch
  - create
  - update
  - patch
  - delete
```

From the side RoleBinding:

```
apiVersion: rbac.authorization.k8s.io/v1
kind: RoleBinding
metadata:
  name: full-access-namespace-rb
  namespace: aws-book
roleRef:
  apiGroup: rbac.authorization.k8s.io
  kind: Role
```

```
  name: full-access-namespace
subjects:
- apiGroup: rbac.authorization.k8s.io
  kind: Group
  name: admin-group
```

The good thing is that you can validate the role and user binding using an open-source tool called `rbac-lookup`.

`https://github.com/FairwindsOps/rbac-lookup`

Once you configure the tools, all you have to do is run the next command:

```
rbac-lookup admin-group -o wide
```

In the last section of this chapter, I will explain the tools used for CI/CD with Kubernetes.

## Kubenetes CI/CD Tools

The following are some tools:

- **Argo**

  Free, open-source software designed to help Kubernetes users manage workflows, clusters, and GitOps operations.

  `https://argoproj.github.io/`

  Argo provides four different solutions.

- Argo Workflows

- Argo CD

- Argo Rollouts

- Argo Events

  However, the focus is on the Argo CD that will allow you to deploy to Kubernetes.

- **Tekton**

With Tekton, developers can design, test, and deploy applications in cloud and on-premises environments using a single framework.

```
https://tekton.dev
```

- You can use the version control built-in pipeline, for example, github action, gitlab pipeline, or bitbucket pipeline.

- You can use Jenkins.

The free and open-source software that facilitates the development, deployment, and testing of cloud-native apps on Kubernetes. Amazon, GCP, IBM Cloud, Azure, Red Hat OpenShift, and Pivotal are some of the many supported cloud providers.

```
https://jenkins-x.io/
```

I will give a complete example of how the deployment will be on Kubernetes. One of the most common tools to deploy is Flux (`https://fluxcd.io/`).

Flux is a tool for synchronizing Kubernetes clusters with configuration sources (such as Git repositories) and automating configuration changes when new code is ready to deploy.

1. The first step is to use Flux, so let's do that. I will use Helm, which is much easier than the standard installation.

   ```
   helm repo add fluxed https://charts.fluxcd.io
   kubectl apply -f https://raw.githubusercontent.com/fluxcd/
   helm-operator/master/deploy/crds.yaml
   kubectl create ns flux
   ```

   There are different ways to connect Flux to Git. One of them uses the Git token API, and you can follow the instruction here to create a token in GitHub. See Figure 10-35.

***Figure 10-35.*** *Creating a personal token, Github*

Additionally, here is the step mentioned in GitHub documentation:

https://docs.github.com/en/authentication/keeping-your-account-and-data-secure/creating-a-personal-access-token

Another way is that Flux utilizes an SSH key to establish a connection to the Git repository. Existing SSH keys can be used to generate a Kubernetes secret.

Failing that, use fluxed's GitHub key to set things up. Since I already have a pair of keys, I plan to use the private key to generate a Kubernetes Secret.

Once you are done, run the following Linux command. On Windows use set instead of export.

```
export GITHUB_USER=<username>
export GITHUB_TOKEN=<access-token>
```

Currently, the following commands can be used to bootstrap Flux and install it on your cluster.

The following command will establish the aws-book-repo repository in your GitHub account, populate it with configurations for the Flux components, and bootstrap those settings into your cluster under the namespace flux we created earlier.

```
flux bootstrap github \
 --owner=$GITHUB_USER \
  --repository=aws-book-repo \
  --branch=main \
```

```
--path=./flux-config/config-path \
--personal
```

Next, make sure the FluxCD toolkits have been installed in your cluster by running the following scripts:

```
kubectl get deployment -n flux
```

You now have the following components of the Flux toolkit already installed on your cluster:

- *Source Controller*: In a Kubernetes cluster, the controller obtains artifacts. The Source Controller may receive and act upon incoming alerts, such as those generated by Git commits and Helm chart uploads.

- *Helm Controller*: This is in charge of looking after Helm equipment.

- *Kustomize Controller*: This controller's job is to compare the actual state of the cluster with the ideal state indicated by Commit manifests pulled from the Source Controller and bring the two into harmony.

- In addition to facilitating garbage collection for removed resources and monitoring the well-being of currently deployed resources, the Kustomize Controller enables dependency ordering and health evaluation.

- *Notification Controller*: This processes incoming and outgoing communications. Its function is to establish links with other services, including those provided by GitHub and GitLab. Its job is to inform the controllers in the GitOps toolkit whenever there are changes to the source code.

Copy the following URL to check if Flux has created the GitHub repo:

```
https://github.com/your-github-username/aws-book-repo
```

The next step is to automate the deployment; Flux will help you generate the needed files, but we need to clone the Git repo locally.

```
git clone https://github.com/your-github-username/aws-book-repo
```

Then, we must change the directory to flux-config/config-path and run the following command:

```
cd flux-config/config-path
```

One must first tell Flux where the forked podinfo repository is before it can be used to keep an eye on it. One way to do this is by creating a GitRepository manifest that specifies the repository's URL, branch, and interval for monitoring.

```
flux create source git podinfo \
  --url=https://github.com/$GITHUB_USER/podinfo \
  --branch=master \
  --interval=30 s \
 --export > ./flux-config/config-path/podinfo-source.yaml
```

Use the following command to generate a Kustomization manifest, which will instruct Flux to look in the specified directory for the deployable manifests:

```
flux create kustomization podinfo \
  --source=podinfo \
  --path="./kustomize" \
  --prune=true \
  --validation=client \
  --interval=5 m \
  --export >./flux-config/config-path/podinfo-kustomization.yaml
```

Once the files are created, you need to push the changes to Git by using the following command:

```
git add.
git commit -m "new updates"
git push
```

If anything is added to the repo, Flux will notice the change.

Here are some useful Flux commands:

- When executing the following, you can see Flux bringing the cluster's state into conformity with the one specified in the manifests.

  ```
  watch flux get kustomizations
  ```

- Running the following will permanently halt Kustomization monitoring:

  ```
  flux suspend kustomization <kustomization_name>
  ```

- This resumes the previous command:

  ```
  flux resume kustomization <kustomization_name>
  ```

# Summary

In this chapter, I covered Kubernetes and Amazon EKS; moreover, I covered the Kubernetes objects and the most important commands that will be used daily.

Kubernetes is one of the most common DevOps tools; almost all companies use it. Nevertheless, each company uses it in different ways and integrates it with various tools. The beauty of these tools is that every day is a learning experience.

The chapter covered the most common CI/CD tools used by Kubernetes; for sure, there are other tools that can be found online, but these are popular ones.

In the next chapter, I will show you how to use Kubernetes for real projects so you can see a complete integration between the DevOps tools and how to use them within one solution to reach a goal.

# CHAPTER 11

# DevOps Projects

I have included this chapter to help you better understand how to work with the DevOps tools I covered in earlier chapters about CI/CD, IaC, Amazon AWS, EKS, and more.

How do you use all these concepts together to create something outstanding? DevOps is a mentality; as I mentioned earlier, you could go to three different companies using the same tools, but each might choose to configure and use these tools in different ways. This is the beauty of DevOps.

In this chapter, I will create three different projects; you can find the source code for each in my GitHub repository at `github.com/OsamaOracle`.

These projects will not depend on one Amazon AWS service. I will cover different AWS services, and the source code for each will include a complete Readme file to help you understand the project's purpose.

To understand the idea of DevOps and the purpose of this book, you should apply and try these solutions by yourself.

The following are the requirements for this chapter's projects:

- Amazon AWS; create an account at `https://aws.amazon.com/console/`

- GitHub Account; create an account at `https://github.com/GitHi`

- AWS CLI installed and configured; follow the steps at `https://docs.aws.amazon.com/cli/latest/userguide/getting-started-install.html`

- Terraform; use the latest version at `www.terraform.io/`

- VS Code, which you can download at `https://code.visualstudio.com/`

I covered how to install each of the tools mentioned in earlier chapters; make sure you have configured the tools and are ready to start your first DevOps project.

© Osama Mustafa 2023
O. Mustafa, *A Complete Guide to DevOps with AWS*, https://doi.org/10.1007/978-1-4842-9303-4_11

I will also review common commands here so you will not need to repeat them in each project step; you can fork the GitHub repository and make the necessary changes.

With all that said, let's get started. The first thing you'll want to do is to clone my GitHub repository.

# Cloning a GitHub Repository

There are three options to clone a repository to your local machine: SSH, HTTPS, and good old-fashioned download. Let's quickly run through them here.

## SSH

Setting up SSH for GitHub will allow you to clone the repo each time with no password or username; all you have to do is configure the GitHub once, and you are done.

The first step is to set up an SSH key and generate an SSH key; if you are using Linux, all you have to do is run the following commands:

1. Run the `ssh-keygen` command.

   ```
   ssh-keygen -t rsa
   ```

2. The command will ask you where you'd want to save the key, so choose a location.

   In parentheses is a proposed default filename and directory. Here is an example of a typical `.ssh/id_rsa` file location: /home/user name. Press Enter to accept the path. Or, provide the critical path and filename and hit Enter.

3. To prevent unwanted access to your private key, however, you need to set a passphrase, but it's optional.

4. Repeat the passphrase when asked to verify it.

5. Now create the SSH key, go to the previous path, and copy the `id_rsa.pub` content.

6. Go to GitHub, as shown in Figure 11-1.

*Figure 11-1.* *GitHub setting*

7.  On the next screen, you need to choose to add the SSH key, as
    shown in Figure 11-2.

***Figure 11-2.*** *GitHub SSH key*

8.  On the next screen, copy the public key by clicking New SSH key, as shown in Figure 11-3.

***Figure 11-3.*** *Adding the SSH key to GitHub*

# HTTPS

Now that the generic steps have been done, HTTPS is simple if you clone the repository using this option.

You will need the GitHub username and password when you close the GitHub repository. See Figure 11-4.

***Figure 11-4.*** *HTTPS GitHub link*

You should be all set now to start on the first project.

# Project 1: Creating an AWS Endpoint

The project consists of the following:

- A Lambda function that stores a request payload into the DynamoDB datastore

- A Lambda function that is triggered by an EventBridge rule each seven days

The solution contains several GitHub Action workflows that automate deployment using Terraform. Workflows use a remote S3 backend to store Terraform state files. See Figure 11-5.

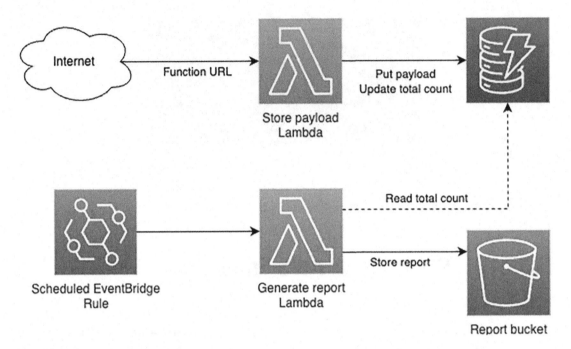

*Figure 11-5.* *Project architecture*

Here is the project link: https://github.com/OsamaOracle/AWS-endpoint.

# Repository Structure

Figure 11-6 shows how to view the GitHub folder structure.

| | | |
|---|---|---|
| 📁 | .docs | creation of an endpoint in AWS where data can be sent in a JSON format |
| 📁 | .github/workflows | creation of an endpoint in AWS where data can be sent in a JSON format |
| 📁 | app | creation of an endpoint in AWS where data can be sent in a JSON format |
| 📁 | backend | creation of an endpoint in AWS where data can be sent in a JSON format |
| 📄 | .gitattributes | Initial commit |
| 📄 | .gitignore | creation of an endpoint in AWS where data can be sent in a JSON format |
| 📄 | LICENSE | creation of an endpoint in AWS where data can be sent in a JSON format |
| 📄 | README.md | Update README.md |

*Figure 11-6.* *Repository structure*

Here's a breakdown of the folders and files:

- `.docs` contains all the pictures in the Readme file.

- `.github/workflows`

  - `deploy-app-to-aws.yaml` is the GitHub Action pipeline to allow the app to be deployed.

  - `deploy-backend-to-aws.yaml` will be run only once to create the back end for Terraform.

- App

  - `Main.tf` will create all the required Amazon AWS resources such as policy, Lambda, and CloudWatch

  - `Output.tf` is the function URL's output once Terraform is deployed.

  - `Variable.tf` is the value will be used as the main file.

  - Src folder

    - `generate-report-lambda-function` is the Python function that generates a report via Lambda.

    - `Store-payload-lambda-function` is the function that will store the endpoint in the datastore DynamoDB.

- Backend is where the terraform state file will be saved and deployed automatically via GitHub action.

## How Do You to Use the Solution?

To save a payload, send a POST request to the function URL (you can also find it in the store-payload Lambda function resource in the AWS console).

```
> curl -i \
  -d '{"key1":"value1", "key2":"value2"}' -H "Content-Type:
  application/json" \
  -X POST https://e4aj24hziroq2sjpdzw4riwxeyOhssvf.lambda-url.eu-
  central-1.on.aws
```

> **Note**    The function URL supports only POST requests on the root path. Any other requests will be rejected.

Figure 11-7 shows the output of the previous command.

```
λ ~/ curl -i \
  -d '{"key1":"value1", "key2":"value2"}' -H "Content-Type: application/json" \
  -X POST https://e4aj24hziroq2sjpdzw4riwxey0hssvf.lambda-url.eu-central-1.on.aws
HTTP/1.1 200 OK
Date: Sun, 05 Feb 2023 22:13:03 GMT
Content-Type: application/json
Content-Length: 19
Connection: keep-alive
x-amzn-RequestId: 764bc1ea-9848-44be-9b53-2b478c5e75fa
X-Amzn-Trace-Id: root=1-63e029ef-2d263f0a02889ded610269df;sampled=0

{"status_code":200}
λ ~/
```

***Figure 11-7.*** *POST output*

You can confirm that the payload was stored successfully using the AWS DynamoDB console (Figure 11-8). Please open it and retrieve all the items from the payload-datastore table.

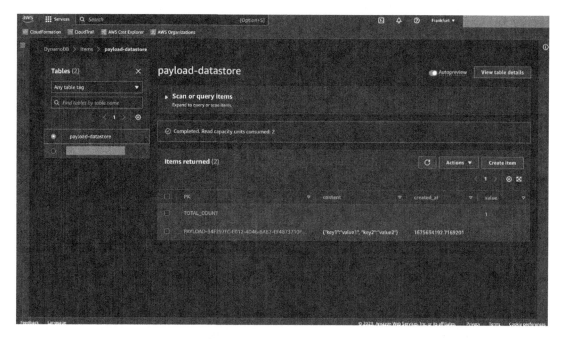

*Figure 11-8.* *DynamoDB datastore*

In some period, the generate-report Lambda function will be triggered automatically and generate a report with the total count of items in the datastore, as shown in Figure 11-9.

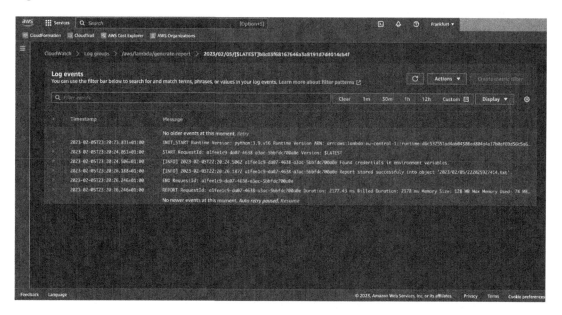

*Figure 11-9.* *A report with the total count of items in the datastore*

# How to Deploy the Solution to AWS

To deploy the solution to AWS, follow these steps:

1. Fork the repository or push the source code to GitHub.

2. In the project, select Secrets and Variables ➤ Actions ➤ Variables (Figure 11-10), and configure the following environment variables:

   - `TF_BACKEND_STATE_BUCKET` is the name of a bucket where the Terraform state will be stored.

   - `TF_BACKEND_STATE_KEY` is the name of an object where the Terraform state will be stored.

   - `TF_BACKEND_LOCKS_DYNAMODB_TABLE` is the name of a DynamoDB table where Terraform locks will be stored.

   - `REPORT_BUCKET_EXISTS` is the flag that shows if the report bucket already exists; if set to false, Terraform configuration will automatically create a new one.

   - `REPORT_BUCKET_NAME` is the name of the bucket where reports will be stored.

   - `AWS_REGION` is the desired AWS region. See Figure 11-10.

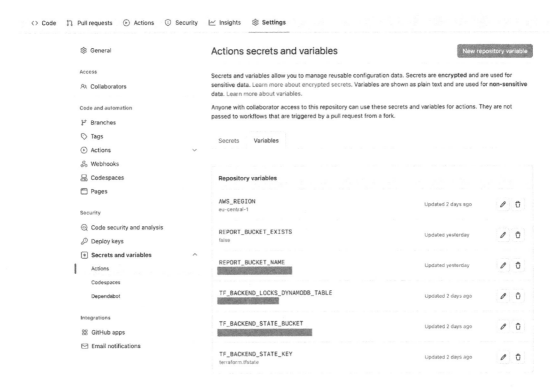

**Figure 11-10.**  *Defining the GitHub variable*

3.  In the project, select Secrets and Variables ➤ Actions ➤ Secrets
    (Figure 11-11), and configure the following secrets:

    •   AWS_ACCESS_KEY_ID is the AWS Access Key that will be used for
        Terraform configuration deployment.

    •   AWS_SECRET_ACCESS_KEY is the AWS Secret Access Key that will be
        used for Terraform configuration deployment.

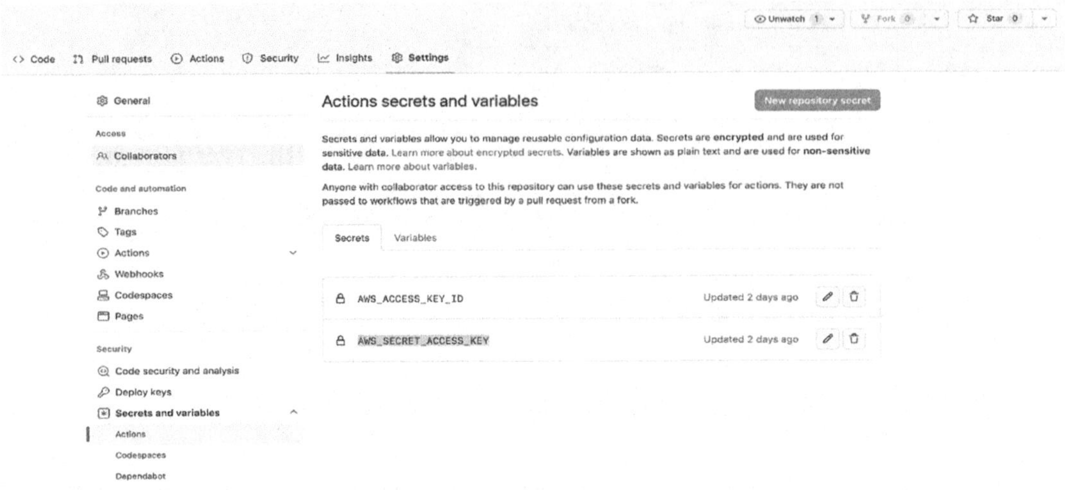

**Figure 11-11.**  *Defining an access key and secret as a secret inside GitHub*

4.  Run "Deploy Terraform backend to AWS workflow" (Figure 11-12),
    which creates the needed resources to store and maintain the
    Terraform state and ensure it finished successfully.

**Figure 11-12.**  *GitHub workflow action*

5.  Run "Deploy application to AWS workflow" (Figure 11-13), which creates application resources, and ensure it finished successfully

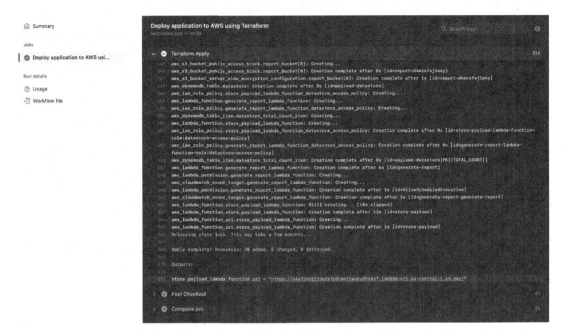

***Figure 11-13.*** *Terraform runs automatically without human interaction*

At the end of the Terraform Apply step, you will see the function URL, like `https://<random-string>.lambda-url.<region>.on.aws/`. This URL can be used to store a payload in the data store.

After running the deployment workflow, you can check that it has created two Lambda functions, as shown in Figure 11-14 and Figure 11-15.

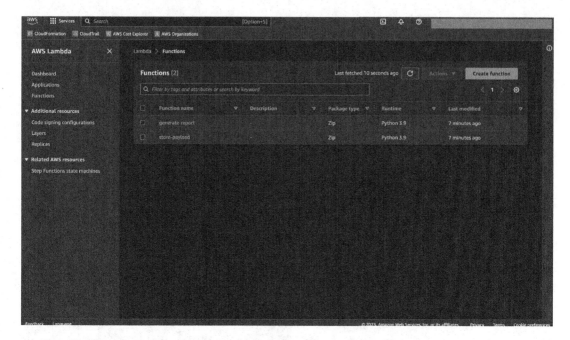

***Figure 11-14.*** *Lambda function deployed by GitHub action*

To see an initial report, open the configured S3 Report bucket in the AWS console.

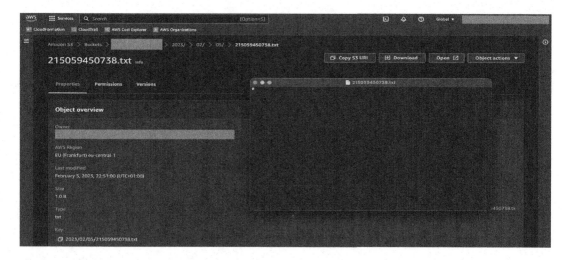

***Figure 11-15.*** *S3 report generated by Lambda*

# Project 2: Creating an EKS Instance and Deploying an Application to the Cluster via Terraform

This repo contains the example app from `https://dotnet.microsoft.com/en-us/learn/aspnet/hello-world-tutorial/intro`, a simple Dockerfile, and a Helm chart for it. See Figure 11-16.

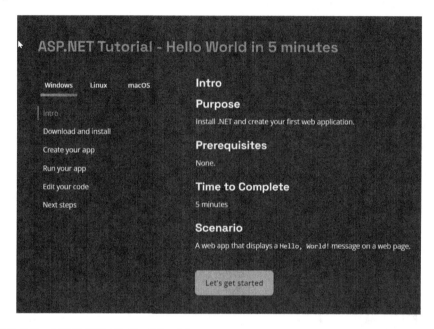

***Figure 11-16.*** *ASP.NET Hello World*

The goal is to deploy the included application (under `app/`) to the EKS cluster you created using the provided rudimentary Dockerfile and Helm chart in a namespace named with your first name.

The objective of this project is to do the following:

- Enable HPA for the deployment and set the target utilization to 80 percent for CPU and 85 percent for memory.

- Set a CPU request to 150m.

- Make the application highly available.

- Expose the application via a service to the cluster.

- Expose the application to the Internet. You can use the Route 53 zone already created in the provided AWS account in region eu-west-1.

- Make the application's index page show `Hello {GREET_VAR}` instead of "Hello world," where `GREET_VAR` is an environment variable. The variable should get its value from the `values.yaml` file.

The Terraform code will deploy the following AWS resources:

- Virtual private network (VPC)

- Subnet (public subnet, private subnet)

- NAT gateway

- EKS cluster

- ECR private repo, which will be used for Docker

The following are EKS features:

- AutoScaler is enabled.

- One worker node for a cluster is set up in a private subnet.

- One worker node for a cluster is set up in a public subnet.

## How to Run the Code

The code, this time, will not be deployed using any pipeline; on the other hand, it will be deployed manually using the Terraform code shown here:

```
terraform init
terraform plan
terraform approve --auto-approve
```

## Delete the Resource

```
terraform destroy --auto-approve
```

In this code, some stuff needs to be done twice or manually; when you deploy the code, the ECR will start creating the image. Therefore, it's essential to run the code twice.

- Terraform will fail the first time it tries to deploy the code because the ECR was created but the image is not built yet; you need to access the AWS account via ECR and then choose the repo, view the push command, and run them manually.

- Copy ECR ARN and paste it under value.yaml, which is located under the challenge directory. See Figure 11-17.

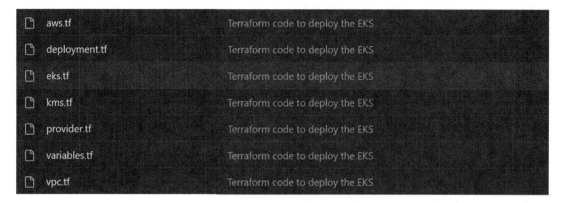

**Figure 11-17.** *Repostoiry structure*

Here's a breakdown of the structure:

- Aws.tf defines the provider needed and which region the EKS will be deployed in.

- Deployment.tf creates the ECR repository in AWS, plus the policy required to use the ECR.

- Kms.tf creates the EKS secret encryption key.

- EKS.tf will be responsible for deploying the EKS and creating the worker node; I am using terraform-aws-modules/eks/aws, a stable external module.

- Provider.tf defines the version for each component used inside our code.

- Variable.tf contains all the variables that can be changed during the process to make our code more reusable.

- Vpc.tf is a virtual private network responsible for creating the subnets.

Here's the project link: `https://github.com/OsamaOracle/Terraform-eks-helm-deployment`.

# Project 3: Creating AWS Resources Using Terraform

This project aims to demonstrate the IaC–Terraform usage but by using the module and creating a different AWS resource using IaC.

The following modules are created:

- AWS network, VPC, subnets, NAT gateway, Internet gateway

- EKS

- AWS RDS, MariaDB

- Elasticache, Redis Cluster

- SSM parameter store

- S3 buckets

- EC2 instances

- EC2 key pair

- Web Application Firewall (WAF)

- Load balancer

- IAM policy for EKS

The Terraform code is built by a module; utilizing modules may save time and prevent expensive mistakes by reusing configuration generated by you, other team members, or other Terraform practitioners who have released modules for you to utilize.

When you create a Terraform module, you can recall it in the following way:

```
module "vpc" {
    source                  = "./vpc"
    vpc_cidr                = var.vpc_cidr
    public_list             = var.public_list
    private_list            = var.private_list
    public_security_group   = var.public_security_group
    private_security_group  = var.private_security_group
```

```
    alb_name            = var.alb_name
    prefix              = local.prefix
}
```

Each module has input that allows you to choose from it; the Terraform module is a folder containing a set of configuration files used consistently. By enclosing collections of related resources in Terraform modules, you can write less code overall for associated pieces of infrastructure.

Here's the project link: https://github.com/OsamaOracle/AWS_infrastructure_project.

Another example of the module in this project is rds, as shown here:

```
module "rds" {
    source              = "./rds"
    subnet_list         = module.vpc.private_subnet_ids
    security_groups     = [module.vpc.vpc_security_group_private]
    cluster_name        = var.cluster_name
    master_username     = var.master_username
    master_password     = var.master_password
    engine              = var.engine
    engine_version      = var.engine_version
    instance_class      = var.instance_class
    dbname              = var.dbname
    username            = var.username
    password            = var.password
    port                = var.port
    allocated_storage   = 20
    skip_final_snapshot = var.skip_final_snapshot
    multi_az            = var.multi_az
    environment         = var.environment
}
```

The input of the module is different this time from the VPC because each module has its information, and each AWS service has its mandatory requirements. See Figure 11-18.

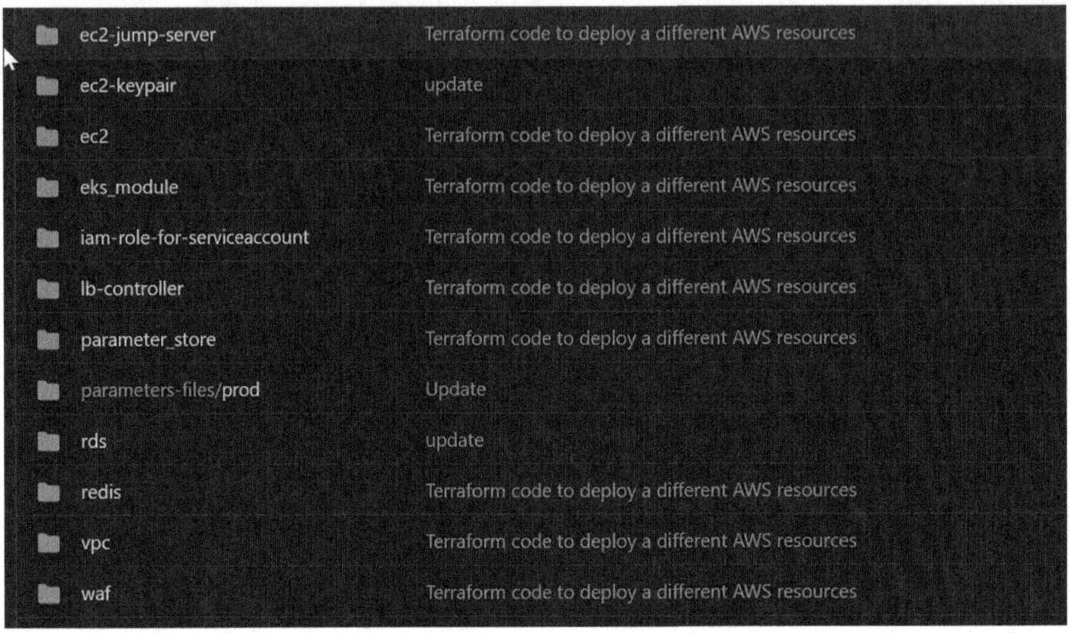

| 📁 | ec2-jump-server | Terraform code to deploy a different AWS resources |
| 📁 | ec2-keypair | update |
| 📁 | ec2 | Terraform code to deploy a different AWS resources |
| 📁 | eks_module | Terraform code to deploy a different AWS resources |
| 📁 | iam-role-for-serviceaccount | Terraform code to deploy a different AWS resources |
| 📁 | lb-controller | Terraform code to deploy a different AWS resources |
| 📁 | parameter_store | Terraform code to deploy a different AWS resources |
| 📁 | parameters-files/prod | Update |
| 📁 | rds | update |
| 📁 | redis | Terraform code to deploy a different AWS resources |
| 📁 | vpc | Terraform code to deploy a different AWS resources |
| 📁 | waf | Terraform code to deploy a different AWS resources |

*Figure 11-18.* *Terraform module folders*

Each one of these modules contains two necessary files.

- Main.tf

- Variable.tf

The main file will contain a resource that will be created; for example, see Figure 11-19.

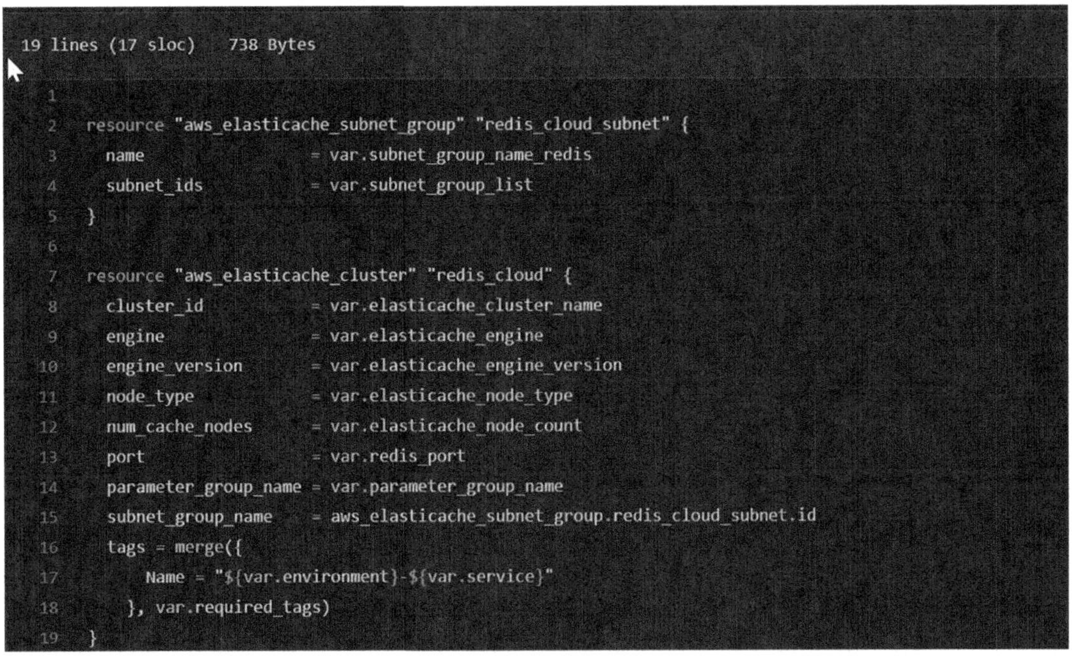

```
19 lines (17 sloc)   738 Bytes

  1
  2   resource "aws_elasticache_subnet_group" "redis_cloud_subnet" {
  3     name                   = var.subnet_group_name_redis
  4     subnet_ids             = var.subnet_group_list
  5   }
  6
  7   resource "aws_elasticache_cluster" "redis_cloud" {
  8     cluster_id             = var.elasticache_cluster_name
  9     engine                 = var.elasticache_engine
 10     engine_version         = var.elasticache_engine_version
 11     node_type              = var.elasticache_node_type
 12     num_cache_nodes        = var.elasticache_node_count
 13     port                   = var.redis_port
 14     parameter_group_name   = var.parameter_group_name
 15     subnet_group_name      = aws_elasticache_subnet_group.redis_cloud_subnet.id
 16     tags = merge({
 17       Name = "${var.environment}-${var.service}"
 18       }, var.required_tags)
 19   }
```

***Figure 11-19.***  *Inside the module file main.tf*

# How to Run the Code

The code, this time, will not be deployed using any pipeline; on the other hand, it will be deployed manually using the Terraform code shown here:

```
terraform init
terraform plan
terraform approve --auto-approve
```

Inside the project is a file called backend.tf; this file will allow you to upload the state file to Amazon S3. The bucket must be created before running the code.

```
# terraform {
#   backend "s3" {
#     bucket = aws_s3_bucket.backend_bucket.id
#     key    = "terraform.tfstate"
#     region = "eu-central-1"
#   }
# }
```

# Project 4: Creating a CloudFormation Project

In this project, we will use another IaC service, AWS CloudFormation. Before implementing this project, it's important you understand the concepts we will repeat from earlier projects, but this time using IaC.

We will do a couple of things in the code. First, we will "harden" Linux. Hardening Linux, or any other operating system, increases the system's safety by incorporating preventative measures. Linux distributions consist of many parts that must be constructed with great care. As a consequence, there may be lots of untied ends. A machine's security risks increase in proportion to its complexity.

In addition, log files offer a history of actions taken by the Linux OS, programs, and the system, which may help diagnose problems and, in this case, deploy a CloudWatch agent.

This project aims to prepare a hardened, logging configured, and highly available server that hosts a simple application to echo sent requests; all of this will be done using IaC and CloudFormation. Table 11-1 provides a succinct rundown of each step of the project and its purpose.

***Table 11-1.*** *CloudFormation Project Summary*

| Project Step | Purpose |
| --- | --- |
| Basic infrastructure and VM setup | Working CloudFormation template that deploys the essential infrastructure required to set up the instance |
| Application setup | Application code and setup options |
| Logging setup | Script to set up logging mechanism on the system |
| Hardening | A script that hardens the OS to be resistant to general cyberattacks |
| Final output | CloudFormation script Implementation plan and documentation |

The code will first set up the network that includes the VPC and the subnets, as shown in Figure 11-20.

```
AWSTemplateFormatVersion: '2010-09-09'
Description: 'Deploy a secure and highly available EC2 instance with cutom request echo application in an autoscaling group'
Parameters:
  ClassB:
    Description: 'Class B of VPC (10.XXX.0.0/16)'
    Type: Number
    Default: 19
    ConstraintDescription: 'Must be in the range [0-255]'
    MinValue: 0
    MaxValue: 255
  Emails:
```

***Figure 11-20.*** *CloudFormation section where it will set up a VPC*

Next, we will set up the EC2 based on a predefined AMI from the AWS market and deploy it to the previous VPC, and we will set up an SSH key (which can be changed, and you can use your key), as shown in Figure 11-21.

```
  SSHPublicKey:
    Description: 'SSH key pair for user custom admin user'
    Type: String
    Default: ssh-rsa AAAAB3NzaC1yc2EAAAABJQAAAQEA0v8IaRtSlyZuSoRmrYPKMA8oKVbzqAYloBmM
v90lem67+//3jfdO+xMDJyKvZKcHeg8Zx/ZFIP6poGWc63nGwQW6zrfH/isvxPg9
nKVZP3t5pZ6GR1aBVrGTuiogiQhmyPW8wzy2vDzim8l2vyoD6f4xW5mLQ5s+S0Ew
wciVYWs6sah6gdMrOraXfSYJo5LLa0P6VSlnJbTrqGUzLvGmH9iwwNFfqrMJQf+v
FKeebfMSTR2oHN/rQcfDywUOqd4jb4KIncKiEHHnqs4cXmOUKlKO2Dke2DM1Rbvc
kb9oAOq/EzuF067T3MwzYcMDuIikf1GMZ1TUo5H2bEdRkJRHYw==
    ASGMinCount:
```

***Figure 11-21.*** *SSH key for the Ec2*

Then we will set up a small application to have Nginx do an echo and run a bash script that will do a simple hardening; the bash is already uploaded to my S3 bucket.

https://osamaoracle.s3.eu-west-2.amazonaws.com/Hardening/
restricted_user.sh

Next, I will configure the CloudWatch agent, which requires a configuration based on my setup, and I will use the one that has already been uploaded to the S3 bucket.

https://osamaoracle.s3.eu-west-2.amazonaws.com/Logging/cwagent-
config-2.json

Then I will deploy the application and configure the Nginx web server based on the configuration that was already written and uploaded to my S3 bucket as a template for this project.

# Project Architecture

Figure 11-22 shows the project architecture.

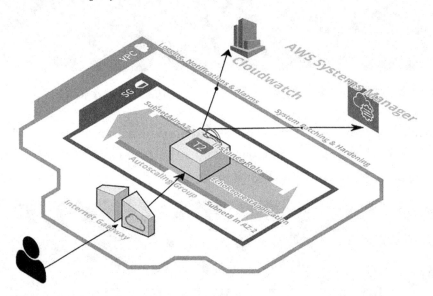

***Figure 11-22.***   *Project architecture*

The basic architecture consists of the following:

- One VPC

- Two public subnets

- One Internet gateway

- One AutoScaling group

The single autoscaling group spans two availability zones (AZs), with one subnet in each availability zone, so the loss of one AZ/data center does not affect the availability of the solution, and the application remains up.

Logging will be configured for all critical logs and stored in CloudWatch; the operating system will also be hardened to resist cyber threats.

# Application Setup

A Python-based Flask application has been set up on the instance responsible for echoing the request sent by a user.

The application has been set up to restart upon the system reboot automatically.

## Logging

A CloudWatch agent to monitor system stats has been set up on the instance.

## Hardening

Ubuntu 18.04 OS has been hardened as follows:

- Encryption has been set up on the underlying volume.

- A custom admin user has been created.

- A custom-restricted user has also been created.

- The IP banning system has been implemented to thwart relevant cyberattacks on the system via SSH and application ports.

- System packages also get upgraded every month.

Here is the project link: `https://github.com/OsamaOracle/Complete-AWS-Project`.

# Summary

In this last chapter, I shared projects using different DevOps techniques and the same tools used in other chapters, but with each project, I showed you how to use these tools differently.

The more you practice DevOps, the more things you will learn every time; it's essential to apply and practice DevOps to allow you to understand the tools and how to use them.

# Index

## A

© Osama Mustafa 2023

O. Mustafa, *A Complete Guide to DevOps with AWS*, https://doi.org/10.1007/978-1-4842-9303-4

## B

Printed in the United States
by Baker & Taylor Publisher Services